# DEVIL IN THE GROVE

"A powerful and well-told drama of southern injustice."

—*Chicago Tribune*

"After reading Gilbert King's excellent book on a little-known and horrifying incident in which four young black men were rounded up and accused of raping a white woman, readers cannot help but be awed by the bravery of those who took a stand in the late 1940s and early 1950s."

—*San Francisco Chronicle*

"A thoroughgoing study of one of the most important civil-rights cases argued by Thurgood Marshall in dismantling Jim Crow strictures. . . . Deeply researched and superbly composed."

—*Kirkus Reviews* (starred review)

"The story's drama and pathos make it a page-turner, but King's attention to detail, fresh material, and evenhanded treatment of the villains make it a worthy contribution to the history of the period, while offering valuable insight into Marshall's work and life."     —*Publishers Weekly*

"In the terrifying story of the Groveland Boys Gilbert King recreates an extraordinary moment in America's long, hard struggle for racial justice. *Devil in the Grove* is a harrowing, haunting, utterly mesmerizing book."

—Kevin Boyle, author of
*Arc of Justice: A Saga of Race, Civil Rights, and Murder in the Jazz Age*

"A taut, intensely readable narrative."    —*Boston Globe* (Book of the Year)

"Gripping. . . . Lively and multidimensional."     —*Dallas Morning News*

"A compelling chronicle."                       —*Booklist*

"The tragic Groveland saga—with its Faulknerian echoes of racial injustice spinning around an accusation of rape—comes astonishingly alive in Gilbert King's narrative. It is both heartbreaking and unforgettable."

—Wil Haygood, author of
*King of the Cats: The Life and Times of Adam Clayton Powell, Jr.*

"This is a haunting and compelling story, one of many in the campaign for racial justice. Gilbert King unmasks the near impossibility of defending four black men, deliberately and falsely accused of raping a white woman in Lake County, Florida, where Klan-infested white supremacists styled themselves law enforcement, while they murdered, maimed, lynched, and tortured to justify their raw power. Readers familiar with Dixiecrat culture will recognize how the trumped up case against the Groveland Boys wasn't an isolated instance as much as a Southern pastime, and they will be absorbed by complex events taking place in the backwoods and the courtrooms where local lawyers, the NAACP, and Thurgood Marshall soldiered. This book is important because it is disturbing. And in that regard we cannot walk away from the story it tells."

—Phyllis Vine, author of *One Man's Castle*

"Its rich case history captures the beginning of the end of the most extreme forms of racism, when violence ran rampant, aided by public authority, when the federal government was distant at best, and when a small group of courageous activists risked all for justice. Very few books combine this depth of research and narrative power about a subject of such pivotal significance."

—Ira Katznelson, author of
*When Affirmative Action Was White*

"Gilbert King's gut-wrenching, and captivating, narrative is civil-rights literature at its best—meticulously researched, brilliantly written, and singularly focused on equal justice for all."

—Michael G. Long, author of
*Marshalling Justice: The Early Civil Rights Letters of Thurgood Marshall*

"Gilbert King has done a remarkable job of weaving together history, sociology, law, and detective work of his own, to reveal facts that even I, one of the defense counsel in the case, had not been aware of until now."

—Jack Greenberg, Alphonse Fletcher Professor of Law, Columbia University, former Director-Counsel, NAACP Legal Defense Fund

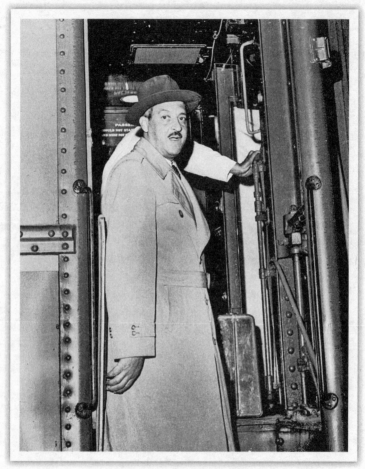

(*Courtesy of Cecil Williams*)

# DEVIL IN THE GROVE

Thurgood Marshall, the Groveland Boys,
and the Dawn of a New America

## |||||||||||||| GILBERT KING ||||||||||||

HARPER ● PERENNIAL

NEW YORK ● LONDON ● TORONTO ● SYDNEY ● NEW DELHI ● AUCKLAND

HARPER ● PERENNIAL

A hardcover edition of this book was published in 2012 by HarperCollins Publishers.

HarperCollins books may be purchased for educational, business, or sales promotional use. For information, please e-mail the Special Markets Department at SPsales@harpercollins.com.

FIRST HARPER PERENNIAL EDITION PUBLISHED 2013.

*Designed by Lisa Stokes*

The Library of Congress has catalogued the hardcover edition as follows:

King, Gilbert.
   Devil in the grove : Thurgood Marshall, the Groveland Boys, and the dawn of a new America / Gilbert King.—1st ed.
      p.  cm.
   ISBN 978-0-06-179228-1 (hardback)
   1. Discrimination in criminal justice administration—Florida—Groveland. 2. Groveland (Fla.)—Race relations. 3. Rape—Florida—Groveland. 4. African Americans—Civil rights. 5. Marshall, Thurgood, 1908–1993. 6. National Association for the Advancement of Colored People. I. Title.
HV9956.G76K56   2012
305.896′073075922—dc23

                                                                    2011033757

ISBN 978-0-06-179226-7 (pbk.)

21 22 23   OV/LSC   30 29 28 27 26 25 24 23 22

*For Lorna, Maddie, and Liv*
*and in memory of Matthew P. (Matty) Boylan*

# | CONTENTS |

# | PROLOGUE |

Flag outside the NAACP offices at 69 Fifth Avenue, New York City. (*Library of Congress, Prints & Photographs Division, Visual Materials from the NAACP Records*)

ALL HIS LIFE, it seemed, he'd been staring out the windows of trains rumbling toward the unknown. Again, he was seated in the Jim Crow coach, hitched directly behind the engines, where the heavy heat bore the smell of diesel. Still, the lawyer sat proud in his smart double-breasted suit, a freshly pressed handkerchief dancing out of his pocket, as the haunting Southern landscape of cypress swamps, cotton fields, and whitewashed, tin-roofed shanties flickered by. Traveling alone, he hunched his six-foot, two-inch frame over case files; a cigarette dangling from his lips, he scribbled some notes on a yellow legal pad. He would rewrite the draft before he typed it up later; he worked meticulously. A federal clerk once told him that with just one look at the smudges or erasures on a lawyer's pleading he'd know if it was written by a white man or a Negro. It was a remark Thurgood Marshall never forgot. In cases like his there was too much at stake for him to be filing any "nigger briefs."

The trains he rode bore grand names like the Orange Blossom Special, the Silver Meteor, and the Champion, and their rhythms ran in Marshall's Baltimore blood. Both his father, Willie, and his uncle, Fearless, had been porters on the Baltimore & Ohio Railroad, and to help pay for college, young Thurgood himself had worked as a waiter in a B&O dining car. The railroads were for him and his family a source of pride, and status, but on trips like these, when he was riding alone, they also summoned in Marshall an old sadness. His wife, Buster, unable to bear the children he had longed for, had one year for his birthday given him the electric train set she had hoped someday to present to her husband and their son. With the train, and with an engineer's hat perched atop his head, Marshall entertained the boys in their Harlem apartment building instead.

By the mid-1940s, Marshall, the grandson of a mixed-race slave named Thorney Good Marshall, was engineering the greatest social transformation in America since the Reconstruction era. He had already devoted more than a decade of his career to overcoming the "inherent defects" of a Constitution that had allowed, by law, social injustices against blacks, who had been denied not only the right to vote but also equal rights and opportunities in education, housing, and employment. With his far-reaching triumphs in landmark cases he argued before the U.S. Supreme Court, Thurgood Marshall would indeed redefine justice in a multiracial nation and become, as one civil rights pioneer described him, the Founding Father of the New America.

Before achieving those victories, however, Marshall fought countless battles for human rights in stifling antebellum courthouses where white supremacy ruled. Neither judges nor juries in the Jim Crow South had much interest in Marshall's nuanced constitutional arguments. To Marshall, the representation of powerless blacks falsely accused of capital crimes became his opportunity to prove that equality in courtrooms was every bit as vital to the American model of democracy as was the fight for equality in classrooms and in voting booths.

On Marshall's journeys, when the moon lit the passing landscapes of the South, he customarily drank bourbon, and he enjoyed the company of the night porters—they'd joke and talk together in segregated cars atop suitcases and the occasional casket. Or, sitting in the coach car, Marshall would drift in and out of sleep to the lullaby of the locomotive, its plaintive cry announcing every crossing as it rolled onward, southward, closer and closer to benighted towns billeting hostile prosecutors, malicious police, and the Ku Klux Klan. In the rhythm of the rails came the whipping of the wind as again the dream descended on him, and in the wind the massive black flag unfurled outside the offices of the National Association for the Advancement of Colored People (NAACP), and as a pall fell over Manhattan's Fifth Avenue, he read again the message, in stark white letters on the flag's flapping black field: "A Man Was Lynched Yesterday."

The photographs were always horrifying: shirtless black victims, their bodies bloodied, eyes bulging from their sockets. Of all the lynching photos Marshall had seen, though, it was the image of Rubin Stacy strung up by his neck on a Florida pine tree that haunted him most when he traveled at night into the South. It wasn't the indentation of the rope that had cut into the flesh below the dead man's chin, or even the bullet holes riddling his body, that caused Marshall, drenched now in sweat, to stir in his sleep. It was the virtually angelic faces of the white children, all of them dressed in their Sunday clothes, as they posed, grinning and smiling, in a semicircle around Rubin Stacy's dangling corpse. In that horrid indifference to human suffering lay the legacy of yet another generation of white children, who, in turn, would without conscience prolong the agony of an entire other race. "I could see my dead body lying in some place where they let white kids out of Sunday School to come and look at me, and rejoice," Marshall said of the dream.

Seventeen-year-old Norma Lee Padgett had that look—chin held high, lips pursed—when in her best dress she slowly rose from the witness box to identify for the jury the three Groveland, Florida, boys whom she had accused of rape. Like the "sworn truth" of the fictitious Mayella Ewell, the white teenage accuser in Harper Lee's *To Kill a Mockingbird,* Norma Lee's dramatic testimony against the Groveland Boys tore a county apart. Her pale index finger extended, it dipped from boy to boy as she spoke out each name, like a young schoolteacher counting heads in class, and her breathy cadence sent a chill through the courtroom.

"*. . . the nigger Shepherd . . . the nigger Irvin . . . the nigger Greenlee . . .*"

And like Harper Lee's heroic lawyer, Atticus Finch, Thurgood Marshall found himself at the center of a firestorm. It would bring the National

Guard to Lake County, Florida, where mob violence drove hundreds of blacks from their lives in Groveland, and in the aftermath it would prompt four sensational murders of innocents, among them a prominent NAACP executive. Despite the fact that Marshall brought the Groveland case before the U.S. Supreme Court, it is barely mentioned in civil rights history, law texts, or the many biographies of Thurgood Marshall. Nonetheless, there is not a Supreme Court justice who served with Marshall or a lawyer who clerked for him that did not hear his renditions, always colorfully told, of the Groveland story. The case was key to Marshall's perception of himself as a crusader for civil rights, as a *lawyer*, willing to stand up to racist judges and prosecutors, murderous law enforcement officials, and the Klan in order to save the lives of young men falsely accused of capital crimes—even if it killed him. And Groveland nearly did.

By the fall of 1951, Marshall had already filed and had begun trying in lower courts what would become his most famous case, *Brown v. Board of Education*, when he was again riding the rails toward Groveland. It was on such a journey to the South that one of Marshall's colleagues noticed the "battle fatigue" setting in on the lawyer. "You know," Marshall said to him, "sometimes I get awfully tired of trying to save the white man's soul." Battling personal demons as well as the devils who brought bullets, dynamite, and nitroglycerin into the Groveland fray, the lawyer saw death all around him in central Florida. So intense did the violence in Groveland become that on one of Marshall's visits, J. Edgar Hoover insisted that FBI agents provide the NAACP attorney with around-the-clock protection. Usually, though, Marshall negotiated Florida alone, despite the number of death threats he daily received.

A fellow NAACP lawyer thought of Marshall as a "suicidal crusader," because he involved himself in such explosive criminal cases in the South at an exceptionally crucial time in the history of the blacks' struggle for equal opportunity. Suicidal or not, Marshall was unquestionably irreplaceable in the mission of the burgeoning civil rights movement. And Marshall's colleague too got swept up in the enthusiasm and commitment. "Thurgood says he needs me," the NAACP associate told his wife. "If he needs me, I'm going. If I get killed, I get killed. But I gotta be on that train. . . ."

Marshall would later say, "There is very little truth in the old refrain that one cannot legislate equality. Laws not only provide concrete benefits, they can even change the hearts of men—some men, anyhow—for good or evil." Thurgood Marshall might never have spoken those words if he hadn't defended the Groveland Boys. The case made a lasting impact on both him and the NAACP's Legal Defense Fund. It also became the impetus behind the NAACP's capital punishment program, which eventually led to the Supreme Court ruling that capital punishment was unconstitutional as well as to the Court's later decision to invalidate the death penalty for rape.

The victories came only after many train rides to towns where no hotels or restaurants accommodated people of Marshall's race. Local blacks would welcome him, though, with hospitality and tears of gratitude. They'd clean their houses spotless for his stays. He'd join his hosts at their dinner tables and tell them stories from his travels that brought laughter to the night. He'd eat their modest offerings of salt pork and poke salad with such aplomb you'd think he was dining on his favorite she-crab soup over drinks with friends back in Harlem. The women would have lunches packed and delivered to him at court each day. Broken-down cars would get "glued together" to taxi him back and forth. Later in the day, word would spread: "Men are needed to sit up all night with a sick friend." You'd hear it whispered everywhere. They'd all know what it meant. They were lining up armed guards to keep Marshall safe from night-riding Klansmen while he slept.

Alice Stovall, Marshall's secretary at the NAACP, recalled the effect Marshall had on blacks when he showed up at courthouses in small Southern towns. "They came in their jalopy cars and their overalls," she recounted. "All they wanted to do—if they could—was just touch him, just touch him, *Lawyer Marshall*, as if he were a god. These poor people who had come miles to be there."

Southern juries might be stacked against blacks, and the judges might be biased, but Thurgood Marshall was demonstrating in case after case that their word was not the last, that in the U.S. Supreme Court the injustice in their decisions and verdicts could be reversed. He was "a lawyer that a white man would listen to" and a black man could trust. No wonder that across the South, in their darkest, most demoralizing hours, when falsely accused men sat in jails, when women and children stood before the ashy ruins of mob-torched homes, the spirits of black citizens would be lifted with two words whispered in defiance and hope:

"Thurgood's coming."

Interior of the Morton Funeral Home, Columbia, Tennessee, showing vandalism of the race riots in February 1946. (*Library of Congress, Prints & Photographs Division, Visual Materials from the NAACP Records*)

*November 18, 1946*

I F THAT SON of a bitch contradicts me again, I'm going to wrap a chair around his goddamned head."

One acquittal after another had left Tennessee district attorney general Paul F. Bumpus shaking his head in frustration over the NAACP lawyers, and now Thurgood Marshall was hoping to free the last of the twenty-five blacks accused of rioting and attempted murder of police in Columbia, Tennessee. The sun had been down for hours, and the start of a cool, dark night had settled over the poolrooms, barbershops, and soda fountains on East Eighth Street in the area known as the Bottom, the rickety, black side of Columbia, where, nine months earlier, the terror had begun. Just blocks away, on the news that a verdict had been reached, the lawyers were settling back into their chairs, fretfully waiting for the twelve white men on the jury to return to the Maury County courtroom. They'd been deliberating for little more than an hour, but the lead counsel for the defense, Thurgood Marshall, looked over his shoulder and knew immediately that something wasn't right. Throughout the proceedings of the Columbia Race Riot trials, the "spit-spangled" courtrooms had been packed with tobacco-chewing Tennesseans who had come to see justice meted out. But the overall-clad spectators were equally intrigued by Marshall and his fellow NAACP lawyers: by the strange sight of "those niggers up there wearing coats and talking back to the judge just like they were white men."

Marshall was struck by the eeriness of the quiet, nearly deserted courtroom. The prosecution's table had been aflutter with the activity of lawyers and assistants throughout the trial, but none of them had returned for the verdict. Only the smooth-talking Bumpus had come back. All summer long he'd carried himself with the confidence that his Negro lawyer opponents were no match for him intellectually. But by relentlessly attacking the state's case in a cool, methodical manner, Marshall and his associates had worn Bumpus down, and had already won acquittals for twenty-three of the black men on trial. The verdicts were stunning, and because the national press had defined the riots as "the first major racial confrontation following World War II," Bumpus was no longer facing the prospect of humiliation just in his home county. The nation was watching and he had begun to unravel in the courtroom, becoming more frustrated, sarcastic, and mean-spirited as the trial progressed.

"Lose your head, lose your case," was the phrase Marshall's mentor, Charles Hamilton Houston, had drilled into him in law school. Marshall could tell that his adversary, seated alone at the prosecutor's table, was in the foulest of moods as he was forced to contemplate the political ramifications of the unthinkable: his failure to win a single conviction against black lawyers defending black men accused of the attempted murder of white police in Maury County, Tennessee.

The shock from the summer's not-guilty verdicts had worn off by

November, and Marshall sensed that the white people of Columbia were becoming angrier and more resentful of the fact that this Northern Negro was still in town, making a mockery of the Tennessee courts. He'd watched patiently as Bumpus stacked the deck in his own favor by excusing every potential black jury member in the Maury County pool (there were just three) through peremptory challenges that did not require him to show cause for dismissal. And Marshall had paid close attention to the desperation in Bumpus's closing statement to the jury, when the prosecutor warned them that if they did not convict, "law enforcement would break down and wives of jurymen would die at the hands of Negro assassins." None of it surprised Marshall. He was used to, and even welcomed, such tactics from his opponents because they often helped to establish solid grounds for appeals. But Marshall also noticed that the atmosphere around the Columbia courthouse was growing more volatile.

A political cartoonist for the *Pittsburgh Courier* now doing public relations work for the NAACP had been poking around the courthouse and had come to believe that the telephone wires were tapped and that the defense lawyers were in danger. Learning this, Marshall refused to discuss any case details or sleeping arrangements over the phones, and the PR representative reported back to Walter White, the executive secretary of the NAACP, that "the situation in the Columbia Court House is so grave that anything may happen at any time." White issued a memorandum to NAACP attorneys, demanding "no telephone calls be put through to Columbia or even to Nashville [where Marshall was staying] unless and until Thurgood says that it is safe to do so." White noted that "we are dealing with a very desperate crowd" and want nothing to "jeopardize the lives of anyone, particularly persons as close and as important to us as Thurgood and his three associates." White even contacted the U.S. attorney general's office and warned that if anything happened to Marshall while he was in Tennessee, it would "create a nation-wide situation of no mean proportions."

Marshall's associates didn't need Walter White to warn them of any danger they might be in. They were local Tennessee lawyers who had investigated enough lynchings in these parts to know that the death threats they received from the citizens of Columbia were to be taken seriously. Sitting to one side of Marshall at the table was a forty-seven-year-old poker-playing highbrow with a faint Caribbean accent named Zephaniah Alexander Looby, who came to Tennessee by way of the British West Indies. At fourteen years of age and living in Dominica, Looby found work as a cabin boy aboard a whaling ship, and two years later, in 1914, "broke and bedraggled," he jumped ship in New Bedford, Massachusetts, with the dream of becoming a lawyer. He eventually received his degree from Columbia Law School in New York and taught economics at Fisk University in Nashville until the call of civil rights law beckoned and Marshall put him on the Columbia case.

To Marshall's left was the lone white attorney on the case, the young, hotheaded Maurice Weaver, who reveled in the danger of standing up to white authority and racism; on more than one occasion throughout the Columbia Race Riot trials he had nearly come to blows with prosecutors. Marshall and Looby enjoyed having Weaver around, in part because the two black attorneys were inherently polite and gracious in court whereas Weaver was something of a lightning rod for white anger. Whenever prosecutors or witnesses referred to a black as "that nigger," Weaver loudly interrupted with objections, insisting that the person be referred to as "Mr. or Mrs." for the record. Bumpus seethed.

Weaver also endeared himself to Marshall because the Tennessee lawyer liked to drink, though at one point during the trial, his provocative nature had become not only distracting but dangerous, and Marshall was forced to intervene. Weaver's teenage and very pregnant wife, Virginia, decided that she'd like to see her husband at work and asked to ride along with Looby's associates and black reporters. Locals were speechless when the pregnant white girl hopped out of a car packed with Negroes and marched straight into court. Marshall, observing the commotion, pulled her aside and told her to take a Greyhound bus to court next time. "You almost started another lynching here in the courthouse," he warned.

As the jury of twelve began filing back into the courtroom, Looby and Weaver searched their tired, sullen faces for a hint of the verdict. Marshall was on edge; he remembered how colleagues and friends had urged him not to return to Columbia. Over that "terrible summer of 1946," he'd been running a constant fever while working in courtrooms that had no bathrooms or drinking fountains for blacks. The long hours, relentless travel, and Tennessee heat were taking their toll, but Marshall would not slow down. By July the lawyer's body had finally wilted. Mid-case, he succumbed to exhaustion and a debilitating pneumonic virus that led to a long stint in a Harlem hospital, followed by weeks of doctor-ordered bed rest. Still, from his bed, and against everyone's wishes, Marshall continued to lead late-night telephone strategy sessions with Looby and Weaver until he could no longer stay away—and no one was going to stop him from boarding a train to Nashville. "The Columbia case," he said, "is too important to mess up. And I, for one . . . am determined that it will not be messed up."

M ARSHALL WAS IN New York on February 26, 1946, when a desperate call from Tennessee came into the NAACP offices, describing a full-blown race riot in Columbia. An emergency meeting was called and Marshall learned that the trouble began the previous morning when a black woman, Mrs. Gladys Stephenson, went into a Columbia appliance store with her nineteen-year-old son, James, to complain about being overcharged for shoddy repairs to a radio. After loudly proclaiming that she'd take the radio elsewhere, Gladys exited the store with her son. But twenty-eight-year-old radio repair apprentice Billy Fleming did not appreciate the threatening look he got from James on the way out.

"What you stop back there for, boy, to get your teeth knocked out?" Fleming asked, before racing over and punching James in the back of the head.

James's boyish looks were deceiving. A welterweight on the U.S. Navy boxing team, he barely flinched and countered with several punches to Fleming's face, sending him crashing through a plate-glass window at the front of the store.

Bleeding profusely from his leg, the army vet came up fighting, and other whites joined the melee, shouting, "Kill the bastards! Kill every one of them!" One man went after Gladys, slapping and kicking her to the ground and blacking her eye. A few minutes later police arrived and carted mother and son off to jail. After pleading guilty to public fighting and agreeing to pay a fine of fifty dollars each, the two were about to be released when Billy Fleming's father convinced officials to charge both Gladys and James with the attempted murder of his son; the two were held by police in separate cells. As the news spread that James Stephenson had gotten the better of Billy Fleming and sent him wounded to the hospital, Maury County became galvanized. A mob began to gather around town and outside the jail, and by late afternoon the sheriff was hearing talk that a group of men were planning to spring the "Stephenson niggers out of the jail and hang them."

Carloads of young, white workers from the phosphate and hosiery mills in nearby Culleoka (where the Flemings lived) began arriving at the square, and more volatile World War II veterans joined them. Rumors that rope had been purchased had reached the Bottom, and Julius Blair, a seventy-six-year-old black patriarch and owner of Blair's Drug Store, had heard enough.

He'd seen firsthand what white mobs in Columbia were capable of in recent years, around that courthouse down the block. He'd been there when they'd taken one man out of jail and lynched him back in '27, and more recently, there was young Cordie Cheek. The community was still raw over Cordie's killing. The nineteen-year-old had been falsely accused of assaulting the twelve-year-old sister of a white boy he had been fighting with. The boy paid his sister a dollar to tell police that Cordie had tried to rape her, but a grand jury refused to indict and Cordie was released and abducted that same day by county officials, who took him to a cedar tree and hanged him. Julius Blair was well aware that it was Magistrate C. Hayes Denton's car that had driven Cordie to his death; yet, undeterred, Blair marched into Denton's office and demanded that Gladys and James Stephenson be released. "Let us have them, Squire," Blair told him. "We are not going to have any more social lynchings in Maury County."

Blair managed to convince the sheriff to release the Stephensons into his custody and arranged for them to be dropped off at his drugstore early that evening. By then, though, blacks in the Bottom had gone past being intimidated by the hooting and honking of armed whites circling the area in cars; they weren't going to stand passively by this time while another Cordie Cheek lynching unfolded. More than a hundred men, many of them war veterans, took to the streets with guns of their own, determined to fight back at the first sight of a mob moving toward the Bottom. Armed and angry, they told the sheriff in no uncertain terms that they were ready if whites came down to the Bottom. "We fought for freedom overseas," one told him, "and we'll fight for it here."

True to his word and hoping to avoid any more trouble, the sheriff released the Stephensons that evening, and Blair arranged for the two of them to be whisked out of town, "blankets over their heads" for their protection. "Uptown, they are getting together for something," Blair told them.

The nearby white mobs meanwhile did not disperse, and blacks in the Bottom were growing more fearful as the night progressed. Drinking beer and circling in cars, whites fired randomly into "Mink Slide," as they derisively referred to the Bottom. Blacks, drinking beer on rooftops, were also firing in response and by bad chance hit the cars of both a California tourist and a black undertaker. When half a dozen Columbia police eventually moved into Mink Slide, a crowd of whites followed behind. They were welcomed by shouts of "Here they come!" and "Halt!" and then, in the confusion, came a command, "Fire!" and shots were exploding from all directions. Four police were struck with buckshot before they retreated.

Reports of the skirmish roused whites around town. Columbia's former fire chief headed toward Mink Slide with a half gallon of gasoline and the intent to "burn them out," but he was shot in the leg by Negro snipers as he stole down an alley. With the arrival of state troopers and highway patrol reinforcements, the whites finally outnumbered the blacks and moved into Mink Slide, where they ransacked businesses until dawn, fired machine guns into stores, and rounded up everyone in sight. "You black sons of bitches," one patrolman shouted, "you had your-alls' way last night, but we are going to have ours this morning."

Just after 6 a.m., gunfire from the street rained into Sol (son of Julius) Blair's barbershop. "Rooster Bill" Pillow and "Papa" Lloyd Kennedy, hiding in the back, saw armed officers coming and were said to have fired a single shotgun blast before they were overpowered and taken into custody. They were stuffed with other blacks from the Bottom into overcrowded cells at the county jail and interrogated without counsel for days. Two prisoners were shot dead "trying to escape."

Mary Morton had watched helplessly as state patrolmen barged into her family's funeral home on East Eighth Street and arrested her husband. From the street she heard the sound of breaking glass and the building being ransacked. A short time later she saw the same officers, laughing and joking, return to the street. Once they were out of sight, Morton went inside to discover the parlor furniture broken and slashed, clothes torn to pieces, and the entire interior doused with embalming fluid. With horror, she laid eyes on a defaced casket. Photographed soon after, the image of that casket would be published in newspapers across the country and ultimately come to symbolize the Columbia riot of 1946. Across its lid, in large letters, "KKK" was crudely scrawled in chalk.

Mary Morton tried to pick up the phone, but patrolmen caught her, cursed her, and threatened to throw the phone out on the street. Police had declared war on the black citizens of Columbia, and the highway patrolmen, instead of trying to bring order to the town, had joined in with vigilante mobs. The Tennessee State Guard had cordoned off the area, but they did nothing to stop the destruction and violence in Mink Slide. The Maury County jail had become a deadly destination for Mary Morton's husband and other leaders of the black community. Officials would soon shut down telephone service into and out of Mink Slide, but not before Mary Morton managed to make her call. After the police moved on, she phoned a friend in Nashville. She implored him to get word to the NAACP immediately.

Nine hundred miles north, in New York, a lanky lawyer in suspenders was called into a meeting. He grabbed his coffee and settled into a chair. He heard another all-too-familiar story of violence and cruelty in the South, and he knew that once again order would be restored, as always, with blacks' "blood running in the gutters." An editorial in the *Columbia Daily Herald* proclaimed that the "situation is in the hands of the state troops and state police. . . . The white people of the South . . . will not tolerate any racial disturbances without resenting it, which means bloodshed. The Negro has not a chance of gaining supremacy over a sovereign people and the sooner the better element of the Negro race realize this, the better off the race will be." In Marshall's early days at the NAACP, emergency meetings would sometimes end with the unfurling of the ill-omened black flag, alerting New Yorkers that yet another man had been lynched. The flag's gloomy stain over the city usually meant that Marshall would be back on a train, alone, again riding toward trouble.

And nine hundred miles south, in Columbia, Tennessee, where the town's blacks were holed up in their homes and jail cells, there rose whispers of relief: the lawyer was coming.

T HE TWELVE white men on the jury took their seats in the box, and the foreman rose to announce the verdict against Rooster Bill Pillow for shooting and wounding a state highway patrolman. The courtroom was still.

"Not guilty."

Marshall, Looby, and Weaver sat in quiet shock. In the last acquittals, Weaver had loudly slapped a defendant's knee in excitement and leapt from his chair to shake hands with jurors who appeared to be just as stunned as everyone else in the courtroom. "This makes me proud to be an American!" he'd shouted. Marshall wanted no celebratory outbursts this time.

Papa Kennedy's verdict was next. Marshall was expecting Kennedy would be going to jail, for unlike Pillow, Kennedy had been surly and impudent throughout the trial—at one point telling Bumpus to "shut up" in open court. But the jury rejected the charge of attempted murder and convicted Kennedy on a lesser count that enabled him to leave the courthouse free on bail.

Marshall and his lawyers rose from their seats, wanting nothing more than to leave town quickly. Because of the constant threats and concerns for his safety, Marshall had been staying in Nashville, almost fifty miles to the north, and driving back and forth each day with Looby and Weaver. Tagging along was reporter Harry Raymond, who'd been covering the trial for the *Daily Worker*, a New York newspaper published by the Communist Party of the USA. He described the moments after the verdict as tense, and he expected "something serious, something of a violent nature, to happen." On his way to telegraph the verdict to his newspaper, Raymond noticed one agitated, heavyset spectator rushing out the doors and declaring that something must be done about the failure of the jury to convict.

Raymond knew the NAACP lawyers had been threatened with lynching, and had been told their bodies would "wind up in Duck River," which they had to cross each day on the way to court. The white reporters covering the trial pleaded with Raymond to leave town with them, but he had a feeling the story of the Columbia Race Riot hadn't ended with the verdicts, and he chose to ride back to Nashville with Marshall and the NAACP lawyers.

With their heads down, the lawyers humbly exited the courtroom. Gone was Marshall's usual swagger. There were no pictures or proclamations on the courthouse steps. Marshall walked briskly. Looby tried to keep up with him as best he could on his bad leg; he'd spent months in a cast after being struck by an automobile and was still limping noticeably. Marshall waited impatiently as the lawyers, with Raymond tagging along, hopped into Looby's car. They drove a few blocks to Mink Slide, where they picked up soft drinks and crackers at Julius Blair's drugstore—the epicenter of the race riots nine months earlier. After some congratulatory handshakes, Blair urged them to get moving. Marshall, though, wanted to do some private celebrating.

Maury County was a dry county, but Marshall had become acquainted with the local bootlegger, so there would be just one stop to make before they headed north to Nashville. The sedan stole down a dirt road at just about eight o'clock in the evening. The bootlegger, however, had disappointing news. "I just sold the last two bottles to the judge!" he told Marshall. The four men headed for Nashville, empty-handed.

With Marshall at the wheel, Raymond beside him, and Looby, in part because of his bad leg, in the back with Weaver amid piles of law books and case files, the four men heaved a collective sigh of relief as they headed out of Columbia. They had seen the signs posted around town during the trials:

**NIGGER READ AND RUN. DON'T LET THE SUN GO DOWN ON YOU HERE. IF YOU CAN'T READ, RUN ANYHOW!**

To Marshall, they recalled a message he had received mid-trial from Walter White: "Take care of yourself and keep your feet in running order." The sedan had just crossed a bridge over Duck River when they came upon a car parked in the middle of the road. Marshall honked the horn and waited, but the car did not move, so he drove around it and headed for Nashville. Inside the sedan it was quiet; unspoken went the fear that something was amiss. Then, piercing the silence, the sound of a siren screamed from behind.

"Thurgood," Looby said. "That siren. It's a police car!"

"Is it following us?" Marshall asked.

"Yes. It's coming after us fast."

"You'd better stop the car, Thurgood," Weaver said.

Marshall turned his head and was troubled to see three cars following them. The first, carrying highway patrolmen, roared past the sedan and forced Marshall to jam on the brakes. Quickly, eight men, some in police uniforms and some in civilian clothes, converged on the sedan. Marshall saw that a few of them had their hands on their guns while others shone flashlights on the men inside. Reporter Harry Raymond kept his mouth shut, but he knew this wasn't a routine police stop.

The lawyers and Raymond were ordered out of the car. They froze as one cop approached.

"You men the lawyers for the National Association for the Advancement of Colored People?"

"Yes, I'm Thurgood Marshall. This is Maurice Weaver and this gentleman is Alexander Looby."

The cop looked them over. "Drinking, eh?"

"I beg your pardon," Marshall replied.

"I said you've been drinking. Celebrating the acquittal. Driving while intoxicated."

Weaver interjected that this stop was a civil rights violation and, furthermore, it was obvious none of them had been drinking.

"Stay out of this, Weaver," the cop said. "You're a white man and have no business in this car anyway."

The police then asserted their right to search the car and Weaver demanded that they produce a warrant. Using flashlights, Marshall was able to read the "John Doe" warrant signed by a deputy sheriff, charging the lawyers with transporting whiskey in violation of "county local option law."

"Look," Marshall told Weaver. "Let's watch him. Don't let him put any liquor in there, 'cause this is a dry county."

The police search of the car turned up nothing, so they decided to search the lawyers.

"You got a warrant to search us?" Marshall asked.

"No," the officer responded.

"Well, the answer is no," Marshall said.

The police let the lawyers return to their vehicle, and this time Looby took the wheel.

"You weren't driving this car, were you?" one cop asked Looby.

"I'm not answering your question," Looby replied.

The cop then looked to Marshall, who said, "I'm not answering your question, either."

Confused about what to do next, the police argued over who had been driving the car when it was stopped. "That's the one! The tall yaller nigger!" one of them insisted with certainty, and the officers approached Marshall, who was asked to show his license.

The cop took one look. "Get out," he said. "Put your hands up."

Marshall was dumbfounded. "What is it?" he asked.

"Drunken driving," the officer responded.

"Drunken driving? You know I'm not intoxicated," Marshall said. "I haven't had a drink in twenty-four hours!"

"Get in the car," one of them said.

With guns drawn and flashlights glaring, four men hustled Marshall into the backseat of a nonofficial sedan.

"Keep driving," they shouted back to Looby and Weaver as they placed Marshall under arrest. With Marshall wedged into the backseat, the car sped away, back toward Columbia. As they picked up speed, the four law enforcement agents were quiet and all business. They drove into the darkness. Walter White had warned Marshall, as had Looby and Weaver, about these Tennessee men and their "Master Race preachments." Marshall knew that the Ku Klux Klan in Columbia was deeply entrenched in the local police; he knew its members served as sheriffs and magistrates. He had read the NAACP reports. This wasn't the Klan of "cowardly hood," rather, it "wears cap and visor, and shining badge. . . . It is the LAW. It arrests its stunned victims, unlisted."

Marshall had no idea where they were going. For years his dark humor had horrified young lawyers and assistants when he would go into great detail about what Southern police or the Klan did with uppity Negroes in the woods. Now Marshall was the uppity Negro, alone, and he wasn't in a joking mood. Looking out the window of the sedan, he could see the cedar trees as the headlights flashed across them. It was under a cedar tree just down the road that hundreds of townspeople had gathered around young

Cordie Cheek in his last living moments. They had watched and cheered as officials pulled down Cordie's pants and castrated him before forcing him up a stepladder and hanging him. Pistols were passed around the crowd; they were fired until all the bullets were gone.

The car began to slow. The lawmen were quietly mumbling and pointing; then the driver turned left down a dirt road, toward "the famous Duck River." Marshall knew that nothing good ever happened when police cars drove black men down unpaved roads. He knew that the bodies of blacks—the victims of lynchings and random murders—had been discovered along these riverbanks for decades. And it was at the bottom of Duck River that, during the trial, the NAACP lawyers had been told their bodies would end up.

The sedan was lumbering forward, bouncing down the dirt road, when Marshall caught his first glimpse of the men waiting down by the river. The headlights illuminated their stern faces. The car slowed, then stopped. Suddenly headlights appeared behind them. Had word spread about the lynching of the NAACP lawyer? Glimpsing the glare of the lights behind them, one of the policemen in Marshall's car stormed out of the sedan to confront the driver of the second car. Marshall craned his neck to see; he recognized the limp.

It was Looby!

Instead of driving to Nashville as the police had ordered, Looby had spun a U-turn and followed the police sedan. As soon as it turned left off the main road, he knew Marshall was in trouble. He'd been teaching at Fisk University, just down the block from where the Maury County officials "arrested" Cordie Cheek, threw him into a sedan, and drove him to these same woods along Duck River. Well, they'll have to kill me, too, Looby thought. He wasn't going to leave Marshall to the devices of murderous law enforcement officers.

Once again the policemen ordered Looby to leave the scene. Waiting to be arrested, or worse, the slight, gimpy lawyer stood his ground; he refused to budge. He'd had these same police and town officials on the witness stand, and he'd wanted to question each one of them about the lynching of Cordie Cheek so that he could rightfully raise the issue of self-defense during the trial, but the judge had refused to allow it. Now Looby spoke his mind: he wasn't leaving without Marshall, he said. Livid, the deputies and police conferred to the side. Whatever the plan had been, there were now too many witnesses, and there was sure to be another riot if things got out of hand with the lawyers. The police returned to the car and made a loop back up to the main road, with Marshall's eyes lingering on the lynch party waiting by the river, while Looby, the man Marshall called a Rock of Gibraltar, followed close behind with Weaver and Raymond. This time the police drove Marshall back to the courthouse in Columbia, where he was pointed toward a magistrate's office.

"You go over there," one of the policemen said. "We'll be over."

"No, you won't. I'm going with you," Marshall replied, reminding the police that they had placed him under arrest. "You're not going to shoot me in the back while I'm 'escaping.' Let's make this legal."

"Smart-ass nigger," one said, and they shuffled Marshall up to the second floor of the courthouse, with Weaver trailing behind to serve as Marshall's lawyer. Once there, they met Magistrate Jim "Buck" Pogue, a small, bald man not more than five feet tall.

"What's up?" Pogue asked police.

"We got this nigger for drunken driving," one officer told him.

Weaver was fuming. He accused the officers of being "frame-up artists" and demanded that Pogue examine Marshall.

Pogue looked Marshall up and down. "He doesn't look drunk to me," he observed.

"I'm not drunk," Marshall exclaimed.

"Boy, you want to take my test?" Pogue asked.

Marshall paused and looked quizzically at the magistrate. "Well, what's your test?"

"I'm a teetotaler," Pogue said. "I've never had a drink in my life. I can smell liquor a mile off. You want to take a chance?"

Marshall stepped forward. "Sure," he said, and leaning his tall, lanky frame down to Pogue till his mouth was just an inch from the magistrate's nostrils, Marshall blew so hard he "almost rocked this man."

Pogue took a deep whiff and exploded at the police. "Hell, this man hasn't had a drink. What are you talking about?"

The arresting officers quickly filed out of the office.

"What else is there?" Marshall asked.

Pogue told him that there was nothing else and stated that those officers had come to the wrong man if they wanted to frame Marshall. He said he was the one magistrate in Columbia who had refused to sign warrants for the arrests of Negroes during the February trouble, and then he extended his hand to Marshall, saying, "You're free to go."

Marshall quickly left the courthouse for the second time that day. He noticed again that the streets were deserted. This time, however, he understood why. "Everybody," Marshall realized, "was down at Duck River waiting for the party."

He and Weaver hurried over to the Bottom, where Looby and Raymond were waiting at Sol Blair's barbershop. They made sure Marshall was okay, but they also suspected Marshall wasn't out of danger just yet. The officers, they figured, had probably been hoping to bring Marshall before Magistrate C. Hayes Denton, who surely would have locked Marshall up for the night. Then, in "the pattern of all recent Maury County lynchings," it would only have been a matter of storming the jail with some rope and finishing the job.

Looby thought it likely the officers might not yet be ready to give up on their party. He came up with a plan of his own. "Well, Thurgood," he said, "we'll put you in another car."

They decided to send a decoy driver out with Looby's car, which would head toward Nashville, while Marshall and Looby in a different car sneaked out of town on back roads. Sure enough, Marshall watched members of the mob turn the corner and follow Looby's car; then he and Looby drove off in another direction. He would later learn that Looby's car was indeed pulled over, and when the pursuers discovered that Marshall wasn't in it, "they beat the driver bad enough that he was in the hospital for a week."

In another car, Maurice Weaver made it back to Nashville that evening along with Harry Raymond, who immediately began typing his story for the *Daily Worker*. "I am certain . . . a lynching was planned," he wrote. "Thurgood Marshall was the intended victim."

Walter White was convinced that had Looby obeyed police orders and continued driving to Nashville on that November night in 1946, Marshall "would never have been seen again."

Safely back in Nashville and his heart still pounding, Marshall made a late-night phone call to U.S. Attorney General Tom C. Clark to tell him what had happened.

"Drunken driving?" Clark asked.

"Yes."

Clark paused. He had come to know Marshall well since being appointed attorney general in 1945 by President Truman, and he had just one question for the man who would one day replace him on the U.S. Supreme Court.

"Well," Clark asked, "were you drunk?"

"No," Marshall asserted, "but exactly five minutes after I hang up this phone I'm going to be drunk!"

# The Metropolitan

l. 2, No. 47　　　　　　　　　Harrisburg, Pennsylvania, December 6, 1946　　　　　　　　　1

## .ocal NAACP Sponsors Mass Meeting for South Carolina Brutality Victin

### Isaac Woodward, War Veteran, Victim of South ern Police Attack and His Attorney, Frankli Williams to Appear at Greater Zion.

**Local N. A. A. C. P. Mass Meeting Held for S. C. Brutality Victim**

Harrisburg. Pa., Dec. 6—

A mammoth mass meeting under the auspices of the Harrisburg Chapter of the N. A. A. C. P. for the benefit of Isaac Woodard, South Carolina brutality victim will be held tonight at 8 P. M. at Greater Zion Baptist Church, according to an announcement of Rev. F. D. Gholston, president of the local chapter.

Both the victim and his Attorney Franklin Williams will appear and speak on the program. Woodard was blinded by an at-

tack made upon him by Police Chief Lynwood L. Shull of Batesburg, S. C. Woodard a war II veteran was on a bus at the time on an interstate journey. Shull who was arraigned before the U. S. District Court in South Carolina for violating the civil rights of Woodard, has recently been released on bond. The NAACP is raising funds to prosecute the case. Mrs. Goldie Watson., President of the Philadelphia Bi-Partisan Committee and members of the State FEPC will also speak at the mass meeting. All organizations and citizens interested in furthering the cause of Civil Liberties and protecting members of minority groups from Southern brutality are invited to attend

*Attorney Franklin Williams*

*Isaac Woodard*

NAACP attorney Franklin Williams and blinded World War II veteran Isaac Woodard went on a nationwide speaking tour to raise money and awareness of the brutality Woodard suffered at the hands of law enforcement agents in the South. (*Courtesy of Schomburg Center for Research in Black Culture, Franklin Williams Papers*)

N IGGER BOY, WHAT are you doing here?"
　　Marshall had been standing under the sweltering sun on the far end of the platform. He had stomach pangs from hunger and he tried to make himself look small, but the white man had come straight toward him, eyes cold and firm, the gun on his hip in plain sight.

"Waiting for the train," Marshall told him.

The man eyed him up and down, suspicious of the suit.

"There's only one more train comes through here," the man told him, "and that's the four o'clock—you'd better be on it because the sun is never going down on a live nigger in this town."

His appetite gone, Marshall's eyes followed the man as he turned away. "So I wrapped my constitutional rights in cellophane, tucked 'em in my hip pocket . . . and caught the next train out of there," the lawyer recalled.

One trip bled into another, and he never felt safe until he was riding the rails north again: sitting with a glass of bourbon in his hand, waiting for the porter to bring him a good cut of meat. Outside the parlor car window, the whitewashed shacks eventually gave way to factories and highways and row houses with white marble steps . . . until he finally stepped off the train in the entirely different world of New York. Pennsylvania Station, with its colossal pink granite columns and glass and steel train sheds, was one of the largest public spaces in the world, its grandeur awing the millions of travelers and commuters who daily passed through it. "One entered the city like a god," architectural historian Vincent Scully noted. Yet the anonymity of strolling across the breathtaking ten-story vaulted concourse like any other man wearing a fedora and hauling his briefcase and luggage suited Marshall just fine. Standing out in a crowd on a train platform was something Marshall was happy to leave behind him in the South.

From Penn Station, Marshall hailed a DeSoto Sky View taxi and headed up the west side of Manhattan to his Harlem apartment. Though the Great Depression had put an end to the Harlem Renaissance, the concentration of blacks in the fifty-by-eight-block area created a dazzling energy and culture that continued to thrive in Harlem in the postwar 1940s; it was still "the Negro capital of America." Uniformed black soldiers on leave from World War II swarmed the uptown streets, flocking to popular clubs like the Savoy Ballroom at night and bars like the Brown Bomber during the day. Past the Victoria and Apollo theaters on 125th Street, Marshall crossed over tracks laid on cobblestone, where trolley cars encouraged commuters to "Ride the Surface Way."

Thurgood and his wife, Buster, in their twenties, childless, and already married for seven years, had come to New York in the fall of 1936. Like so many blacks who had migrated from the South, the young couple had come to Harlem, but not to escape Jim Crow. Thurgood had been offered a job with the NAACP, where he'd share a Manhattan office with his mentor, Charles Hamilton Houston. The money wasn't good. Houston himself was living at the YMCA in Harlem, and he pulled in nearly twice Thurgood's two-hundred-dollar salary each month. The Marshalls had packed their bags in Baltimore and headed north to stay with Thurgood's aunt Medi and uncle Boots (Denmedia and Clarence Dodson) on Lenox Avenue—in the heart of Harlem in the waning moments of the Renaissance. It was the place to be.

FATS WALLER PARKED on a piano bench for the night in a Harlem flat, fedora perched on his head and a flask within easy reach. He popped and rolled his eyes and wiggled his brows between verses as the dancers—maids, elevator operators, and other working-class blacks who lived uptown—brushed against him, fighting for space to unwind. Men were patted down on entry, but Fats had to remind some of them to behave, mid-song, until the words were said so often they crept into his lyrics: "Put that gun away!" Lights dimmed with colored bulbs hung over the dance floor, a space cleared of furniture except for a table and chairs to accommodate a five-hour poker game. Bourbon and gin flowed. The floors shook, and from the kitchen the sweet smell of yardbirds (chicken) and grits wafted in the air. All night long piercing laughter and shouts rose above Fats's voice until the lights continued to dim and he was singing and playing swing and stride piano in darkness.

A lively young couple, Thurgood and Buster reveled in the Harlem nightlife. They had looked for a place of their own but quickly realized they were going to have to compromise. With a total population more than double what it is today, the buildings and tenements uptown were overflowing with "roomers": residents who rented sleeping space in apartments where living and dining rooms were converted into bedrooms at night. To help pay the rent, many tenants held rent parties; they would simply throw up a sign with the date and their address, and for a dollar or so guests could gain entry.

> **We got yellow girls, we've got black and tan**
> **Will you have a good time?—YEAH MAN!**

The tradition of the rent party, which thrived during the Harlem Renaissance, continued into the forties out of economic necessity. Because famous clubs like Connie's Inn and the Cotton Club did not allow black customers, and Small's Paradise, though not segregated, had high door fees that ensured mostly upscale white audiences, much of the great live music at the time was not accessible to blacks. This spurred musicians like Waller and Louis Armstrong to play at rent parties—not just for the extra cash but also for the joy of performing at lively parties with enthusiastic black crowds.

After a few weeks with Marshall's relatives, the young couple found a place of their own on 149th Street. It was small and cramped, but they weren't sharing it with people twice their age, and with Charlie Houston holed up at the YMCA, neither Buster nor Thurgood was complaining, even though money would be tighter. To make ends meet, Buster realized she'd have to contribute. Light-skinned, with wavy hair and soft brown eyes, she'd been a student at the University of Pennsylvania when she met Thurgood at a restaurant in Washington. Marshall claimed it was love at first sight, but eighteen-year-old Vivian Burey disagreed, claiming that the Lincoln University student and self-avowed ladies' man "was so busy arguing and debating with everybody at the table that [he] didn't even give me a second glance." The daughter of a Philadelphia caterer, Vivian had an ample chest that had earned her the nickname Buster in her teen years—a nickname that she maintained throughout her life. She had pluck and a radiant smile, and her intelligence and outgoing personality helped her to acclimate to New York as easily as her husband did.

Soon after they arrived in New York, Buster became involved with the Harlem cooperative grocery markets that had been sprouting up after the Great Depression to develop black economic power. Her work with the co-op helped lower the couple's food bills each week and added a few extra dollars to their cash flow. Despite the excitement and prestige that Marshall's work for the NAACP added to both his and Buster's lives, financially they remained strapped. Still, the young couple had to laugh as they looked forward to better days and a bright future together. In the midst of helping Charles Houston prepare briefs for the NAACP's first test case on educational segregation before the U.S. Supreme Court, Thurgood and Buster found themselves delivering groceries around Harlem and Washington Heights for extra cash.

Soon Houston was lessening his workload in New York and preparing to return to Washington. Marshall was proving himself more than competent and hardworking, and Houston had no qualms about handing more responsibilities to his protégé. With Houston set to leave in July 1938, Marshall was about to be handed control of the NAACP's legal office. He'd receive a $200 raise, so he'd now be earning $2,600 per year. "How much is that a week?" a frugal Buster wanted to know.

In the days before Houston departed, he and Marshall went for a walk outside the office. The two could not have been more different. Houston was serious and tightly wound, whereas Marshall was folksy, familiar, and always laughing. But they shared a commitment to hard work and thorough preparation, and Houston wanted Marshall to know that he'd continue to counsel and support his former student. Houston warned Thurgood about the difficulties of working under Walter White, the executive secretary of the NAACP. White wasn't a lawyer, but he liked to think he was at times, and he didn't shy away from voicing opinions on legal strategies. White also had an ego, and Houston wanted Marshall to know that it would probably take some time before he'd see a reasonable salary that was worthy of the work he'd be doing. "You know how much money you're making," Houston said. Marshall just nodded.

"And you can imagine how much money I make. And I still say you have more goddamn fun than I do."

With that, Marshall let out one of his hearty, high-pitched laughs. "Ain't no question about that!" he said.

Not long after Marshall's promotion, Buster realized that the tiny flat on 149th Street wasn't going to do for the couple anymore—not with her husband's newfound social status. She began asking around, talking to some of the other NAACP wives, and before long she had her sights set high on the bluff.

O N  T H E  W A Y  home from Penn Station after another grueling trip south, Marshall sat in the DeSoto, eyeing the wide sidewalks in front of the Super Food Markets and Harlem tenements with "To Be Demolished" signs posted by the New York City Housing Authority, as the taxi approached Sugar Hill. In this renowned neighborhood of Harlem, Marshall lived alongside the successful artists, intellectual elites, and wealthy blacks who, pursuing their dream of the "Sweet Life," had gravitated there during the Renaissance. If Harlem was the black capital of America, Sugar Hill was its cultural soul. It contained "perhaps the most modern and beautiful residential areas for Negroes in black America," and it was home to musicians like Duke Ellington, Louis Armstrong, and Lena Horne, the writer Ralph Ellison, and actor Paul Robeson. At the heart of Sugar Hill was 409 Edgecombe Avenue, a thirteen-story neo-Georgian building on Coogan's Bluff that towered over the town houses and tenements of Harlem. The poet Langston Hughes spoke of "two Harlems," and he clearly had 409 Edgecombe in mind when he wrote of those who "live on that attractive rise of bluff . . . where the plumbing really works and the ceilings are high and airy." Its residents included Aaron Douglas, the Kansas-born,

Parisian-trained artist who became known as the "father of black American art"; W. E. B. DuBois, author and civil rights activist; and Walter White, Marshall's boss. A 1947 issue of *Ebony* magazine commented that the building attracted so many black elites "that legend, only slightly exaggerated, says bombing 409 would wipe out Negro leadership for the next 20 years."

One resident at 409 had leadership skills that were disputed by no one, though she was not whom DuBois had in mind when he wrote of the exceptional "talented tenth" who would save the Negro race. Madame Stephanie St. Clair, known to most as "Queenie," was purported to be the Numbers Queen of Harlem and, at one point, the richest black woman in America. In New York by way of Martinique, Madame St. Clair—abrasive, unsmiling, and tough as nails—had managed to withstand the violent efforts of Dutch Schultz and any other mobsters who'd tried to horn in on her gambling operations and territory.

The building had its share of society parties hosted by Gladys and Walter White—their thirteenth-floor apartment was called "the White House of Harlem"—and at times it fostered a fraternity atmosphere. The Baltimore couple fitted right in. At one of White's parties, Marshall couldn't stop laughing as he watched his new friend, world heavyweight boxing champion Joe Louis, chase the actress Tallulah Bankhead as she ran screaming down the hallways of 409 with the fighter in close pursuit. For the most part, however, and in stark contrast to the life he lived away from home, Thurgood Marshall's life at 409 was a quiet one.

On weekends, the young Marshalls attended upscale Harlem supper clubs like Happy Rhone's Paradise on 143rd Street and Lenox, the "NAACP's unofficial after-hours headquarters," where the leaders of the burgeoning civil rights movement during World War II held court with black intellectuals, literati, and entertainers. Richard Wright, author of *Native Son* and the 1941 winner of the Spingarn Medal, the NAACP's prestigious award "for the highest achievement of an American Negro," was another of Marshall's "sassiety" Harlem neighbors who moved in the same circle at the time. Thurgood also socialized with a friend from his college days at Lincoln University, Langston Hughes, who had come to New York years before and was one of the leading voices of the Harlem Renaissance. Like many intellectuals and activists who joined the NAACP's fight for equal rights, both Wright and Hughes were drawn to communism, and for decades Marshall had to navigate the complex relationship between communist supporters in the Civil Rights Congress—a communist front organization dedicated to civil liberties—and J. Edgar Hoover's FBI, which, Marshall knew, could destroy the NAACP with just a few well-timed words during the Red Scare.

The Marshalls eventually settled on a modest one-bedroom flat on the ninth floor at 409 Edgecombe, where they mostly socialized on weekends with a couple they knew from their college days—eating and drinking together late into the night, and playing card games. (They called their little group "the Pokenos," after the card game Po-Ke-No.) With Thurgood traveling so frequently and often being gone for long stretches, Buster kept herself busy with social affairs and Urban League activities in Harlem. In many ways they were living a dream life—a young, attractive, educated couple with a desirable place to call home in the greatest city on earth. In private, however, the Marshalls were struggling with disappointments. Buster had miscarried again. Married for more than a decade, she'd been unable to carry a baby to term, and sadness was turning to frustration and grief.

"Buster had a weak uterus," said Marshall's secretary, Alice Stovall, adding that Buster had become pregnant "quite a few times because she said she knew how much Thurgood wanted children." Everyone around them had children, it seemed, and Buster's sense of self-worth had become wedded to her fertility problems and the notion that she was disappointing her husband. She was unable to shake the sadness that enveloped her.

Thurgood compartmentalized the pain and occupied himself increasingly with work and travel. On the rare mornings when he was in New York, he'd ride the elevator down to the white-tiled lobby, where Nathan the doorman would hold open the tall glass doors as Marshall stepped onto Edgecombe Avenue. High on Coogan's Bluff, Marshall could look out over the Harlem River to Yankee Stadium on his way to work. More impressive, though, was the view of the Polo Grounds, where the New York Giants baseball team played their home games. The stadium hosted the first game of the 1946 Negro World Series, in which the Kansas City Monarchs beat the Newark Eagles, 2–1. They did so without their former star, Jackie Robinson, who had been signed by the Brooklyn Dodgers before the season and was lighting up the International League with the Montreal Royals in preparation for his 1947 debut, when he would break baseball's color line by becoming the first black to play in America's major leagues. In that 1947 season, when Brooklyn Dodgers president Branch Rickey wanted a black lawyer to help put Robinson's financial affairs in order, he sent the rookie to Thurgood Marshall.

Before heading downtown to the NAACP offices, Marshall would stride past Colonial Park and down Seventh Avenue to the Hotel Theresa at 125th Street, the "social capital of Negro America." On June 19, 1946, nearly a quarter million people turned out for a parade there on 125th Street to wish Joe Louis luck in his rematch that evening with Billy Conn at Yankee Stadium. Louis was greeted all along 125th Street with music, floats, honking horns, and large signs that read, "Good Luck, Joe." Before the fight, Louis famously said of the lighter Conn, "He can run, but he can't hide," and in the eighth round, before the first television audience to witness a world heavyweight championship, Louis finally found Conn, landing a vicious right-uppercut, left-hook combination that sent the Pittsburgh fighter onto his back for the ten count.

*Ebony* magazine kept an office at the Hotel Theresa, Walter White did his WLIB radio show there, and just across the street from the hotel, the black newspapers the *Chicago Defender* and the *Pittsburgh Courier* had offices. Marshall often met with reporters or addressed women's groups at the hotel. In Theresa's coffee shop he sometimes sat with Joe Louis, ate mushroom omelets, and rubbed shoulders with the likes of Bumpy Johnson, the notorious bookmaker for Madame St. Clair. But it was Marshall who commanded the attention of the staff. A waitress there remembered that "they treated him like a movie star." She recalled, "He was so handsome in those days." The waitress recalled, too, how Julia Scott, the manager of the coffee shop, used to wait on Marshall "because she was afraid we'd spill coffee on him or cause some embarrassing accident because we were so nervous in his presence. 'You girls stop staring at Mr. Marshall,' she'd say when he came in."

Despite the difficulties at home, Marshall was riding high in 1946. In May the thirty-seven-year-old attorney became the thirty-first Spingarn medalist, joining the likes of Wright, Robeson, DuBois, author and activist James Weldon Johnson, and the American contralto Marian Anderson as recipients of the esteemed award. Next to Wright, Marshall was the youngest person to receive the Spingarn Medal, conferred in recognition of his "distinguished service as a lawyer before the Supreme Court of the United States . . . particularly in the Texas Primary Case which conceivably may have more far reaching influence than any other act in the ending of disenfranchisement based upon race or color in the country." In this 1944 case, *Smith v. Allwright*, involving an all-white primary, the U.S. Supreme Court justices voted 8–1 in Marshall's favor, ruling that blacks "cannot be legally barred from voting in the Texas Democratic primaries." One Spingarn Medal Award Committee member noted that Marshall's work in the case "brought about the most beneficial results for the Negro since Emancipation." Marshall was also cited for his attack on the Jim Crow travel system and unequal educational opportunities as well as for his battle to win for blacks "basic human rights and justice in the courts."

In May 1946 Walter White wrote a note to Marshall, informing him that because the company making the Spingarn Medal would be unable to create a new die in time for the June ceremony in Cincinnati, the NAACP would instead be presenting him with a replica gold-plated medal. "Lest you think we are trying to pull a fast one on you," White went on to explain, the company would be casting a solid gold medal that Marshall would receive "as soon as it is delivered." Marshall returned the note after writing a two-word response: "Oh yeah."

THURGOOD MARSHALL SMOKED three packs of cigarettes a day. By mid-June of 1946, however, Marshall's body was failing him. He was drinking steadily and not getting much sleep, and his constant travel to Columbia, Tennessee, where temperatures soared over a hundred degrees, had left him exhausted, with no time for exercise—not that he'd ever shown any interest in exercise. Nor did his preferred diet of fried food and red meat do him any favors. He was laughing less, talking in muted tones, and to friends and associates, he was not himself. Sensing something might be amiss with his health, Marshall arranged NAACP staff participation in the Blue Cross Hospitalization Plan, which, he said, at "very reasonable rates" would relieve employees of "that mental worry of wondering where the money is coming from to meet the bills."

Two weeks later, more than seven hundred delegates joined thousands of members in Cincinnati for the NAACP's thirty-seventh annual conference, at which, on the closing night, Marshall would receive the Spingarn Medal. Onstage, Marshall was seated beside Joe Louis and Colonel Benjamin O. Davis, the famous Tuskegee airman. Next to Louis, Marshall looked gaunt and run-down in his dark pinstripe suit and spectator shoes: a stark contrast to the smiling, muscular fighter. Still, Marshall managed to rise to the occasion. Standing before his mentor, Charles Hamilton Houston, he made it clear that the medal was "an award coming to one person in recognition of the work of a large group of lawyers who have always worked together in a spirit of wholehearted co-operation and without any hope of reward other than that of seeing a job done." After his acceptance speech Marshall introduced the lawyers he'd been working with on the Columbia case, Z. Alexander Looby and Maurice Weaver, as well as Mrs. Gladys Stephenson, whose broken radio had started the riots back in February. The case had exhausted Marshall, and listening to Mrs. Stephenson onstage as she told her story reminded him of the oppressive heat and stress he had been enduring. Indeed, he'd just come from Columbia, where he'd been "carrying around a fever ranging from 103 to 104 degrees" over the last week, and the fever had not abated in Cincinnati. It was so bad, Marshall said, that he "was only able to be out of bed two or three hours a day."

After the convention, when Marshall returned to New York, he could not get out of bed at all. Seeing his condition as critical and even "grave," Walter White was worried. He wanted to avoid sending Marshall to Harlem Hospital—a place, he noted, that had earned such a reputation for the "callous and inadequate treatment" of black patients that it inspired a folk saying: "When any member of your family goes to Harlem Hospital, telephone the undertaker." White thus reached out to some of his society friends and associates in an attempt to have Marshall admitted to Mount Sinai Hospital. It was not to be. Citing red tape, overcrowded conditions, and the inability to "build a room" for Marshall on such short notice as the excuses offered by the hospital, White concluded that Marshall, in his hour of need, was not admitted because of his race.

So it was that Marshall found himself in Ward 2D at Harlem Hospital, where the doctors could not figure out the cause of his illness. They first suspected a tumor, or "cancer of the lung," and White, alarmed at the critical nature of Marshall's prognosis, notified the NAACP's board of directors that the lawyer's condition was "due solely to the fact that he has worked himself almost to death without any thought of self."

Marshall had hoped to keep the news of his admission to Harlem Hospital quiet, but it wasn't possible, especially when the hallways began to buzz over the large plant and cards that Marshall had received from Eleanor Roosevelt. When Roosevelt was First Lady, she had been drawn to the cause of racial justice, and as a board member and activist for the NAACP, she had lobbied her husband on many race-related issues from civil rights to the Costigan-Wagner antilynching bill. Franklin Delano Roosevelt, for his part, was less than enthralled with his wife's alliance with the NAACP, and the White House attempted to maintain a distance between the president and Eleanor's activism on behalf of blacks. Marshall himself had felt the president's chill when Attorney General Francis Biddle phoned FDR to discuss the NAACP's involvement in a race case in Virginia. At Biddle's instruction, Marshall picked up an extension phone to listen in, only to hear FDR exclaim, "I warned you not to call me again about any of Eleanor's niggers. Call me one more time and you are fired." Marshall later recalled, "The President only said 'nigger' once, but once was enough for me."

Eleanor Roosevelt nonetheless continued her work with the NAACP during and after the FDR administration. Appalled by the riots in Columbia, Tennessee, she worked closely with Marshall to get a reluctant Justice Department involved. A plant and cards simply betokened her esteem and admiration for a man at the front lines in the country's civil rights battle. Roosevelt, however, wasn't the only one who had learned that Marshall had checked into Harlem Hospital. Marshall's wife, Buster, was at home in Sugar Hill one day in July when a Railway Express man showed up at the apartment on Edgecombe Avenue with a package from the men Marshall was defending in the Tennessee riot case. "You know," the deliveryman told Buster, "I'm from Tennessee, and from the smell I know what's in here, and I would sure like to have some of it." Inside the box was a "twenty-pound, country-cured ham" and a letter that read, "Dear lawyer . . . The wives all wanted to send you flowers, but we knew what you'd rather have."

The doctors at Harlem Hospital continued to run tests. Marshall, still unable to get out of bed, did not show any improvement. It had been determined that Marshall did not have a tumor, and eventually the doctors settled on a diagnosis of a mysterious, pneumonia-like virus—"Virus X," as Marshall called it. The diagnosis afforded the thirty-eight-year-old little comfort. Just a few years before, Fats Waller, whose exaggerated facial expressions and mannerisms Marshall often affected while telling a story, had died of pneumonia on a train down south shortly before his own fortieth birthday. The doctors ordered that Marshall be confined to bed for six weeks without visitors, and if he then showed any improvement, he would be allowed to return to work, but "not more than three hours a day every other day." After a month Marshall slowly began to regain some of his strength. He was no longer running a high fever, but his doctors refused to allow him to return to work. White visited him in mid-July and noted that Marshall was "far from out of the woods yet." White also noticed that Marshall's spirits nonetheless seemed to be rising, as he'd asked White to deliver a message to the NAACP staff: "Give them the bad news that I'll live," Marshall said.

By early August, Marshall's doctor, Louis T. Wright, the first black surgeon at Harlem Hospital and himself a Spingarn medalist in 1940, had "ordered" Marshall to leave the country; Wright felt that the lawyer would benefit from an extended leave, preferably in a tropical climate, where he could relax and recover. From NAACP donors, White secured five hundred dollars for Marshall's medical bills, and sent Thurgood and Buster to stay with William H. Hastie, another fellow Spingarn medalist and one of Marshall's former professors at Howard University Law School. Hastie had just been appointed the first black governor of the U.S. Virgin Islands by President Truman.

Marshall rested for a week in the Virgin Islands. For no longer than that could he resist working on the proposed budget for the NAACP's Legal Defense Fund. Against doctor's orders, he was also on the phone each night with Looby so that they could discuss legal strategies and the day's proceedings in the Columbia Race Riot case. He reported to White, however, that he was "taking it more than easy" and the only exercise he was getting was from losing money at poker, which "is no effort for me."

By mid-August Marshall had nearly recovered. Taking advantage of the excellent climate, he and Buster visited Cuba, Haiti, and Jamaica. "I will have a difficult job to persuade Buster to leave," Marshall wrote to White. "I am not too anxious to leave myself, but I understand that my welcome is about worn out, so I better leave before being run out." He told White not to pay attention to the "deliberate falsehoods" that Hastie had been spreading about Marshall's "descent upon the Virgins," despite the fact that White thought it would take a "month of steady explanation" to answer Hastie's accusations.

Months would pass before Marshall regained full strength, but he nevertheless returned to Columbia, despite his doctor's warnings. In November he won in Tennessee, but more important, he survived not only a mysterious virus but also a lynching party. Walter White, in his autobiography *A Man Called White*, wrote, "It is doubtful whether any other trial in the history of America was ever conducted under more explosive conditions." But White wrote those words in 1948, one year before Thurgood Marshall became involved in his most deadly and dramatic case ever. It would far surpass the Columbia Race Riot trials in its explosive conditions, and its consequences would have an impact on the NAACP's Legal Defense Fund and its staff for decades to come.

# |3| GET TO PUSHIN'

Willie Padgett rests his foot against his 1940 Ford sedan as he shares a laugh with Deputy James Yates. (*Photo by Wallace Kirkland/Time & Life Pictures/Getty Images*)

NORMA LEE WORE a pink farm dress on the worst night of her life. Blond and seventeen years old, she pushed the wedding ring back onto her finger; tossed a compact, powder, and perfume into her purse; and sauntered outside her daddy's house to where Willie was waiting beside his run-down 1940 Ford. He opened the door for her and Willie's eyes went right to Norma's bare legs as she slid her thin body across the tattered seat. With only one stop to make, Willie pulled away from the Tyson farmhouse as the Florida sun was setting, and minutes later he idled the old Ford in front of Frisz's Bar and Grill, where he ran inside and picked up a bottle of whiskey for the big dance.

On July 15, 1949, the front pages of newspapers across the country bannered frightening news for Americans. President Truman had called an emergency meeting with "top Cabinet, military, atomic and Congressional leaders" on a matter so secret that none of the participants would comment "for the good of the country." As it turned out, Russia, aided by spies who worked on the Manhattan Project, was just weeks from successfully testing its first atom bomb, a near replica of the U.S. Fat Man design, years earlier than analysts had expected. The United States was already in the throes of the Red Scare, and Americans' fears of atomic warfare and the spread of communism intensified.

The same day another headline in the papers announced that the celebrated stage star and singer Paul Robeson had been a member of the Communist Party for years, and was "ambitious to become 'the Black Stalin'"—or so a former communist testified at the House Un-American Activities Committee hearings in Washington, D.C. The witness stated further that the Communist Party planned to set up a black republic through an armed revolt in the South, extending from Maryland to Texas, and that Robeson had been assigned "certain secret work that was intercontinental."

On that mid-July Friday, twenty-three-year-old Willie Haven Padgett, his work on the farm done for the week, was blissfully unaware of the portents of nuclear warfare or the creeping threat of communism. He was looking forward to a Friday night of drinking and dancing and getting whatever else he might in the backseat of his car before the sun came up. Born and raised among the lower-class whites of Tattnall County, Georgia, Willie had moved with his family to Bay Lake, Florida—a clannish stretch of truck farmers who mostly lived off the land in scattered wooden shacks a few miles south of Groveland. He hadn't made it past grammar school, so he had already put in years of hard work in the family's fertile Lake County soil when he met a frail but comely girl up the road named Norma Lee Tyson.

Still, Willie was nervous, despite the fact that this was hardly their first date. He'd met the Tyson girl the year before, when she was just sixteen years old, and he and Norma had married a few months later. But things had been rocky from the start, and the two had separated even before their first anniversary. Norma's father, Coy Tyson, had had a lot to do with that. He didn't much care for the freckled, bucktoothed kid who asked for his daughter's hand in marriage, and Coy Tyson certainly didn't like the fact that his daughter was often left at home while Willie caroused all night all over Lake County. Rumors around town had it that the short-tempered Willie got rough with young Norma—that he slapped her around at times—and Bay Lake locals knew Coy Tyson wasn't going to stand for behavior like that. Willie realized he had to watch his step with Norma these days, because the Tysons were not to be messed with, and tonight might be his last opportunity to make things right with Norma Lee.

One thing working in Willie's favor was that Norma, despite her age, wasn't exactly an innocent farm girl—not even in the eyes of her father. Her reputation around town was "not good," according to one white woman who knew her, and "a bad egg" is how another local described her. For Norma had been seen "cavorting with Negroes"—one sure way for a white girl to tarnish her reputation—and this may have been why Coy Tyson was willing to give Willie another chance with his daughter. The Padgetts and the Tysons alike had thought the young couple would benefit by a temporary separation; both had some growing up to do.

By the summer of 1949, Norma was living at her father's house and Willie had moved back onto his mother's property about a mile down the road from the Tysons. The monotony of long hours on the farm and the haunting daily reminder that he had failed so early in his marriage had Willie looking forward to the weekend as a chance to patch things up with his teenage bride. There was a dance at the American Legion hall in Clermont, about sixteen miles away, and if Willie could get his jalopy of a car to run—and if Coy Tyson would approve—he could show Norma a good time out on the town.

For Norma, even if she and Willie were having troubles, the idea of going out dancing with him on a Friday night was still preferable to another night at home with her father. Why should Willie always be out having a good time? Why should she be always the one stuck at home?

After picking up a bottle of whiskey at Frisz's, the Padgetts arrived at the American Legion hall in Clermont around 9:30 p.m. They found a table with Willie's sister and her husband, and mixing with young farmers and war veterans still in their twenties, the young couple drank whiskey, danced, and gabbed until 1 a.m. After a last dance, they left the hall and headed for Willie's old Ford.

Willie tried to start the car, but the engine wouldn't turn over. According to Norma's later account, they had to "get it pushed off" in order to leave the unpaved parking lot. As they rolled down the road into darkness, both of them roaring drunk, Norma announced she was hungry, as she hadn't had anything to eat that night; so they decided to drive to Burtoft's Café, a "dine-and-dance spot" in Okahumpka, to grab a sandwich. With farmland and pastures flickering by the car window, they passed what was left in the bottle of whiskey back and forth. They had traveled some miles north toward Okahumpka when it dawned on Willie that Burtoft's Café probably wouldn't be open at this hour. Norma decided they should turn around; she was tired, she just wanted to go home.

Willie slowed the car. The road was deserted, and Willie's hopes were empty. Nothing magical was happening between him and Norma—all they shared was frustration and youthful impatience and confusion. Maybe it would never work out between them. What would they be, then? Neighbors? Willie didn't see himself ever leaving Bay Lake, and Norma wasn't going anywhere, either. Seventeen years old, thin, and pretty, but a prisoner in her daddy's house, sitting around all day and night with her daddy whispering in her ear that Willie Padgett's no good. Another man was sure to come along, come to rescue her. Willie had seen the young veterans practically leering at Norma when he was dancing with her. No doubt they were whispering, too, wondering where things stood and how long it would be before Norma was free of him. Well, she was still Willie Padgett's wife. At least in name she was.

Good and drunk now, Willie took another swig of whiskey before handing the bottle to Norma. Then, slowing the car, he made a right turn down a dirt driveway, but he didn't get far. He struggled with the wheel to pull up beside some mossy oaks, and stopped at a fence gate. The Ford's engine rattled the dashboard. The headlights illuminated the white, sandy road before them. Despite the shining moon, it was undeniably dark and uncomfortably quiet, with no signs of cars coming from either direction. Norma Lee, in her pink cotton dress, sat on the front bench seat, her delicate body pressed against the door, while she waited for Willie, the boy she called "Haven" in happier moments, to rest his hand on the gearshift and turn the car back around so that she could finally go home.

S AMUEL SHEPHERD WAS having car troubles of his own that night. He and his friend Walter Irvin, both twenty-two-year-old army veterans from the same outfit, had started out the evening in his father's 1937 Ford, but the car was not acting right in Groveland. So Samuel drove them back to the Shepherd house in Bay Lake around 9:30 p.m.;

there he hoped to swap the old Ford for his brother James's Mercury. James, who was married to Walter's sister, ultimately consented to the switch, on the promise they'd have the car back before James had to leave for work in the morning. The two friends gassed up the tank and headed east for a night out.

The town of Eatonville was only six miles north of Orlando and thirty-five miles east of the town that Samuel and Walter called home. Yet it was worlds away from Groveland. After the Civil War, many black soldiers, not content to be swept into the undesirable parts of a town, chose to settle in one of dozens of race colonies that had begun to spring up across the nation. There blacks could live a life that was virtually free of racial friction. In 1887, Eatonville became the first incorporated African-American community in America. According to its most famous resident, the writer Zora Neale Hurston, who gained fame during the Harlem Renaissance, Eatonville was something of an oasis for blacks—"a pure Negro town . . . where the only white folks were those who passed through." She described it as "a city of five lakes, three croquet courts, three hundred brown skins, three hundred good swimmers, plenty guavas, two schools, and no jailhouse." (In 1949, after traveling the world and after decades in New York, where she'd moved in the same Harlem circles as Thurgood Marshall, Hurston had returned home after being falsely accused of molesting a ten-year-old boy. The charges were ultimately dropped, but the damage to Hurston's reputation was irreparable, and unable to make a living with her pen, the talented, outspoken, and now broke Eatonville resident was working as a housemaid in Florida.)

For Samuel Shepherd and Walter Irvin, a night out in Eatonville was a welcome respite from the discriminating ways of Jim Crow and the continual racial harassment they'd endured while growing up together in Lake County. On their arrival in Eatonville, the two friends swaggered into Club Eaton—a renowned nightspot on the Chitlin' Circuit where well-known black musicians such as Duke Ellington, Ella Fitzgerald, Billie Holiday, and a young local boy named Ray Charles performed during the segregation era. Samuel and Walter ate a light supper, drank a few beers, chatted with girls, and played the jukebox. Then they decided to see what was happening at Club 436 in nearby Altamonte Springs. There the two army buddies ordered a quart of beer. After an hour or so, because Irvin had to get up early to work with his father in the orange groves under Florida's unforgiving summer sun, and as he wanted to get at least a few hours of sleep, they finished their beer and drove approximately forty miles west, over a hot, flat land dotted with wild orange trees and live oaks swathed in Spanish moss.

It was long past midnight, and Samuel and Walter were just a few miles north of Groveland when they came upon a 1940 Ford by the side of the road. Samuel slowed the Mercury, and as he passed the car he saw a young white couple inside. About fifty yards farther on, Samuel stopped and turned the Mercury around. Willie had emerged from the Ford and was shouting something as Samuel and Walter rolled up to his car. Shepherd stuck his head out the window. "Need any help?" he asked.

"Yes," Willie answered. Shepherd put the Mercury in park, Irvin got out, and Willie explained that the car's battery was dead and that he needed a push to jump-start the car. Norma, still inside the Ford, interrupted the men's discussion several times, telling Willie to get in the car so that they could get the engine started and get home. "OK, in a minute," Willie told her.

Finally, Shepherd and Irvin went around to the back of the Ford, and Willie hopped in next to Norma. The two army veterans leaned in and began pushing, to no avail. One of the rear wheels was still lodged in sand. Samuel and Walter stopped to rest. "Get to pushin'," Willie ordered them, popping his head out the window. Samuel didn't like his tone.

Frustrated, impatient, Norma and Willie got out of the car to find out why the two black men had ceased their effort. Samuel tried to explain that it was no use: The battery was dead; they had given it a try but the car wasn't budging. They were both sweating and breathing hard, and Shepherd was annoyed. He had stopped to help and didn't appreciate being bossed around by Padgett. To ease the tension, Norma smiled at the two friends and extended the whiskey bottle to Samuel. He gratefully took a swig, then passed the bottle to Walter, who handed it back to Norma. Willie glared as his eyes followed the bottle, and when Norma extended it to him, he erupted. "Do you think I'm gonna drink behind a nigger?" Willie spat.

That was it for Samuel Shepherd. He'd had enough; after going out of his way to help this drunken cracker, Shepherd wasn't about to abide his insults. He grabbed Willie by the shirt. Willie tried fighting back, but, drunk and scrawny, he was no match for Samuel. In just a few seconds Willie was flat on his back, either knocked out or passed out, in the ditch.

The two friends stood for a moment, their eyes set on a motionless Willie Padgett lying sprawled in the grass beside a pasture fence. They hadn't hurt him too badly, and he'd had it coming, but this was Lake County, and they could see the picture. Cross a white man wrong in these parts and you're like to find your own black self lying dead in a ditch. Norma Lee Padgett, still clutching the near-empty bottle of whiskey, steadied herself on the sand and clay. Bathed in the bright moonlight and the glow from the Mercury's headlights, she knew. She knew nothing good would come of this. They all knew.

# |4| NIGGER IN A PIT

Charles Hamilton Houston. (*Library of Congress, Prints & Photographs Division, Visual Materials from the NAACP Records*)

H ER NICKNAME WAS "Big East," and, like her friend Thurgood Marshall, she was a force to be reckoned with. Nearly six feet tall, exotic-looking, athletic, and graceful, Evelyn Cunningham was a black reporter and columnist with the *Pittsburgh Courier*, and was known around New York for her "high heels, red hair, mink coat and attitude."

"When Evelyn Cunningham entered a room, you knew it," said Charles Rangel, the congressman from New York, longtime Harlem resident, and former desk clerk at the Hotel Theresa. Cunningham's other nickname, "the Lynching Editor," stemmed from her days as a stringer for the *Courier*, when she traveled through the South to cover the same racial atrocities and trials that claimed the attention of Marshall and the NAACP. "I wanted to do hard news," Cunningham said, "and he [the *Courier* editor] started worrying about me and I said, 'Well, I get killed somewhere it's not your fault. Can't nobody sue you 'cause you weren't even there. Chicken!'" Like Marshall, Cunningham loved the travel and the excitement of working for a cause she believed in—civil rights. "I think I did my best writing during that period of danger," she said. "Went to jail a couple of times, I was threatened, I was almost raped, all the bad things . . . really bad."

Cunningham claimed she conned her editors into assigning her to the dangerous stories she wanted to report. "I said, 'You know, they don't lynch women. I got an advantage being a woman. Everything they're doing, they're doing to men.' And they bought that!"

Hard as Marshall and Cunningham worked on the road, in New York they found occasion to play. One night they decided to visit an illegal after-hours club that didn't open until three in the morning. It was filled with smoke, sultry bebop music, and the "not particularly savory" people that Marshall usually steered clear of. But after a few drinks, the lawyer loved being in the middle of it. With a cigarette dangling from his lips and a drink in his hand, Marshall was enjoying himself, Cunningham recalled. They were having a great, noisy time when, suddenly, police descended on the club from all directions. It was a raid. The music stopped; people screamed and scattered. Thinking quickly, Cunningham accosted a cop she recognized, telling him, "You can't arrest this man. He is very, very important, he's with the NAACP, you've got to let him go." The officer permitted Cunningham to lead Marshall through a side door, out to the street. Big East was trying her best to get him away from the scene as fast as possible, but Marshall apparently wasn't ready for the night to end. Cars rolled by, with horns honking, as police jostled men into waiting wagons. Espying his fellow club patrons in handcuffs and custody, the boisterous, slightly inebriated lawyer spun around in his tracks and bellowed, "I would like to defend these guys—these cops got no right doing this!" Big East grabbed him by his coat sleeve and dragged him away. "Time to go home," she said, convinced that Marshall would have surely gotten himself arrested. "He was a bit high," she recalled.

That he was out so late at night in New York while living at 409 Edgecombe was no surprise to friends, who observed that Marshall's relationship with his wife had "become distant and lifeless." Buster had by now become accustomed to Marshall's constant travel and days, or weeks, away from home. They had been married only a few years in 1933 when Marshall was in his final year at Howard University Law School and his professor Charles Hamilton Houston approached his prize student with a proposition. Houston had been asked by the NAACP to defend George Crawford, a Virginia man accused of murdering two white women, and Houston invited Marshall to assist with the case. It was an opportunity Marshall could not pass up. He assisted Houston more than diligently, working long hours in the Howard law library. He also caught the eye of Walter White, the executive secretary of the NAACP, who observed a "lanky, brash young senior law student" who was always present. "Amazed at [Marshall's] assertiveness in challenging positions taken by Charlie and the other lawyers," White recognized young Thurgood's "great value to the case in doing everything he was asked, from research on obscure legal opinions to foraging for coffee and sandwiches." The opportunity not only to study under Houston but also to work alongside the legal giant was a life-changing event for Marshall. Although they were unable to win an acquittal for Crawford, they did together prevent a death sentence. That in itself was worth celebrating, for both men knew that when blacks were charged with killing whites in the South, a life sentence was a victory. "You've won," Marshall later said, "because normally they were hanging them."

The following summer Houston had another proposition for Marshall, who had just graduated as valedictorian from Howard University Law School. The NAACP was sending Houston on a fact-finding mission to study and document the inequalities in schools for both black and white children in the South, and Houston wanted his young protégé to accompany him. It was something Marshall had to talk over with Buster first. They'd been living together with Marshall's parents in a small house on Druid Hill Avenue in Baltimore, patiently waiting for the day when Marshall would graduate from law school, hang a shingle, and start making a name for himself. Buster had meanwhile been selling bread in a Jewish bakery and women's hats in a clothing store, among other jobs, to help make ends meet. Complicating the decision was a scholarship offer from Harvard Law School for Marshall to study for an advanced law degree. Marshall, however, could not resist the opportunity to travel with his mentor. He'd study for the Maryland bar exam when he returned.

Having packed Houston's six-cylinder Graham-Paige with their luggage and bags of fruit, the two men set off from Washington, D.C., on a journey that took them through the Carolinas, Georgia, Alabama, Louisiana, and Mississippi. Traveling not as lawyers but as journalists and social scientists, they documented public facilities and schools for blacks in rural areas of the

South that, to both men, seemed to have been lost in time. With a still camera as well as a rented, handheld silent movie camera they compiled a visual record of the poverty they encountered. An endless string of ramshackle schools on dusty roads, where children sat on floors of tiny classrooms with broken windows and potbellied stoves, demonstrated indisputably that the segregationist states were by no means meeting the "separate but equal" standard established by the U.S. Supreme Court in the nocuous *Plessy v. Ferguson* decision in 1896. "Motion pictures," Houston wrote, "humanize and dramatize the discrimination which Negroes suffer much more effectively than any corresponding amount of speech could do. . . ."

Riding alongside Houston in the car, Marshall smoked cigarettes and typed observations on a well-worn Remington portable that he balanced on his knees. "Conditions," Marshall wrote, "were much worse than we heard they were"—conditions like streets with human waste running through poorly drained ditches, because there was no plumbing in the black parts of town. The trips—they made two of them—had a profound impact on Marshall. Not only had he now seen with his own eyes the "evil results of discrimination" that his mentor had tried to describe to him in classrooms, but the course of his life had been significantly altered. Houston's incessant credo took hold of the impressionable young man: "A lawyer's either a social engineer or he's a parasite on society."

Marshall went back to Maryland, where he passed the bar, then struggled to find paying clients at his own private practice during the Depression. Most blacks in Baltimore had little money, so Marshall mostly practiced poverty law for the lowest of fees. The more successful blacks were reluctant to hire black lawyers, as they thought their suits would be better represented by white lawyers who had relationships with opposing counsel and judges. So it didn't matter how smart or how competent Marshall was. His race alone prohibited him access to the legal sphere where Baltimore's higher socioeconomic class conducted business and forged relationships—a sphere that even the least competent of white lawyers could enjoy by virtue of their skin color.

Charles Hamilton Houston had to ask only once for the young lawyer to join him in New York at the national headquarters of the NAACP.


B Y THE MID-1940S, the NAACP had become overwhelmed with casework. For years Thurgood Marshall and the association had been planning an all-out attack on segregation, one they hoped would reverse the separate-but-equal doctrine established by *Plessy*. To get there, the NAACP's Legal Defense Fund (LDF) had been filing numerous lawsuits around the country to combat inequalities in teachers' pay, housing, transportation, the armed forces, and higher education. Despite the relocation of the NAACP to more spacious offices in the Willkie Memorial Building in midtown Manhattan, a rash of recent hirings had left Thurgood Marshall's LDF short on space.

Since his arrival at the NAACP in 1938, Marshall had been forced to share an office, first with his mentor, Charles Hamilton Houston, and later with various LDF counsel over the years. He was, Marshall wrote in a 1947 memo to Walter White, "the only executive who shared offices." That was after he'd been shuttled into a small fourth-floor office in Freedom House with two young females, attorney Constance Baker and sociologist Annette Peyser—the three of them shared the single phone. Marshall told White conditions had become unbearable; it was impossible to concentrate with three people in the same office working on different types of cases, "answering the telephone and/or dictating." Marshall was, he wrote, "at the end of my rope."

Though sympathetic, White was not especially disposed to accommodate the less than punctilious Marshall. He had already made it clear to Marshall that he did not appreciate some patterns of behavior in the LDF offices, most notably an "overfamiliarity and casualness" and the use of first names between executives and secretaries or stenographers during office hours that Marshall permitted. W. E. B. DuBois, who had left the organization in 1934, was nevertheless around the office enough to observe Marshall's "unbuttoned office manners to be outlandishly bad." It was a charge the lawyer could not deny. Victories were celebrated, often on Friday afternoons, when Marshall would pull a bottle of whiskey from his desk drawer and proceed to hold court. Imitating judges, opposing counsel, or dim Uncle Tom witnesses, he'd punctuate his tales from the civil rights battlefront with one of his famous deadpan grins or bawdy punch lines. He relished racial humor, like the story about the slave who stole a turkey from his master, then ate the whole bird—and just as the master was about to deliver a whipping, the slave pleaded, "You shouldn't beat me, massuh. You got less turkey, but you sure got more nigger."

"He could tell some pretty off-color jokes which would be, if they were told by someone else, embarrassing," recalled Mildred Roxborough, who began a long career with the NAACP as a secretary in the early 1950s. "But you would find yourself responding to them because of the way in which he told them."

In an office where the work was hard, usually depressing, and often tragic, Marshall was inclined to using sophomoric or gallows humor to alleviate tension. One associate recalled an occasion when Marshall, in the course of doing research, came across a story in a nineteenth-century newspaper about a black man who'd been doing railroad construction in the Midwest and had fallen into a ditch. The absurdity of the headline gripped Marshall, who kept reading it aloud from his desk, over and over, as if it summed up the black man's condition then, and now: "Nigger in a Pit . . . Nigger in a Pit . . . Nigger in a Pit . . ."

The letters from the South that arrived at the NAACP offices often brought cries for help or pleas for justice, and Marshall commonly read them to his staff, even if the LDF could not offer help. A letter, at once touching and humorous, that he received in May 1949 from Charles Jones in Hog Wallow, Georgia, was typical:

Mr. Turgood.

I see by the Courer [Pittsburgh Courier] that you ar the No. 1 negro of all Time, so I take my pen in han as you must be the man I have been lookin for all these yers.

You see Mr. Turgood I has great trouble an goin to church don't seem to make it better. The Courer say you has scared the white folks down hear in the South and has them on the run. Well, maybe so but you has them runnin after me and I am ritin to try to get you to make them run in the other road away from me. They is shootin and beating and tarfeatherin all around here getten closer to me all the time just las week over in the next county and I hop you will come quick because these white folks down hear don't ack like they heard of Supreme court or any court or anything. They is runnin wild and we shure could use the No. 1 negro of all time or somebody to stop them from mistreatin us.

You all is in Harlem an if the goin get tough you can duck in the next basement an nobody no wher you has gon, but down here aint no place to hide they just grabs you and yore number is up or down. Please Mr. Turgood if you are No 1 of all time you can do it you are the one we ben watin for since I was born please help these white folks is mighty mean and mighty close on my heels

yours for a little while anyway
Charles Jones X

*PS Mr Turgood I rite this for Charlie he cant read or rite but he got real good sense. His wife Essie Mae*

Gloria Samuels was Marshall's secretary in 1949. She acknowledged the use of first names at work as Walter White had observed, as well as occasions of laughter, but the fourth floor was not typically so casual as the executive secretary seemed to believe. The workload was far too heavy to be abandoned in laughter, and productivity was no just cause for White's worry.

"Mr. Marshall was very dedicated and careful," Samuels said. "He always wore a suit and tie every day, and he was surrounded by serious young lawyers doing important work. We worked late whenever we had to. Even Saturdays. That was part of the job." Mildred Roxborough confirmed Samuels's observations. "When he was working, you didn't joke," she said. "You didn't waste time. You had an assignment he gave you and he expected it to be completed. It was inviolate that you did that work and you produced and you performed."

Constance Baker, a black woman who was in her last year at Columbia Law School when she was hired by Marshall as a law clerk in October 1945, thought Marshall was ahead of his time in his hiring practices. Baker, who married in 1946 and became Constance Baker Motley, remembered Marshall's "total lack of formality" during her interview, in which he mostly told stories about women lawyers he had known and admired, especially black women who had mustered the courage to enter the white-male-dominated legal profession. That same year Marshall also hired a white woman, Marian Wynn Perry, as an associate counsel, no matter that in 1945, as Motley noted, "nobody was hiring women lawyers." Marshall's hiring practices were not a conscious attempt to achieve diversity on his staff: he just didn't think about it, said Motley, noting that Marshall's mother, Norma, who taught at a segregated elementary school in Baltimore, was one of the first black women to graduate from Columbia University's prestigious Teachers College. She pawned her engagement and wedding rings to help fund Thurgood's law school education at Howard University (his brother Aubrey went to medical school). Marshall had nothing but respect for serious women who were committed to achievement. "His mother was a professional," Motley said. "So the idea of a woman in a professional job, he didn't see anything wrong. In fact, there were women in his class at law school. He didn't think anything strange of a woman being a lawyer."

Evelyn Cunningham, who later became a noted Harlem columnist and feminist, referred to her friend Thurgood Marshall as one of the "first feminists."

B Y THE LATE 1940s, Marshall was logging some fifty thousand miles each year as he swooped into cities and towns across the South, usually alone. The postwar years marked the beginning of a more violent era in the American South, and Marshall's willingness to ride into a hornet's nest of racial conflict in pursuit of his well-stated goal—to dismantle Jim Crow—only cemented his growing legacy as a crusader for justice. Marshall relished his role as Mr. Civil Rights—it suited his gregarious, larger-than-life personality—and he was acutely aware that when he stepped off the train, his only sword was "a piece of paper called 'The Constitution.'" He had grown into a celebrity, and wherever he went he was treated like one. Men respected him and wanted to drink with him and listen to his stories; women simply fawned over him. More and more frequently, after conferences on the road, he did not return home to Harlem, and Buster. To avoid crisscrossing the country, Marshall found it reasonable not to detour back to Manhattan—"no sense in coming back to New York," as he wrote in a letter—and his correspondence vaguely hinted at a need for privacy. On most of his business trips he stayed with friends or associates, but on one occasion he wrote to West Coast civil rights attorney Loren Miller, stating, "I do not want to burden you and Juanita again," and asking for "a suggestion as to a good place near Los Angeles as to where one can go and rest and hide."

Daniel Ellis Byrd, the handsome and extroverted former member of the Harlem Globetrotters basketball team who went on to become field secretary with the NAACP in Louisiana, worked on several desegregation suits with Marshall. The two were close friends and Byrd liked to tease Marshall about his predilection for the ladies. Byrd once wrote to inform Marshall that he had to rearrange the lawyer's itinerary, since he had scheduled Marshall to give a speech on Mother's Day in New Orleans. Byrd wrote, "It has been suggested, however, that since you are not an authority on making a Mother's Day Address, that you would be much more successful, and the occasion would prove more pleasant for you, if you were permitted to 'undress' someone's fine Mother, on Mother's Day (smile)."

In New Orleans, Marshall usually stayed at the home of A. P. Tureaud, a Creole attorney who had also studied law at Howard under Charles

Hamilton Houston. At one time the only black attorney in Louisiana, Tureaud filed countless equal pay and desegregation lawsuits in parishes around the state on behalf of the NAACP, and he spent decades fighting nearly every one of them in court. Tureaud lived in the Seventh Ward, a largely Creole section of New Orleans, and around the corner from his home was one of Marshall's favorite restaurants, Dooky Chase's, where he and Tureaud often conducted business over gumbo and fried chicken in the upstairs meeting room. Otherwise they'd work, as they were doing one evening when, in Tureaud's French Quarter office, Marshall decided he needed a break and headed for the bar downstairs to get a drink, although he knew the bar was closed to blacks. It was the kind of behavior that had earned Marshall one of his nicknames, "Nogood." Tureaud and Byrd continued working and as the hours passed without Marshall reappearing, they began to worry. They worried even more when they could not find Marshall in the bar or anywhere else. Disheartened, they returned to the office, only to find Marshall sitting at the desk going over briefs. The next day on the stairway, Tureaud ran into the strapping white owner of the bar, and his heart jumped. "Say, where's that big tall black fellow that came into my place last night?" Tureaud said that he didn't know. "Well," the owner said, laughing. "If you see him and he ain't busy, ask him to stop by again tonight. He sure had some funny stories."

I N FEBRUARY 1949, with the volume of criminal cases coming through the NAACP threatening to paralyze the LDF, Marshall issued a memorandum that established three rules to be applied "to the types of criminal cases we accept . . . (1) That there is injustice because of race or color; (2) the man is innocent; (3) there is a possibility of establishing a precedent for the benefit of due process and equal protection in general and the protection of Negroes' rights in particular."

The memo also addressed a "misunderstanding" that had arisen when one of his LDF attorneys, Marian Wynn Perry, argued against "limit[ing] ourselves on the second point" and Marshall had to remind her that the NAACP was not a legal aid society. Although he acknowledged that a defendant's innocence was a matter of judgment, he also reasoned that "any experienced lawyer reading the record in a case can usually detect whether a man is obviously guilty or whether he is apparently innocent." He further exhorted his staff to "put no more credence in a convicted defendant's protestation of innocence than we do a confession of guilt. Neither is sufficient in itself for either point." Perry ultimately agreed that she would "obey orders."

Marshall's core strategy for the LDF in education, equal pay, or transportation cases hinged upon the careful selection of the plaintiffs, as the aim was to try their cases in favorable courts in order to establish precedents, usually through the appeals process. So it was absolutely imperative that the organization not be embarrassed by any defense they mounted. They could ill afford any mid-trial setbacks or surprises. While Marshall expected to lose criminal cases before juries, he also expected the LDF's cases to firmly establish grounds for appeals on record. The LDF would thus have strong equal protection cases that it could appeal to the higher courts. To Marshall, it was therefore essential that his lawyers strongly believe a potential client had been wrongly accused. On occasion, prisoners who'd escaped from chain gangs in the South would show up at the NAACP offices, and Marshall was adamant about turning them away, lest the organization be charged with "harboring an escaped felon." Sometimes a lawyer would nonetheless listen to a convict's horrific story and attempt to persuade the governor of the state from which the prisoner had fled "not to sign extradition papers."

In the summer of 1949, Jack Greenberg, a twenty-four-year-old Jewish kid with a cherubic face and a buzz cut who had recently been hired by Marshall as a staff attorney for the LDF, sat at his desk listening to a black woman's shocking tale: Her son had just been sentenced to ten years in a Richmond, Virginia, prison for stealing a bag of peanuts. The sentence seemed exceedingly harsh to Greenberg, who suspected that race had played a role. Though he had grown up in an area of the Bronx where "no blacks lived anywhere nearby" and his family was not involved in civil rights, his parents had instilled in him "an abiding concern for those who are disadvantaged." Astounded by the woman's story, Greenberg marched into Marshall's office and urged his boss that they take the case. Marshall was nonplussed. He nodded at Greenberg, then telephoned an attorney he knew in Richmond and asked him to look into the situation. A little while later Marshall called Greenberg back into his office to tell him that, as it turned out, the bag of peanuts was "one of those enormous burlap bags, the size of a flatbed truck." As Greenberg digested this new information, Marshall added one more detail. With "pursed lips and a raised eyebrow," Marshall noted that the defendant had "hijacked the truck along with it."

IN DECEMBER 1940, Eleanor Strubing, a thirty-two-year-old housewife, socialite, and former fashion model from Greenwich, Connecticut, claimed that her Negro butler and chauffeur, Joseph Spell, had kidnapped her, written a ransom note, tied her up, then raped her four times before dragging her to a car and driving to Kensico Reservoir in adjacent Westchester County, New York, where he'd thrown her off a bridge into the water and then pelted her with rocks. The newspaper coverage was predictably sensational. The front page of the *New York Daily News* featured a picture of Strubing in a bathing suit adjacent to a photo of Spell, arranged so that the brooding butler appeared to be staring straight at the vulnerable socialite. The provocative story led to rumors that "panic-stricken Westchester families were firing their black servants."

The then thirty-two-year-old Marshall interviewed Spell in the Greenwich town jail. He left convinced that the butler was telling the truth when he claimed that Strubing had not only consented to but also initiated a sexual liaison one evening when her husband was out of town. The sexual encounter began in the living room, until Strubing became worried that someone might see them through the window, at which point they retreated to the garage. They proceeded to have sex in the car, but "the sex stopped" as Strubing's fears of pregnancy loomed. The two then did go for a drive, only again Strubing panicked and ordered Spell to stop the car. She then walked home by herself. She did not report the alleged crime to police for hours.

"He was supposed to have raped this woman four times in one night," Marshall recalled. He recalled, too, the incredulity at the LDF when the story hit the newspapers: "All the secretaries, all of 'em, came and said, 'Hey, defend that man. We want to see it. Four times! Ha ha. Ha ha. Four times in one night. Yeah, bring him in here, let us see him.' I told 'em, get out of my office."

The case was important, Marshall said, because winning Spell's freedom would strengthen the security of "thousands of Negro domestics, chauffeurs, maids and butlers throughout the country whose jobs are jeopardized by this case." After presenting his findings to the NAACP, Marshall announced that the organization would defend Spell "to the limit of our resources."

Once the trial began it was revealed that police had found neither the rope nor the ransom note; nor had a Greenwich doctor found any evidence of rape. Strubing herself seemed out of sorts when questioned on the stand, stating, "I'm sure he raped me three times. But I can't remember now. On a stone floor—or something. It's so confused." The facts of the case were confused enough that the prosecution offered a plea bargain. Marshall, however, argued that Spell was "not only innocent, but [in] a position where everyone else knows he is innocent." With a possible thirty-year sentence hanging in the balance, Spell put his faith in the advice of his lawyer.

In his closing argument, the state's attorney asked that the "lust-mad Negro" be convicted lest "shame and disgrace" fall upon Mrs. Strubing. The all-white jury of six men and six women deliberated from noon until nearly midnight on February 1 and voted unanimously to acquit Joseph Spell of all charges. Very little uproar followed the verdict, aside from the reaction of some of Strubing's society friends, who telegraphed the governor to state they "resent bitterly this acquittal which casts such an unfair slur on her character." Spell could muster only "What a relief!"

Thurgood Marshall appreciated that the rape accusations against the butler might afford the LDF secretaries some amusement, but the vast majority of cases that crossed Marshall's desk were painful, often horrible tragedies that he would never even consider showing to the women in the office. The most unsettling involved teenage and preteen girls from black communities who were raped and often beaten or killed by advantaged, even prominent white citizens and law enforcement personnel in the South. Frequently the accused men would not be indicted, or else they'd stand trial (on reduced charges of unlawful carnal knowledge) before a jury of their peers, who were not about to take the word of poor blacks over that of white policemen, doctors, insurance collectors, or plumbing contractors. Most frustrating to Marshall was the fact that the NAACP did not have sufficient funds to provide legal assistance; also, many of the rape cases simply did not fit the criteria that Marshall himself had defined for the LDF. Outraged by the inhumanity of whites who abused their power or authority, and moved deeply by the suffering of their poor black victims, Marshall could only apologize that he and the organization could not do more, in the affectively written letters he sent to regional NAACP personnel, as well as to the families of raped, beaten, and sometimes murdered adolescent girls.

Limited though the NAACP was in its ability to force prosecution on those who perpetrated crimes against defenseless blacks, the legal arm of the organization had more options available when it came to defending black men charged with rape upon white women. W. J. Cash, in his seminal exploration of Southern culture, *The Mind of the South*, wrote that while "the actual danger of the Southern white woman's being violated by the

Negro has always been comparatively small . . . much less, for instance, than the chance that she would be struck by lightning," it was "the most natural thing in the world for the South to see it as very great, to believe in it, fully and in all honesty, as a menace requiring the most desperate measures if it was to be held off." In Cash's estimation, the Southern rape complex "had nothing immediately to do with sex," but rather with the feeling among Southerners that if blacks were to advance beyond their severely circumscribed social station, they might "one day advance the whole way and lay claim to complete equality, including, specifically, the ever crucial right of marriage." Thurgood Marshall understood perfectly the mind of the South, and he knew he had to act fast when it came to rape cases in the South, because a lynching could quickly turn the defense of the accused into a plea for the prosecution of his murder.

A T THE CONCLUSION of Joseph Spell's rape trial in Connecticut, Marshall returned home to Harlem barely long enough for a meal with Buster before he was back at Pennsylvania Station, his bags packed for a three-day train ride to Oklahoma. Buster could do little more than shrug when Marshall had told her he'd be going back on the road, and in the coming decade his absences would become only more frequent. Buster, for her part, would come to rely on the constant assurances from fellow NAACP wives and 409 Edgecombe neighbors like Gladys White and Minnie Wilkins that Thurgood was safe, in good spirits, and heading homeward soon.

The long train trip to Oklahoma gave Marshall the opportunity to bone up on briefs from his next criminal case—a gruesome one, in which he'd be defending a sharecropper who had confessed to a savage mass murder that had shocked all of Oklahoma. A year earlier, a young white couple, Mr. and Mrs. Elmer Rogers, and their four-year-old son, Elvie Dean, were butchered to death on New Year's Eve in their home in Choctaw County, Oklahoma, before their farmhouse was burned to the ground. Almost immediately after the crime a white convict who had been out on furlough confessed to the murders. Newspapers reported that the prisoner had also visited bars and brothels in the area, and both the prison warden and Governor Leon Chase Phillips were severely criticized. To stem the controversy, the governor had the warden fired, then sent a special investigator to Hugo, the Choctaw County seat, to defuse the increasing political fallout. Despite the prisoner's confession, the investigator arranged for him to leave the state for Texas.

Two weeks later the investigator announced that he had found the "real" killer: a Negro sharecropper named W. D. Lyons.

Under the supervision of the governor's aide, Special Investigator Vernon Cheatwood, Lyons was beaten over his head and body with a blackjack while Cheatwood and other police officers interrogated the prisoner for several days. Despite the beatings, Lyons refused to admit his involvement in the murders—until Cheatwood produced a pan of bones. He placed the pan in Lyons's lap and growled, "There's the bones of the baby you burned up."

The sleep-deprived Lyons was forced to scrutinize the teeth, bones, and charred remains of the young child and his mother. It proved to be too much for the superstitious sharecropper to bear. Lyons confessed, in his words, because "they beat me and beat me until I couldn't stand no more, until I gave in to them. . . . "

A confession in hand, Cheatwood and the police then chauffeured Lyons back to the farmhouse, where one of the murder weapons—an ax that had somehow escaped notice in prior investigations—was found in the ashes. Threats of being burned and beaten with a pick hammer prompted a second confession from Lyons at the crime scene.

Marshall's appetite for a coerced confession case was buoyed by his recent victory at the U.S. Supreme Court the year before. In *Chambers v. Florida*, Marshall argued that the confessions used to convict four transient blacks in the murder of a Florida man should have been ruled inadmissible because they had been "extorted by violence and torture," in violation of the Fourteenth Amendment. In a unanimous decision, the nine justices overturned the Florida court's convictions, thus handing Marshall his first win before the Supreme Court. In delivering the opinion of the Court, Justice Hugo Black wrote an eloquent passage that, his widow later recalled, he "could never read aloud without tears streaming down his face."

> *Today, as in ages past, we are not without tragic proof that the exalted power of some governments to punish manufactured crime dictatorially is the handmaid of tyranny. Under our constitutional system, courts stand against any winds that blow as havens of refuge for those who might otherwise suffer because they are helpless, weak, outnumbered, or because they are nonconforming victims of prejudice and public excitement. Due process of law, preserved for all by our Constitution, commands that no such practice as that disclosed by this record shall send any accused to his death. No higher duty, no more*

*solemn responsibility, rests upon this Court than that of translating into living law and maintaining this constitutional shield deliberately planned and inscribed for the benefit of every human being subject to our Constitution—of whatever race, creed or persuasion.*

Marshall was cautiously optimistic that he could at least establish on record that Lyons's confessions were coerced and, if nothing else, take the case (now with precedent) before a sympathetic Supreme Court on appeal. First, however, he had to navigate the dangerous and highly charged atmosphere in Oklahoma. On this trip—unlike his trips to the South with Houston, which were essentially fact-finding missions involving little conflict or even contact with whites—Marshall was coming to Choctaw County to fight. Word of his imminent arrival had already spread through town; the situation grew only more volatile, and for Marshall, perceived by whites as the enemy, more dangerous. As a deputy sheriff said in the court hallways at one of Marshall's Tennessee trials, "We are going to teach these Northern Negroes not to come down here raising fancy court questions." The law may have been on Marshall's side, but law enforcement wasn't.

Upon his arrival in Choctaw County after a six-hour bus ride, Marshall was whisked away by blacks who felt it necessary to hide him under armed guard and to move him from place to place during his stay. For word had gotten out that "a Nigger lawyer from New York" was trying the case, and the small black community feared for Marshall's life. An aged, obstinate widow fearlessly took him in. Marshall noted that she serenely proclaimed, "I ain't scared," and snored all night while he lay awake, sweating, afraid. "I think I remembered every lynching story that I had read about after World War One," he recalled. He was unable to sleep; the ghastly photographs appeared, and Marshall pictured himself in each one—his crumpled body dumped in a ditch at the center of town, or hanging from a tree—the white children in their Sunday clothes, pointing, grinning, and rejoicing.

Marshall became convinced that Lyons had been made a political scapegoat in the governor's attempt to avoid the fallout he'd face if it was shown that furloughed prisoners had been responsible for three murders in his state. The yearlong delay before trial only confirmed Marshall's suspicions that prosecutors were "scared to try the case," because usually, when blacks confessed to murdering whites, justice was swift and unmerciful.

As the trial was getting under way, Marshall wrote to Walter White in New York, telling him that the courthouse was jammed with more than a thousand people, many of whom had come in trucks and wagons, to see "a certain Negro lawyer—first time in this court—so sayeth the bailiff." Marshall added that white schoolteachers had even brought their classes to court, the judge remarking that it was good for children to be able to witness such "a gala day." "Imagine it," Marshall wrote, "a Negro on trial for his life being called a 'gala day.'" He noted that the "jury is lousy. . . . No chance of winning here. Will keep record straight for appeal."

Before the first day of testimony, Marshall appeared before an "informal" county judge who smoked a big cigar as he announced that there were "two nationalities" involved in this case and that he did not want any disorder. He did not alleviate Marshall's unease about the reception a black New York lawyer might expect in Oklahoma. The Lyons case was called, and Marshall was introduced; he took a seat at the counsel table and, as he told Walter White, "the building did not fall and the world did not come to an end."

After the noon recess, however, the crowd "about doubled" and "the fireworks started," as Marshall moved to have the first confession excluded from evidence because police officers had beaten the defendant. All morning the officers had maintained, under oath, that Lyons "was not struck, or injured in any manner." But when the county prosecutor called Lyons to the stand, the defendant shocked everyone in the courtroom by testifying that the prosecutor himself had witnessed the torture—a charge the prosecutor denied before the judge. The court went silent as the normally reticent sharecropper met the prosecutor's eyes. "Oh, yes, you were there," Lyons said. The prosecutor's face reddened. "Why," he stammered, pushing a finger in Lyons's face, "I stopped them from whipping you."

The response in the courtroom was tremendous. The spectators erupted in a noisy buzz; the county judge rapped his gavel on the bench in an effort to bring order to his court. Marshall moved quickly, making certain that the court record showed the prosecutor had conceded that Lyons was beaten while in custody. No one in the courtroom had ever seen anything like it before: a black man in a Jim Crow state standing up in court and talking to powerful white people without the slightest form of deference—all the while looking them straight in the eyes. And he wasn't done.

With Special Investigator Vernon Cheatwood on the stand, Marshall asked him about his interrogation of W. D. Lyons, to which Cheatwood replied that he had questioned Lyons for "six or seven hours but never raised his voice, never cursed him, and positively never struck him with anything." The special investigator admitted to putting the pan of bones in Lyons's lap, but went on to deny owning a blackjack or any kind of club.

After a hotel clerk testified that Cheatwood had instructed him to "go up to my room and get me my nigger beater," Marshall saved his best for last. He called two white relatives of the slain woman, including Mrs. Rogers's father, who testified that Cheatwood had shown him his blackjack and admitted that he'd beaten Lyons for "six—either six or seven hours . . . [saying] I haven't even got to go to bed."

One Oklahoma newspaper reported that after Marshall's grilling, the special prosecutor stepped down from the witness stand "shaking as though suffering from palsy." Marshall himself noted, "Boy, did I like that. And did the Negroes in the Court-room like it. You can't imagine what it means to those people down there who have been pushed around for years to know that there is an organization that will help them. They are ready to do their part now. They are ready for anything."

Marshall was exhilarated by the theatrics that criminal cases before a packed courtroom could summon. He'd committed himself and the NAACP to chiseling away at the apartheid systems of the South, but the work was painstakingly slow, and victories in voting rights and interstate transportation cases generated little cause for attention outside the East Coast conference rooms of lawyers and editorial writers. Cases in criminal courtrooms, though, generated immediate excitement, and so did the Negro lawyer from the North who could bring spectators to their feet with his words. Not just black spectators, either; for whites, too, "stopped us in the halls and on the streets to tell us they enjoyed the way the case was going and that they didn't believe Lyons was guilty." Marshall reported to Walter White that "90% of the white people by this time were with Lyons. One thing this trial accomplished—the good citizens of that area have been given a lesson in Constitutional Law and the rights of Negroes which they won't forget for some time. Law enforcement officers now know that when they beat a Negro up they might have to answer for it on the witness stand. All of the white people in the Court room passed some mighty nasty comments after the officers lied on the stand. Several told the officers what they thought of them out on the halls."

The white people in the courthouse halls might have believed that Lyons was innocent, but the whites on the jury were not prepared to say so. After five and a half hours of deliberation, they returned with a guilty verdict. Marshall was not surprised. "We are in a perfect position to appeal," he stated, noting that the prosecution had asked for the death penalty, whereas the jury's sentence of Lyons to life imprisonment for a crime that resulted in "three people killed, shot with a shot gun and cut up with an axe and then burned—shows clearly that they believed him innocent."

The Lyons case reaped a harvest of publicity, which was augmented by the statement of E. O. Colclasure, the father of the murdered white woman. He told the press that he did not believe W. D. Lyons was guilty; he opined further that the Oklahoma police and prosecutors had conspired to frame the sharecropper. Moved by Thurgood Marshall's argument in court, the still grieving father joined the NAACP.

Confident he could reverse the verdict on appeal, Marshall boarded a train for the long trip back to New York. Despite the loss, he was becoming more optimistic about what had happened in Oklahoma. Every visit to a Jim Crow courtroom confirmed to him that the American justice system was wholly stacked against powerless blacks—but he was seeing tiny cracks in the veneer. Guilty verdicts with recommendations of mercy instead of death sentences. Police officers indicted on brutality charges. Hope where there was none before. Criminal cases could affect people in unexpected ways. They raised awareness, increased NAACP membership, and if handled properly, they could bring in money. Lots of it. "I think we should aim at $10,000," Marshall wrote to White. "We could use another good defense fund and this case has more appeal tha[n] any up to this time. The beating plus the use of bones of dead people will raise money." Between the Spell case in Greenwich and Lyons in Oklahoma, Marshall was optimistic about the future. "The NAACP did all right this month. . . . We have been needing a good criminal case and we have it. Lets [*sic*] raise some real money."

# | 5 | TROUBLE FIXIN' TO START

The Southern Knights of the KKK, led by Bill Hendrix in 1949. (*Courtesy of the State Archives of Florida*)

NORMA PADGETT DIDN'T make it home that night.

The first glare of another warm July sun had just come up over the high and dry pastures of Okahumpka, Florida, when Clifton C. Twiss and his wife, Ethel, up early as usual, heard a car coming up the road. The motor shut off for a moment, then started back up again, and when they looked out the window they saw a thin girl walking away from a small, dark car toward the fork. Clifton picked up his binoculars to get a closer look and then passed them to his wife. The car, with a white man driving, sped away. Unusual thing to see this time of morning, they thought—young, blond girl dressed nicely, pacing back and forth along the newly paved road, a purse slung over her shoulder. They kept an eye on her, curious as to why this waifish teenage girl would be up at six o'clock on a Saturday morning out here in Okahumpka—a town that wasn't much more than an intersection in Lake County. It was odd, they thought, but she didn't appear to be in any trouble. The couple, seeing her dropped off by the side of the road, decided she must be hitchhiking or waiting for someone, so they went about their morning rituals, stirring their coffee and reading the morning paper, and occasionally glanced up the road at the girl in the pink dress with the purse.

At about 6:45 a.m. nineteen-year-old Lawrence Burtoft, who was finishing his shift as watchman at his father's Okahumpka restaurant, looked out the window and saw the girl standing by the crossroads of Leesburg and Center Hill. He didn't know her by name, but he'd seen her in the restaurant before and knew that she was from Bay Lake, a small community of mostly dirt-poor farmers about twenty miles south, and he wondered what she was doing up here by the cattle pens in Okahumpka so early in the morning. She looked as if she was waiting for somebody. Burtoft got dressed and went outside to pick up the fresh bread that was dropped off each morning before daylight.

"Good morning," the girl said as Burtoft approached. After they'd exchanged greetings, she asked if anybody might be coming along who'd be able to take her back to Groveland. Burtoft told her no and offered her some water or a cup of coffee. She declined, but they went inside the restaurant anyway. Sitting across from Norma Lee at a table, Burtoft slowly sipped his coffee and tried to figure out, without prying, what had brought this girl out here to the middle of nowhere.

After a few minutes of small talk, Norma indicated that there had been some trouble. She told Burtoft that she'd been out last night with her husband, Willie Padgett, and his car had broken down on the way toward Groveland. Some black men, she said, had come along in a car and pulled over, to see if she and Willie needed any help.

Burtoft had just finished his coffee when the girl told him the black men had hit Willie over the head and carried her away in their car.

Burtoft's eyes studied the girl. "Did they hurt you?" he asked.

"No," she said, adding only that her feet hurt from walking such a long way.

Burtoft noticed a tear in the girl's dress; it had gotten caught on a barbed wire fence, she explained. Burtoft remarked nothing in the girl's behavior to suggest that she'd been kidnapped by some black men a few hours earlier. Except for a few tears and an occasional sniffle, she "looked to be in a pretty calm condition for her husband to be lying down dead beside the road."

The two sat inside the restaurant for fifteen minutes or so, with Norma waiting patiently until Burtoft had finished his breakfast before she asked him to help find her husband. Burtoft detected no urgency in her voice, and as he rode his bike to his parents' house to get their car, it struck him how strange it all was: Norma Lee so calmly relating how her husband might be lying dead at the side of the road to Groveland.

When he returned to the restaurant in the family car, he and Norma Lee drove south, back toward Groveland. Burtoft's reluctance to pry was vying with his curiosity. His heart raced as he began to register the reality of what the girl had told him.

"Do you think you would recognize them?" he asked.

"No," she said. She didn't think she could, as it was too dark, although she did note that one was extremely dark and one was "high yellow."

A few miles down the road, Norma asked Burtoft to pull over. He followed the girl into the high grass alongside the road, any moment expecting to stumble over the body of her husband. But they found nothing. Norma admitted that she did not know exactly where to look, but they did drive farther on. When it became apparent to Norma Lee that they had now driven too far, Burtoft turned the car around and headed back to Okahumpka. Having convinced Norma Lee that they should report the incident to the police in Leesburg, five miles to the north, Burtoft had driven about a mile or so when they came upon another car at the roadside. Two men emerged from the parked car and flagged them down. Burtoft stopped; he recognized one man, Curtis Howard, a classmate from Leesburg High School, and he had seen the other one, short and lean, more than once on the dance floor, but not with Norma. Willie Padgett came over to his wife; they didn't speak a single word to each other.

Strangely calm, Burtoft thought. Only minutes before, Norma Lee had been half expecting to find her husband dead. And Willie Padgett couldn't have been certain his wife was alive, either. Burtoft had anticipated a more emotional reunion, but Norma simply got into the other car while Willie thanked Burtoft for his time and trouble.

"You're quite welcome," Burtoft said, still dazed as he watched the two men drive off with the girl.

&gt;&lt;

S HERIFF WILLIS MCCALL was on his way back from an Elks Club convention in Cleveland, Ohio, with a deputy, a prisoner, and some friends when he stopped his sturdy Oldsmobile 88 in Citra, a small Florida town, home to the pineapple orange, about an hour and a half north of Groveland. Standing outside the Olds in his tall, white Stetson hat, the lumbering forty-year-old sheriff savored a long swig from a Coca-Cola bottle; he'd been driving for hours. The trip had been a getaway from the never-ending job of maintaining "lawanorder" in Lake County, but he had managed to conduct a little business in Ohio, picking up a prisoner in Columbus to face break-in and assault charges in Lake County court. McCall had been away from Florida for only a few days, but he couldn't resist the urge to check in on his domain. He reached down and powered on the police radio.

"We're probably too far away to get anything from Tavares on this thing," he said as he started up the car and bucked his six-foot, three-inch frame behind the wheel. As he drove south into citrus country, the radio cackled beneath the lull of the heavy engine until McCall thought he could make out the voice of his deputy, James Yates, in distress. Something about a shooting in Lake County. McCall stiffened behind the wheel, then reached for the radio and managed to get Reuben Hatcher, the county jailer, on the other end.

"What's the trouble?" McCall asked after identifying himself.

Hatcher was breathing hard and trying to compose himself. "Boy, I've never been so happy to hear anyone's voice," he told McCall, adding that "there's a lot of trouble fixin' to start . . . some of the people down there are making all kinds of threats."

McCall tried to make sense of Hatcher's panic but he could barely make out the jailer's voice on the radio. He wanted to know exactly what had happened in Groveland. Only his radio had gone silent. It was a long couple of minutes till it cackled again. Then nothing, a static hiss. Finally, with heavy clarity the words came.

"A white housewife . . . raped by four negroes . . ."

With his passengers sitting in stunned silence, Willis McCall's ears pricked up. Black suspects were in custody, he was told, but a mob was forming in Groveland and there was a "pretty high feeling" around the county. McCall stared straight down the highway, one hand gripped tight on the wheel as he pressed his foot down on the accelerator. He knew Lake County better than anyone and he could sense the distress on the other end of the radio. Night was coming; he needed to get back fast. The sheriff had one more thought, which he was able to relay to the jailer.

"Call Yates and tell him to get the Negroes out right away," he said. "Hide them in the woods."

M CCALL HIGHTAILED IT to his split-level farmhouse in Eustis, threw the Oldsmobile into park, and began unloading luggage from his trunk to the garage. Night was falling, and he knew now that a large mob of heavily armed men was forming in Groveland, and another in Mascotte twenty-five miles to the south. A gang of blacks, he'd been told, had raped a young, white Lake County girl, and as the news quickly spread, cars were rapidly gathering. Vengeance charged the county air. McCall knew how it would end, unless Yates got the Negroes hidden in the woods. Say nothing more on the radio, McCall had told his deputies: men at the Leesburg station might be listening, and McCall wanted no chance of a tip-off that might lead to a roadblock or ambush. He needed to secure the suspects because in darkness, he knew these south Lake County men would head north to Tavares. He was sure of it. They'd storm the jail, and there'd be no stopping the lynching.

The sheriff was hoisting his luggage from the trunk when two cars pulled up to his house. In the first car he could see Deputy Yates and another man, Captain Bill Allison, a warden of the prison camps in Tavares. Deputy Leroy Campbell pulled the second car in behind them. Joining the sheriff in front of the house, Yates told him the Negroes were lying down in the back of his car; he'd ordered them to keep their heads down, so no one had seen them as they drove through town. Yates added that they had confessed to raping Norma Padgett.

Willis McCall was quiet. He walked toward the rear of Yates's car. His wife, Doris, had stepped outside, and he could hear his sons, Malcolm and Donnie, laughing and playing inside—the two boys oblivious to their father's mood and the deputies' tension. McCall peered inside his deputy's car. He could see two prisoners crumpled together on the floorboard, handcuffs joining their wrists. He opened the rear door and immediately recognized the faces of Samuel Shepherd and Walter Irvin, the two army veterans from Groveland who had been picked up by Lake County deputies early that morning. As the door swung open, the dazed prisoners could hear the echo of children's laughter at the same time they caught a glimpse of the "Big Hat Man" who stared down at them. They were all of them in a world of trouble.

๑๛ ๑

WITH SHEPHERD AND Irvin still slumped down on the floor in the back of the car, Yates and another deputy sped north toward Florida State Prison, in Raiford, some two hours away. McCall fired up his Olds and headed in the opposite direction, toward Groveland, where he aimed to quiet any mob he might encounter. He never made it. Just outside the city limits, he spotted a motorcade of twenty-five cars moving toward Tavares, their headlights blazing a path to the jail. McCall, certain they meant business, spun his car around. After following them for a few miles, he gunned the engine and, pulling ahead of the convoy, he took the lead into Tavares. He had his revolver at hand on the seat next to him.

McCall parked the car and hurried to the back of the courthouse. He left his gun behind; with more than 125 men "armed to the gills" coming toward him, a revolver would be no deterrent. McCall recognized many in the mob as Bay Lake farmers, men he knew, and he knew a show of force was likely to provoke them into violence. If he was going to prevent a lynching, McCall was going to have to do it with his wits and personality.

"Willis, we want them niggers."

Flowers Cockcroft, thirty-five, the "husky, brash" son of a Lake County watermelon farmer, stepped forward and spoke for the mob. The sheriff removed his hat and, attempting to meet their rage with a smile, talked fast and acknowledged as many of the men as he could by name. "I can't let you people do this," he said, looking toward Cockcroft. "You fellas elected me to uphold the law, and I've got to do it."

McCall was answered by men in the back of the mob hurling obscenities, but he dared not show any fear. He lowered his voice. "I may be in sympathy, and I know you're stirred up about this thing," he said. "You've got a right to be. But you don't have a right to take the law into your own hands. These Negroes are going to be held and tried in court."

"Look, McCall," one man shouted, "we're going to fix them niggers right now or none of our women is gonna be safe."

Even as the sheriff continued to reason with them, he could sense they were determined in their purpose and he feared they might be on the verge of storming the jail. His reputation around Lake County might be enough to hold them off, but only if he changed his tactics. "The prisoners you want are no longer here," McCall told them. "They've been taken elsewhere."

From the back, jeers and shouts of "Liar!" pierced the night. The mob thought McCall was bluffing; they demanded to be let into the jail. A few minutes of heated discussion later, McCall agreed to allow a small delegation inside to search the jail cells for two black prisoners. He pointed to two men at the front of the lynch mob; Willie Padgett and his father-in-law, Coy Tyson, stepped forward. Padgett would at least recognize the men who had beaten him and abducted Norma the night before, and Coy Tyson couldn't wait to lay eyes on the men who'd raped his daughter. Flowers Cockcroft, the self-appointed spokesman of the mob, also joined them. McCall had negotiated an agreement, and Deputy Campbell led the three men into the courthouse while the sheriff and a few nervous deputies waited outside with the rest of the mob.

IN HIS CELL on the top floor of the jailhouse, sixteen-year-old Charles Greenlee was still trying to figure out what was happening to him. He had just arrived in town the night before from Gainesville, where he and his friend Ernest Thomas had been washing dishes and flipping burgers together at the Humpty Dumpty Drive-In. The twenty-five-year-old Ernest had been looking to come home to Groveland and he'd convinced his younger friend that plenty of orange-picking work awaited both of them in the groves of Lake County.

At six feet tall, Charles looked older than his age, but he still had the wiry frame and the fears of a teenager. Leaving home hadn't been easy for him. His close-knit family had endured a summer of unimaginable agony. In May, Charles's four-year-old sister had been killed when she was struck by an Atlantic Coastline train passing on the tracks close by their home in Pine Top, near the Georgia border, in Baker County, Florida. His grief-stricken thirty-two-year-old mother, Emma, was already inconsolable when, in the cruelest of fates, just weeks later her two-year-old daughter was killed on the same tracks. The family had been irreparably damaged. Charles's own grief had compelled him to leave.

On the morning of July 15, in Zuber, Florida, Charles and Ernest had hitched a ride south on the back of a University of Florida truck. They'd caught a few more rides, and eventually some white men in a Dodge truck had dropped them off in Mascotte. They had walked the remaining couple of miles along the train tracks to Groveland. Both of them were filthy, and since their plan was for Charles to stay at the Thomas house, they decided he should wait in the train depot while Ernest picked up some clean clothes at the Thomases' home for Charles to wear. He had been waiting about an hour and a half when Ernest returned in a 1941 Pontiac with two packages of cookies, a bag of peanuts, and a bottle of soda water, but no clean clothes. For those, Charles would have to wait a few more hours, until

Ernest's mother got home from her job running a beer joint in Groveland.

The idea of loitering in the rail depot of an unfamiliar town at night, when he was all sweaty and caked in road dust, made Charles more than a little anxious. So, when he spotted a .45 Colt revolver with a four-inch barrel beside his friend on the front seat of the Pontiac, he asked, half jokingly, if Ernest would let him meanwhile hang on to the gun. To Charles's surprise Ernest agreed. He handed over the gun, then drove off in the Pontiac. Charles would never see his friend again.

At nightfall, beside a tomato shed near the station platform, with his suitcase for a pillow, Charles did manage to sleep for a few hours. Sometime after midnight he awakened to the buzz and bites of mosquitoes. Tucking the revolver in his belt, he headed across the street to L. Day Edge's gas station. There he filled his soda bottle with water at a drinking fountain, and there the flashlights of two Edge Mercantile night watchmen spotted him.

"Is there anywhere a fellow can get something to eat?" Charles asked the watchmen.

"Hold still a minute, boy," one said, drawing his gun. Charles instinctively raised his hands in the air.

They marched Charles across the street, back to the depot, where they rifled through his suitcase. They examined his Social Security card and driver's license. They questioned him about the gun, which, as it turned out, wasn't loaded. Because he didn't want to involve Ernest in the inquiry, Charles said the gun belonged to his father up in Santa Fe, Florida, north of Gainesville. They were about to release him when another man from the filling station appeared.

"What road camp you break out?" the man asked. Charles patiently explained where he had come from, but the man was cautious. "You don't know what that boy done done," he told the watchmen. "You better hold him till morning."

One of the men stepped into a phone booth, and not long after, at about 3 a.m. George Mays, Groveland's chief of police, arrived. He decided it was best to put Charles in for the night. The two night watchmen brought to the jail more cookies and another bottle of water for him; they also told him they'd like to "work out something with the gun" if he was interested in selling it. So Charles hadn't worried. The men were treating him well, and they would soon enough discover he hadn't done anything wrong. Charles had figured he'd be out of jail by morning.

But he wasn't. The next morning, deputies James Yates and Leroy Campbell arrived at the jail, both of them in a foul mood.

"Stand up, nigger," Campbell had said as they'd entered the cell, and immediately they'd begun peppering the teenager with questions: "Where are the boys you were with last night?" "Where's the car?" "Was it an old Buick or a new Buick?"

Charles was confused. "I wasn't in any car," he replied, adding that he hadn't been with any boys last night, either. The deputies made the boy drop his pants, as Yates was looking for "anything to indicate he was connected with the rape." When he failed to find anything, dissatisfied, he walked away in a huff.

"You're lying," Yates growled.

Soon after, Charles became aware that a crowd of men was gathering around the jail. He'd heard a few remarks from outside about "what they would do and what they would not do if they got ahold of this boy Greenlee." Then he heard footsteps approaching.

Chief Mays led a young white couple over to Charles's cell. Standing there shirtless, Charles lowered his eyes to the floor as Willie and Norma Padgett looked him up and down.

"He's not one of the boys," Willie said.

Norma turned to Mays. "He looks like one of the boys," she said.

Willie took another look. "He is not one of the boys," he said again, then left with Norma.

Returning a few minutes later, Willie quietly asked Charles if he'd been with any boys the night before. Charles replied that he didn't know what boys Willie was talking about. "The boys what took me out of the ditch last night," Willie said.

"No, sir," Charles answered. "I wasn't one of them." Willie described them in more detail and again asked if Charles had seen them. Charles responded that he hadn't seen anyone last night "but the men who had put me in jail."

Willie Padgett appeared satisfied and left the jail, but others arrived to question Charles further about some boys in a car the night before. He had no idea why until finally Chief Mays told him: "Boy, if you don't know it, you in trouble. Some boys raped a white woman last night and robbed a man. If I don't hurry up and get you away from here they gonna take you out and kill you."

With the clamor outside the jail growing, Charles begged Mays to "hurry up and take me away." The police chief told him that some cars were on the way.

At about the same moment, Elma Lee Puryear, the mayor of Groveland, saw about fifty Bay Lake men standing outside the jail as he was driving by. Feeling uneasy and suspecting they "might cause some trouble," he learned from a Lake County deputy that the crowd believed the jail was housing a Negro who had raped a Bay Lake girl the night before. Puryear and the deputy determined that the Negro should be moved from the rickety Groveland jail. They hustled the teen outside, past the gathering mob, and into the mayor's car. Charles was transferred to Tavares without incident.

At Tavares, Charles found himself in the bullpen, where he saw, among the prisoners, "two colored boys who were all beat up." Their faces were swollen and bloody; they sat slumped in resignation; they said nothing. One of them, Charles noticed, "had a big hole knocked in the back of his head." When the prisoners were served supper, the two beaten ones were removed from the cell. The taller of the two returned before Charles had finished his meal. He removed his shirt; bruises and welts covered his upper body.

The turn in Charles's fate was hard for him to fathom. He had never been in any serious trouble with the law. The day before, he and his friend Ernest had set out for Groveland, where they'd be sure to find decent jobs picking citrus. They'd even lined up a place to stay. Most important, Charles had traveled with the blessing of his parents, who hoped that by striking out on his own he'd have a chance for a fresh and optimistic start in a new town. When his father told him, "Go ahead and try," Charles felt ready for an adventure. But not for this one.

Night had fallen. Charles Greenlee had been in the supposedly more secure county jail in Tavares for about nine hours when the angry shouts of a much larger crowd had the prisoners on the top floor stirring. Unlike his fellow inmates, Charles had some idea why the mob had gathered, and he was scared for his life. He could hear some men moving from cell to cell. When they reached the bullpen, he immediately recognized Willie Padgett, the man who had talked to him earlier that day in Groveland. Padgett recognized Charles, too; just as he had told Norma, he now told her father that Greenlee wasn't one of the boys.

"That's the boy they picked up in Groveland for carrying a gun," Padgett said. Charles sighed in relief; he began to think this whole misunderstanding would be cleared up soon.

Except that Leroy Campbell was eyeing him with suspicion and menace. The "stout white man dressed in a white shirt with bloody specks, felt hat, brown summer pants, revolver strapped to his hip, and a small brown badge on his belt" was one of the deputies who had grilled him in Groveland, and at Tavares he'd been conducting the two brutalized colored boys back and forth from the bullpen.

After searching the basement and the other floors in the courthouse, the three Bay Lake men—Padgett, Tyson, and Cockcroft—were finally satisfied that Samuel Shepherd and Walter Irvin had been moved to Raiford, just as the sheriff had said. Still, they weren't happy, and they left the building grumbling. The mob outside assured Coy Tyson that they'd take care of things their way if the law failed him and his daughter. Willis McCall urged them all to go home.

"You've got families and responsibilities," he told them. "I'm sure you have many things to do on a Saturday evening besides sit here and argue with me about some nigras. I've secured them, and that's all there is to it. I've got to follow the law. Now, you fellas give it up and go on about your business. Some of your wives are probably waiting supper, or they may be wantin' for you to take 'em out to a movie or something."

Slowly, and to McCall's great relief, the crowd began to disperse.

By the end of the weekend, Sheriff Willis McCall would be proclaimed a hero in newspapers across the country for successfully preventing a lynching in Lake County. The *Orlando Sunday Sentinel* trumpeted McCall's fortitude before the mob under the headline "Lake County Bride Kidnapped," while a paper as far away as Eugene, Oregon, shouted, "Sheriff Staves Off Lynching." Even the *New York Times* noted that the "fast talking" sheriff moved quickly to "disperse a mob of about 100 armed men who came to take two Negroes from his jail." The *Miami Herald* praised McCall's "steadfast courage," but added, "the whole setting smells Ku Klux Klan."

A steady Florida rain had begun to fall as the dispirited Bay Lake vigilantes returned to their cars and trucks with their rifles and ax handles. McCall decided that now would be a good time to talk to the young boy who was the third suspect in the rape of Norma Padgett. He rode the slow elevator in the courthouse up to the jail on the top floor.

For both Sheriff Willis McCall and Charles Greenlee, their evening of fear was far from over. And their weekend would be anything but quiet.

B Y THE SUMMER of 1949, Walter White, who had been suffering from a heart ailment, had become the focus of a damaging controversy within the NAACP. After admitting to an affair with Poppy Cannon, a white South African socialite, White divorced his wife of twenty-seven years, Gladys, a black woman, and married Cannon in June. The interracial marriage did not sit well with the black press, and the distraction was causing a rift within the NAACP, where "all hell broke loose." Roy Wilkins, editor of the *Crisis*, the organization's official organ, and, like Marshall and White, a resident at 409 Edgecombe Avenue, thought it best that White not attend the NAACP's annual convention. White had become a lightning rod for criticism among those who had previously viewed him as a race leader, and the blond-haired, blue-eyed Negro who "dressed like a tweedy English country squire" and was known as "Mr. NAACP" did not make things any easier for himself that summer. He wrote a provocative piece for *Look* magazine's August issue, "Has Science Conquered the Color Line?" in which he pondered the benefits of hydroquinone, an antioxidant that could be used to remove melanin from human skin, and wondered whether the ability to turn dark skins pale might "solve the American race problem."

For his part, Marshall felt White was entitled to marry "whomever he wished provided she consented," but that did not stop White from considering Marshall "obstreperous" and even "mean-spirited" at the time. Marshall had never shied from confronting White about his lack of a law degree, and he bristled whenever the executive secretary attempted to exert his influence in the LDF's legal affairs, especially when White began traveling to Washington to observe Marshall's arguments before the Supreme Court—during which proceedings White would sit "within the rail," a section reserved only for members of the Supreme Court bar.

"Now look," Marshall told him, "you're not supposed to be in there, and they know you're connected with me, and one of these days they're going to find out you're not a lawyer. And I'm gonna get blamed for it. And it's going to affect my standing. And I don't believe in letting anything affect my standing in the Supreme Court. So I'm telling you, don't let me catch you sitting there again. If you do, I'm going to tell the guard."

"You wouldn't," an indignant White replied.

"Try me," Marshall said.

Not long after that exchange, Marshall spotted White again within the rail. Marshall quietly approached a guard and, pointing to White, whispered, "See that fellow over there? I don't think he's a member of the bar." The guard politely requested White to move to the spectators' section in the rear of the court.

The next time Marshall appeared before the Supreme Court he was pleased to note that White had chosen not to defy him. That is, until he discovered the executive secretary even more exclusively seated. At White's behest, Justice Hugo Black arranged for him to sit as a guest in the judge's box. Marshall could only shake his head. "So he won, anyhow," he said.

Despite the fact that White still had the full support of Eleanor Roosevelt, he ultimately decided to take a leave of absence in the summer of 1949, leaving Marshall and Wilkins, now the acting secretary, responsible for day-to-day operations at the NAACP. Aside from the teachers' pay, voting, education, and transportation cases that constantly occupied the LDF in its multipronged legal attack on Jim Crow, a steady stream of capital rape cases continually flooded its offices. Marshall had long been aware that such charges raised serious human rights issues, since the death penalty for rape was "a sentence that had been more consistently and more blatantly racist in application than any other in American law."

Since sex cases involving race were complicated and controversial, Marshall always worried over their potential to "crowd out other important work." He had also learned, however, that headline-grabbing press coverage of the NAACP's more salacious criminal cases produced an increase in both membership rolls and financial donations more immediately and more dramatically than the segregation cases that they'd labor on quietly for years. As special counsel, Marshall was the public face of the NAACP, and he too was capturing headlines. His presence inside and outside courtrooms around the country on behalf of defenseless blacks seeking justice had cemented his reputation as Mr. Civil Rights. He was collecting important victories before the Supreme Court, including *Shelley v. Kraemer* (1948), wherein the Court, siding unanimously with Marshall, ruled that the enforcement in a state court of a restrictive covenant that barred "people of the Negro or Mongolian Race" from owning property violated the equal protection clause of the Fourteenth Amendment. Marshall's name was being splashed across the headlines of every major newspaper in America, and on radio broadcasts he was being hailed as "the Joe Louis of the courtroom."

On July 17, 1949, the day after Samuel Shepherd and Walter Irvin stopped to assist Willie and Norma Padgett on a lonely stretch of road just north of Groveland, Florida, Marshall was 2,500 miles away with Wilkins in Los Angeles, where the delegates to the NAACP Annual Convention were still buzzing about Walter White. Half of them, Wilkins noted, "wanted to lynch Walter for leaving Gladys, and the other half wanted to string him up for marrying a white woman." The organization's attempt at damage control on the West Coast required most of the executive staff and LDF lawyers, so the national office in New York was working with a skeleton crew. Marshall had left only one young lawyer behind at the home office, associate counsel Franklin Williams, in the event that any legal emergencies arose.

The Groveland Boys. *From left to right:* Sheriff Willis McCall, jailer Reuben Hatcher, Walter Irvin, Charles Greenlee, and Samuel Shepherd. (*Library of Congress, Prints & Photographs Division, Visual Materials from the NAACP Records*)

B Y THE HUNDREDS, blacks cleared out of Groveland on the backs of citrus trucks. Others took blankets, food, and water and fled with their children into the pine leaf forests, surer than rumor that the Ku Klux Klan would be coming from all directions to burn down Stuckey Still, the black enclave west of Groveland.

Not satisfied that he had appeased the mob at the jail for the night, Sheriff McCall took some highway patrolmen down to Groveland, where he was troubled to see that the Bay Lake men hadn't gone straight home to their wives and families as he'd suggested. Their numbers, in fact, were growing. The sheriff estimated that some 250 men had gathered in the streets, around their cars and trucks, and more vehicles were spilling into town by the minute, their horns blaring. The streets of Groveland were noisy with dangerous excitement. Two of the rapists may have made it to Raiford, but that didn't mean the night was over.

Ernest Thomas had seen the writing on the wall, what with Norma Padgett claiming she'd been raped by "four niggers" and his friend Charles Greenlee in jail, where a large crowd was aching for a lynching party. Ernest wanted out and hopped on a bus heading north that morning.

Disappointed that they had left the Tavares jail empty-handed, Coy Tyson and Flowers Cockcroft made it clear to the "sullen, glint-eyed" mob that they still had some business to settle. And they'd settle some of it in Stuckey Still, an area just outside Groveland where blacks lived in wooden, weather-beaten shacks on small plots of land dotted with palm scrub and pines. By nightfall, however, most of the blacks had already evacuated.

McCall was trailing cautiously behind a cluster of cars when a volley of shotgun blasts rang out. In a din the cars sped off in all directions and disappeared in clouds of dust. Stunned, the sheriff's gaze followed the trajectory of the shots. It took him to their target: the Blue Flame, the juke joint owned by Ethel Thomas, Ernest's mother. As he was assessing the damage to the cinder block shack—the windows had been blown out by "15 loads of buckshot"—McCall discovered one man inside: he'd been roused from his sleep but was uninjured. The sheriff figured the shooting at the Thomas place had at least blown some steam off the mob. He monitored the area for a while, but apparently the Bay Lake rabble had headed home to sleep things off. The rest of the night was mostly quiet around Groveland.

B OY," LEROY CAMPBELL said, stepping toward Charles, "I believe you lying. That gun what you got came from Groveland."

Not long after Campbell had escorted Coy Tyson and Willie Padgett out of the courthouse, the stocky, forty-year-old part-time truck driver and deputy returned to the fourth floor; it made Charles Greenlee nervous that the deputy was eyeing him again. The mob may have left the precincts of the courthouse, but the boy did not feel that the danger had passed. Not with this deputy, who'd barked "nigger" at him that morning in Groveland, standing outside the bullpen, glaring in at him. He'd come and go, Charles noticed, and he'd murmured words that Charles could barely make out:

something about the gun; Charles thought he'd heard Ernest Thomas's name. Sitting on the floor, his bare back against the wall, Charles tried to snatch some sleep as the hours blurred, and every set of bootsteps he'd hear on the cement floors of the Tavares jail caused his heart to race. But the stocky deputy, Leroy Campbell, had come to pay him another visit, still focused on the gun.

Charles could make out other men in the shadows, including Reuben Hatcher, the fifty-three-year-old jailer with a big ring of cell keys, but still he was shocked when they grabbed his arms and dragged him down to the basement. The room was clammy, with exposed water pipes and a dirt floor. One of the men handcuffed him to an overhead pipe so that his feet just barely touched the ground. Charles, still shirtless, hung from the pipe as Deputy Campbell loosened the sixteen-year-old's pants and pulled them, along with his undershorts, to the floor.

Charles looked Deputy Campbell in the eyes, and he knew how and where the two men in the bullpen had been beaten swollen and bloody. Campbell picked up what looked to be a piece of rubber hose about a foot and a half long; he inserted his meaty hand through a cord on one end so that it wouldn't slip from his grasp. Without saying a word, the deputy started whipping the boy hard across the chest. After three or four blows, Campbell asked again if Charles was lying. "Were you one of the boys?" he snarled.

"No," Charles answered, just as Deputy James Yates stepped out from behind Campbell and reared back with another piece of leaded hose. He slashed across the boy's pelvis. Then twice; and again. Charles could see that Yates was "trying to hit me in my privates," and he'd tried to keep his legs crossed, but when Campbell set to whipping the hose across his arms and face, the boy, stunned, let his legs drop, giving Yates some clean shots to his groin.

"Are you one of the boys that raped the woman?" Campbell asked repeatedly, each time punctuating the question with another swing of the hose.

"No!" Charles screamed.

Blood began to pour from Charles's nose and mouth. He felt his eye swelling shut. He felt something sharp stinging the soles of his feet; Yates had smashed a Coca-Cola bottle and scattered the broken glass in the dirt beneath the boy's bare feet. The stocky deputy was doing most of the questioning, except for a few interjections from Yates when Campbell paused between blows, catching his breath. Behind the two deputies stood a third man, Charles noticed; he seemed to be "directing the traffic."

The interrogation of Charles Greenlee continued for about forty-five minutes, with the teen slipping in and out of consciousness. Campbell, his voice rising as the force of his blows increased, was unrelenting. "Did you rape that woman?" he snapped at the beaten boy yet again.

There was only one way to stop it: "Yeah," Charles answered.

The men behind him stirred and mumbled. Deputy Campbell let his arms drop slowly to his sides. Without blows, he asked a few more questions: Was he with those other boys? Did they rob that man? Did they pull a gun on the girl?

"Yes," Charles said. To all of it.

Campbell let the hose fall to the floor. He stared a long minute at the boy, then pulled the gun from his holster and pointed it at Charles's belly. "Better start saying your prayers," he advised.

The jailer, Reuben Hatcher, wanted Campbell to show some mercy. "Shoot him in the stomach and he will die quickly," he said.

Charles Greenlee—one eye puffed shut, blood pouring down his face, broken glass imbedded in his feet—finally broke. He began sobbing like his tortured mother, who all summer long suffered the unbearable pain of losing her two daughters on the railroad tracks. Quivering between gasps for air, he begged Campbell not to kill him.

Savoring the moment, the deputy took his time before he shoved the gun back into his holster. But Charles could not escape the menace in his gaze even as Hatcher uncuffed him from the pipe. His wrists burning and bloody, Charles was bending over to pull up his pants when a hard kick from behind knocked him to his knees. He fell forward and lay, a crumbled heap, in the dirt. That's when he recognized one of the men in the shadows staring down at him. It was the Big Hat Man, Sheriff Willis McCall.

Crowding around him now, the men led Charles to the elevator. McCall was all business. Like Samuel Shepherd and Walter Irvin, the young boy from Santa Fe had confessed to raping a white woman—and he'd catch up with Ernest Thomas yet. Just as the elevator was about to ascend, Charles was treated to a hard kick "in the privates"; he doubled up on the floor, unable to move or breathe. The elevator rose to the fourth floor. Campbell dragged the boy to a cell and locked the confessed rapist in.

WILLIS V. McCALL was Lake County born and bred, and like Charles Greenlee, he knew the anguish families endured after the death of children. His parents had seen a daughter and two sons die before Willis was born, and as a boy living at his father's "heart yellow pine house," he'd experienced the tragedy of his younger brother's drowning in a nearby lake. The son of a dirt farmer, McCall had spent his "scratch-hard childhood" working long hours in the fields, plowing, and chopping and picking cotton, often barefoot. Those Bay Lake men riding through Groveland weren't much different from his father, McCall knew, but he had also determined early on, perhaps because of a deep-set fear of poverty, that he wasn't going to walk in his father's shoes. For he also had smarts and ambition. By the age of twenty-one, he had not only acquired a wife—he'd married his girlfriend, Doris Daley, a local Umatilla girl—but also accumulated some cows, and he soon turned a small-time milking operation into the Bluebird Dairy, a business venture complete with state-of-the-art pasteurizing machinery, the first in Lake County.

In the mid-1930s, at the age of twenty-six, McCall had sold his dairy and taken a job with the U.S. Department of Agriculture as a fruit and vegetable inspector, in an industry that had been taking more than its share of lumps. Aside from countless bank failures at a time when citrus prices hit record lows during the Great Depression, central Florida was also devastated by hurricanes, a Mediterranean fruit fly outbreak, and the coldest winter freeze in the state's history. Yet over the next nine years, McCall would witness a remarkable rebound in central Florida's citrus industry—one that would enable the state to overtake California as the largest harvester of citrus, thanks to a series of government programs, contracts, and interventions.

The Civilian Conservation Corps, one of President Franklin D. Roosevelt's work relief programs, built railways and highways in Florida that, once completed, made it easier and faster for growers to ship fruit to other parts of the country. Then, in 1945, the National Research Corporation developed a new method of concentrating orange juice and won a $750,000 government contract to prepare more nutritious and better-tasting food products for U.S. soldiers overseas. The company created the Florida Foods Corporation to fulfill the contract, but the war ended shortly thereafter, and the army canceled its order; so the corporation, its research and development completed, shifted its focus to the consumer market, setting up a new entity that would ultimately become Minute Maid Company. It wasn't long before America's freezers had the six-ounce tins that brought Florida orange juice to their kitchen tables just by adding water, and Willis McCall couldn't drive anywhere in Lake County without passing a roadside sign that read "This Is a Minute Maid Grove." That same year, too, the federal government allowed farmers to begin spraying crops with DDT; the toxic synthetic pesticide, used during World War II to control typhus and malaria, proved to be extremely effective against citrus insects that had long menaced Florida orange groves.

With Lake County on its way to becoming one of the richest counties in the nation, USDA inspector Willis McCall was able to foster relationships with the powerful citrus barons of central Florida. In the mid-1940s, the issue most crucial to citrus growers was labor. More groves were sprouting up everywhere in the region; the trees were healthier, the crops more bountiful. Business was good, especially for growers large enough to do their own packing, shipping, and processing. But profits depended on keeping the cost of labor down, because labor represented by far the largest proportion of costs. Since the 1920s, black migrant workers had been coming to Florida from two directions: Georgia to the north, and the Bahamas to the south. Poor whites, too, streamed south into Florida for seasonal jobs picking and packing in the citrus groves. As the industry began to lengthen the production period, however, migrants, both black and white, started settling in the area. Still, in the early to mid-1940s with the country at war, even the combination of an influx of workers and new settlements of permanent workers could not offset the chronic labor shortage in the area.

Imposing, gruff, intelligent, and focused, Willis McCall, in his country boots and wide-brimmed Stetson, caught the eye of some local bankers and citrus barons as the kind of man who understood their needs as businessmen—a man with a "tough reputation in the groves." Before the citrus boom, Lake County was rife with lumber mills and turpentine stills, where forced labor thrived and camps were often guarded at gunpoint to prevent workers from escaping. Camp bosses ruled with an iron fist. They were hard men who frequently resorted to beating workers to satisfy production demands, and despite a steady flow of European immigrants arriving in America in the early twentieth century, blacks were still the preferred workers. "No white people from any country . . . will . . . submit quietly to such treatment as the common Negro," read an editorial in the Christmas 1904 edition of *Southern Lumberman*. Willis McCall was a throwback to the bygone days of Lake County.

When the incumbent sheriff died in office in early 1944, McCall threw his hat into the ring with the backing of the county's big citrus men and began campaigning. He was a natural. Quick-witted and folksy, with a big, round face, McCall was capable of showing extraordinary self-confidence as well as a self-effacing, aw-shucks modesty around voters. Even his opponents swore he could "charm a snake." He branded himself "the People's Candidate." Smiling, with one of his meaty hands placed affectionately on a man's shoulder while shaking hands with the other, he inspired trust and a feeling of safety. "People have confidence in me," he said. "They know where I stand."

After knocking off five challengers in a primary, McCall won a tight race against interim sheriff and former Pittsburgh Pirates pitcher Emil Yde to become the new sheriff of Lake County in May 1944. One of his first moves as sheriff was a lightning-quick response to a newspaper allegation that McCall's campaign had been financed by gambling interests and that McCall himself would prove to be a "sell-out in politics." To prove the paper wrong, McCall raided a warehouse where he destroyed, he claimed, eighty-six slot and pinball machines belonging to his alleged financial backer, the county's "King of Slots." The *Leesburg Commercial* subsequently stepped back from its allegations, stating somewhat apologetically in an editorial, "It looks very much like we have a fine sheriff in Lake County."

Cleaning up the slots racket and sweeping punchboard lottery games out of Lake County's taverns, however, were mostly symbolic gestures on McCall's part, rather than demonstrations of a morally driven, sustained attack on illegal gambling. For the new sheriff was presiding over a county where *bolita* was king. A lottery game also known as Cuba, *bolita* ("little ball" in Spanish) employed one hundred Ping-Pong-type balls with numbers on them, which were tossed in a sack and then pulled out blindly, one by one, in a nightly or weekly "throw." Players might bet as little as a nickel on their selected numbers, and the last numbered ball to be pulled from the sack was the winner. Depending on who was running the game, the payoff was roughly from 70–1 to 90–1. *Bolita* thrived in Hispanic and black communities, a fact that wasn't lost on McCall. "Just as long as you got a little handful of 'em together," he said of the blacks of Lake County, "you gonna have a little *bolita*, a little moonshine, and a whole lot of sex. Anybody that don't know that, don't understand 'em."

The game also lined the pockets of politicians and law enforcement officials wherever it was played, and bloody turf battles frequently erupted over who controlled the game and who got the payoffs—from the "cracker mob of Central Florida" right up to the king of *bolita*, Santo Trafficante Sr., the renowned Mafia boss from Tampa.

Some of McCall's critics and political opponents accused him of turning his back on the *bolita* business and allowing it to thrive. Others argued that the amount of money generated—supposedly under the nose of a sheriff who liked to boast of his awareness in regard to every activity in all 1,100 square miles of Lake County—would not be possible unless McCall had reached some kind of financial understanding with moonshine and *bolita* racketeers. Indeed, one of McCall's deputies later acknowledged that the sheriff and his deputies controlled gambling in Lake County "from the back door of the county jail." It was no surprise to McCall's foes and critics when the *Tampa Tribune* reported that nineteen slot machines seized by state beverage agents had turned up in various Lake County Elks Clubs where McCall had active memberships. And a past president of the county's branch of the NAACP admitted that his own mother was a *bolita* collection agent for McCall.

What is certain is that Sheriff Willis V. McCall, from his first day in office, understood that citrus was the engine that drove Lake County's economy, and he focused nearly all his efforts on issues surrounding labor. With so many young men serving in the military and the demand for citrus products increasing with every month, growers were scrambling to find enough hands to work in the groves. Every able body was needed, and in January 1945, Florida governor Millard Caldwell sent letters to all sheriffs in the state, urging them to "use their good offices" to take vigilant action to enforce "work or fight" laws that were designed to "prevent loitering, loafing and absenteeism." To further incentivize Florida law enforcement, Caldwell's statute allowed sheriffs to pocket all of the fines they collected up to a yearly maximum of $7,500. McCall had his mandate. Still, despite the additional money collected from fines, journalists wondered how the sheriff was able, on a mere four-digit salary, to accumulate the vast stretch of land on which he later built his ranch in Umatilla.

Despite the chronic labor shortage in the groves, wages were kept low, and with the new sheriff enforcing the work or fight laws, citrus barons had in the blacks of Lake County "a ready pool of [cheap] involuntary labor that could be tapped whenever whites faced any sort of labor emergency." Within days of receiving Governor Caldwell's letter, McCall arrested forty citrus pickers for vagrancy when they did not show up to work on a Saturday. The next month, another picker, Mack Fryar, similarly failed to appear on a Saturday after having put in a full week's labor. McCall, without a warrant, entered Fryar's home and placed him under arrest. Fryar protested, but McCall was in no mood to explain: "None of your damn jaw, come on with me," the sheriff said and, unprovoked, whipped out his blackjack and knocked Fryar out cold in front of his wife and fourteen-year-old son.

McCall then dragged the supposedly delinquent picker to his car and hauled him off to jail in Tavares, where he was held for days before receiving any medical treatment.

Pickers like Fryar were assessed exorbitant fines, which trapped them in debt peonage, a condition not unlike slavery. The "Florida bail bond racket" was, according to a former Orlando newspaper editor, the "most lucrative business in the state." The bondsmen worked hand in glove with employers to secure labor in exchange for fines and bond costs. Citrus grove foremen informed bondsmen how many men were needed, and workers were "secured from the stockades." If workers attempted to flee across state lines, they could be recaptured "without the formality of extradition proceedings." They had no choice but to work to pay off their fines at whatever grove or camp they were taken to, and they often worked under the supervision of armed guards, as they might on a chain gang.

In April 1945 six pickers accused the sheriff of brutality—McCall had gotten wind that they were attempting to organize citrus pickers to protest a mandatory seven-day workweek at A. S. Herlong & Company in Leesburg—so it didn't take long for Sheriff McCall to come to the attention of the NAACP. Complaints mounted at the NAACP that McCall's main function in law enforcement "appears to have been to dragoon the colored peons used in the county's citrus fields and packing plants." The NAACP, observing "a pattern of beating and abusing" on the part of the sheriff, contacted the U.S. Justice Department. The FBI was ordered to open a civil rights investigation. The federal field agents were stymied, however, when the pickers and their families suddenly began disappearing: fleeing Lake County for faraway states like Texas and Missouri, or, in the case of the Fryars, as far north as Harlem. (The Fryars managed to sell their chickens, but left behind all their possessions.) Local whites had made it clear that blacks could expect consequences and possible mob action if they stirred up trouble for the sheriff and the county by talking to J. Edgar Hoover's men. Thus was Sheriff Willis McCall able to successfully dodge charges, as the FBI abandoned its investigation due to lack of evidence.

Emboldened by the support he received from both the citrus growers and the whites in Lake County, McCall became more audacious in his arrests—audacious enough to make headlines in the winter of 1948. The local groves had slashed fruit-picking wages by 20 percent, an action that brought an out-of-town union organizer named Eric Axilrod from the Congress of Industrial Organizations (CIO) to Mount Dora. At a public meeting Axilrod encouraged pickers to protest the wage cuts by staging an "Easter

Holiday" strike in order to prevent "the return to eight cent boxes of fruit." When McCall arrived on the scene with some of his deputies and spotted Axilrod's "Don't Starve Tired" circulars, he immediately handcuffed and arrested the organizer, then paraded him in front of more than one hundred men as a lesson to any pickers who might be considering joining a union. "Look at his wrists!" McCall bellowed before carting Axilrod and six pro-union workers off to jail, where they sat for days. The activist's father posted a thousand-dollar bond, and on Axilrod's release, McCall warned him and his "communist infiltrated groups" never to return to Lake County. Axilrod forfeited the bond and drove straight to Alabama, with McCall's deputies tailing behind to make sure the union rabble-rouser left the state of Florida.

I'M WILLIS MCCALL and you're a damn liar!"

In 1948, thirty-four-year-old reporter Mabel Norris Reese hadn't been in Lake County for very long when "this great big hulk of a man in a ten-gallon hat burst through the door." She was still trying to understand the Jim Crow world that she found herself in after her husband, an Ohio newspaperman, purchased the Lake County weekly newspaper, the *Mount Dora Topic*, the year before. It wasn't long, either, before Reese, as the *Topic*'s editor, had her first run-in with Sheriff McCall. She'd written a story about McCall's "political shenanigans" in his first term as sheriff, when he'd claimed to raid the warehouse of Lake County's King of the Slots. As it turned out, the King had not been one of McCall's backers, but rather a political opponent, who in fact had gotten out of the slots business by then. Nor had McCall smashed to pieces any pinball and slot machines, according to the King, whose garage was housing only machine parts he hadn't disposed of yet. McCall, the King told Reese, had put on a show and tried—unsuccessfully—to pin a slot machine rap on him.

Patiently producing her notes for the irate and intimidating sheriff, Reese showed him direct quotes by his accuser and explained that she was only reporting the words of others. McCall was not satisfied. He left the office in a huff, and at every store and office up and down the quaint, tree-lined business streets of Mount Dora, he stopped to recommend strongly that they not advertise in the *Topic*.

For several days following Axilrod's release and banishment, McCall was apoplectic. The CIO, effectively barred from Lake County by the sheriff, hired pilots to buzz the citrus groves in small planes. From out of the sky, leaflets fluttered to earth. They accused McCall of running union organizers out of the county at gunpoint and resorting to "Hitler's gestapo technique" by using the sheriff's office to intimidate workers in order to drive them back to their "cut-rate jobs," all in violation of the law.

Mabel was at home when she received a tip that a black picker who had been spotted talking with a labor union representative had gotten into some trouble. On arriving at the black laborer's house, she found him bandaged from head to foot. The beating, he told Mabel, had been executed by two of McCall's deputies, one of them his right-hand man, James Yates. "Now let that be a lesson to you," the picker had been warned. "Don't talk to any of these organizers again."

That "lesson" was exactly the hard-line stance that whites in Lake County had come to expect from their sheriff, and the threat of a union-organized labor strike in the groves and packinghouses of Florida's interior citrus belt during the height of the harvest season spelled bad news for any opponents hoping to unseat Sheriff Willis McCall. McCall had shown that he was, according to the CIO, willing to throw up a "big 'red scare' trying to hide the illegality and one-man campaign of intimidation," and he was not afraid to play hardball with blacks, either. More worrisome to McCall were the sustained efforts on the part of the NAACP to unsettle his, and central Florida's, political way of life. The Democratic Party had controlled Southern politics since Reconstruction, and most general elections were determined by the outcomes of Democratic primaries. For McCall, as for many sheriffs and politicians in the South, once they'd made it through the all-white primaries, Republicans usually did not have the numbers to challenge.

In the landmark case *Smith v. Allwright*, Thurgood Marshall had argued before the U.S. Supreme Court in 1944 that it was unconstitutional for the state of Texas to ban blacks from voting in the Democratic Party's primary. The Supreme Court agreed and overturned the party's practice of all-white primaries, a ruling, Marshall noted, that was "a giant milestone in the progress of Negro Americans toward full citizenship." He later assessed the *Smith v. Allwright* victory to be "the greatest one" of his career.

When the Court's decision was announced in June 1944, a raucous party broke out at Manhattan's NAACP office. Phones were ringing off the hook, and the secretaries made a game of transferring the various, ceaseless press and congratulatory calls around the office in circles. Marshall cracked a bottle of bourbon with his staff—and managed to miss a call from Supreme Court justice Frank Murphy, who later told Marshall that "a guy had the right to get drunk at a time like that."

Attorney General Tom Clark made the victory even sweeter when he "told the other states they'd better fall in line or he'd whack them one." It was indeed a watershed moment that, Marshall knew, would usher blacks closer toward full citizenship and enable them to vote in primaries everywhere once and for all. He knew, too, that the South would not acquiesce to the Court's decision without a fight, as by reflex states erected legislative hurdles to slow the tides of change. Still, with blacks in Texas no longer prohibited by law from voting, a revolution in Southern politics had truly begun, as had the dismantling of white supremacy at the ballot box.

Meanwhile, not far from Lake County, a quiet but relentless NAACP man was about to make Sheriff Willis McCall's life difficult. A schoolteacher from Mims, Florida, Harry Tyson Moore had been closely following the *Smith v. Allwright* case because he himself had had the opportunity to work with Thurgood Marshall on an equal pay case in Brevard County a few years earlier. Not long after the Supreme Court's 1944 ruling, Moore and some of his NAACP associates organized the Progressive Voters League, which mounted an aggressive campaign to register blacks onto the voting rolls in Florida. By 1948, he had brought nearly seventy thousand new black Democratic voters into the system, and with Florida's black population growing significantly every year, Moore's voter registration drive represented the single greatest threat to the citrus belt, to the Southern way of life, and to Willis V. McCall.

It was no coincidence that the Ku Klux Klan held five rallies in Lake County in the weeks leading up to Election Day to show their support for McCall as well as presidential candidate Strom Thurmond of South Carolina, who was running as a member of the splinter group of segregationist Southern Democrats who became known in 1948 as the Dixiecrats. Clearly, any CIO-backed candidate for sheriff was going to have a tough time getting black voters to the polls. To make it tougher, on the eve of the election 250 hooded Klansman formed a motorcade that snaked its way through Lake County, "warning blacks not to vote if they valued their lives." Trailing behind the motorcade in a big Oldsmobile, his trademark white Stetson visible to all, was the incumbent sheriff himself, "making no attempt to interfere" when the Klansmen stopped to burn a cross in front of a black juke joint in Leesburg. The evening ended in a field just north of Lake Okahumpka, with Klan speeches and a barbecue. It may as well have been a celebration of what would prove by a landslide to have been the inevitable—the reelection of Willis V. McCall. Thus began his most eventful term as sheriff of Lake County.

## |7| WIPE THIS PLACE CLEAN

State Attorney Jesse Hunter, Sheriff Willis McCall, and Deputy James Yates visit the remains of Henry Shepherd's home. (*Photo by Wallace Kirkland/ Time & Life Pictures/Getty Images*)

G ROVELAND WAS A ghost town.

Mabel Norris Reese slammed down the phone and sped south to see for herself.

"Everything was silent," she observed. The reporter for the *Mount Dora Topic* had never seen anything like it. Blacks had simply vanished. She wasn't there long when she heard the roar of the engines in the distance and experienced a "scary feeling" when a long line of cars rolled into town, and it was only as the noise grew louder that she began to get a glimpse of anyone. "People would rush inside and shut their doors, pull their blinds," she said. Blacks ran for the woods "or streaked for miles into the groves." Mabel tried to count the cars; there were more than two hundred vehicles, she observed, many with license plates from Polk and Orange counties. Her instincts told her to get home to Mount Dora to be with her husband and young daughter, but as a reporter, Mabel sensed trouble. She couldn't leave.

INSTEAD OF DRIVING back home to Eustis after the Saturday night ruction of the Bay Lake men, Willis McCall commandeered a room at the Groveland Hotel in the event that they were planning another ride. The night, though, was mostly quiet, and the sheriff even managed to get a few hours of sleep in the old hotel on Cherry and Main streets. On Sunday morning he went with his deputies to survey Mascotte and Stuckey Still for damage, but apparently only Ethel Thomas's bar, the Blue Flame, had been shot up. At mid-morning Groveland had the eerily quiet atmosphere of a town deserted, as if warnings of a landfall by a powerful hurricane from the Atlantic had driven the residents away. It was clear to McCall that a black exodus wouldn't have occurred without good reason, and his instincts told him to hold on to his room key at the hotel—that more trouble might be yet to come. A few miles to the south, in the Bay Lake homes with telephone service, white farmers and their wives were spreading word to friends and relations that four Lake County Negroes had raped Coy Tyson's seventeen-year-old daughter.

McCall kept himself busy. Annoyed that Ernest Thomas had managed to skip town before he'd had a chance to talk to him, McCall telephoned the Gainesville Police Department and the sheriff of Alachua County to put them on the lookout for the young black man wanted for kidnapping and rape. He interviewed Norma and Willie Padgett to ascertain their version of events since Friday evening, and he concluded a meeting with State Attorney Jesse Hunter by assuring the prosecutor that he'd find more than sufficient evidence, beyond the accusations of the young Bay Lake couple, to show that a kidnapping and rape had occurred in Lake County. He'd already gotten confessions from the prisoners, and Deputy James Yates was collecting physical evidence including tire tracks and shoe prints from the crime scene; a physician in Leesburg had examined Norma. He'd bring the attorney a case rock-solid, McCall told Hunter, and he'd get Ernest Thomas.

By mid-afternoon Groveland was getting unquiet. "Knots of men stood about on the main street, hard-eyed and watchful," and McCall noticed that the automobiles—some parked, others cruising the streets—had come from neighboring counties, as well as from Georgia. It was common Klan practice to use outside Klaverns on "rides" or "jobs" in cars with the license plates intentionally obscured so that local riders could not be easily identified. At dusk, a twenty-car procession rolled into Groveland; flyers advertised the cause. Headlined "Ideals of the Ku Klux Klan," they extolled the virtues of white supremacy under the logo of Dr. Samuel Green's Association of Georgia Klans. An Atlanta obstetrician and Grand Dragon, Green boasted that the Klan was once again growing by "leaps and bounds" in its purpose to establish "a beachhead in Florida." Outraged by President Truman's espousal of civil rights legislation, Green had promised that any Yankee attempt to force equality between the races would oblige Americans to "see blood flow in these streets. The Klan will not permit the people of this country to become a mongrel race."

Willis McCall sensed events could easily escape his control. Hailed as a hero in the morning's papers for preventing a lynching on the steps of the Tavares jail, the sheriff knew that he and his handful of deputies would be powerless should the four hundred to five hundred men now milling about in the business section of Groveland decide to make a second move on Stuckey Still. He knew, too, that in countless instances in the South angry mobs had pressured, sometimes at gunpoint, local sheriffs who were holding black men accused of raping white women to walk away from their jails. What usually followed were lynchings "at the hands of persons unknown." (The NAACP defined "lynching" as an illegal killing by three or more persons claiming to be serving justice or tradition.) The case in Groveland was uncomfortably similar to events seventeen years earlier in Scottsboro, Alabama, when two white women accused nine black youths of rape and Sheriff M. L. Wann headed off a lynch mob outside the Scottsboro jail, declaring, "If you come in here I will blow your brains out," before he called in the National Guard. In his stand against the KKK, Sheriff Wann may have been a hero to the North, but under mysterious circumstances he was also shot dead one year later by a white man who was never apprehended. Willis McCall realized fully how fine was the line he'd have to walk between the requirements of the law and the unspoken expectations of the Klan. For neither politicians nor the powerful citrus barons held sway over white mobs bent on vengeance in the matter of Negroes, the flower of Southern womanhood, and rape.

A group of Lake County's leading citizens met with McCall to voice their concern over developments in Groveland. Among them was Norton

Wilkins, one of the owners of Groveland's B&W Canning Company, the largest employer of any canning operation in the state. With more than five hundred plant workers, mostly women, who famously dressed in nurses' uniforms, and countless more pickers in the groves, B&W was, in 1949, shipping a million cases of canned fruit and 250,000 boxes of fresh oranges and grapefruit annually. Wilkins was concerned that Klan violence would lead to a mass exodus of blacks, which would have a disastrous negative impact on production, and profits, at his plant. Also present was L. Day Edge, a wealthy businessman and former state senator with extensive real estate holdings in the county. His family had once owned a turpentine still, which stood on all the land that was now called Stuckey Still; when the still shut down, Edge gave the "colored people their homes and property for being so faithful in his service." In attendance as well were Groveland's mayor, Elma Puryear (who had on Saturday transported Charles Greenlee from Groveland to Tavares), and a few other prominent Lake County residents. Fearing that the gathering restive mob intended more damage than a few potshots at a black juke joint, they discussed a course of action for "protecting lives and property of persons in the colored section of Groveland." They ultimately agreed that McCall should place a phone call to Florida's governor, Fuller Warren, to request assistance. Within minutes, Warren notified the National Guard, informing commanders that following the rape of the Bay Lake girl, the "situation was getting out of hand" in Groveland.

By 11 p.m. troops had arrived from the National Guard in Leesburg and Eustis. At McCall's behest, they were dispatched to strategic locations in black sections of town, mostly for, as McCall told them, "psychological effect." The commanding officer on the scene observed five hundred armed men in cars stalking the streets of Groveland, and Lieutenant James Herlong saw immediately that his twenty men were far outnumbered and stretched too thin over the potential areas of disturbance. He phoned the governor to request additional troops. By midnight, some seventy more guardsmen were spreading over the vacant lots and open fields around Stuckey Still.

Around 1:30 a.m., McCall observed that the unwelcome cars in Groveland had begun to disperse—the local whites were returning to their homes in Bay Lake. The presence of the National Guard had gone a long way toward preventing any further mayhem, the sheriff was convinced, and once he was confident the threat had passed, McCall relieved both the Eustis and the Leesburg units from duty. At daylight, he and State Attorney Hunter met in the sheriff's office with several reporters and a photographer from the Associated

Press. Hunter and McCall had succeeded not only in maintaining law and order in Lake County, but also in averting a labor crisis in the citrus groves; they wore smiles of accomplishment. Outside the courthouse, however, some men from Bay Lake were again milling around in a restless manner, and the sheriff's teeth gritted behind his smile. He still had work to do, as word had obviously made it out of Tavares that the third rapist was being held in the county jail. While the affable Jesse Hunter entertained the reporters, McCall slipped upstairs with his deputies Leroy Campbell and James Yates.

The prisoners had just been served breakfast. Charles Greenlee, half dazed by the beating he'd endured at the hands of McCall's deputies, was sitting in his cell. Crusted in dried blood, his shirtless body ached; his eye was swollen shut. He could barely crane his neck when he heard the familiar footsteps of Deputy Campbell. For the second time in twenty-four hours, the boy was told that he'd have to be moved to a more secure jail or else he'd be facing a lynching. He didn't doubt it was true. The deputy took Charles upstairs, where, according to the plan devised by McCall, Campbell and Yates had the boy change into a prisoner's work outfit before they took him downstairs to McCall. The sheriff shoved a scythe into the boy's hands and told him to walk, "as if he was a trusty going out in the yard to cut grass," all the way out to an unmarked blue 1948 Ford in the parking lot. Limping stiffly along, grimacing in pain, the glass cuts in the soles of his feet burning more with each step he took, he finally reached the patrol car. Campbell grabbed the scythe from the boy's hand and told him to lie down out of sight on the floor. Campbell and Yates hopped in the front, and the three of them began the long ride to the state prison at Raiford.

Later that day, McCall received a telephone call from the manager of a Leesburg radio station who wanted to confirm a news story before he put it on the air. McCall listened intently; the manager had been informed that one of the prisoners in the Lake County rape case had been seized from two deputies and lynched. The sheriff was shaken: Had a mob gotten to Greenlee? Had somebody gotten wind of the transfer and tipped off the Klan? Or had Campbell and Yates themselves? Immediately the sheriff called Raiford and learned that less than two hours after the deputies had left Tavares, Charles Greenlee had been safely delivered to the Florida State Prison, where he'd joined Samuel Shepherd and Walter Irvin behind bars. McCall's sigh of relief was abbreviated by the noise of the crowd loitering outside the courthouse walls.

The reporters had come to see the "High Sheriff" who had prevented a lynching just two nights before, and McCall was determined to convey the cool confidence of a man who had his county under control. The local papers had already reported that he had confessions from three of the rapists; that morning's edition of the *Ocala Star-Banner* had run the front-page headline "Three Negroes Confess to Rape Near Groveland." As the news had spread about the sheriff's call upon the National Guard to quell a potential riot, journalists had begun descending on Lake County, pressing McCall with questions about reports of Klan activity around Groveland. McCall answered that he didn't know much about the cars that had rolled into town from Orange and Polk counties; nor was he around when any KKK literature was distributed, he said.

McCall was more interested in conveying the message that he had three rock-solid confessions, and that he would have four if he hadn't been so busy trying to hold back the mob on Saturday; but for that, he would have apprehended Ernest Thomas by now. "There'll be no lynching of Negroes in Lake County as long as I am sheriff," McCall proclaimed. Indictments, he told reporters, would be coming down soon, and he wanted it to be known that the prisoners would be treated well and they'd receive a fair trial. "We're not going to run anything over on them," he said. Although he conceded that there might be more "demonstrations" over the next night or two, he wasn't expecting any violence. McCall was telling the reporters, especially the Northern ones, exactly what they wanted to hear, and he was basking in the adulation.

Willis McCall was also a man who did not shy away from speaking his mind, even with reporters. In fact, he divulged to them that he had received a call from a woman at, of all places, the New York office of the NAACP. (Most likely, it was from LDF attorney Constance Baker Motley, who would, a few years later, help write briefs for Thurgood Marshall for *Brown v. Board of Education*.) She wanted to know what the sheriff's department was doing to protect the black citizens of Groveland. "I told her we were looking after them all right," McCall announced to reporters, "and I said we'd take care of half of those in Harlem if they wanted us to. Then I hung up."

AT SUNSET, ON Monday, July 18, a mob of more than one hundred men was spotted just a few miles north of Groveland. They'd set up a roadblock and were stopping cars, searching for blacks. Rumor reached McCall's office that the "Ku Klux Klan was planning to wipe out the entire Negro community of Groveland." The sheriff grabbed a handful of deputies and made a dash to Stuckey Still, where they waited with the National

Guard, watching as cars loaded with whites circled the streets. Suddenly there was a volley of gunshots as riders began firing their guns indiscriminately into houses. Most of the black residents had already cleared out of the area, but some continued their nightly retreat into the swamps and woods, fearful of more violence. Joe Maxwell wasn't one of them. He had stayed behind with his family, in the small house that he had built himself, determined to ride out the night. Maxwell had recently returned from military service; with a wife and three small children to provide for, he was planning on being in the groves the next morning, where it was entirely possible he'd be working for some of the same whites night-riding in that long line of cars menacing Stuckey Still. He could hear the roar of the motors, the ugly shouts of fired-up men.

There were at least three cattle trucks packed full with men, all of them screaming and hollering, their guns poking out from the slotted sides. Behind them followed countless cars with long guns poking out the windows. Maxwell heard a frightening cry: "That's old Joe Maxwell's house over there!"

Maxwell told his children to hide under the bed, and trying to keep them safe, he piled mattresses up around them. He "heard a window break and that's when they shot in the house," Maxwell later recalled. Shotgun fire pelleted a bag of crayons just inches above his six-year-old daughter's bed. Glass shattered everywhere. The screams of Maxwell's children inside counterpointed the horrific rebel yells from outside.

McCall and his deputies sped toward the shooting. When someone warned, "You better not go down there, they'll kill you," he replied, "I don't have any choice."

Shots were echoing nonstop in the dark, but the sheriff could make out the flickering figures of men running in the glare of headlights. "Sons of bitches," he said. "Now they got me mad."

The sheriff jumped out of his car and fired a tear-gas canister into the crowd—to no effect; the mob just moved farther ahead. McCall reloaded the tear-gas gun and fired at a truck; this time the smoke cleared the crowd from the area. When the sheriff and his deputies made an attempt to follow the mob, the wind blew the tear gas back at them and they were temporarily incapacitated.

By this time reporters had also made their way to the scene. The mob had parked along Route 50 to regroup and clear their eyes. Deputies Yates and Campbell and Lieutenant Herlong of the National Guard joined McCall, and together, with reporters in tow, they approached the mob.

McCall recognized many in the crowd as the same Bay Lake men who had descended on the Lake County Court House two nights before, including Flowers Cockcroft, the man who had accompanied Coy Tyson and Willie Padgett up to the jail in their search for Shepherd and Irvin. Cockcroft, the proprietor of a general store and filling station in Mascotte, had sold out all of his ammunition earlier in the day; he was leading the mob.

"You fellas don't want to do this!" McCall shouted. "You're breaking the law, and I want you to know I'll arrest you. You got no business here. Go on home."

A voice pierced the darkness. "We wanna wipe this place clean of niggers!"

The men were riled up, and McCall could sense that they were in no mood to abandon their plan as they had two nights ago at the jail and the night before when the National Guard had appeared. The men were shouting McCall down; his threats of arrest were making no impact on them. He tried one more time to appeal to reason, telling them that their families would suffer if they did anything rash. "Don't go out there and do something you're going to be sorry for."

But they didn't retreat. Exasperated, McCall huddled with Herlong. The sheriff and the guardsman had to come up with a plan—fast. As McCall surveyed the crowd, among the unmasked faces he sighted many men he knew, some of them as law enforcement officers, like C. E. Sullins, the police chief in Clermont. Groveland's Curtis Merritt was one of the leaders, as was Wesley Evans, the stout, illiterate citrus grove caretaker the sheriff himself had on occasion recruited: proficient with a leaded hose in his treatment of black pickers, Evans proved to be useful in helping the law obtain confessions from black suspects in the basement of the Lake County Court House. McCall also recognized Sumter County's deputy sheriff, James Kimbrough—he'd be forced to resign when state patrolmen identified his car as the source of shots being fired at black residences—and Klansman William Jackson Bogar, who "was the chief of the Klokann Committee," an investigative unit within the Klan. McCall had attended meetings with Bogar at the Apopka Klavern of the Association of Georgia Klans, where many central Florida law enforcement officials were initiated into the Ku Klux Klan. As one reporter noted, it was impossible "to tell where the mob left off and law enforcement began."

Mass arrests being out of the question, McCall and Herlong were considering a more prudent alternative when, behind them, one of the riders offered his solution to a guardsman. "Why don't you take that peashooter and go home," he said. "You look like a Boy Scout." In reply, the guardsman popped several loud rounds from his M3 submachine gun into the ground and asked the rider if that sounded like a peashooter. The air was thick with smoke and tension.

McCall and Herlong decided they'd best confer with the apparent leader of the riders, Flowers Cockcroft. After a few minutes of bargaining, the obdurate Cockcroft nodded, but his eyes hardened. Apparently he and McCall had struck a deal. Herlong ordered the guardsmen to withdraw.

If the guardsmen were confused by Herlong's order, reporters were more so, especially as the sheriff appeared to be unprepared to make any arrests. One writer from the Associated Press asked McCall for the names of the rioters. "I don't know the names," McCall replied. "I don't know who they are." Pressing McCall, the reporter asked why a mob firing weapons into homes of blacks in Stuckey Still warranted no arrests. McCall brushed him off.

Word of the inquisitive reporter reached Cockcroft, who confronted the sheriff. "Where is that son of a bitch that wanted our names?" Cockcroft demanded. Knowing that "all hell would break loose" if he fingered the journalist, McCall merely shrugged. And Cockcroft fumed: "I'll tell him my goddamn name and I'll fix his ass, too." As if on cue, the rioters began threatening all the newsmen, telling them to get out of town and warning them not to print any lies about what was happening in Lake County.

McCall urged Herlong to execute his order and withdraw his troops "down the road toward Leesburg and wait out of sight." The sheriff, as agreed, pulled his deputies back; reporters tagged along for safety. Cockcroft stood glaring while the law and the Guard withdrew. Then he turned to his men. "Go and get more ammunition," he barked, "and clear the streets of women and children."

The cattle trucks, again packed with armed men, started rolling away, with dozens of cars following behind. The National Guard and Lake County law did not pursue. In less than half an hour, driving along "miles of clay roads into the backwoods farmlands" of Bay Lake, the rioters were igniting bottles of gasoline and tossing them through the windows and onto the roofs of the Negroes' deserted homes. By the time McCall and the journalists caught up with them, a church had been shot up and two houses were in flames. A third, the home of confessed rapist Samuel Shepherd, was smoldering—it had already burned to the ground. The Klan and the Bay Lake whites watched in indifference as the flames licked the pines and the heat exploded the crackling sap. A nine-year-old girl, "Little" Rochelle Hunter, was separated from her family as she fled from the mob. Terrified by the angry shouts and explosions, she hid for hours, then fell asleep alone in the woods. (The missing Valree girl turned up the next afternoon when she returned to the site of her charred home to look for food.)

At midnight, Lieutenant Colonel Harry Baya arrived in Bay Lake with more than two hundred National Guardsmen from Tampa. He immediately reported to McCall, who refused to identify any of the men involved in torching the Negroes' homes, although "he knew all of the ringleaders who were responsible for the mob's actions." The sheriff allowed that many of the men were from Bay Lake and were related to either Norma Tyson or Willie Padgett, but he was unwilling to have any of them arrested or even brought in for a conference. McCall justified his refusal to identify or arrest Coy Tyson, Flowers Cockcroft, and fellow Klansmen like William Jackson Bogar as necessary steps in ensuring peace and preventing a full-blown race riot. Handled his way, McCall reasoned, the riders, by torching deserted houses in the Negro section of Bay Lake, were able to blow off steam without causing any bloodshed.

Baya's meeting with Flowers Cockcroft was no more satisfying. Cockcroft's riders would take no further action against the blacks as long as the National Guard maintained its presence, but once it withdrew, they would resume until they accomplished their goal of "terrorizing the negroes" and driving out "five or six negroes whom they believed were undesirable." Cockcroft added that he could not speak for any of the other "out of county" people who were pouring into Groveland by the carload, heavily armed. Nonetheless, the riot and its evident destruction of the Negroes' homes, and especially the Shepherd property, seemed to have appeased Cockcroft's mob for the time being, and by 1:30 a.m. Lake County had quieted down again.

Cockcroft had advised his men that their work was done for the night, that they should return to their cars and disperse. Muttering darkly, he had given a glimpse of his true resolve to a lingering reporter.

"The next time," he said, "we'll clean out every Negro section in south Lake County."

IN GROVELAND, L. D. Edge, Norton Wilkins, Mayor Puryear, and other prominent white citizens and business owners brooded over the terror unfolding in their community. Whatever racial views they held, they held them secondary to economic interests, and the shooting, razing, and torching of homes in black communities could have devastating economic consequences. Edge and Wilkins both owned businesses that relied heavily on black labor in a county where labor shortages were already a serious problem. Puryear, who owned a number of homes that he rented out in black neighborhoods, "had all of his life savings tied up" in the Negro economy.

For these pillars of the white community, the situation in Groveland's black enclaves was unfolding in a manner uncomfortably close to the events of the Rosewood Massacre in Levy County, Florida, twenty-six years earlier. With law enforcement in Rosewood complicit in the rioting, white owners of turpentine and lumber mills, whose businesses would be devastated by a black exodus, appealed to the governor for help. The sheriff, however, insisted that it was unnecessary to call in the National Guard, as he had the situation under control. Any control he may have had, though, he lost when hundreds of unmasked Klansmen joined local whites in driving out black residents by gun and torch. The vigilantes destroyed every Negro home in Rosewood.

The trouble that began in Rosewood in January 1923 bore eerie similarity to what occurred on Friday night in July just outside Okahumpka after Willie Padgett left the dance hall with his seventeen-year-old estranged wife. In Rosewood, neighbors discovered twenty-two-year-old Fannie Taylor bruised and beaten in her own home one morning; she'd claimed that a black man had forcibly entered her home and assaulted her. Coupled to the rumors that the white girl had also been raped was the dubious report that an escaped prisoner was hiding in the same area. Both stories spread like wildfire throughout Levy County, and a mob of hundreds gathered. Torching homes, the mob sent blacks fleeing into the swamps. The violence escalated when blacks attempting to defend their homes fired back at the mob. Churches were burned. A white turpentine mill owner, W. H. Pillsbury, helped blacks escape the area—he even hid a black man in his home—at the same time that he pleaded with whites to cease the riot. Unfortunately, rioters learned that Pillsbury was harboring a Negro. They made the black man dig a grave; then they shot him dead. One woman was shot in the face while hiding under her house; Fannie Taylor's brother-in-law took credit for her death. An undetermined number of blacks were killed in the rioting, but no escaped convict was ever found. Nor was it ever proved that a rape, or even an assault, had occurred. In a forced migration, the blacks who survived the massacre moved on, never to return, and the white businesses that depended on their labor or patronage suffered tremendous losses.

Twenty-six years later and a little more than one hundred miles to the south, L. D. Edge and Norton Wilkins and their cohort of wealthy business owners wanted no repeat of Rosewood in Groveland.

ॐ ॐ

"THEY TELL ME my chickens and ducks are all gone," Henry Shepherd said.

The father of Samuel Shepherd had holed up with his family at a daughter's home in Orlando and was listening to the radio when he learned that his house had been burned to the ground during the violence in Groveland the night before.

Not long ago Shepherd had been a proud, successful farmer. He had raised a large family and dramatically improved its economic lot by rising from tenant farmer to landowner, but events over the last few years had left him broken and despondent: a "ravaged ghost" of a man, who was often heard to mumble that he wanted "no more trouble." Henry Shepherd was convinced that the previous night's terror in Groveland was more about him than about his son Samuel's alleged rape of Norma Padgett. His own neighbors, he later learned, were the very men who'd thrown lit kerosene-filled bottles through his windows.

To Henry Shepherd, a lifetime picking fruit in groves owned by wealthy whites in Groveland did not seem like much of a future. Though forced labor and peonage conditions continued in Lake County, there had also been a movement toward "Negro self-emancipation" over the last several years. Some blacks had purchased swampland around Bay Lake as cheaply as eight dollars an acre, and in their spare time drained the swamps and cleared the land to create sustaining farms. Once the land was drained, the surrounding acreage was automatically relieved of water, and white farmers bought up the adjacent land at bargain prices. The unintended consequence of the wasteland drainings was a breakdown in segregation in Bay Lake. As a result, Henry Shepherd's northernmost land bordered the Padgett farm. The two families were no strangers to each other.

Determined to escape the backbreaking work in the groves, Shepherd lived thriftily and augmented whatever meager savings he could muster from tenant farming with Samuel's army allotments. In 1943, for $255, he purchased fifty-five acres of swampland in Bay Lake. Working tirelessly to drain the swamp, not to mention enduring countless snakebites on his legs, he was eventually able to cultivate rich Florida soil. Before long he had good crops, hundreds of chickens, and a few cows, while his wife, Charlie Mae, had "the best preserve cellar in the area." He also built a relatively modest six-room house on the property.

Not by intent, Shepherd also drew the resentment that festered among the poor white farmers in Bay Lake. Neighbors tore down Shepherd's fences, thus allowing cows to graze on his farm—and to destroy his crops just before harvest. Shepherd confronted them, but to no avail, and when it happened again he called upon Sheriff McCall to help him with the dispute. McCall merely confirmed what Shepherd already knew: "No nigger has any right to file a claim against a white man."

For want of any legal recourse, Charlie Mae tried appealing to civility. She suggested to Oscar Johns, whose cows had again ravaged Shepherd's crop, that they might come to some sort of agreement regarding compensation for loss. Johns responded by cussing and threatening to kill her.

The harassment continued. Fences were torn down and rebuilt, crops replanted. And the Shepherds refused to leave Bay Lake.

Despite the setbacks, Henry Shepherd continued to prosper, in part because the older of his six children worked on the family farm rather than in the citrus groves: another irritant to many whites. So was Shepherd's refusal to allow his teenage daughter, Henrietta, to do service in the home of a white neighbor who, Shepherd knew, had attempted to rape a prior teenage maid. When James Shepherd, the oldest son, found work as a mechanic and started driving a late-model Mercury around town, the Shepherds had become, in the eyes of local whites, "too damned independent": an "uppity nigger" family with two cars outside their house.

Envy of Shepherd's prosperity and growing bargaining power intensified when Samuel, home from the army in 1949, did not return to the citrus groves but worked with his father instead. The sight of that "smart nigger" Samuel, still in his military uniform, driving around town in his brother's Mercury, rankled whites. It was about time "that somebody put both Henry and Sammy in their places."

Terence McCarthy, a British economist and writer studying peonage in the South, arrived in Groveland in the aftermath of the rioting. On a tour of Stuckey Still and Bay Lake, his driver, a Klansman, pointed out the ashy remains of Henry Shepherd's home. McCarthy noted "three twisted bed frames warped by the fire's heat, a smashed camp cot, an upturned stove"; he could hardly believe anyone had ever lived there. Marauding neighbors had stolen Shepherd's chickens and Charlie Mae's preserves. When McCarthy asked why, his driver replied, "They should never let those niggers live here. We should keep 'em together where we can keep our eyes on 'em and not let 'em buy white man's land." McCarthy learned that whites in Groveland (who accounted for about 60 percent of the town's population of one thousand) were tolerant of blacks, as long as they continued to work in white-owned citrus groves. "The Negroes do most of the work around here," the Klansman told McCarthy. "It's these nigger farmers—they've got to go." Black farmers like Henry Shepherd and his family threatened, "by their example, the whole system of servitude and forced labor which is the base of the local economy," McCarthy wrote. He noted that the whites he spoke with were less interested in seeking revenge for the rape of Norma Padgett than in seeing the demise of "all independent colored farmers."

A FEW OF HENRY Shepherd's children, reluctant to leave the farmhouse undefended, had decided to stay in Bay Lake. Worried by the radio report of the riot, Shepherd went back to Groveland the next day to look for them. He arrived at his property and discovered that more than a thousand dollars in tools and equipment had been looted, as well as a hand drill press, a gristmill, and thousands of auto parts. He found his family; they were still hiding in the woods.

And his son Sammy was locked up in jail, staring at a death sentence. No one in his family was safe. "I keep getting orders to stay away from Groveland," Shepherd said. "They say the mob is after everyone in my family and that they was going to kill us." Henry Shepherd knew he had to leave his farm, and he knew he could never return. As proud as he was of his house and the farm that for six years had supported him and his family, he knew he had no choice but to walk away. "My family is all scattered," he said.

Terence McCarthy, after seeing the burned ruins of Henry Shepherd's house, wondered what would become of the other blacks who dared to desert the groves and independently farm land they had purchased. His Klansman driver didn't have to wonder. "They'll get out, be driven out or be killed, especially around Bay Lake."

THE MOB HAD disbanded, but Groveland was restless, impatient for justice. One Lake County resident bluntly told a newspaper, "We'll wait and see what the law does, and if the law doesn't do right, we'll do it." Both Sheriff McCall and State Attorney Jesse Hunter hoped to forestall mob violence by ensuring that the wheels of justice moved swiftly in the Groveland rape case. Hunter began drafting indictments. On Tuesday, July 19, however—before any charges were made, before any details of the alleged crime had been announced to the public, and while the National

Guard was still patrolling the area to prevent any further mob and Klan violence—the *Orlando Morning Sentinel* published prominently on its front page an editorial cartoon titled "No Compromise!" It featured a drawing of "The Lake County Tragedy" depicting four empty electric chairs, side by side, with a sign over them reading "The Supreme Penalty."

As Sheriff McCall had let it be known that the New York office of the NAACP had contacted him about the violence around Groveland, the *Morning Sentinel* addressed the possibility of an NAACP defense in an editorial:

> *If smart lawyers or agents of different organizations seek to hamper justice through the employment of legal technicalities, they may bring suffering to many innocent Negroes.*

The paper also reported that Norma Padgett had been "bludgeoned" by her assailants; that all three prisoners had confessed to rape; and that Norma had identified Shepherd, Irvin, and Greenlee. While none of it was true, the *Morning Sentinel* editorial effectively captured the sentiment among most Lake County whites, especially in its implicit warning, or threat, that unless the accused men were, as McCarthy wrote, "offered up as a 'legal' blood-sacrifice . . . evil will befall the rest of the Negro community."

Mabel Norris Reese did her part as well to assure Lake County residents that lynching was unnecessary because McCall and Hunter would efficiently see to it that the rapists be executed soon by the state of Florida. In her editorial "Honor Will Be Avenged" in the *Mount Dora Topic*, Reese wrote, "It was a sorry thing that happened to the young couple. The trampling of their honor must be avenged [and that] revenge will be accomplished by a more frightening and awful means than a mob has at its command."

Sheriff Willis McCall, fearful of more violence, was not eager to release the National Guard, but by Tuesday morning he was butting heads with the battalion commander, Lieutenant Colonel Baya, over a host of issues. For one, Baya knew false rumors were being circulated—that the blacks who had fled Groveland were now arming themselves and preparing to return—in order to allow groups of deputized whites to stop vehicles and confiscate weapons from blacks. For another, the commander knew that McCall, who had issued orders in writing that "any persons bearing arms shall be disarmed and turned over to the sheriff," was himself ignoring this edict if the persons were white. For a third, the sheriff not only had refused to furnish Baya with the names of the mob's ringleaders but also had declined to apprehend them himself, being "too busy trying to catch the Negro who had gotten away."

Because McCall was unwilling to arrest or implicate white rioters, on the grounds that such action "would result in a terrific race riot," Baya wanted to withdraw his two hundred plus troops. He contacted Governor Warren, recommending that political pressure be put on McCall to pick up the ringleaders and take "positive action against them."

Willis McCall had been up all night and most of the morning. The hot Florida sun was beating down when he parked his car in front of the Groveland Hotel. He trudged to his room, where he hoped to catch a few hours of sleep before sundown, in the event that the Bay Lake men, and maybe the Klan, should night-ride again. He'd talked with Coy Tyson, and told him that the rioting had to stop—that Tyson had to make it stop. They'd made their point, McCall told him—houses had been burned to the ground, property destroyed—but if they rode out looking for trouble again, McCall couldn't guarantee he'd be able to keep them out of jail. He told Tyson he had three Negroes locked up at Raiford, and he and Jesse Hunter were going to see to it that all three boys were found guilty and sent to the electric chair for raping his daughter. He'd get the fourth one, too, McCall promised.

Coy Tyson talked it over with some of the ringleaders. He reported to the sheriff that they "had agreed to stop any further violence." With that news, McCall phoned Governor Fuller Warren. He convinced the governor that he had the situation in Groveland under control. But, he added, he'd like to keep the Guard around through the weekend, just to be safe.

# | 8 | A CHRISTMAS CARD

Sheriff McCall and Deputy Yates (*behind him*) confer with the National Guard in Groveland. (*Photo by Wallace Kirkland/Time & Life Pictures/Getty Images*)

YOU CAN EITHER jump into the river, or take what is in this gun."

Standing at the rock's edge, the white man held the pistol steady and waited for the boy to make his choice. James Howard, helpless, watched his sobbing fifteen-year-old son—hands and feet bound by rope—shuffle back off the edge of the embankment, watched him plunge into the cold, deep water of the Suwannee River, where he disappeared.

The lynching of Willie James Howard in January 1944 occurred more than a decade before the fourteen-year-old black youth Emmett Till was beaten and shot, and his body then dumped in a river in Tallahatchie County in Mississippi for reportedly whistling flirtatiously at a young white woman. Tens of thousands of mourners viewed Till's disfigured body in an open-casket funeral in Chicago, and the ensuing investigation and trial of two white men accused of the murder generated an unprecedented amount of media coverage and outrage that crossed racial lines. Both suspects were acquitted, and young Emmett Till became a civil rights martyr.

By contrast, the killing of Willie James Howard barely attracted any attention inside or outside Florida, and presented Thurgood Marshall with one of his earliest introductions to violence and whitewashed investigations in Florida. In December 1943 Willie had a job sweeping floors at Van Priest's Dime Store in the sleepy city of Live Oak. He was a precocious boy with a round face and a sweet singing voice, and his good-natured disposition had prompted his family to nickname him "Giddy Boy." It also prompted Willie to present his coworkers at the dime store with Christmas cards.

Among the recipients of Willie's cards was a fifteen-year-old cashier at Van Priest's named Cynthia Goff, a student at the town's all-white high school. Offended by the black boy's gesture, she reported it to her father, Phil Goff, a former member of the Florida House of Representatives and the postmaster in Live Oak. Willie, meanwhile, aware that he had displeased Cynthia, wrote her a note in which he attempted to explain himself. He gave Cynthia the note on New Year's Day 1944. It read:

*Dear Fried:*

*Just a few line to let you hear from me I am well an hope you are the same. this is what I said on that christmas card. From W.J.H. with L. I hope you will understand what I mean. that is what I said now please don't get angry with me because you can never tell what may get in some body I did not put it in there my self. God did I can't help what he does can I. I know you don't think much of our kind of people but we don't hate you all we want to be your all friends but you want let us please don't let anybody see this I hope I haven't made you made if I did tell me about it an I will for get about it. I wish this was an northern state I guess you call me fresh. Write an tell me what you think of me good or bad.*

*Sincerely yours, with,*
*From. Y.K.W* [you know who]

*For Cynthia Goff*
> *I love your name. I love your voice,*
>> *For a S.H.* [sweetheart] *you are my choice.*

Willie Howard's choice of Cynthia as his sweetheart incensed the Goff household. According to Lula Howard, the boy's mother, on the morning of January 2, Phil Goff and two other white men arrived at the Howards' house and asked for her son Willie. When the two men tried to drag Willie off the porch, Lula Howard struggled to hold on to her boy—until Goff pulled a gun on her. She released Willie, who was then shoved into their car.

The three men drove to the Bond-Howell Lumber Company. There they picked up the boy's father, James Howard, a company employee, and then drove the father and son down a red clay road in the woods. They stopped at an embankment on the Suwannee River. Inside the car, once the boy admitted that he'd written the letter to the girl, Goff and the two white men bound the fifteen-year-old's hands and feet with rope. When James Howard tried to speak to his son, he was ordered, at gunpoint, to keep his mouth shut.

The next order forced James Howard to remove his son from the car and stand him up several feet from the riverbank. With the boy in place, bound and now crying, Goff asked him if he understood "the penalty of his crime."

Willie sobbed. "Yes, sir."

By now, James Howard knew his boy would find no mercy in these woods, and finally permitted to speak, he said to his son, "Willie, I cannot do anything for you now. I'm glad I have belonged to the Church and prayed for you."

Goff allowed the boy a last request, and Willie asked his father to take his wallet from his pocket. The postmaster lifted his gun and forced the boy to choose between a bullet and the Suwannee. Bawling and terrified of the gun, Willie staggered backward and toppled over the rock's edge, into the river, where the deep, dark water swallowed him.

The three white men returned James Howard to the lumber company. In the Bond-Howell office Lula had been waiting, hysterical, for about an hour. Looking "terribly afraid of something," James Howard told his wife, "Willie is not coming home." He would say nothing more.

Later that evening, Phil Goff and his two friends, along with James Howard, appeared before the Suwannee County sheriff to give an affidavit. The three white men claimed that they had taken Willie James from his home in order to have his father punish him for the offensive note he'd written to teenager Cynthia Goff. The three men had bound the boy's hands and feet only to prevent him from trying to run from the whipping he deserved, but the boy had become hysterical. He'd refused to be humiliated by anyone, including his own father. He had stated he'd "rather die," and with that he had jumped into the river and committed suicide. The three men entered their signatures on the affidavit, which James Howard was also required to sign so as to indicate that he agreed with the version of events therein. A second document stated that James Howard had recovered the body of his son and that he did not desire a coroner's inquest.

Three days later the Howards sold their house and moved to Orlando.

The lynching of Willie James Howard soon came to the attention of Harry Tyson Moore, who had grown up just outside Live Oak and had attended school with Lula Howard. With two daughters, Peaches and Evangeline, close in age to Willie James, Moore was infuriated by the murder of a fifteen-year-old boy. On learning that James Howard was willing both to testify he had been threatened into signing the affidavit and to provide the true version of the events surrounding his son's death, Moore, who was president of the Florida State Conference of the NAACP, contacted the national office. To Moore's surprise, not only had the New York office already caught wind of the lynching but also Thurgood Marshall was already working on the case.

Armed by Moore with an eyewitness to the lynching, Marshall wrote a letter to Governor Spessard Holland requesting an investigation. The governor assured Marshall that protection would be provided for James Howard during his testimony, in light of which Holland roundly condemned the murder but at the same time warned Marshall not to get his hopes up, stating, "I am sure you realize the particular difficulties involved where there will be testimony of three white men and probably the girl against the testimony of one negro man."

Marshall also called upon the left-leaning Florida senator Claude Pepper to exert his influence in the case. Invoking patriotism, Marshall reminded the senator that the War Department had recently confirmed stories of American servicemen who had been tortured by the Japanese in Philippine prison camps and argued that the lynching of a fifteen-year-old boy would taint America's international reputation: "the type of material that radio Tokio [sic] is constantly on the alert for and will use effectively in attempting to offset our very legitimate protest in respect to the handling of American citizens who unfortunately are prisoners of war." Claude Pepper refused to get involved.

In Florida, Harry T. Moore continued to press for action, even though past experiences in lynching investigations had convinced him that it would be "a waste of time to seek help from state authorities." On May 8, 1944, the state of Florida convened a grand jury in the death of Willie James Howard. Sheriff Tom Henry did not appear pleased that the boy's father showed up to testify. Nonetheless, Howard's testimony failed to return an indictment against Phil Goff and his two friends. Moore could have predicted it; the case would not even go to trial.

Still, Moore refused to quit. Commenting upon the grand jury proceedings, he wrote to Marshall, "We are forced to wonder if the sheriff himself is not involved in this crime. It is very probable that he at least has tried to help cover up the facts in this case." Nor was Marshall ready to give up on Willie Howard. He dispatched new affidavits to Attorney General of the United States Francis Biddle and requested a federal investigation. A few weeks later, Tom C. Clark, the assistant attorney general, replied that the Justice Department had begun a preliminary investigation into the boy's death. Weeks turned into months, months into a year, and the Justice Department had not yet any progress to report. Moore could not hide his disappointment; in a letter to Clark he opined, "The life of a Negro in Suwannee County is a very cheap article."

The death of Willie James Howard was effectively shelved in 1945. Beyond the Justice Department, Moore and Marshall had nowhere to go. The process of the case, frustrating in the extreme from its deplorable beginning to its unjust end, was a repulsive reminder to Moore and Marshall of the ruthless measures men took to protect the flower that was "Southern white womanhood." It was a lesson no doubt made more bitter that same year in the case of a Suwannee County constable who had forced a black man, again at gunpoint, to jump off a bridge to his death by drowning in the Suwannee River. Not surprisingly, a local grand jury refused to indict. In federal court, however, the constable was tried—and convicted, but not of murder. The sentence—for civil rights violations—did not satisfy Harry T. Moore: "Thus a man gets off with only a year in jail and a fine of $1,000 for committing first degree murder. So long as these conditions exist in America, our democracy is little more than 'sounding brass or a tinkling cymbal.'"

Moore's tireless work did not go unnoticed by the national office of the NAACP in New York. "Your letters on lynching and mob violence in which you point out cases within your own state are excellent and help us focus the attention on the need for Federal legislation," wrote Gloster B. Current, director of branches. Current, like Marshall, knew that the state of Florida, despite recording a higher number of lynchings and registering more members of the Ku Klux Klan than any other state in the South, inexplicably remained in the shadows of Dixieland in the 1940s. Florida was epithetically "south of the South," and racial incidents that would have likely attracted national attention had they occurred in Mississippi or Alabama somehow managed to escape scrutiny because they'd taken place in the forgotten land of sun and surf. The postwar years would find Moore involving himself in more and more criminal cases, including the (often confessed) rapes of black teenage schoolgirls and maids by whites who'd be sprung from jails not by angry lynch mobs but by family members posting bail. Without Moore's voice, his agitating letters, and his telegrams of protest, the all-too-frequent atrocities committed in his backyard would have been that much easier to conceal or ignore.

He would raise that voice, too, when another Florida sheriff demonstrated his contempt for the civil rights of blacks and justice for all, in Groveland in 1949.

SEVENTY-FIVE MILES TO the east, in the small town of Mims, just off the Atlantic Ocean, Moore had been following the events in Lake County with much distress but little surprise. As the NAACP's executive secretary in Florida, he'd been traveling the state for more than a decade: holding meetings, raising money, investigating lynchings and incidents of police brutality, and then pressuring politicians into action. Without pay, he'd worked for the black people's cause on weekends and in whatever spare time he could manage outside his teaching job in the Brevard County school system. Both he and his wife, Harriette, also a teacher, were forced out of the jobs they'd held for twenty years because Harry was deemed, in the summer of 1946, a "troublemaker and Negro organizer."

Insightful yet quiet, unassuming, and mild-mannered, Moore composed his public speeches with passion and focus, but his delivery, soft-spoken and understated, reflected the manner of the man and contrasted sharply—and for evangelistic Southerners, unfavorably—with the customary fire-and-brimstone, church-pulpit rhetoric. Moore, however, was not about to allow an uninspiring delivery to impede the urgent messages he wanted to spread. Recruiting his teenage daughter to speak on his behalf, every night after dinner he would rehearse her delivery of his words, which she had memorized, so that she could dramatically place a pause or drive home a point to stirring effect. Evangeline was nearly paralyzed with fear the first time she spoke at a Baptist church in Lake County, but she finished the speech as perfectly as she had practiced it. Moore began traveling the state with his family in their blue Ford sedan, with Evangeline dividing her time between homework and the demanding work of the NAACP.

The Moores lived in a three-bedroom, one-story wooden frame home that Harry had built in 1926. Approximately forty-five feet long and twenty-two feet wide, it was propped up on wooden blocks nearly two feet off the ground. The house had a large front porch that stood behind four wooden columns at the end of a white sand driveway off Old Dixie Highway. Orange, grapefruit, and palm trees brightened up the landscape close to the house. Whereas most of the black laborers in Mims lived in wooden shacks on small parcels of scrub, the Moores' house sat on nearly eleven acres of land and was set deep in an orange grove. Whites referred to it as the place where "that rich Professor Moore" lives. Though far from rich, a family with two educated, working parents in a home packed with books was no doubt more exceptional among the blacks in Mims.

Harry's political activism continued to render him unemployable, but after nearly two years of job searching, in May 1948 Harriette was offered a teaching position in Palm Beach County, about two hours south of Mims. The Moores decided to rent a bedroom in a private home in Riviera Beach during the school year so that they could keep the house in Mims. Still, they had some financial belt-tightening to do, especially with two girls enrolled at Bethune-Cookman College in Daytona Beach. While Harry had always planned to live off his grove when he retired, he had not been planning to retire in his mid-forties. Nor was he planning, whatever his circumstances, to retire from the cause he had dedicated his life to: the civil rights of the Negro in Florida.

Born in Florida in 1905, Harry T. Moore was just three years older than Thurgood Marshall, and both men had started working for the NAACP, though at a distance of a thousand miles from each other, before their thirtieth birthdays. Moore founded the Brevard County chapter of the NAACP in 1934, the same year that Marshall began assisting Charles Hamilton Houston in civil rights suits. What introduced Moore to Marshall three years later had its roots in the Margold Report, a study commissioned by the NAACP that would ultimately lay out a legal strategy for racial reform.

In 1930, the NAACP hired the Harvard-educated lawyer Nathan Ross Margold to study areas in which legalized segregation might be most vulnerable to attack in the courts, and finding discrimination in the financing of public schools to be especially assailable, Margold advised the NAACP to "boldly challenge the constitutional validity" of black schools that were systematically underfunded in direct violation of the Fourteenth Amendment's equal protection clause; for in every case, when states exercised their discretion to spend public funds designated for elementary and high schools, appointments to white schools significantly exceeded those to black schools. After studying the report, Houston devised a long-term plan whereby the NAACP would establish over a number of years a series of precedents in courts across the South regarding inequalities in public school budgets and facilities—to demonstrate that "the law functioned to sustain white supremacy."

Harry Moore had been following events at the national office of the NAACP closely, and in 1937 he wrote a letter informing Walter White that the association's Brevard County branch had hired a lawyer to file suit for equal pay for teachers in that county. When the letter landed on Marshall's desk, the young lawyer could barely contain his excitement. It was exactly the type of case he and Houston were looking to pursue, and it appeared that Moore not only was fully committed to the lawsuit but also had already done much of the legwork. The letter occasioned the first of many meetings between Marshall and Moore over the next decade, some of them at Moore's house in Mims. There Moore played host to Marshall (in part because the local hotels were closed to blacks) as they prepared the case against the Brevard County school board. Marshall said of Moore, in a letter to Walter White: "He seems to be a fine sort of fellow," if "under tremendous pressure because of his actions in the teachers' salary case." Moore in many ways perfectly complemented the ebullient, self-assertive, larger-than-life New York lawyer Thurgood Marshall in that the erstwhile teacher was exactly the selfless, committed, and detail-oriented sort of person on whom the attorney depended. The two men thrived on their mutual respect. In time the school case in Brevard County would inspire similar lawsuits in counties across Florida, and Harry T. Moore would be the first to credit their success to Thurgood Marshall's energy and dedication. "Thurgood was the savior," said Dr. Gilbert Porter, Moore's friend and colleague. "We never started winning any cases until he came. But after he won a few, all you had to say to a white superintendent, 'Well, I'm gonna talk to Mr. Marshall,' and they'd cooperate."

Marshall's visits to Florida had an undeniable impact on Moore. With even more ardor he discharged the monotonous tasks at his local branch—collecting signatures, raising a few dollars here and there from the poorest blacks in the state—because he saw it did make a difference. He spent hours at night bludgeoning countless typewriter ribbons, writing letters to politicians and membership reports to the New York office, whose field administrators saw in Moore a valuable point man in a state with unlimited potential for growth. In the postwar decade Florida would also prove to be a state with a boundless capacity for racial inhumanity, even by measure of the rest of the South, and Marshall and Moore would find themselves challenging law enforcement officers and elected officials determined, without conscience, to whitewash some of the most horrific lynching cases of the twentieth century.

From 1882 to 1930, Florida recorded more lynchings of black people (266) than any other state, and from 1900 to 1930, a per capita lynching rate twice that of Mississippi, Georgia, or Louisiana. But neither Marshall nor Moore needed statistics to know that by World War II, Florida still ranked high among the most violent states in the South. Jack E. Davis, a University of Florida history professor who studied racial violence in the South, concluded that "a black man had more risk of being lynched in Florida than any other place in the country." Alarmingly, despite the shocking and heinous nature of the lynchings in Florida, the crimes and the cover-ups generated little attention, let alone outrage—beyond the black newspapers. The state of Florida—that tropical vacation territory lying south of Georgia and, it would seem, of the Jim Crow South—appeared to be immune to media scrutiny.

HARRY T. MOORE saw no hero in the newspaper accounts of Willis McCall's stand against mob violence in Groveland following the supposed rape of Norma Padgett by four black men. To Moore, the devastation of the black homes and property occurred not in spite of the sheriff's brave watch but because of his blind eye: it simply wasn't plausible that McCall neither knew nor could discover the parties responsible for the rioting in Lake County. On Wednesday, July 20, 1949, Moore sent a telegram to Governor Fuller Warren urging "prosecution of mob leaders responsible for terrorism and vandalism against innocent Negro citizens of Lake County."

Warren at least seemed to be more sympathetic to the Negro cause than his predecessor, the segregationist Millard Caldwell, who viewed the murder of blacks as a political nuisance, and once had his executive secretary request a local judge to launch an investigation because "[l]ynching of negroes is really beginning to give the Governor a terrific headache. . . . "

Fuller Warren had won the 1948 election by running as a moderate and promising to ease racial tension and violence in Florida. He'd denounced the Klansmen who paraded through Lake County on election night (with Sheriff Willis McCall following behind) as "hooded hoodlums and sheeted jerks," and Moore cautiously held out some hope for the new governor. Warren had admitted to being a former member of the Ku Klux Klan, but renouncing his past, like many a politician before and since, he'd stated that he had joined years before "as a favor to a friend" and that he "never wore a hood." Moore did not adopt a wait-and-see approach with the new governor. On July 22, 1949, two days after his original telegram to Warren in regard to Willis McCall, Moore wired a second message to the governor, in which he used the sheriff's own words to make his point. "Since mob leaders are known," Moore wrote, "we again urge that they be arrested and vigorously prosecuted for the damage done to innocent Negro citizens. . . ."

Moore's telegram was intercepted by a staff person at Warren's office. "Have written him enough," the aide scratched across the top and filed the telegram away.

W ITH HUNDREDS OF National Guardsmen camped around Stuckey Still, Mascotte, and Bay Lake, and with only one arrest (for public intoxication), Tuesday night had passed without incident. Convinced that speedy indictments of the three Negroes in custody would significantly curb the violence around Groveland, McCall and State Attorney Jesse Hunter had met with Judge Truman G. Futch on Wednesday, July 20, to expedite the formal charges against Samuel Shepherd, Walter Irvin, and Charles Greenlee for the rape of Norma Padgett. By late afternoon the grand jury, which included the first black ever to so serve in Lake County, had been seated in the courtroom to consider the evidence. Norma Padgett told the court she'd been raped by four men. Willis McCall testified that he had confessions from three of them. By midnight, Hunter had his indictments.

The only reporter present, Mabel Norris Reese of the *Mount Dora Topic*, who'd been invited by the state attorney, was impressed with the strength of the case against the accused. She had only praise for "sage and trial-trained Jesse Hunter" and Sheriff Willis McCall, who, she wrote, had "earned a badge of honor" for the way he conducted himself during Lake County's "eye-blackening rape case."

Things were beginning to quiet down around Groveland. McCall could finally focus on hunting down the fourth rapist.

୨ ୫

FRANKLIN WILLIAMS HAD been following press reports of the violence in Groveland from the NAACP's midtown Manhattan office, but with most of the staff counsel still in Los Angeles for the annual conference, he could do little more than gather information so he'd be prepared to answer any questions Thurgood Marshall might raise. Constance Baker Motley had already spoken with Sheriff Willis McCall about protecting blacks in Lake County from rioting whites; the conversation had not gone well. Harry T. Moore, down in Mims, had learned that Shepherd, Irvin, and Greenlee had been indicted for rape with a trial date set for Monday, August 29. That left barely a month to prepare for a capital case that would most likely sentence three men to the electric chair, and they didn't even have legal representation yet. Moore had dispatched a young black lawyer from Tampa to Florida State Prison in Raiford for the purpose of taking down statements from Shepherd, Irvin, and Greenlee.

Marshall returned to a New York office in chaos. The phones were ringing nonstop with calls from the Florida branches about the assaults upon the Negro communities in Lake County, as well as from NAACP members who had concerns about events at the annual convention in Los Angeles, where delegates had just passed a resolution to permit its board of directors to weed out known communists from local branches. Marshall had begun a tricky political dance with FBI director J. Edgar Hoover. With Hoover's agency being the key to the public's perception of the Red Scare, Marshall was eager to demonstrate the NAACP's (anticommunist) patriotism. At the same time, Marshall's gravitas and popularity with the press exerted pressure on Hoover to reshape the image of the FBI as a government agency with no commitment to the civil rights of blacks. Each man uttered his public statements about the other's organization with politic caution.

Behind the discreet public statements, though, lay decades of tension. Marshall had seen, time and again, the FBI arrive at the scene in the aftermath of a lynching, and time and again leave without any suspects. Moreover, Marshall had learned, the bureau's agents in the aftermath of a lynching evinced so much antagonism toward the black victims and witnesses that the latter simply would not talk to the FBI, out of fear that any information they provided would be relayed to local law enforcement and thus put their lives in danger. Marshall had aired his complaints against the FBI in an appearance before the President's Committee on Civil Rights: "You don't investigate a lynching in the same way you investigate a hot automobile. . . . You have more local feeling to overcome. You have more unwillingness of people to talk." Agents, he said, needed special training, and most important, Marshall stated, they must "themselves believe in the enforcement of civil rights."

After a black army veteran, Isaac Woodard, had been beaten and blinded in South Carolina in early 1946, Marshall seethed when he was yet again informed that an FBI investigation had been unable to acquire sufficient evidence to pursue the case further. That summer had borne witness to a rash of lynchings across the South—all of which had gone unsolved (if not uninvestigated)—and a frustrated Marshall wrote a letter to Tom C. Clark, asking the attorney general to investigate the bureau itself. "The FBI has established for itself an uncomparable [*sic*] record for ferreting out persons violating our federal laws. . . . [This] extends from the prosecution of vicious spies and saboteurs . . . to nondescript hoodlums who steal automobiles and drive them across state lines. On the other hand, the FBI has been unable to identify or bring to trial persons charged with federal statutes where Negroes are the victims."

Clark, in turn, forwarded Marshall's letter to Hoover. Furious, the FBI director fired back, "I have found from previous dealings with [Marshall] that he is more careless to the truth and facts in the charges which he makes against the FBI." He added, "I believe that Mr. Marshall's obvious hostility to the Bureau dominates the thinking of his associates in the legal operation of the National Association for the Advancement of Colored People." Hoover then challenged Marshall to provide specific names of Southerners who believed they had been wronged by the FBI—a challenge Marshall refused to meet.

By all accounts, Hoover cringed at the start of every civil rights investigation, before "rushing pell-mell" into them at the urging of "vociferous minority groups." Satisfied that the FBI had put together a very strong case for prosecutors, with "clear-cut, uncontroverted evidence of conspiracy" in lynchings, Hoover himself became apprehensive of Southern courtroom justice when all-white juries either acquitted defendants or refused to indict suspects altogether. For it was the bureau that bore the brunt of criticism in such cases, not the prosecutors or juries who chose to ignore sound evidence. In Hoover's estimation, such cases, perceived by the public as losses, weakened the FBI's reputation.

When Walter White attempted to arrange a meeting between Marshall and Hoover in the hope that they might come to a truce, Marshall was not optimistic. "I . . . have no faith in either Mr. Hoover or his investigators," he wrote to White, "and there is no use in my saying I do." Hoover simply refused to meet. White persisted, however; in the face of the mounting anticommunist fervor he felt the NAACP needed to be viewed by the FBI as a bastion of democracy, not as a target. In April 1947, putting together an NAACP anticommunism position pamphlet, White requested a patriotic encomium from J. Edgar Hoover, who replied that it would be his "pleasure." Hoover offered: "Equality, freedom and tolerance are essential in a democratic government. The NAACP has done so much to preserve these principles and to perpetuate the desires of our founding fathers." A few months later, White finally persuaded Marshall to travel to Washington to meet Hoover, and the director, in his turn, extended an olive branch of future cooperation. It didn't take long for Marshall to win Hoover over "with his charming, good-ol-boy, 'I'm a little ol' Baltimore lawyer' persona, which worked so well with southern sheriffs and politicians." He made it clear to Hoover that the NAACP could help him avert criticism that the FBI was uninterested in race crimes, and Hoover recognized the value that an endorsement from someone of Marshall's stature in the black community would have on the public's perception of the bureau and, concomitantly, on the agency's reputation. Marshall asked only that the FBI recommit itself in cases where the civil rights of blacks were clearly violated.

By the time the Groveland case memos first crossed Hoover's desk, the director was disposed to write, "Give this matter your full attention," across the bottom, ordering a full investigation. Soon thereafter, FBI field office directors were reporting to Hoover that "Thurgood Marshall of the NAACP complimented the Bureau on its hard work in this case." The two men appeared indeed to have reconciled their differences. The NAACP's Jack Greenberg took a more cynical view. "The Association and Hoover were using each other," he said.

Just days after the alleged rape, Florida newspapers
were calling for capital punishment of the Groveland
Boys. (*Library of Congress, Prints & Photographs
Division, Visual Materials from the NAACP Records*)

BLOODHOUNDS HAD PICKED up the scent of Ernest Thomas. Willis
McCall had led more than one thousand armed men into a cypress
swamp in northern Florida where they had the fourth Groveland Boy
trapped. Around dusk, one group of men on horseback spotted Ernest running across a field two hundred yards in the distance. When they yelled at
him to stop, he only ran faster, and six to eight men, spurring their horses to

full speed, started firing their guns, McCall noted, "like you see in a western movie."

E RNEST THOMAS NEVER made it back to the train depot in Groveland on the night of July 15. He'd left behind the mosquito-bitten sixteen-year-old Charles Greenlee with a gun tucked into his pants, and then he'd as good as disappeared. He was nowhere to be found the following day. Something must have spooked him by the time the sun came up. He may have heard about Samuel Shepherd and Walter Irvin being picked up by Lake County deputies early that morning for the rape of a white woman, or heard about the mob gathering outside Groveland jail, where Charles Greenlee had landed in a cell. There was talk around town that Ernest had returned to Groveland with an eye to getting more involved in the *bolita* business—perhaps running it from his mother's juke joint, the Blue Flame—and in that, he had maybe upset certain parties, Henry Singleton in particular. The owner of the only other alcohol-serving Negro juke joint in town, the Blue Moon, for years Singleton not only had run a lucrative *bolita* operation but also had managed to stay on the good side of Sheriff Willis McCall. Had Ernest Thomas and Henry Singleton perhaps faced off in a confrontation the night before? Might that have been why Ernest had thought it wise to leave Groveland the following morning on the first bus out of town?

A picture began to emerge after Richard Carter, a reporter for the *Daily Compass*, a short-lived leftist newspaper in New York, arrived in Lake County to investigate. Carter had been reporting on the dockside rackets of New York's waterfront when he turned his sights to Groveland. With a keen understanding of organized crime and its political and economic effects, Carter quickly focused on the *bolita* business in Lake County in an attempt to understand why Ernest Thomas might have fled Groveland on the morning of July 16.

In the course of his investigation, Carter discovered that Ernest Thomas had been "peddling *bolita*" in Gainesville for a man named Leroy McKinney, when the two men decided "that there was money to be made by paying odds higher than the traditional 70–1 on a winning *bolita* number." By returning to Groveland, Carter learned, Ernest had hoped to expand his *bolita* business, but he would need a partner in Groveland, so he turned to George Valree, "a bearded, fantastic Negro, who had amassed a fortune in voodooism." Valree owned two houses in Groveland. In one of them "he looked into his crystal ball" for both local blacks and wealthy whites who came from miles away to pay for his clairvoyant services. The other house "was known to be the headquarters for *bolita* in South Lake county." Business was so good that Valree "had recently bought himself a Cadillac."

Ernest Thomas, according to Carter, had worked out a "cozy arrangement" with Valree, who began sending business to him. But the new partnership didn't sit well with the "well-entrenched local *bolita* hustler" in Groveland, Henry Singleton. In addition to running his own juke joint, Singleton had his hand in bootlegging and the numbers game, and "the law enforcement officers whom Singleton paid for protection" were not pleased with the new competition, Carter wrote. Ernest Thomas would not be allowed to come back into Lake County and take money out of their pockets. Not without a fight. "Things were coming to a head in the *bolita* war," Carter wrote, when Singleton and Thomas ran into each other on the night of July 15 and quarreled on the streets of Groveland. "Thomas was feeling his oats and Singleton was resentful," but Singleton had a powerful Lake County ally who had a definitive interest in the *bolita* dealer's continuing prosperity. All Singleton would have to do was pick up the phone and call Willis McCall and let the sheriff know he was having some *bolita* trouble.

Three nights after the alleged rape of Norma Padgett, a Bay Lake mob had torched both of George Valree's homes to the ground. Ernest Thomas had already fled Groveland in fear for his life. And Henry Singleton no longer had to worry about the crystal-gazing seer or the cocky Ernest Thomas cutting into his *bolita* throws.

B Y THE END of the week, the mobs having finally vacated the streets of Lake County, Willis McCall had released the National Guard: and with the three confessed rapists now indicted and secured at Raiford, the sheriff turned his mind to Ernest Thomas. A phone call to the Gainesville Police Department apprised the sheriff that Ernest had been seen in town recently with his wife, Ruby Lee. Promptly, with his deputy James Yates, McCall was heading up to Gainesville.

Ruby Lee Thomas claimed she had not seen her husband since the day he had left for Groveland. "It was obvious she was lying," McCall noted, and after spending the next day pursuing leads that went nowhere, he decided to further question Ruby Lee. As it happened, she was not home, and for the first and "only time in the whole investigation," as McCall would later say, "I violated the law." A letter in the Thomas mailbox caught his eye. It "was not sealed very well and came open with very little effort." It was from Ernest Thomas. The letter told Ruby Lee where her husband would "be until things cooled off" and how she could reach him, under the assumed name of Willy Green, at an RFD mailing address with a box number in Shady Grove, which lay about two hours northwest of Gainesville, near the Georgia border. Thomas would be staying there, he said, "with some kin folks" deep in the swamps.

The letter being a sure lead, McCall contacted Simmie Moore, the sheriff of Madison County, as well as the sheriffs in neighboring Lafayette and Taylor counties, and together they formulated a plan. Once McCall and Yates, who both had no jurisdiction beyond Lake County, had been deputized by local sheriffs, they set out on their manhunt along with several patrolmen from nearby Perry and Mayo. They'd narrowed Thomas's whereabouts to a tenant house on a woodland farm near an old turpentine still, where they decided to lie low until their quarry had "settled down for the night"—they'd move in on Thomas when he was sleeping.

They broke into the tenant house at three in the morning on July 25. They found Thomas's clothes and a few personal effects, but not Thomas himself. He had switched to another house nearby, but he'd heard the lawmen's commotion. Roused from his sleep, he had slipped out a window and made a dash for the woods. McCall admitted, "We had not cased the place as well as we would have liked."

The lawmen put in a call to the State Road Camp at Perry for bloodhounds. An hour later trucks arrived with men, dogs, and horses; by then Ernest Thomas had had a two-hour head start. The hounds picked up Thomas's scent at the house where he'd slept, then led his pursuers through a "cotton patch and through a hog pen, and . . . through a big swamp." The posse knew they were on Ernest's trail in the swamp when one of the dogs found where Ernest had "cut his breeches legs off"; the hound got so excited, he pulled the leash out of the hand of the Perry prison camp inmate. For six miles they pursued the trail, until the dog gave out and they had to send back to their camp for more hounds. This reprieve allowed Ernest Thomas a little more time to put some distance between himself and the posse, but by early afternoon the dogs had again picked up his scent. The sheriffs continued the chase. As the hours passed, however, they recognized that the black fugitive's apparent familiarity with the backwoods and swamps of Madison County had made of him elusive prey.

Word of Thomas's escape had spread by then, and the posse grew. Since before nightfall cars had been descending on the area, and men were being deputized in groups to join the manhunt. McCall made sure that the men of Bay Lake and Groveland had been alerted, in the event that any of them might still be seeking justice for the rape of Norma Padgett. With more than a thousand armed men having answered the call, they were able to encircle the farmlands and cypress swamps where they believed Thomas had hidden. Around dusk, a group of men on horseback spotted Thomas briefly and gave chase, firing their guns and ordering him to halt. Again Thomas escaped his pursuers. He disappeared into a thick cypress pond, where the dogs less effectively followed his scent and darkness hindered the search. Still, the posse had him confined, and by daylight on Tuesday, July 26, when they resumed the chase, every road Thomas might have hoped to cross had been blocked off. His sole recourse was the swamp.

In his legless dungarees, a dirty white flannel shirt, and a pair of muddy tan slippers, Ernest Thomas had been worn down by lack of sleep and his unending flight beneath a ruthless sun. He'd run twenty-five miles, at least, when he found himself in an area of densely wooded pines at the edge of the swamp; he was not far from Moseley Hall—a black section of Madison County in which he hoped to be able to disappear. The hope evaporated when he saw the cars and the armed men patrolling the road. He retreated deeper into the woods, and sitting down, his back against a tree, he drifted into sleep. Nearby, so did one of the bloodhounds in his pursuit. Sheriff McCall had no way to determine if Ernest had befriended the dog asleep at his side or if the dog was guarding the quarry until the posse arrived. The sheriff couldn't ask Ernest because the posse's first sight of him asleep prompted a volley of shots that rang out across the swamp. Around 11:30 a.m. on Tuesday, July 26, Ernest Thomas's lifeless body lay crumpled in a pool of blood, clay, and pine needles. A broken, half-empty pack of Camels was sticking up from the one pocket of his shirt.

The next day, McCall and Yates drove Norma and Willie Padgett to Madison County in order to view the body of Ernest Thomas at the T. J. Beggs Funeral Home. Also present was the state attorney Jesse Hunter. Norma approached the casket. "That is him," she said, staring down at the corpse. No matter that Ernest's face and head were riddled with bullets, she further affirmed, "I would know that face anywhere. He is the one that had the gun and he is the one that drove the car." Willie Padgett never said a word.

Two days after the shooting, at a coroner's inquest, a string of witnesses paraded before county judge Curtis Earp. Almost all of them testified they had been close enough to observe that Thomas was armed and had attempted to fire a .32-caliber Harrington & Richardson revolver when he was discovered; yet virtually none of them could say or even approximate, not with "so much excitement" at the scene, how many shots were fired or who was actually present to fire them when Thomas was killed. One of them claimed he was close enough to hear Thomas's last words, "Don't shoot, white man, don't shoot," but not to see who did the shooting. Nor could he say how many shots had followed, although he did attest that with all the bullets flying, one of the dogs was shot.

On the one hand, Willis McCall told reporters that Thomas was "belligerent as the devil. He had a loaded pistol in his hand and he had his finger around the trigger"; on the other, under oath, McCall stated he had been nowhere near the spot where Thomas was killed, telling investigators, "I was across on the opposite side of the swamp when the shooting occurred." He didn't know who fired the fatal shots, he later told reporters, "but it was a bunch of good fellows."

Called as a witness before the inquest, Sheriff Simmie Moore stated that when he arrived at the scene, Thomas was already dead with a bullet hole in the back of the head, two bullet holes in his right temple, and bullet wounds in the forehead, "above the eyes." Moore had laid down newspapers "because it was a little bloody" and covered Thomas with a cloth. The actual number of bullet wounds sustained by Ernest Thomas was never clearly established, although the *Baltimore Afro-American* estimated that "nearly 400 slugs" were found in the body. The coroner's report found that "there were other holes in the body" and that Ernest had been "shot with buckshot, as well as with rifle or revolver bullets."

At the end of the testimony, Sheriff Moore was recalled as a witness in the Ernest Thomas inquest. Apparently Moore had been discomposed by the chronic amnesia that had plagued witnesses throughout the hearing, and he wanted something on the record to show which sheriffs were in the vicinity "when this negro was shot." When asked, Moore replied, "Sheriff McCall of Lake County, and Sheriff Towles of Taylor County."

"How many deputy sheriffs were down in that area?" the state attorney then asked.

"One," Moore said.

"Who was that?"

"Sheriff McCall's deputy."

Ormond Powers, a reporter for the *Orlando Sentinel*, had been covering the Groveland story and he told Milton C. Thomas, a former editor from the newspaper, that he had become frustrated with what he perceived were "glaring flaws" in Willis McCall's versions of events. To start, Powers had never seen any of the confessions McCall claimed to have obtained from the Groveland Boys. He just printed what the sheriff and his deputies told him, but he doubted the defendants had so freely admitted their guilt. Powers believed that reporters were "being told just the things they [law enforcement] wanted written" and that his own "probing questions were never welcomed." The *Sentinel* reporter also suspected that Ernest Thomas's involvement with *bolita* was the reason the young man had fled Lake County, not the fact that Norma Padgett claimed to have been raped. Powers had questions for Sheriff McCall about the specifics of Thomas's resistance at the time the Groveland native was gunned down, and those questions "have never been answered."

The reporter had come to suspect that McCall was "desperate to seal Thomas's lips" and that the reason for such an extensive manhunt "was for the purpose of shutting up Thomas permanently." Officers in northern Florida, Powers believed, "could have taken Thomas," but Powers suspected "a plot to GET Thomas—and they did. The 'they' in this case being organized gamblers."

The authorities, Powers said, viewed Thomas as a "definite threat to the established and entrenched gambling set-up in that section of Lake County," and the posse was organized to make "absolutely sure Thomas had no chance to TALK." The reporter also observed, "It seemed there was relief that Thomas was dead." Finally, Ormond Powers told the editor that McCall "was present—and probably shooting—when Thomas was killed," and that "this might have been cold-blooded murder."

THE CORONER'S JURY found that Ernest Thomas had been "lawfully killed" and ruled his death a justifiable homicide. Two hundred miles to the south of Moseley Hall, many of Thomas's neighbors found the evidence supporting the jury's ruling to be suspect. One of Groveland's white elected officials "broadly hinted" to a reporter that it was unlikely that Ernest Thomas had attempted to shoot his way out of the swamp, as "Thomas was a bright, well-dressed, college-educated man. He wasn't a rough of any sort." Beyond dispute, though, was the fact that the "Groveland Four," as the newspapers referred to the Lake County rapists, were now the Groveland three.

After the inquest, on the drive back to Bay Lake, Willis McCall asked Norma Padgett to hold out her hand. He'd retained a token from the crime scene: something to ease the pain of the seventeen-year-old farm girl. Norma extended her pale, white palm. The sheriff plunked into it a .38-caliber slug that had recently been pumped into the black body of Ernest Thomas.

IT DIDN'T TAKE much for Franklin Williams to convince Thurgood Marshall that events in Groveland resembled a Little Scottsboro and that NAACP counsel ought to intervene. On first hearing, the case for the most part fulfilled the three requirements Marshall had established to guide his staff. For one, the injustice stemmed from race. Second, while the innocence of Shepherd, Irvin, and Greenlee might be open to question, Marshall had argued enough cases to be suspicious of confessions obtained by law enforcement in Southern jails—especially if the crimes carried a death penalty. Lastly, the case obviously raised due process and equal protection issues.

Williams presented a persuasive argument, but the New York office was shorthanded. With White, Wilkins, and Marshall's assistant special counsel, Robert Carter, unavailable, options were limited. In 1949, Constance Baker Motley was still "learning to try cases," under Marshall, and the prospect of dispatching her to Florida to try a criminal case did not appeal to Marshall. Nor could he enlist a more experienced attorney like William Hastie, the former dean of Howard University School of Law and cousin to Charles Hamilton Houston, as Hastie was still serving his term as governor of the Virgin Islands. (President Truman would soon appoint Hastie to the U.S. Court of Appeals for the Third Circuit, thus making him the nation's first black appellate judge.)

In the end, Marshall assigned the case to Franklin Williams himself. Williams had argued *Watts v. Indiana* with Marshall before the Supreme Court a few months earlier—another instance when the NAACP was shorthanded—and the young lawyer effectively convinced the justices that a murder confession had been obtained involuntarily. So it was that Williams found himself on a plane to central Florida.

The thirty-one-year-old assistant special counsel had been hired by the NAACP in 1945, when he'd impressed Walter White by passing the New York state bar examination *before* receiving his degree from Fordham University Law School. Williams, a native of Flushing, Queens, New York, and like Marshall, an alumnus of Lincoln University, had served in a segregated unit of the U.S. Army during World War II, his military experience being particularly useful to Marshall at a time when the NAACP was handling numerous cases in which black servicemen appeared to have been unjustly court-martialed. Like all counsel under Marshall, though, Williams had soon found himself working on briefs and appeals for cases involving school desegregation, restrictive covenants, and transportation. A 1946 case that had especially commanded Williams's attention concerned a young former sergeant in the U.S. Army, Isaac Woodard, who had been maimed by police just hours after receiving his honorable discharge.

On February 13, Woodard, in uniform, had boarded a Greyhound bus at Camp Gordon, near Augusta, Georgia, and was heading to South Carolina to pick up his wife so they could travel on to New York together to visit his parents. Not long into the trip he and the bus driver got into a dispute over Woodard's need to use a drugstore bathroom during a stop. The argument was brief, but when the driver stopped again in Batesburg, South Carolina, Woodard was removed from the bus and taken to a nearby alley, where the policemen beat him with their nightsticks. They then arrested Woodard for disorderly conduct and threw him into a cell, where he was again drubbed with a nightstick, by the chief of police, Linwood Shull. When Woodard awoke the next morning, both eye sockets had been ruptured and his corneas irreparably damaged, but police denied him any medical attention for two days. Woodard had already been blinded for life when, two days after the beating, he was dropped off by police at a hospital in Aiken, South Carolina. The substandard medical care he received there resulted in amnesia, and it was several weeks before his relatives, who had reported the sergeant missing, were able to find him.

While Williams was eager to take Woodard's case, which certainly met Marshall's guidelines, he knew that any investigation would be difficult given that his client was both blind and unable to remember many of the details of his ordeal. Eventually Williams managed to locate a student from the University of South Carolina who had been on the bus with Woodard; the student identified Shull as the arresting officer. With that the NAACP immediately began publicizing Woodard's story. When Walter White met with President Harry Truman during "that terrible summer of 1946" after several high-profile lynchings of black soldiers in the South had caught the nation's attention, Truman "exploded" on being informed that the state of South Carolina had simply dismissed the Woodard incident. Truman ordered the Justice Department to investigate; the indictments of Shull and his officers followed shortly thereafter.

The blinding of Isaac Woodard enraged the public. Orson Welles campaigned on his radio broadcasts for punishment of the police officers; Woody Guthrie recorded "The Blinding of Isaac Woodard." To raise awareness further, the NAACP sent Woodard on a national tour with Franklin Williams to speak about the soldier's beating and blinding at the hands of police. The pair made an unforgettable impression. Woodard, who had begun to regain his memory, was initially terrified to address an audience he could not see, but from the outset of the tour his account of the pride he felt at serving his country in the Pacific, which earned him a Battle Star and a Good Conduct Medal, deeply stirred his audience, as did the poignant rendering of his anticipation as he boarded the bus, believing he was only hours away from seeing his wife, and then his desolation over the loss of his memory and sight. The soldier was "a good platform person," according to Williams, who would follow Woodard's story with a passionate appeal for funds.

Williams was good on the platform, too. Thin and handsome, with a chiseled face and dark, deep-set eyes, he dressed in sharp, tailored suits, often with a bow tie and fedora. What he lacked in experience the urbane young lawyer more than made up for in confidence, and his substantial intelligence matched his forceful presence. Williams perfectly projected the NAACP's desired public image. As the newest attorney on a staff that included Thurgood Marshall, Robert Carter, and Constance Baker Motley, Williams was proving himself a worthy addition in his tireless advocacy on behalf of Isaac Woodard. When Woodard and Williams appeared at Harlem's Lewisohn Stadium, at a rally cochaired by heavyweight fighter Joe Louis, twenty thousand people attended, and the event pulled in more than twenty-two thousand dollars for Woodard's aid and an "antimob violence fund."

The case against Woodard's attackers was less successful, and Williams witnessed Southern justice as he sat beside Isaac Woodard in court. The judge in the trial, a proponent of civil rights, was so outraged by the U.S. attorney's inept and uninspired efforts to make a case against the defendants that he declared it "disgraceful." Adding insult to injury, Shull's defense lawyers outright shouted racial epithets at Woodard in the courtroom. The jury needed not even a half hour to find Shull and the police not guilty on all charges; the gallery burst into applause.

Williams could barely believe what he had witnessed. Marshall had always returned from his trips down south with colorful stories of crazy sheriffs, violent mobs, and vicious death threats, and Williams had laughed at Marshall's mockery along with the rest of the legal staff in the comfort of the NAACP's midtown offices. But Williams could find nothing funny in his acquaintance with that Southern landscape. The stories he could tell of his experiences with Woodard below the Mason-Dixon Line would, Williams said, "make your hair stand on end."

Still, Williams was beginning to appreciate Marshall's strategy in regard to criminal cases in the South, where local law enforcement, prosecutors, judges, and juries all guaranteed that the scales of justice would tip in favor of white supremacy. You fought, as Marshall repeatedly reminded his staff, so that you lived to fight another day, whether by filing an appeal to a higher court or simply by recognizing that when an all-white jury handed a black defendant a life sentence instead of the death penalty, you had in a sense won, because the jurors believed your client to be innocent. For Marshall, the fight was never over with a jury's verdict. For him the Supreme Court was as level a playing field as you'd find in the land: that was the courtroom he wanted to fight in. Williams, too.

Yet here Williams was, on a plane, heading back down to that strange, lawless other land where people didn't take kindly to niggers wearing suits and talking back to judges just like they were white men.

# | 10 | QUITE A HOSE WIELDER

Willie Padgett, Mabel Norris Reese, and Jesse Hunter. *Life* magazine photographer Wallace Kirkland protected Norma Padgett's identity by hiding her behind Hunter. (*Photo by Wallace Kirkland/Time & Life Pictures/Getty Images*)

DON'T WORRY, MAMA. I haven't done anything."

Walter Irvin spoke calmly, then walked past his sobbing mother toward Deputy James Yates and the patrolmen who were waiting outside the house to take him and Samuel Shepherd away. He had only gotten a few steps from the front door when Willie Padgett darted from a black sedan and charged.

"You little son of a bitch. You were there. You had better get my wife or I am going to kill you."…

Irvin, confused, told Padgett he didn't know anything about his wife.

"Yes you do," Padgett fumed, and as he rushed toward Irvin, Deputy Yates and Deputy Leroy Campbell pulled the sputtering Bay Lake farmer away and sat him back in the car.

The patrolmen ushered Shepherd and Irvin into the backseat of another car, and a caravan of squad cars sped its way through Groveland. Meanwhile, James Shepherd's Mercury, which Samuel had been driving the night before, was confiscated by the police; Deputy Campbell had it taken to a filling station, where a search was begun on it for evidence. By then the caravan, which had been heading toward Mascotte, had turned onto a deserted clay road. Four or five miles got the patrol cars to a secluded spot. They stopped alongside the road.

It was Yates who opened the door on Irvin's side. "Get out of the car, boy," he ordered, and Irvin did.

"Why did you rape that white woman?" Yates demanded, but Irvin didn't have a chance to answer. Yates smashed him across the forehead with a nightstick.

Shepherd had watched his friend collapse on the road before he, too, was ordered out of the car. The patrolmen were standing in a semicircle before him. "Better talk," Yates advised, and Shepherd replied that he didn't know anything.

At that the patrolmen converged on both Shepherd and Irvin, who had pulled himself up from the ground. With some patrolmen holding the two of them and others beating them with blackjacks and fists, Shepherd and Irvin ended up eventually on the roadbed. Curled up, they were kicked repeatedly, then dragged again to their feet.

"Nigger, you the one that picked up this white girl last night?" someone asked.

"What white girl?" Irvin replied before being struck again.

"Well you might as well tell us you're the one did it," another one said, "'cause we gonna beat the hell out of you until you tell us you did do it."

Shepherd's vision was blurring, and Irvin was drifting in and out of consciousness. As best they could, they denied having anything to do with the missing white girl.

One of the patrolmen brought Willie Padgett over to the beaten men and asked if he was sure these two were "the right ones." Padgett paused, grimacing at all the blood.

"The hell with it," the cop said, lifting his blackjack and bringing it down hard on skull and bone.

WHEN FRANKLIN WILLIAMS arrived in Orlando, before he could even think about investigating the Groveland case he had to attend to the basics of housing and transportation. Blacks traveling by car commonly relied upon *The Negro Motorist Green Book* as a guide. The eighty-page booklet, published by Victor H. Green & Company in New York, under the sponsorship of Esso and the Ford Motor Company, listed by city and state the names and addresses of hotels, restaurants, taxi services, and gas stations that would accommodate blacks: thus it aimed to "solve your problems" if you happened to be traveling in unfamiliar territory, especially in Jim Crow states. The 1949 *Green Book* confirmed Williams's suspicions. Not a single hotel in Lake County was open to blacks. Further, because he had been advised not to spend too much time near the courthouse in Tavares—Willis McCall country—especially after dark, Williams's misgivings far exceeded the assurance of the *Green Book*'s tagline, "Now We Can Travel Without Embarrassment."

Through the NAACP's network of Florida branches, Williams lined up a room at an Orlando "tourist home," akin to a black-run bed-and-breakfast. It was here that Williams met and befriended Joe Louis, who was visiting Orlando for a boxing exhibition. On learning of the Groveland case, Louis aided Williams in his work with some ready cash and subsequently donated five hundred dollars to the NAACP for the defense of the Groveland Boys. A picture of Louis and Williams appeared in the *New York Post* below the caption "Slugs for Equality," for news of Ernest Thomas's killing had made headlines in Northern newspapers, like that in the July 27 *New York Times*, which ran "Posse Kills Negro, Florida Fugitive; He Was Hunted in Groveland Rape Case."

In New York, too, Thurgood Marshall, after consulting with Williams in Florida, attached his notable name, for the first time publicly, to the Groveland case. He fired off a telegraphed request for a federal investigation to U.S. attorney general Tom Clark, stating, "This wanton killing by a deputized mob is worse than a lynching." He followed with a protest to Governor Fuller Warren of Florida, charging, "There is serious doubt that the man killed was in any manner connected with the alleged rape." The national press accounts of Marshall's actions included his phrase "alleged rape," which was another first, for until then, except for black newspapers, coverage of the events in Groveland had eschewed the word *alleged* in connection to the plight of Norma Padgett on the night of July 15.

In Florida, in order to proceed with the investigation, and working with a limited NAACP budget, Williams had to retain a lawyer who was a member of the state's bar: not any easy task, given that the state registered a total of less than two dozen black lawyers, with most of them practicing in

Miami or the larger cities and none of them in Lake County or any county nearby. Williams nonetheless managed to find two young law school graduates—William Fordham from Tampa and Horace Hill, a Howard University Law School graduate, from Daytona Beach—who had been admitted to the Florida bar the year before. Of course, they had been reading the papers, too, and were not so sure they wanted to be involved in a Lake County rape case. Williams, though, could detect the excitement in twenty-four-year-old Hill at the prospect of working alongside an attorney from the national office of the NAACP and Thurgood Marshall's legal defense team. Still, fully aware of the Lake County rioting, the renegade posse, and especially the vindictive Big Hat Man sheriff, Hill was reluctant. "My aunt wanted to know if I had lost my mind," Hill recalled. "I even called my parents, and they wanted to know whether or not I was crazy, and they said how dangerous it was."

On Friday, July 29, the smooth-talking, persuasive Franklin Williams was driving north to the Florida State Prison in Raiford not only with his new recruit Horace Hill but also in Hill's 1948 Chevrolet and with Hill's wife, Dorothy, whom Williams had convinced to serve as their stenographer. And with William Fordham, too. By late afternoon they'd arrived at the prison farm known as "the Rock" and had settled in a room where they met the three defendants one by one. Although Fordham, who had previously been dispatched to Raiford by Harry T. Moore, had tried to prepare the New York attorney for the visit, Williams was profoundly shocked by his first sight of Samuel Shepherd, Walter Irvin, and Charles Greenlee. It had been nearly two weeks since they had been transported to Raiford, but their faces and bodies still bore the effects of the beatings they'd suffered in Lake County. "Their heads were a mess" and caked with "encrusted dry blood," Williams observed. "Their hair was a mess. It was shocking to me that in a state prison, they had not even been able to wash their hair." Bruises, scars, and swellings were the badges of their brotherhood.

Samuel Shepherd was the first to be interviewed. After taking the lawyers through events on the evening of July 15, when he and Walter Irvin had driven to Eatonville for a few beers, he described what happened the following morning. Samuel had just dropped off his sister-in-law at the beauty parlor in Groveland when he stopped by Walter Irvin's house around 7 a.m. to see if his friend had gotten up on time for work. At the same moment, two Florida Highway Patrol cars and a third, black car pulled up in front of the house, and several white men emerged, among them the deputies Campbell and Yates. "Where is the guy that was with you last night?" Yates asked

Shepherd, and what began with that question led to the beatings he and Irvin endured on the deserted clay road outside of Groveland.

"They must have beat us about a half hour," Shepherd told the lawyers, who were at once riveted and appalled by his testimony. After the beating, he and Irvin were shoved back into the patrol car. Irvin's shirt was drenched in blood, and when he reached his hand up to his head he felt "a big chunk knocked out of it." A patrolman told them to scoot up to the edge of the seat so their blood wouldn't drip onto the upholstery. As did Irvin, Shepherd opened his mouth to show Williams's team his broken teeth and lifted his shirt to reveal still numerous bruises.

Then Shepherd continued, telling the lawyers how Yates and Campbell in their black sedan led the caravan to the place where Padgett's car had broken down on that Friday night after the dance. Ordered out of the car, Shepherd and Irvin stood beside Deputy Yates, who was trying to match their footprints to those in the sand and clay. After examining Shepherd's shoes, which Shepherd avowed he'd worn the night before, Yates once more studied the ground, and declared, "These are not your tracks." Similarly questioned, Irvin, who was still bleeding profusely from his head, admitted that he had in fact been wearing a different pair of shoes. Frustrated, Yates returned the men to the patrol car, which delivered them to the Tavares jail.

They had been locked in a large cell with other inmates, who could plainly see that Irvin, sitting in a corner on the floor with his hand pressed against his head, was unable to stop his wound from bleeding. One of the prisoners remarked that it looked like the police had tried to kill them, but Irvin, understandably, was in no mood to talk. Hours had passed when Yates and Campbell showed up at the bullpen. The interrogation of Samuel Shepherd and Walter Irvin was not over yet.

"Nigger, you are gonna tell us the truth or we are gonna beat the hell out of you," Campbell warned. "We will make you tell it."

They were in the bowels of the jail. Irvin surveyed the basement room; a number of pipes ran the length of the room, which housed "a lot of motors." The deputies hoisted Irvin up; they cuffed his hands to an overhead pipe. As Irvin stood only five foot two, his feet did not reach the floor. Satisfied that Irvin was hanging securely, Yates and Campbell took turns beating him with a leaded rubber hose.

"They hit me across my back, shoulders, head, arms and hindpart," Irvin told Williams and the two young black lawyers, but neither Yates nor Campbell had any questions for him. Campbell just "kept on trying to get me to admit that I had raped some woman, which I would not admit because I did not know what they were talking about."

Tossing aside the rubber hose, Campbell pulled out his gun and taunted Irvin, saying "he would get a thrill out of blowing my brains out." But instead he stepped aside for another man, who held Irvin up by the chin and with his fist made a punching bag of Irvin's face. Then the man reared back and with his "high top boots," Irvin said, he "kicked me in the privates."

They dumped Irvin in a cell. It was Shepherd's turn next, and the deputies now led him down to the basement, where he, too, endured another brutal beating. "My mouth was bleeding where a front tooth went through my lip," Shepherd recounted. "I have three teeth broken in the back of my mouth. Nobody at the prison camp has looked at it, though I asked to see the doctor when I first came here."

Williams wanted to know about another critical issue, the much-publicized confessions of the three defendants in the case. Shepherd said he had never signed anything, but the repeated beatings had wrenched an oral confession from him—particularly the blows delivered by the man in the high-topped riding boots, whom he recognized as Wesley Evans, a regular customer at the dairy in Groveland where Shepherd had once worked. Evans had asked for a few cracks at the prisoner, and with a hose he was so vengefully smashing Shepherd's face and chest that Yates, deeming him "quite a hose wielder," wondered if Evans might be related to Norma Padgett. Evans said no, he wasn't related, but he did pause to allow that both Norma and Willie Padgett were "good friends," before continuing to slash away at Shepherd. Two nights later, Wesley Evans would be standing among the ringleaders of the mob that burned the Shepherds' house to the ground in Bay Lake.

"They tried to make me say that I had been with the group of fellows that raped a white woman," Shepherd said. "It was terrible the way I was whipped, there was just knots all over me. They said they were not going to stop whipping me until I said that I was the one. I kept telling them I was in Orlando where I was. Finally, when I couldn't take it anymore, I said yes." Shepherd said yes, he raped Norma Padgett, and the men dropped their hoses. Yates told Shepherd he could have "saved all the beating" if he had just said yes the first time they asked.

Williams cataloged the still visible evidence of Shepherd's injuries: scars on his head, broken teeth, tooth puncture of upper lip, lash scars across back and chest, scars on the wrists, which supported Shepherd's claim that he had been cuffed to a metal pipe above his head. Irvin evidenced similar injuries: body scars, wide bruises, lash marks, scars across the wrists. Also, Williams noted, Irvin's "right jaw appeared to be fractured."

After the beating Shepherd, too, was returned to the fourth floor of the jail, where, like Irvin, he was locked in a separate cell. Irvin, however, did not remain long. Again he was removed to the basement for a second round of beating by Campbell and Yates; for Irvin had not yet confessed. At the end of it "I was bleeding pretty bad," Irvin told Williams, but to the end he had refused to admit to raping Norma Padgett. The deputies took him back to his cell; on the way up "one of them kicked me in the balls," Irvin said.

Around 6 p.m., Yates and Campbell informed the two exhausted, beaten black men that "a mob was on its way"; they were "lucky," said the deputies, in that they were going to be taken away from the jail so they wouldn't be killed. Handcuffed together, Shepherd and Irvin were led to a car and ordered to lie down in the backseat so as not to be seen. They could hear the chaos on the police radio, which relayed that colored people were being beaten and killed in the vicinity, while the black sedan made its way to a watermelon field in the woods. There the two prisoners were handcuffed with their arms wrapped around a small pine sapling. They'd expected to be doused in gasoline and set afire, but instead they simply waited. A young girl on horseback passed by; the deputies stayed by the sedan. After a half hour or so, Shepherd and Irvin were again stuffed into the back of the car, then driven to Eustis. The sedan had pulled into a driveway when they heard a voice shout, "Where are those niggers at?"

The door on Shepherd's side of the car was flung open, and immediately a tall man in a white Stetson was bashing the prisoner with a large, heavy flashlight and stomping him with his boots. Already displeased—the sheriff had just gotten home from Ohio only to find that all hell had broken loose in his county—McCall became only more provoked when Shepherd entreated him to stop: the sheriff started "really kicking him then." With venom to spare, McCall went round to the other side of the sedan and with the flashlight gave Irvin a taste of it across his arms and legs. The deputies then resumed their journey with Shepherd and Irvin. In about two hours they arrived at Florida State Prison in Raiford.

The third prisoner in the Groveland rape case, Charles Greenlee, did not escape a trip to the basement of the Tavares jail. He, too, had wounds to show. Because of his young age, Horace Hill's wife, Dorothy, was asked to step out of the room while the lawyers examined the boy. Williams recorded that Greenlee's left eye was "red and bruised"; his right cheekbone bore a double scar and he had "scars all around his neck"; also scarred was the groin area, and his testicles were still swollen; his feet had numerous cuts. The examination complete, Hill's wife returned to take down the rest of Greenlee's statement. When he had finished he said to Williams, "All of this is true. I know nothing about this rape. I don't even know Samuel and Irvin."

The lawyers closed their notepads. What Williams had suspected had proved to be true: Sheriff Willis McCall and his deputies had tortured the three Groveland boys in order to secure the confessions that supported the sheriff's boast to the press, no matter that one of them, Walter Irvin, had refused to confess even to stop the beating. Individually, the three men's stories were remarkably similar in their descriptions of their torturers and of the basement below the jail in Tavares. But, while Greenlee's denial that he had ever seen Norma and Willie Padgett on the evening of July 15 was convincing enough, the account that the two army buddies related of their whereabouts that night was indeed problematic, as it included an encounter with the alleged victim and her husband.

After assuring the three defendants that he would arrange for a physician's visit so as to have a more complete, professional medical report on their injuries, Williams inquired if they had been offered or had sought legal counsel since their incarceration at Raiford two weeks earlier. Apparently, neither at the jail in Tavares nor in the state prison had any officer or official advised them of their right to be represented by a lawyer. The state attorney, Jesse Hunter, had brought Norma and Willie Padgett to Raiford so that the young couple could identify the three suspects, and before the indictment, when he had interviewed each of them, Hunter had asked only if they had lawyers. That both Irvin and Greenlee had replied, naively, that they didn't need lawyers because they hadn't done anything wrong—that it was merely a case of mistaken identity soon to be cleared up—left Williams incredulous. No less naive had been Shepherd's response that he was a member of a church and "was going to tell the thing just like it happened." The defendants' naïveté aside, the oversight on the part of county and state officials bolstered Williams's confidence that his report from the state prison would prompt the NAACP to commit more substantially to the Groveland case, especially since the hunting and gunning down of Ernest Thomas by a posse of more than a thousand armed men, many of them deputized, had already engaged Thurgood Marshall more actively in the fray.

It was when the three prisoners stood up, as the lawyers were preparing for their departure, that Williams noticed, first, Irvin's bare feet and then the bloodstains on the back of his pants, the same pants he'd been wearing the day he was beaten in the Tavares jail. "I have no shoes up here," Irvin told Williams. "I only have my shirt and pants."

Williams and his team had begun the long drive back to Orlando and the attorney from the New York office of the NAACP was still shaken. Unsettled though he naturally was by the defendants' revelations, the injustices they had already suffered, and the physical pain they had endured, it was a comment the sixteen-year-old Greenlee had made in his stuttery, backwoods accent that Williams couldn't shake. The boy had implicitly articulated what every black male since the dawn of slavery in the South instinctively knew about race and sex. It could also explain Ernest Thomas's bolting out of Lake County on the morning of July 16, 1949. On Greenlee's first night in Groveland, when the deputies picked him up at the train depot and put him in jail, they had left him alone in a cell with a cot and without a lock. "Jesus," Greenlee had said, remembering for Williams the night he'd lost his future. "If I, if I thought a white woman had been raped within a hundred miles of [Groveland] and Negroes were suspected, I would have opened the door and left."

WILLIAMS'S STAY IN Orlando was proving to be fruitful. His investigation of the case against the Groveland Boys took him to Terence McCarthy, whose coverage of the story for the *New Leader*, a leftist intellectual weekly newspaper "devoted to the Socialist and Labor movements," had convinced him—as he would convince Williams—that the case had more to do with race and the citrus industry, with intimidation tactics and status, than it did with the alleged rape of Norma Padgett. Henry Shepherd, who had long suffered the ire of his white neighbors, and finally their torch-lit violence, agreed. "I been told by a lot of people it was nothing but jealousy and jealousy is what it was," Shepherd told Williams. Shepherd also had a second theory, one that the World War II veteran Williams understood well: "Sammy is a good boy," Shepherd said. "All the white people will say he was before he went to the army. Since he come back people didn't like Sammy and the Irvin boy driving James's car around. They didn't like no veterans' attitude."

Both Samuel Shepherd and Walter Irvin had recently returned from military service. As U.S. Army regulations allowed soldiers to continue to wear their military uniforms after completing their service, many black veterans did exactly that, perhaps to remind their communities that they, too, had defended their country. They had also been dispatched to foreign

nations, particularly in Europe, where minorities experienced more tolerance and openness than they ever had in America, especially in the South.
So, like many black veterans returning home to states in the South and the
one south of the South, Sam Shepherd and Walter Irvin were not prepared
to return to the fields or citrus groves of Lake County under the conditions
defined by Jim Crow. White Southerners, meanwhile, may have been outraged by the reported egalitarian attitudes of Europeans toward Negroes,
but they were flat-out enraged by stories from France of white women sleeping with American black men; they were thus determined to put returning
black veterans back in their place. After World War I, dozens of Negro soldiers had been lynched in the South, some of them still wearing their uniforms, and in the summer of 1946 the lynchings of black veterans resumed
with a vengeance. Fathers of black soldiers warned their sons not to come
home in their uniforms because police had made a practice of searching and
beating black military men. "If he had a picture of a white woman in his
wallet, they'd kill him," one Mississippi man related.

A veteran himself, and having worked extensively with the blinded
veteran Isaac Woodard, Franklin Williams understood fully the antagonism blacks experienced in the United States on leaving military service.
That veterans Samuel Shepherd and Walter Irvin had still been wearing
their army uniforms around Groveland was bound to incense the whites
of Lake County, Williams knew, and he was also not surprised to learn
that Sheriff McCall had expected them to be picking fruit in the groves
the way black men were supposed to, with poor pay for long hours of hard
labor. Instead, Shepherd and Irvin were driving around town in a late-
model Mercury as if the streets were theirs; to the whites, this was gall-
ingly plain "arrogance." Resentment was general and, according to
Williams, that resentment among rural whites "had been communicated
to them from the sheriff . . . from Willis McCall." Henry Shepherd was
more succinct. He said that to the whites around Groveland, his son was
an "uppity Nigger."

The more Williams poked around the Groveland area, the more he
considered the likelihood that the alleged rape had simply provided the
Lake County Sheriff's Department with an excuse to do some heavy house-
keeping with regard to black troublemakers and potential instigators.
"McCall knew exactly who he wanted to get," Williams said. "He wanted
to get Shepherd and Irvin. He wanted to get them."

✧ ✧

IMMEDIATELY UPON HIS return to New York, Franklin Williams briefed Thurgood Marshall fully on the case of the Groveland Boys: how lucky they were to be alive after the beatings they'd endured; how, two weeks later, "blood was still in their hair and head and the soles of their feet were still cut"; how Shepherd and Greenlee had confessed—but only orally—in order to end their torture, whereas Irvin had not confessed either orally or in writing. None of it surprised Marshall, who had seen enough such cases to know that in the South coerced confessions were more the rule than the exception. Even President Truman's 1946 *Report of the President's Committee on Civil Rights* acknowledged as much, with J. Edgar Hoover testifying that "lawless police action" against blacks was so commonplace in the South that at one particular jail "it was seldom that a Negro man or woman was incarcerated who was not given a severe beating, which started off with a pistol whipping and ended with a rubber hose."

With one suspect dead under legally questionable circumstances and three others severely and lawlessly beaten, Marshall did not hesitate to ratchet up the commitment of the NAACP to the case. He told Williams to enlist the best local lawyer available to try the case, and he told the press, forcefully, "The resources of the association will be thrown behind the defense of these boys, and at the same time, we will insist upon protection of other Negroes in the area." Marshall had served notice to the state of Florida. If local officials with racial bias had been planning to run helpless blacks through their justice system to predetermined convictions, they were going to have to do so against attorneys with formidable backgrounds in both state and federal appeals. Furthermore, NAACP involvement in a criminal case guaranteed it attention in the national press, which would place the prosecuting state attorney Jesse Hunter in the spotlight of newspapers that, unlike Florida's local ones, had no investment in maintaining racial tranquillity and the Jim Crow status quo. By then, at a press conference in New York, Franklin Williams would have already told national reporters that his investigation in Lake County had convinced him not only that the Groveland Boys were "entirely innocent" but also that the "trumped up rape charge" against them had less to do with the riots and destruction in Negro communities than did the resolve of the white mob's ringleaders to intimidate blacks into accepting their designated place in the citrus groves.

While Marshall and Williams attempted to put together a preliminary legal strategy, the New York office of the NAACP advised Harry T. Moore in Florida that the LDF would vigorously defend the three Groveland boys and requested that Moore rouse local public support for the case. Moore immediately sprang into action. He had already sent telegrams to Governor Warren on July 20 and 22 calling for punishment of the parties responsible for the rioting in Groveland, and now, in a letter to the governor on July 30, he demanded a special investigation and a special session of the grand jury "to indict the guilty mobsters." Moore also had Sheriff McCall in his sights. While Moore had commended the sheriff for preventing a lynching on July 16, he had been critical of McCall as well, especially of the county lawman's "lenient attitude toward the mob" in permitting certain of its ringleaders to search the jail for the suspects. Moore had inquired, too, if the sheriff, who'd claimed to have known or recognized all the armed men in the mob, planned to bring charges against those who did not have permits to carry weapons. Now that Moore had learned the defendants had been physically tortured, he composed a circular that he released to the press. It charged that the blacks indicted in the Groveland case had been "brutally beaten by local officers in an effort to force confessions from them" and it called upon Governor Warren to suspend the officers responsible.

Sheriff McCall did not react kindly to Moore's accusations. He had carefully crafted an image of himself for the press as an unimpeachable county official, a man "duty bound" to run the sheriff's office by the rule of law, even if that included his standing up to an angry white mob in order to protect black rapists in his jail. Indeed, obsessed with his public image, McCall clipped every newspaper article that, favorably or not, mentioned his name, and he was quick to correct reporters on issues of fact as well as to dispute any negative statement or opinion written about him—on occasion in person, as he did when he stomped unannounced through Mabel Norris Reese's door at the *Mount Dora Topic* and accused her of writing lies about him. When the *Ocala Star-Banner* reported Harry T. Moore's charge that local officers had systematically beaten the suspects in the Groveland rape case in order to obtain the confessions McCall had been vaunting not three weeks before, the sheriff was apoplectic. "It's a damn lie," was his answer to the charge. "There's absolutely no truth to it."

After the consultations with Marshall in New York, Williams returned to Florida and traveled again to Florida State Prison in Raiford, this time with a physician and a dentist, both black, in order to complete the medical report of the prisoners' injuries. Dr. Nelson Spaulding did the driving, on a hot August day, in his yellow convertible, sporty but with no air-conditioning. When Williams suggested they might at least ride with the top down, the doctor explained that if the police in rural Florida spotted them, three "negroes in a yellow convertible Cadillac," they could only expect trouble. With the top up, Spaulding said, the police "will not notice us."

The evidence, medical and otherwise, gathered by Williams was convincing. Due process in the case of the Groveland Boys had been violated; infractions of the law by law enforcement officers could be substantiated. Williams's interviews thus far had produced sound testimony. But Marshall's man in Orlando had yet to find an experienced lawyer willing to represent three black men accused of raping a white woman in Lake County. Shortly after Williams's first trip to Raiford with Horace Hill and William Fordham, the latter had withdrawn from the case. Although Hill was more than willing to go forward, Williams still needed a seasoned attorney to navigate skillfully a case that would most likely rush the three defendants through a trial to conviction with a death sentence. The case was scheduled to go to trial at the end of August.

In early August, Williams's search for a local lawyer turned up a qualified CIO attorney, but he wanted ten thousand dollars to take the case—a figure well beyond the limited means of the NAACP. Next, a "very distinguished criminal lawyer in Daytona Beach" appeared to be willing to consider representation of the three defendants, until he learned the venue for the trial. Scared off, the white lawyer said to Williams, "You know, Franklin, those clay eating crackers down there in Lake County would just as soon stand off and shoot me with a high power rifle as they would you." Another attorney agreed to take the case but refused to raise any technical issues. He stated that "he would not raise any issue of change of venue or jury selection or anything like that," recalled Williams, who viewed all such issues as being essential to challenge, especially in the very likely event that they would be appealing a guilty verdict in a higher court.

Spessard L. Holland Jr., the twenty-nine-year-old son of the former Florida governor and current U.S. senator, had caught the attention of the NAACP after he'd represented several black migrant workers who had been held in confinement and forced to work in the orange groves. He'd even filed charges with the Justice Department on behalf of the workers. In light of Holland's apparent sympathies with civil rights cases, Williams thought the young white lawyer might be interested in representing the Groveland Boys. He was, and agreed to meet with Williams and Hill the next morning. When they arrived, as arranged, at Holland's office in Vero Beach to discuss the case, the attorney had reconsidered.

"I can't do this, Frank," he said, sitting down at his desk.

"Why not?" Williams asked.

Holland sat in silence, the two black men contemplating him from across his desk. Suddenly he dissolved into tears. Once he'd begun to compose himself, he struggled to explain. "You may not understand this, but my wife is a typical flower of southern womanhood and this is a rape case and I can't take it."

There was nothing more to be said. Williams and Hill left Holland's office for the long drive back to Orlando. If finding a black attorney with criminal trial experience in Florida had proved to be a futile task, that of finding a reputable white lawyer who was willing to risk his career in order to represent three black men accused of raping a white teenager was proving to be herculean.

Days were slipping by. As Judge Truman Futch had already promised the citizens of Lake County a speedy trial, it was bootless to think he might delay the trial to allow a black New York lawyer more time to prepare a defense for three confessed rapists. In the South the bargain between justice and the public was implicit: an expeditious trial with swift punishment by death or else a riot and lynching. With less and less time for the daunting sum of it, Williams had to continue his investigation, locate and interview potential alibi witnesses, and sign on a top-notch criminal lawyer for the defense. Add to that the fact that the New York–based lawyer Williams had little stomach for his necessary, if infrequent, ventures into Lake County either alone or with Horace Hill. If the two attorneys had to speak with someone in the Groveland or Bay Lake area, they would sneak in and out of the county, for they had been duly warned about those trigger-happy, clay-eating crackers. "I was not completely at ease," Williams later recalled. "We just did not tell anybody we were in town."

On one occasion, while preparing to make the dreaded journey from the rooming house in Orlando to Tavares in order to interview a woman who'd had a dispute with Sheriff McCall, Williams had an inspiration: he would ask Joe Louis, who was also in residence, to accompany him. For surely the presence of the world heavyweight boxing champion "would give me some unusual kind of protection," Williams figured, and noted: "Joe would not go."

ON AUGUST 5, at a Federal Housing Authority conference in Washington, D.C., Thurgood Marshall argued that, despite his victory in *Shelley v. Kraemer*, the war to end legalized housing discrimination against blacks went on, and he sharply criticized the FHA "for failing to follow through on the implications" of the Supreme Court's decision. He was not of a mind to be his most patient self when he addressed the conference, as was noted afterward by one NAACP associate, who remarked to Marshall, "You were in rare form last Friday and handed out liberal education all over the place." (During the address, a slightly annoyed government lawyer passed a note to the same NAACP associate that read, "Who's that guy?" Barely had the associate uttered the second syllable of Marshall's first name than the lawyer responded with an "Oh!" and then "closed up like a tongue-tied clam.")

While in Washington, Marshall also pressed the Justice Department and the FBI to initiate a civil rights and domestic violence investigation into the beatings of the three surviving Groveland boys. Marshall by then had been unable to gain support in Washington for a full investigation into the killing of Ernest Thomas; the FBI had conducted a preliminary investigation but concluded "it would appear undesirable to become involved in the killing of Victim Ernest Thomas as there is no indication, with the exception of the statement by Thurgood Marshall, that there was serious doubt that Thomas was involved in the rape. On the other hand, the state has apparently produced evidence to indicate that he was involved in the rape." More successfully, Marshall convinced the Justice Department that the beatings had seriously violated the Groveland Boys' rights.

Within two days the FBI had dispatched Special Agents John L. Quigley and Tobias E. Matthews to the Raiford prison, where they interviewed and photographed Shepherd, Irvin, and Greenlee. Their initial reports back to headquarters prompted J. Edgar Hoover to order a "full and exhaustive investigation into the entire matter of the arrest and mistreatment by the authorities of all the victims." The agents meanwhile continued downstate. They interviewed residents of Lake County by the dozens; they took down statements from witnesses, law enforcement officials, victims of the mob violence, and even Norma and Willie Padgett. In the course of their investigation, Quigley and Matthews began to notice some disturbing elements. For one, "all of the persons interviewed who were allegedly implicated" in the beating and torture of the three Groveland boys "refused to furnish any information whatsoever unless they made it in statement form," thus indicating that Sheriff Willis McCall, deputies James Yates and Leroy Campbell, and Wesley Evans—the four suspects positively identified by Shepherd, Irvin, and Greenlee—had all received legal advice not to provide complete cooperation with the FBI's investigation.

Not surprisingly, the statements of McCall, Yates, Campbell, and

Evans, though totally consistent with one another, differed dramatically from those of the three rape suspects. For example, both deputies and Evans stated that all the interrogations took place in a radio room on the same floor as the jail, rather than in the basement with the three prisoners handcuffed to overhead pipes or, as was the case with Greenlee, in the elevator. Also, whereas Shepherd and Greenlee admitted that they'd confessed to the rape of Norma Padgett only when they could no longer tolerate the painful beatings, and while Irvin stated he did not and would not ever confess to a crime he did not commit, Campbell, Yates, and Evans shared a different account. They claimed that during the interrogations, when the suspects were shown "a pair of pants, a handkerchief and some other evidence," each of them readily confessed to robbery and rape (punishable by death in the state of Florida) and each of them named Ernest Thomas as the fourth accomplice. Further, Irvin and Shepherd, on the one hand, stated that they were seated in the back of Deputy Yates's car when the door was flung open and Sheriff Willis McCall began striking them with a large flashlight; the sheriff, on the other hand, said that when the two black prisoners arrived at his house in the backseat of Yates's car he had simply opened the door and "asked them why they wanted to do such a thing." According to the sheriff, the two army buddies then told him that "the other two made them do it." Finally, none of the Florida highway patrolmen or Lake County law enforcement agents questioned by the FBI had noticed any bruises, marks, or blood on any of the rape suspects when they were transported to Raiford prison; yet special agents Quigley and Matthews themselves not only had observed and photographed evidence of the prisoners' "trauma" but also had taken statements from several prison officials who had documented "numerous bruised marks," cut wounds, broken teeth, and bloodstained clothes at the time the three black men were taken into custody.

Quigley and Matthews took their investigation in Lake County beyond law enforcement personnel and established witnesses to civic officials, politicians, prominent businessmen, and grove owners in this largely rural area of central Florida with a population of thirty-six thousand. What they discovered was a county controlled not by politics, money, the citrus industry, or the law, but by an embittered contingent of the Ku Klux Klan intent upon codifying a racial caste system, through violent means if necessary, that would effectively deny blacks access to political influence, economic opportunity, and social justice.

On August 13, the agents met with Groveland's mayor, Elma Puryear, who had witnessed the gathering of the mob outside the jail on the morning of July 16 and had safely transported Charles Greenlee to Tavares. In his statement to the FBI, Puryear related his efforts to help Groveland's "leading citizens" protect their lives and property from the KKK, which by the evening of July 16 was filling the streets of Groveland. Off the record, Puryear disclosed that most of the trouble around Groveland had been "caused by the people of the Bay Lake region." He also told the agents that certain parties were aware of the FBI's presence in town, and that "word had gotten to them [the town's prominent white citizens] that if they didn't keep their damn mouths shut about what happened around Groveland, their homes and business property would be burned." Neither did Puryear identify in his statement who of those prominent citizens had enabled the blacks to be evacuated to safety, but he did indicate, again off the record, that Norton Wilkins, owner of B&W Canning Company, and L. Day Edge, the wealthy owner of a large mercantile store and formerly Florida's speaker of the House and Groveland's mayor, had been instrumental in the evacuation.

The Edge family, having once amassed a fortune in the turpentine and timber business before the sawmill men "cleared the county of pine trees," had since cultivated in the same fertile soil Lake County's increasingly profitable citrus groves. Citrus baron L. Day Edge had earned a reputation among blacks for his generosity and fairness, and on the morning that Walter Irvin was picked up by Willis McCall's deputies, both he and his father, Cleve Irvin, had been readying themselves for another day's work at Mr. Edge's groves. Agents Quigley and Matthews were thus eager to speak with Edge, who had in fact been quite willing to cooperate with the FBI until he, too, fell under the cloud of threats cast by the county's Klan. Having been informed that if he didn't keep quiet, "he wouldn't have a building left in Lake County"—and having spotted one of the Groveland night riders, Curtis Merritt, "watching the City Hall" to see who might be cooperating with the FBI—Edge had decided it would "very imprudent" for him to meet with the federal agents. Edge, however, did tell Puryear—and the mayor told Quigley and Matthews (off the record)—that Curtis and Bill Merritt along with Wesley Evans, the illiterate, hose-wielding grove caretaker identified by Samuel Shepherd as one of the men in the basement, had been among the ringleaders of the mob violence nearly a month earlier and were behind the current rash of threats being leveled at Groveland's respectable citizens.

In an interview with agents Quigley and Matthews on August 14,

Groveland's chief of police, George Mays, told them he was a "one man police department" and he "absolutely refused to furnish a signed statement form." Informally, however, Mays confirmed it was common knowledge that deputies Yates and Campbell had participated in the beating of the three rape suspects, as had Wesley Evans, who'd been witnessed laughing "heartily" at the banter among some locals about Evans being "quite a hose wielder." Mays also apprised the agents that if anyone were to discover what he had relayed to them, "his life would be in serious danger and he would probably lose his job and have to leave the area."

During the agents' interview with Lieutenant Colonel Harry Baya of the Florida National Guard in Tampa, Matthews and Quigley could sense the frustration that the commanding officer had experienced in trying to bring order to unruly Groveland in July, with much of that frustration being centered upon the unwilling Willis McCall. The sheriff's refusal to identify the mob's ringleaders, let alone take any "affirmative action" in regard to them—because, as he'd informed Baya, he was "too busy" to concern himself with arresting the ringleaders—had baffled Baya, who could not tell for sure whether McCall "knew who they were or not or was just withholding them from him."

In rural counties and parishes across the South, as the FBI was well aware, the sheriff's office was the seat of power. Elected to office by a countywide vote, the sheriff was viewed by his electorate not only as the county's chief law enforcement officer but also as a community leader who shared his electorate's interests. The FBI knew, too, that in Florida in the 1940s and '50s, "County Sheriffs openly joined the Klan, and law enforcement officers boldly attended Klan meetings armed and in uniform," as indeed did some of McCall's good friends like Sheriff Dave Starr of neighboring Orange County. Lake County, though, was Willis V. McCall's personal territory, and he bullied his county like no other sheriff in the state of Florida. Tom Hurlburt Jr., the former chief of the Orlando Police Department, whose father, a citrus buyer, had served as one of McCall's deputies, said, "I believe the only thing more powerful than Willis McCall was the Ku Klux Klan in those days."

Nor was Willis McCall's power unallied with that of the KKK. So it was that Lake County's "leading citizens"—men like Mayor Elma Puryear, Chief of Police George Mays, L. Day Edge, and Norton Wilkins— had no recourse in Sheriff McCall when they received open threats from the Klan. The citrus barons and respected citizens of the county may have been instrumental in McCall's election to office in 1944, but five years and one landslide reelection later, McCall had made Lake County his own. In 1949, McCall's always ambiguous allegiances lay less in his oath of office than in the demands of a restive electorate capable of extreme violence. "Bay Lake region people," Mays told the FBI agents, "were in some manner related to one or the other of the Padgetts. These people are very clannish and stay to themselves, but when any one attempted to molest or abuse their women folk they got up in arms about it and felt that the law should be settled in their own way." McCall knew his constituents, and he knew what they expected of him if he planned on having them keep him in the sheriff's office. McCall held the office until 1972.

B Y MID-AUGUST IN 1949, mainstream newspapers across the state of Florida had joined the black press in the coverage of Harry T. Moore's charges that savage beating at the hands of local law enforcement had coerced the Groveland Boys to confess to the rape of Norma Padgett. Between the press and the FBI—their agents, no doubt in cahoots with the NAACP, snooping all over his county—Willis McCall was livid. Still, he knew he'd have to come up with some explanation for the bruises, blood, and lacerations that had been plainly observed and reported by witnesses. "They might have got in a fight somewhere in prison or somewhere and had a mark or two on them, but they didn't get that in Lake County," the sheriff emphatically told the reporters.

By mid-August, too, Franklin Williams and Horace Hill had in their investigation been collecting increasingly more evidence and testimony that contradicted the "official" narrative being doled out to the press by McCall and State Attorney Jesse Hunter. With just two weeks remaining before the scheduled start of the trial, however, Williams had still not found a defense lawyer for the Groveland Boys. From the New York office, Thurgood Marshall could offer Williams only moral support until the NAACP had a trial lawyer in place, but Marshall meanwhile continued to keep the Justice Department informed of any leads that developed. One of them was startling.

Marshall telephoned Alexander Campbell, the assistant attorney general, immediately upon learning that the "physician who examined the alleged victim of the rape reportedly found that this woman's charges were not true." Campbell in turn informed J. Edgar Hoover, who dispatched a third FBI agent to Florida, to Leesburg, in order to verify the examining physician's "Report of Accident" in the alleged rape of Norma Padgett. No matter that the report bolstered the NAACP's defense case and introduced new issues for Williams's further investigation, and no matter that Williams had yet to find the defendants legal representation: the overwhelming sense in Marshall's office was that neither the judge, Truman Futch, nor State Attorney Hunter would allow a delay of the trial. Indeed, for both the judge and Hunter, with the FBI everywhere in the county asking questions and setting everyone from law enforcement to black pickers and packers on a perilous edge, the trial could not happen soon enough.

Franklin Williams's knottiest problem began to be resolved on August 22, when he met with Alex Akerman Jr., an experienced Orlando trial attorney with something of a maverick's reputation in central Florida. The son of a Republican federal judge in Florida—Akerman Sr. had been nominated by Calvin Coolidge in 1929 and served on the bench until his death in 1948—Alex Jr. was the only Republican member of the Florida legislature. More important for Williams, Akerman was currently representing a black faculty member at Bethune-Cookman College, Virgil Hawkins, in his attempt to gain admission into the University of Florida College of Law, as well as five other black graduate school applicants to the university who had been added to the case. Akerman's concern that the first desegregation lawsuit in the state would be compromised in Florida's supreme court if he were also representing the Groveland Boys made him reluctant to take the NAACP's case. So did the fact that Akerman was just beginning to establish a career in state politics. "I knew that this would be an end to that," he later said.

After a long, fruitless search for an attorney to try a case now only one short week away, Williams was not prepared to accept no as an answer. If desperate in his appeal to Akerman, Williams also argued soundly that the thirty-nine-year-old lawyer had already risked his chances of a political career when he'd initiated the inflammatory, high-profile law school integration suit. Furthermore, the Groveland Boys had no other legal counsel open to them, and the consequence they thus faced was not a denial of admission to a university but a sentence to death in the electric chair—for, Williams insisted, a crime that they did not commit. Their innocence or guilt aside, the three defendants, all of them facing a death penalty, certainly had a right to counsel, and that, for Akerman, made his representation of them the right thing to do. He also appreciated Williams's refusal, for all his frustration and the pressure of time constraints, to settle for some indifferent criminal lawyer who might have signed on solely for the fee. Not that the fee was handsome or, at $1,500, even adequate. Akerman negotiated, and with a handshake he and Williams agreed on a payment of $2,500 for the case. It was more than Williams had expected to pay but less than any other attorney had asked, and the New York office would no doubt be counting on Harry T. Moore to continue to raise both awareness of the case and cash to offset some of the legal costs. In closing, Akerman acknowledged that time was short, although he knew that even if he had a year to prepare for the defense of the Groveland Boys, in all likelihood they'd still be sent to the chair. He promised nonetheless to commit his expertise and energies to the case as well as the assistance of a second attorney, Joseph E. Price Jr., Akerman's nephew, who had graduated from law school the previous June. So Williams might find some comfort in the fact that he was getting two lawyers for the price of one.

As Alex Akerman contemplated the black New York lawyer from the NAACP, he might well have wondered if Franklin Williams realized fully what awaited him in a Lake County courtroom. For weeks Williams, out of concern for his own safety, had been avoiding visits to Groveland and Tavares, where he had yet to step inside the county courthouse. Nor had he yet had occasion to meet Sheriff Willis McCall, although he had seen the handiwork of McCall's deputies on the bodies of the defendants they had interrogated. Likewise, State Attorney Jesse Hunter and Judge Truman Futch were still mostly names to Williams. For the benefit of the New Yorker's education in the courtroom culture of Lake County, Akerman arranged to have Williams and Hill introduced to their opposing counsel, Jesse Hunter, in Tavares the week before the pretrial hearings were to begin.

Jesse Hunter was born in 1879 in Naylor, Georgia, about two hundred miles north of Tavares, but as a young boy he'd moved to Lake County with his family. At the age of sixteen, after just two years of formal schooling, he proved himself qualified to teach at the public school in Mascotte, and at twenty-two he was named principal of a school in Marion County. Always an avid reader, in his spare time Hunter began devouring books on the law, for he'd set his sights on a new career; but first he had to pass the state's bar examination. Unable to fulfill satisfactorily the demands of both his full-time job and his intensive study of law, he resigned his principalship and joined the Railway Mail Service as a clerk on the run from Key West to Jacksonville and back. The schedule—"one full day of work and two days of rest"—afforded him the time he needed for the rigorous study necessary to pass the Florida bar without attending law school. Five years of countless mail runs and mountains of borrowed law books later, Hunter felt prepared.

While he may not have engaged in Socratic debates on the finer points of law or have established a host of law school friendships and future contacts, he had learned a thing or two about self-discipline. And self-confidence.

In 1913, appearing before a justice of the Supreme Court of Florida for the administration of the bar examination, thirty-one-year-old Jesse Hunter had listened as one candidate after another rose and stated the name of the prestigious university where he'd studied law. Then Hunter heard his name called, and with no time allotted for elaboration, the erstwhile mail clerk announced with pride and brevity, "The University of Scuffletown."

Muffled laughter filled the room. The justice, wielding no gavel, shook a box that he'd "filled with odds and ends" to restore order, and asked, "Young man, WHAT college did you say?"

Hunter's reply—"The University of Scuffletown, Your Honor"— brought a pause, then a smile, from the justice. "Mr. Hunter," he said, "that is the best university in this entire country."

Jesse Hunter passed the bar, and that same day so did Truman Futch, another graduate of the "U. of S."—they met; they became friends. The summer of 1913 took Hunter to Tavares, where, on a loan of a few hundred dollars from a friend, he rented "a tin building" around the corner from the courthouse and furnished it with some used chairs, an old desk, and a secondhand typewriter. In that office he practiced law for ten years, until 1923, when he became county attorney. Two years later, Governor John W. Martin appointed him state attorney, a post he had held for nearly a quarter of a century by the time rape and race detonated the riots in Groveland. In thirty-six years of practicing law in Lake County, Jesse Hunter had gotten past being surprised by mobs and murder. Yet he was maybe a bit startled that day late in August 1949 when Alex Akerman walked into his office with two black men.

Certainly Franklin Williams was struck by the presence of the seventy-year-old man who occupied the state attorney's office. "He was almost a caricature of the Southern country boy," Williams observed. "He literally had red suspenders and no jacket, sleeves rolled up." When Hunter advanced to shake Akerman's hand, Williams noticed the sidelong glance the prosecutor cast at him and Horace Hill as Akerman indicated he'd be representing the Groveland Boys. Then, to Williams's astonishment, Hunter asked Akerman, "Where is the third defendant? Aren't these boys the defendants?"

"The dirty bastard," Williams thought, "trying to belittle us like that!" Now outraged—did this country lawyer honestly think Akerman would waltz into the state attorney's office with three black men who were facing the death penalty for raping a white woman, as if they were out on bail?— Williams responded with cold civility, "We are not the defendants. I am an attorney from New York and this is Horace Hill."

After a grunt, Hunter smiled and, with a nod of acknowledgment, said, "Well, come on in and have a Coke with me."

For Williams, that brief exchange between him and Hunter on their first meeting defined their relationship thereafter. "It was very clear to me that he was a sharp character," Williams recalled, adding that he was "never at ease with Jesse Hunter." Hunter's reference to a third defendant may have been merely a momentary lapse of memory, for Hunter had visited all three defendants at Raiford and had more recently questioned them at the arraignment. On the other hand, Hunter's comment may have been a wily attempt to put the two black attorneys off their mental balance, and thus to gain a psychological advantage over them. One thing was certain: Hunter knew that Franklin Williams would be the first black lawyer ever to be sitting on a legal team in any Lake County courtroom. If Hunter's aim had been to keep Williams off his balance in relation to the state attorney's attitudes and intent, he succeeded. "At one moment he [Hunter] would have the most acerbic and bitter racist comment," Williams noted, "and then the very next moment he would be the most pleasant good fellow, country lawyer you had ever met."

On August 25, at the county courthouse in Tavares, the pretrial hearings opened with Judge Truman Futch presiding. They argued motions around a table "in shirt sleeves, drinking cokes and smoking with feet of judge up on the table in front of us," Williams wrote to the New York office. "All very friendly—while deputies swarm all around the joint!" The defense had no expectations of success, but to establish grounds for appeal, Akerman filed, first, a motion to quash the indictments, citing that at the time the defendants were indicted, "lawless mobs were roaming throughout the County of Lake determined to seek and find your defendants and to then inflict grievous bodily injury upon them. . . ." The motion stated, too, that widely distributed newspapers had published editorials and cartoons "calling for and demanding that the extreme penalty of death be leveled" against the Groveland Boys. "Filed too late," Futch ruled.

Akerman then put forth an application for removal of cause for a change of venue, arguing that lynch mob violence, prejudice, and the hostile environment in Lake County would prevent the defendants from receiving a fair trial. With Sheriff McCall and deputies James Yates and Leroy Campbell in attendance, the defense called attention to the apparent "brutal" beatings and abuse "by persons purporting to be law enforcement officials of Lake County." Futch ruled the support of the motion to be "completely irrelevant and immaterial"; furthermore, Futch announced, he would not permit any testimony regarding its substance during the trial.

Next, the defense filed a motion for continuance, citing good faith reasons why the trial should be postponed—namely, the inadequate time to properly prepare a defense, especially given the fact that with the defendants more than a hundred miles away at the state prison in Raiford, their meetings with counsel had been "extremely inconvenient and impractical." Futch considered the motion. Deciding it to be a fair request, he delayed the start of the trial by three days. Jury selection would begin on Thursday, the first of September.

During the remaining days of pretrial hearings Williams and Akerman hoped both to build a case for the defense and to determine specifics of the case being mounted by the prosecution. They thus filed a bill of particulars, which required Hunter to specify what facts the state of Florida intended to prove with regard to the crimes charged in the indictments. The defense attorneys had made a start, albeit late. It would get later.

With the pretrial motions under way, the defendants—Irvin, Shepherd, and Greenlee—had been removed again to the jail in Tavares, to the same cells they'd occupied on the fourth floor a month earlier. The bloodstained sheets on the beds had not been changed, as Williams had noticed with disgust when he'd visited the three defendants. Still, Williams trusted that the Groveland Boys would at least escape abuse during their second stay at the Tavares jail, since the beatings they'd previously endured had been not only well documented but also fully reported in the local and national press, which had laid blame on Willis McCall and his deputies. So it would be in the sheriff's best interest to ensure that the prisoners appear in court with no visible evidence of abuse, or so Williams reasoned—incorrectly, as it turned out. "Every time" the defendants exited the courtroom, on the stairway back up to their cells McCall would kick the three of them repeatedly, although he'd strike Shepherd with special animosity. "Sammie," Irvin said, "he hit Sammie with his fist."

McCall had sat silently with his deputies throughout the August 25 pretrial hearings at the county courthouse. He'd brooded. For more than a month the case had been his. He'd been pursued by reporters; he'd enjoyed celebrity. After all, he had stood up to a lynch mob; he had policed the riots without the loss of a single life. Within hours of the rape he'd had three of the suspects behind bars, and he'd taken care of the fourth one, too. Only now it was Jesse Hunter's case. The sheriff had been sidelined, and worse, he'd had to bear the sight of a black New York NAACP lawyer in a fancy suit sitting before the bar, conferring with the judge and prosecutor about the admission of coerced confessions into evidence: more of the same claptrap he'd read in those "disgusting and disheartening" newspaper articles from up north (he'd clipped them nonetheless). Something had been agreed; Hunter wasn't going to introduce the confessions—as if this weren't Lake County. Then they'd adjourned.

The sheriff and his deputies escorted the Groveland Boys from the courtroom. In the stairwell, the sheriff let out a little of his frustration with a booted foot and his fists. Between blows, McCall demanded, "What are those nigger lawyers putting you up to now?"

The defendants had no answer to the angry question and tried only to protect themselves from the sheriff's rage, which seemed finally to be directed no longer at them but at the defense counsel. "Nigger lawyers better watch their steps," McCall told them, or they'll "end up in jail" along with their clients.

After the adjournment Williams and Hill, along with Akerman, returned to Orlando to take advantage of every minute available to develop strategies and construct a defense. At the same time a tropical storm was heading for South Florida from the Bahamas, and the following day, August 26, what would now be classified a Category 4 hurricane hit land at West Palm Beach and roared north from Lake Okeechobee. By the time it reached Lake County that evening, hurricane-force winds had wreaked havoc in central Florida, with damages running to millions of dollars. Particularly hard hit was the citrus industry; agricultural losses approached $20 million, as the heavy winds uprooted about one-third of the citrus trees—what would have amounted to 14 million crates of fruit. For two days Williams and Akerman were stranded in a rooming house in Orlando without access to the court or the prosecutor's bill of particulars or a working telephone. Residences had been unroofed; the streets were obstructed by fallen pines, downed utility poles, and industrial debris. And the defense case was a shambles.

The prosecution can't have regretted the losses in time and preparation that the storm had cost the lawyers for the defense. Still, the state was hedging its every bet. As Hunter was planning to call Samuel Shepherd's brother James as a time line witness for the prosecution, and in order, therefore, to prevent him from fleeing the county or conspiring with other potential witnesses, the state attorney requested that Judge Futch dispatch

Sheriff McCall to place and hold James Shepherd in the county jail until he had testified at his brother's trial. Never a man for half measures, especially when dealing with blacks, McCall had Samuel's parents, Henry and Charlie Mae Shepherd, jailed as well, and with a phone call north to the sheriff of Alachua County he also had Charles Greenlee's parents detained. It was the sheriff's way of guaranteeing that the families of the Groveland Boys did not get together in an attempt to fabricate alibis for the defendants by scripting a scenario contrary to his own official record on the events of July 15–16.

McCall paid a visit to Ernest Thomas's parents, too. Then he drove them from Groveland to Tavares, where Ethel and Luther Thomas were also jailed until the date of the trial. Jesse Hunter needed Ethel Thomas for the prosecution's case, which hinged in part on establishing Ernest Thomas's whereabouts the night of July 15, and McCall thought it likely that a friendly, private conversation, albeit in jail, would convince the grieving mother to cooperate. Her son Ernest was dead, and with the Klan shooting at the Blue Flame, Ethel Thomas didn't have many options if she wanted to stay in Groveland. If the High Sheriff could see to it that she'd be able to run her juke joint, what harm would she be doing by agreeing to testify for the state?

Henry Singleton need worry no more about the crystal-gazing racketeer or cocky Ernest Thomas cutting into his *bolita* throws. He might have worried a little, though, about McCall, who, as Singleton knew better than most, was not of a mind to do favors for a black man without expecting something in return. So it wasn't much of a surprise to anyone in Groveland that the name of Henry Singleton—bootlegger, *bolita* dealer, nightclub owner, stool pigeon—showed up on the list of witnesses for the prosecution.

# | 11 | BAD EGG

**MRS. WILLIE PADGETT**
*Says She Was Attacked.*

The *New York Post* was the only newspaper to publish a photograph of Norma Padgett at the time of the trial. (*New York Post*)

I F I WERE asked if the woman was raped, I would have to answer 'I don't know.'"

It was not what Willis McCall wanted to hear. He had come to the Theresa Holland Hospital in Leesburg for the physician's report on the examination of Norma Padgett after the alleged rape. He left in a huff—after a brief, unsatisfying conversation with the examining physician, Dr. Geoffrey Binneveld—and headed back to Tavares with a notarized copy of the document and with some bad news for State Attorney Jesse Hunter. The medical evidence did not support Norma Padgett's claim that four men had raped her.

In mid-August, when the existence of the examining physician's Report of Accident was leaked to the NAACP in New York, Thurgood Marshall soon had the FBI scrambling to locate the doctor and the document. It took some digging by Special Agent Watson Roper of the Miami bureau, but on August 30, at the small, private Theresa Holland Hospital in Leesburg, he was querying the young (at thirty) though "highly regarded" Dr. Geoffrey Binneveld on the matter of Norma Padgett. While "the confidential Doctor-Patient relationship" disallowed his providing a signed statement to the FBI without written permission from Norma Padgett, Binneveld did allow Roper to read and take notes on his physician's report.

Norma Padgett had appeared at the whites' entrance to the hospital with her father, Coy Tyson, and her husband, Willie Padgett, on the morning of July 16. In the absence of the senior physician and founder of the hospital, Dr. Howard Holland, Binneveld had attended. The father and husband remained in the waiting room while in an exam room the doctor explained the procedure they'd follow. He noted that the girl appeared to be in "emotional shock" and that, if what she was saying was true, she had not slept in more than twenty-four hours, as she had spent the night hiding and wandering in the wooded area outside Okahumpka. In his external examination he found scratches on both knees and on the palm of her right hand; the soles of her feet were "irritated." When he had proceeded to the pelvic examination, he observed that the labia majora and labia minora were "very red and irritated" and there were "several small mucosal lacerations about posterior fornix" as well. He attributed a small amount of blood present in the vagina to her regular monthly menstrual period, then in its last stages, since he otherwise "found no evidence of tears or wounds in the vagina other than the lacerations mentioned above." Laboratory analysis of a vaginal smear revealed "no spermatozoa were present in the vagina, nor were any organisms resembling gonococci found." Binneveld's conclusion to the report read: "Finding—Traumatic vaginitis," a noninfectious inflammation that might result from vaginal exposure to a condom, soap water, or douches, among numerous other possibilities.

Because he had not examined the accused men, and "since VD is so prevalent among the colored people he treats," the doctor told Agent Roper that he had consulted with a physician and former instructor of his at the University of Virginia School of Medicine. He had recommended that Binneveld put Padgett on penicillin, aureomycin, and some other prophylaxis to prevent any possible venereal infection and that he "give the patient the benefit of the doubt."

Binneveld had of course, by way of Sheriff McCall, provided the state attorney with a copy of the report, and he said that he'd also informed the sheriff "there were no other gross signs of bruises, breaks in the skin, or other signs of violence." The doctor had not, however, discussed with any other party the results of his examination, as he emphatically stated to Special Agent Roper. Nor did Dr. Binneveld—the only physician, insofar as he knew, who had examined Norma Padgett—have any idea how such confidential information might have been leaked to the NAACP or anyone else. Agent Roper's final question for the doctor echoed that of Sheriff McCall the month before: how would he testify should he be called as a witness by the prosecution and asked if Norma Padgett had been raped? The doctor had been pondering the answer to that question for weeks. He didn't have to think about his reply. He'd said it before:

"I don't know."

T HE LAST WEEK of August 1949 brought newspaper reporters from all over the country to cover the trial of the Groveland Boys, a case that the press was calling "Little Scottsboro." Certainly it was strikingly similar in many ways to the infamous 1931 case, in which young white women's accusations of rape by young black men triggered coerced confessions, lynching attempts, and mob violence involving powerful sheriffs, unruly posses, and the Ku Klux Klan in Scottsboro, Alabama. In central Florida, the black papers had been covering the Groveland story since the rioting in mid-July, largely on the basis of information passed on to them by Franklin Williams in the course of his investigation. In late August local reporters were joined in Tavares by correspondents from the *Pittsburgh Courier* and the *Chicago Defender* as well as a few "Northern" writers who had taken an interest in the story. So had the *Christian Science Monitor*, but surprisingly, to Williams, the Associated Press and United Press International had not. Yet while Marshall and the NAACP in New York were trying to focus national attention on the racial tension and racist violence in Groveland, Florida, the big race story that August was unfolding in their own backyard.

On August 27, 1949, in Peekskill, New York, Paul Robeson had planned to perform at a concert for the benefit of the Civil Rights Congress, an organization led by his friend the black communist, lawyer, and activist William Patterson. Earlier that summer Robeson had unpopularly delivered his controversial anti-American speech in France, and at the moment he was about to sing his first selection, hundreds of protestors stormed the stage, pelted the musicians with rocks or slammed them with chairs, and burned the "Dirty Commie" song sheets. Police did little to intervene, but Robeson vowed to return the following week. True to his word, he did, along with twenty-five thousand supporters and hundreds of union members who formed a human wall around the grounds at Cortlandt Manor to protect the performers onstage. A mob of protestors meanwhile threw rocks, overturned vehicles, and shouted epithets like "Kikes!" "Nigger lovers!" and "Go back to Russia!" They burned Robeson in effigy on a nearby hillside; close by they burned a cross.

Five months later, in a speech to the Republican Women's Club of Wheeling, West Virginia, Wisconsin senator Joseph McCarthy would brandish what he claimed was a secret list of more than two hundred known communists working for the U.S. State Department. Thus began the strong wave of venomous anticommunist sentiment that for the next decade would threaten not only government entities, but academia, the motion picture industry, labor unions, and the NAACP. Thurgood Marshall, ever vigilant, would strive continually to safeguard the reputation and activities of the NAACP from the taint of communism. As Roy Wilkins wrote, "We were having enough trouble getting Congress to consider even the most elementary civil rights legislation. The last thing we needed was to give ammunition to red-baiting southern congressmen and senators, who would have loved nothing better than to paint us pink." For all that, neither McCarthy's list nor the HUAC's unduly upset Marshall, who later said, "If you were a Negro and you were not on both of those lists, you should blow your brains out."

That the eyes of the nation were fixed on Paul Robeson and the Peekskill riots late in the summer of 1949 afforded Marshall some relief, for it kept the CRC more fully occupied with its own affairs and thus less disposed or able to insert itself into the Groveland case as it had in the trials of the Scottsboro Boys. Supposedly, "Franklin Williams had falsely accused [the CRC] of trying to steal the case" in Groveland. The accusation may have been false but Williams's suspicions would have been justified, for it would not by any means have been the first case the CRC had tried to steal from the NAACP.

In May 1949, seven young black men in Virginia confessed to the rape of a white woman, and in a series of six trials over a period of eleven days, each one of the "Martinsville Seven" was convicted and sentenced to death. Only after the trials did the NAACP enter the case, at the request of relatives to the condemned men. Sensitive though Marshall was to the fact that the NAACP did not function as a legal aid society, he was equally attuned to opportunities for the establishment of important legal precedents through the process of appeals. The death sentences of the Martinsville Seven offered apparent grounds for appeal in that since 1908, when the state of Virginia instituted use of the electric chair, all forty-five of the men executed for rape had been blacks convicted in attacks on white women. Problems arose when one of the wives of the Martinsville Seven agreed to allow the CRC to represent her husband in an appeal. Marshall was livid.

Marshall and Patterson were deeply divided in their philosophies on both legal tactics and civil rights. Marshall particularly resented the CRC's strategy in high-profile capital cases, which, he believed, "was to go into the local community, spit on the door of the courthouse, cuss at the judge and raise holy cain—and, incidentally, get the men electrocuted." In Marshall's eyes, the CRC existed and operated primarily to raise money, lots of it, for the communist cause—by calling attention to racial and economic oppression under American capitalism and "giv[ing] foreign governments something they can yell about." Unlike the NAACP, the CRC did not apply the bulk of the funds it raised for the actual defense of its clients, what with the production of leaflets, advertising on billboards, and fashioning of "high-powered petitions that the jury will never read" commanding significant expenditures. Patterson, for his part, maintained that nationwide awareness was vital and that "only the movement of the people as a whole guarantees a victory." Nonetheless, Marshall contended, a noisy mass campaign led by an organization that had been cited as subversive and communist by the Truman administration could only be detrimental to the defendants in appeals to higher courts. Ultimately, Patterson pulled the CRC from the defense of the Martinsville Seven. He chose instead to maximize publicity for the case—and raise consciousness of the communist cause—without risking a possible loss in court.

There was no love lost between Marshall and Patterson, personally or professionally. They exchanged letters, and on occasion they attended meetings held by interested third parties hoping to broker a treaty between their two organizations—a futile effort, as both men were equally entrenched in their positions and fiercely committed to their opposing principles. Their relationship was further strained, since both men happened to live at the same address, 409 Edgecombe, in Harlem, although Marshall's demanding travel schedule limited possibilities of chance encounters, or contention, with

Patterson in New York. Of course, Patterson did his own share of traveling, and that late summer of 1949 he was more than contemplating a trip to Groveland. Marshall issued a warning to his neighbor: "These cases, the Groveland cases and any other cases under the jurisdiction of this Association will be carried forward in a lawfullike [sic] manner with the lawful machinery of our Government. We have never been convinced that the Civil Rights Congress is primarily interested in the protection of the rights of Negroes [or] in the particular Negroes involved. . . . We therefore have no intention whatsoever of permitting you to interfere in any of these cases."

Marshall forwarded his letter to Stephen Spingarn, who was working in the White House as assistant to the special counsel to the president, with the following note:

*Dear Steve:*

*I thought you would be interested in the latest developments in the efforts of the Comrades to move in on our cases. These boys never give up and it is a pleasure to crack their knuckles.*

*Sincerely,*
*Thurgood Marshall.*

As THE PRETRIAL hearing proceeded in Groveland, Franklin Williams phoned in the rulings on motions to Thurgood Marshall in New York and updated him on the roster of witnesses and composition of the jury. Williams assured Marshall that in the jury selection process the defense would challenge in any way they could, but he and Marshall both knew that at the end of the day, twelve white Lake County jurors were going to be seated in the box. "I never believed that we would have anything but a verdict of guilty," Williams said. "It never entered my mind. . . . I hoped that we might get life rather than death. But I never believed that these boys would be found innocent."

Marshall had full confidence in Williams, who, he observed, "can come up with more ideas in a minute than most people I know of. And they're darn good ones." Williams was ambitious but also dedicated to the mission of the NAACP—a man who willingly "puts in a real day's work," Marshall said. Nonetheless, Marshall recognized that Williams was facing heavy odds by having been hobbled with the lightning-fast trial date when he'd barely had time to find a Florida lawyer, let alone map out a sound strategy. The want of time would force Williams and Akerman into reactive lawyering once the trial began, and Williams promised Marshall "every bit of energy and effort [would be] directed toward trying to create an error in the case, so that we could get it reversed on appeal." The job, Marshall stressed, was, as always, "to cause constitutional error or to find constitutional error in the process."

Both the prosecution and the defense were required to submit to the court lists of their evidence before the trial began. Jesse Hunter kept it simple; his list included a mere ten items:

1. Handkerchief & lint
2. Cast of left rear tire
3. Cast of right rear tire
4. Cast of left front tire
5. Cast of right front tire
6. Left shoe & cast
7. Right shoe & cast
8. Pants of Walter Irvin
9. Pistol
10. Almanac

The list reflected the simplicity, and strength, of the prosecution's case as Hunter would argue it for the jury, whoever might be sitting on it. Hunter hardly had to worry about jury selection; as Mabel Norris Reese noted in her pretrial coverage, "Jesse Hunter won't have to ask probing questions of the jury because he already knows all about them, and probably he could call any of the 100 or so selected jurymen by their first names." Nor did he have to worry about the credibility of his witnesses or their testimony. He had reviewed thoroughly with the state's witnesses the testimony they would present, from Norma and Willie Padgett to the sheriff's deputies and highway patrolmen. He indeed had reason to feel confident that, as Reese wrote, "Honor Will Be Avenged" in just a matter of days.

If Hunter's list was strategically simple, the evidence for the defense was perforce limited: forty-one local newspaper articles published on specific dates in July and August 1949. The list of witnesses for the defense indicated that they would call only three: Walter Irvin, Samuel Shepherd, and Charles Greenlee. And then they would pray.

Judge Truman Futch had a list of his own. He had posted his "Special

Rules of Court" on telephone poles outside the courthouse. Among the twelve rules for spectators at the trial were bans against loitering in the halls and stairways; the conveyance of bags, bottles, or packages into the courtroom; and hand clapping or outbursts in response to testimony or argument. The judge's rationale, he stated, lay less in any fear of a disruption in the proceedings by the Ku Klux Klan than in his concern that outside "agitators or agents" may have been dispatched to Tavares, perhaps by the NAACP, purposely to start trouble at the trial so that "critics of the south might have something to base criticism upon." Judge Futch had also taken other, more visible preventive measures against the unwelcome presence of any suspect strangers, as Williams and Akerman noticed when they arrived at court on the first day of the trial and viewed the heightened security. "They had deputies who stood every 10 stairs coming up the staircase into the courtroom," Williams recalled. "They were all big characters with guns on. It was a very intimidating scene."

It did not intimidate Mabel Norris Reese, however. Nor did the lawyers for the defense, who had called her as a witness in the pretrial hearings so that her exclusive coverage of the "worst crime in Lake county's history" could be entered on record. On that occasion, under oath, she had indicated that the source for her many articles and editorials about the case had been State Attorney Jesse Hunter. She had also stated that, on the basis of her observations, "there is considerable more satisfaction among the negroes here" in her adoptive South than in her native North and, indeed, she had found no evidence of prejudice in her part of Lake County. On the morning of the trial itself, intercepting Williams and Akerman on their arrival at court, Reese asked them for a statement regarding their expectations in the courtroom. In a rare unguarded moment, Williams responded that he did not hold out much hope for justice in Judge Futch's courtroom and that anyway, the "Supreme Court is the aim." Off the record or not, his comments appeared on the front page of the *Topic* the next day, and the relationship between Williams and Reese continued only to sour thereafter. In the same front-page article Reese looked forward to the relief that would come "to the staunch believers in the wonderfulness that is Lake county when the smudge against her fair name is removed" by the trial, as again she lamented the sensational press stories in the North about beatings and mistreatment of Negroes, which stories, she wrote, strive "to make Lake county sound mean and cruel—unfitted for the God-given loveliness about her." Of course, since Reese relied on Jesse Hunter as her main source of information about the case, she knew that before Lake County could return again to being the "Garden of Eden" it had always been, the prosecution would have to recount the unspeakable events of that night in July "when the true story of what happened to that young Bay Lake couple will be told, probably in unpretty details so that a jury can be convinced."

Relief, for Franklin Williams, at least in regard to the press, came to Tavares in the form of Ted Poston, a black reporter from the *New York Post* who had successfully lobbied his editor to fly him south to cover the trial for the newspaper. Formerly a resident at 409 Edgecombe, he had long been friends with Thurgood Marshall. In fact, Poston had once accompanied Marshall on one of the NAACP attorney's late-night adventures, on this particular occasion to obtain affidavits from blacks who were being terrorized by police in Freeport, New York, then (in the 1930s) a hub of KKK activity. On learning that the Klan-infested police were out looking for two troublemakers from Harlem, Poston was, in his words, "damned scared"; but, as much as he wanted to "get out of town fast," he spent the night dodging the Klan with Marshall as the lawyer continued collecting his affidavits, which he hid in a spare tire, and meanwhile making "more and more outlandish jokes about what [the police would] do to us if they ever caught up with us." The jokes may not have eased Poston's anxiety, but the affidavits enabled Marshall eventually to win from the state attorney general "a restraining order to close down KKK activities" in Freeport. Poston could only admire the courage of a man and attorney who "involv[ed] himself in a case to that degree."

Nor did Poston want for courage, savvy though he also was in protecting himself. In 1933, when he was covering the Scottsboro trial in Alabama for the Harlem-based *Amsterdam News*, each night after court he would sneak out to the railroad tracks in order to deposit his stories "in the mail car of the midnight special." He was evidently not sneaky enough, however, as one night some young white men were waiting near the tracks for the black reporter on the Scottsboro case. They put a pistol to his back and Poston produced fake credentials identifying him as a reverend with the African Methodist Episcopal Church—for which he got a "kick in the pants" but otherwise escaped harm. When Scottsboro had completed the retrial and Poston his assignment, he made a show of reserving a seat on the day coach at the train station so that the ticket seller would be sure to remember him. Then he quietly slipped out of town by bus. He later learned that, as he had feared, about the time the train he'd reserved the seat on was due to arrive, a crowd of angry whites, nearly a thousand strong, had turned up at the depot, obviously not to offer him a friendly good-bye.

Poston's own personal experience of the hazardous link between racial and sexual tensions for black males in the South had drawn him to the story of Norma Padgett and the Groveland Boys from its outset. Born in Hopkinsville, Kentucky, in 1906, two years before Thurgood Marshall, the especially dark-skinned Poston found himself assigned as if by nature to a lower social and economic status among both whites and blacks. At the age of thirteen, he was earning fifty cents a week for tending the fireplaces at the house of a dentist in town. On a particular morning he'd entered one of the rooms to clean out the ashes and lay wood to build a new fire when he encountered there a "grown young lady." She beckoned the boy to her, and with her hand pressed to the front of his pants, she commented on his anatomy, then asked the tongue-tied Poston, "Are you diddling with the *nigger* gals?" Aghast, the boy watched as she disrobed before him, and he trembled, as much with fear as desire, as she coaxed him into sexual intercourse—as she would again the next morning, and the next, for it became "an every morning occurrence." And the boy became increasingly traumatized; even thirteen-year-olds knew what happened to blacks caught with white women. When guilt and fear finally compelled him to tell the woman he was going to quit his job, she replied with a threat. "If you quit, I'm going to tell the doctor you raped me," she said, and for three more years Poston remained a slave to her bidding.

Weeks before the Groveland Boys were brought to trial, Poston had been writing features for the *New York Post* under the series headline "Horror in the Sunny South." As soon as he had picked up the story on Norma Padgett's claims of rape from the newswires, he had begun investigating the case. He had interviewed the family of Samuel Shepherd; he'd spoken with victims of the mob violence. It was Poston who first compared the events in Groveland to those in a similar rape case nearly twenty years before. It was Poston who called it "Florida's Little Scottsboro."

Ramona Lowe, a part-time Florida correspondent for the *Chicago Defender*, also arrived at Tavares to cover the trial. Lowe had been the first reporter to break the story of the gross mistreatment that the Groveland Boys had borne while in Sheriff McCall's custody. If her incendiary pieces on the case had in general won the appreciation of the NAACP, a particular story that ran on the front page of the *Defender* had Marshall and Williams both scratching their heads. In addition to carefully documenting the "seething jealousy" that fueled the resentment of Bay Lake's poor white farmers toward more prosperous black farmers like Henry Shepherd, Lowe claimed that, according to an unnamed source, Samuel Shepherd and

Norma Padgett had been longtime friends. So distraught was Norma over Shepherd's arrest, the source said, she had asserted that should anything bad happen, "I will leave this place [Groveland]. I have known Sam all my life." If Lowe and her source were to be believed, the assertion would certainly alter the complexion of the sheriff's and state attorney's official narrative and would buoy Williams's defense, but in another article, with equal conviction, Lowe had reported that Charles Greenlee had been riding in the car with Irvin and Shepherd on the night of July 15: an affirmation that Williams had determined was simply not true. Lowe's reporting puzzled Williams, but he was happy to have one more journalist on his side covering the trial.

For Marshall and Williams—indeed, for any NAACP defense counsel assigned to a criminal case in the hostile South—the presence of a reporter, even from a black newspaper like the *Pittsburgh Courier* or *Chicago Defender*, helped to ensure their protection. "The theory was," Williams said, "if the world knew you were there, you were safe." (Though it was no guarantee. An FBI informant in a central Florida Klavern later revealed that the *Pittsburgh Courier* was "generally read from the Klan meeting floor.") In the event that the press did not find a trial significant enough to warrant coverage, Thurgood Marshall himself would issue press releases from the NAACP's New York office in which he would announce his own or an associate's arrival and departure times in a given Southern town. With Poston in Lake County, Williams had a major New York newspaper covering his every move and thus, he felt, a "greater modicum of security." For a measure of security, too, Poston reserved a suite in a Negro hotel in Orlando for the duration of his assignment, but each night he would steal out the back door of the hotel to sleep instead at one of three secret private homes. Not a man to take any chances in the South, Poston made sure the defense lawyers had the telephone number of the city editor at the *New York Post* "just in case anything happens."

With trial testimony about to begin, Franklin Williams might have envied the confidence of Mabel Norris Reese that the "true story," however "unpretty" its details, had been uncovered in the case or have wished he could validate Ramona Lowe's discoveries about Norma Padgett's past. Rumors and clues and speculation tantalized the lawyer for the defense with possibilities, but they did not constitute sound evidence for the court, so he had to face what for him was the truth: that for all his interviews and investigation, he still did not know what had happened on that Friday night in July. Certainly suspicion densely clouded Norma Padgett's claim that she'd been raped by the four Groveland boys, and not just among the blacks. Terence McCarthy, the British economist who'd been researching the story for the *New Leader*, told Williams that Groveland's police chief, George Mays, had informed him off the record that Norma Padgett was a "bad egg" and that her denial of acquaintance with the Groveland Boys was suspect—Norma, according to Mays, "had grown up as a child next door" to Ernest Thomas.

Franklin Williams himself had spoken with the Reverend Collis C. Blair, a white Methodist minister in Orlando, who had been in Bay Lake after the rioting. On that occasion, Blair told Williams (as Williams subsequently told the FBI during an August briefing in the New York office of the NAACP), various members of the mob who had "stirred up" the violence and "kept it going" had been pointed out to him, but with no names named. When pressed by Williams as to who they were, the understandably nervous Blair had answered, "The Klan," adding that the men told him "these niggers needed to be taken down a notch." Whatever sympathies Blair may have had with the victims of that violence and whatever horror he may have had of the Klan, the minister knew that the KKK could burn a church with as little compunction as they would a Negro home; he needed to limit his risks.

Sensing that the white minister was holding back perhaps critical information from him, Williams pressed further: Hadn't Blair, a young Methodist from Florida, pursued his religious studies in the enlightened North, at Yale Divinity School? Didn't he acknowledge the church's strategic role in combating interracial violence? With one boy already dead and three others facing the likelihood of execution, would he offer only silence? The lawyer was practically pleading, and the minister, after more than a moment's hesitation, did finally admit that he had had a met with a few people after Norma Padgett had been found walking barefoot up near Okahumpka. With whom? Williams asked. And Blair replied, "Mrs. Padgett, her husband, and mother in law."

Williams, in his conscience, recognized that he could not put Reverend Blair on the witness stand. The substance of Blair's knowledge, vital to Williams's insight into the elusive truth of the case, would have to be imparted in confidence. Williams asked what the Reverend Blair had concluded after talking with Norma and the Padgetts? Blair was neither coy nor evasive. He observed that Norma did not show "any traces of having gone through a bad experience," and seemed "quite thrilled to be the object of so much publicity." As a native Floridian familiar with the Bay Lake community, Blair also found it curious that "none of the family showed any such resentment [toward the Groveland boys] as one would expect." He ultimately admitted to Williams that he had "grave doubts as to whether a rape actually occurred."

Williams passed on the minister's name and telephone number to the FBI, whose agents, the New York lawyer was sure, had gathered information equally valuable to the defense, although the FBI investigation had been "considerably affected" once word of the brutality exerted upon the three suspects by Lake County law enforcement had spread. Williams was of course aware that the willingness of some Lake County residents to talk to the FBI had evaporated in the face of rumors and threats and misinformation to the effect that "the investigation will result in defense material for NAACP attorneys." Williams had in fact attempted to compel agents Quigley and Matthews to testify by serving them an anonymous "Richard Roe and John Doe" subpoena, which was ultimately quashed in the U.S. attorney's office by reason of "the confidential nature of the FBI's investigation." Williams had been frustrated by the state attorney's office as well, in its strategically sound decisions not to call Dr. Geoffrey Binneveld as a witness or to place into evidence his physician's report—and likewise, the (coerced) confessions of the Groveland Boys. Jesse Hunter would rely on the probability that the testimony of a young white woman would trump anything the three Negroes might say in their defense. Judge Futch, meanwhile, compounded Williams's frustration in his rulings not to make the medical report available to the defense and not to allow any testimony about beatings of prisoners at the hands of law enforcement. What the judge called irrelevant Williams considered to be deliberate moves to assure Hunter the convictions he sought.

On Friday morning, September 2, before the commencement of trial testimony, Judge Futch presided over the completion of jury selection and the defense did the best they could with the few challenges still available to them. Over the past few days, as, one by one, the prospective jurors—Lake County farmers and pickers and truckers, with their meaty hands and their worn work clothes—had appeared before the court, Williams, the sharply attired New York lawyer, had recalled again, and more than once, the words of the Daytona Beach attorney who'd refused the case because "those clay eating crackers down there" would as soon shoot you as look at you. In quizzing the potential jurors, Akerman had been trying to gauge what might be their reactions should they see a black man addressing whites in ways they had never witnessed before, thus implicitly challenging the racial power structure as they knew it. "How would you feel about one of these negro lawyers jumping up and objecting?" he'd asked one. To another he'd posed, "And you would feel that it would be proper for them, as defense counsel, to cross-examine witnesses, even though the witness happened to be white?" (One potential juror had become confused when Akerman pointed to Williams and Hill at the defense table: "They are not on trial, are they?" the juror had asked.) Akerman's other primary concern had been to discover if potential jurors were "kin" to any Tysons or Padgetts, and the few who were had been excused. Jesse Hunter, on the other hand, focused largely on any objections the prospective jurors might have to capital punishment; most were "in favor of it."

Most of the prospective jurors, not surprisingly, were also white. Of the three black men whose names had been pulled from the jury pool, only one made it to court: a "gray haired old handyman" whose father-in-law had recently died. The court clerk implored Williams to excuse the "boy" so that he could attend the funeral, adding that the handyman was "one of the best niggers in Lake County." Then all the jurors were white, and by the end of that Friday morning in early September both Hunter and Akerman had announced to Judge Futch that they were satisfied with the jury in the box. While it might have been worse, it was, to Williams's mind, nonetheless terrible. Still, the defense had managed to establish on record that blacks were historically and systematically excluded from jury service in Lake County, so he would be able to tell Marshall on Friday night that the NAACP was well positioned for appeal. It was a small victory and in this trial, Williams feared, most likely his last.

Testimony in *State of Florida v. Samuel Shepherd, Walter Irvin, Charles Greenlee, Ernest E. Thomas* began after a recess on Friday, September 2, 1949. Hundreds of spectators packed into the Lake County Court House, among them a few dozen blacks who filed up to the balcony to a section reserved for coloreds. A few days earlier Mabel Norris Reese had written a news piece under the header "Women Beg for Reserved Seats at Trial," but it was mostly white Lake County men who filled the wooden benches. Ramona Lowe observed: "Through sentiment whipped-up by Florida daily newspapers, the trial has become a side-show for thrill-seeking, sadistic country-bred whites."

Williams and Hill shuddered at the entrance into the courtroom of steely-eyed "Bay Lake Crackers with snuff in their mustache," local men who had been deputized as security police, whose presence was more menacing than reassuring. It was not unlikely that security included some of the very same men who had descended on the courthouse less than two months before with Coy Tyson and Willie Padgett, although Williams could not be sure. When he spotted Willis McCall—strutting around the courtroom like a man in his home at Thanksgiving, shaking hands and welcoming in friends and family—Williams felt a pang of apprehension. McCall "always intimidated me," the lawyer said.

Around 2 p.m., the clang of an iron gate quieted the crowd. A door behind the judge's bench swung open. Slowly, the sheriff's deputies Yates and Campbell paraded the three solemn young black men to their seats at the defense table, and the people of Lake County got their first look at the men accused of raping Norma Padgett. Weeks earlier, at the arraignment, Mabel Norris Reese had noted for her readers that Irvin was wearing no shoes, his "bare feet making a soft, pattering noise as he climbed the steps," but he appeared at the trial in shoes and, like his codefendants, dressed in a suit. That September afternoon the temperature had reached the low nineties and a large electric pedestal fan whirred behind the witness box, the sound promising to drown out any quiet testimony. On the judge's desk lay a pile of cedar sticks; seated, Truman Futch pulled a knife from a drawer and demonstrated, as he would throughout the trial, how he'd gotten nicknamed "the Whittlin' Judge." Oppressive heat, old Southern lawyers in red suspenders, whittling judges, a fearsome sheriff, and a crowd of racist, tobacco-stained crackers on the benches behind him—"it was," Williams observed, "almost to me like a story that I was living through and these were caricatures that I was being exposed to."

A glance up to the balcony did not allay any of Williams's misgivings. In the somber faces of the blacks he read resignation mixed with fear—fear of McCall, "of what he might do and of what he could get away with"— and in no face could he see an expectation of justice. "They were just there watching."

Then Williams spotted the girl: Norma Padgett, seated in the front row beside her husband, her blond locks newly curled, lips tightly pursed. There would be no mercy, either, for the Groveland Boys.

The state attorney called his first witness, whose sole purpose was to attest that he had seen Ernest Thomas on the afternoon of July 26 and that Ernest Thomas had been and was in fact dead. Williams had suspected that the prosecution had a "dying declaration all rigged," but Hunter was content with the testimony. The defense had no questions, and with one of the Groveland Boys out of the way, the state turned to their next witness, the twenty-three-year-old husband of the rape victim, Willie Padgett. Hunter led Padgett through what seemed to Williams a tightly scripted scenario: how Willie had been beaten and robbed on the side of a road near Okahumpka; how he had come to his senses just long enough to see four black men drive away with his wife; how he'd driven miles, to Dean's filling station in Leesburg, where he told the attendant, Curtis Howard, about the attack and abduction. Finding room for doubt in Willie Padgett's story, Williams whispered to Akerman before the Florida lawyer began cross-examination. By the end of his testimony, Padgett had conceded that of the four defendants he was able to identify only two, Shepherd and Irvin, from that night. It was a small gain for the defense, one to be lost in a matter of minutes.

Hunter next called Norma Padgett. Her chin held high, shoulders back, she strolled more than strode to the witness box. She was wearing a dark party dress with a large corsage flower at the hip, and into an ample white belt Norma had tucked a kind of homemade, sleeveless bolero, the bright, wide fabric slung up and over both her shoulders like wings on an angel costume. To Williams and Hill, she seemed to be "promenading" with no sense of shame or discomfort before the court, as if her purpose were to command, and relish, the attention of several hundred Lake County men rather than to testify that she, a white girl still in her teens, had been recently raped by four black men. If initially baffled by the girl's appearance and demeanor, Williams in a moment recalled the publicity that another Lake County girl, Lois Driver, had recently been gleaning in the local and national press. Having won a few local beauty contests—Miss Merry Christmas as well as various agriculturally related titles, like Tangerine Queen—Lois had achieved at least countywide fame when *Ladies' Home Journal* began scouring small towns across America for a series of covers called "Undiscovered American Beauties." The magazine urged photographers around the country to be on the lookout at the beach, football game, church, or high school for a girl "whose face would launch a thousand ships or sell a million magazines." The *Journal* promised it would pay top dollar to photographers and models who made the cut in the highly subjective business of selecting one beautiful girl each month from thousands of entries. In July 1949, as every girl in Lake County was aware, whether with admiration or envy or aspirations, the Undiscovered American Beauty on the cover of *Ladies' Home Journal* was Lois Driver. Franklin Williams was also aware of it, because J. E. Driver, Lois's machinist father, had been summoned and questioned for jury duty on the Groveland rape case (he was not selected). And Norma Padgett was making the most of her moment.

Just as he had led Willie Padgett through his testimony, Jesse Hunter prompted Norma. Evidently he had coached her, too. When he asked Norma to "rise and point out" her rapists, she seemed first to take a few seconds to compose herself for the task as she directed her gaze toward the defendants. She glanced steadily at each of them in turn before she stood and straightened her dress. She eyeballed the Groveland Boys, then, as Williams recalled, Norma slowly raised an arm and extended her index finger, which, again in turn, she pointed at each of the defendants as unhurriedly as she drawled: "The nigger Shepherd . . . the nigger Irvin . . . the nigger Greenlee."

Williams declared it "probably the most dramatic moment in the trial," and he, like everyone else in the courtroom, had been riveted by her every gesture. "Christ," he later recalled, "you could have cut the air with a knife." What Mabel Norris Reese saw in Williams's eyes as he followed Norma's testimony, and indeed throughout the trial, was bitter resentment and hatred. In her articles on the trial, Reese described Williams as being "resentful-eyed" and having eyes "that were so filled with hate as he sat in that courtroom that you could see it, you could feel it."

Akerman and Williams had agreed that the cross-examination of Norma Padgett should be restricted to an attempt to raise reasonable doubt in regard to the identification of the defendants rather than to pursue the possibility that no rape had occurred—a futile tack in light of the admissible evidence. Akerman questioned both the accuracy of the time line in the prosecution's case—she couldn't be accurate, Norma told him, as she "wasn't wearing a watch"—and Norma's apparently absolute certainty as to the identity of her attackers. Norma Padgett proved to be unflappable, however. She left the witness box as confidently as she'd taken it. Whatever Mabel Norris Reese may have read in Williams's eyes, in his mind he knew that Norma Padgett had just sent the Groveland Boys to the electric chair. That delicate white finger of hers had as good as flicked the switch itself.

If Norma Padgett had sent the Groveland Boys to their deaths, the state's next witness was ready to bury their bodies. Deputy James Yates testified that the tire tracks on James Shepherd's car exactly matched those that were found in the roadbed outside of Okahumpka, at the very spot where Norma Padgett claimed she'd been raped. Using FBI procedures as a guide, Yates had made "plaster Paris casts" to determine the match. He had also made casts of footprints found at the roadside where Willie Padgett claimed to have been beaten and robbed; the footprints proved to be an exact match to Walter Irvin's shoes. In cross-examination, Akerman questioned Yates's qualifications as an expert in tire-track and footprint analysis, but the deputy remained confident in his abilities. Yates noted that he must be doing it right because "the sheriff has kept me for 4 years." It was all the jury needed to hear.

The sun had set on Tavares, and Judge Futch, who had whittled through the first day of the trial, declared a recess. The jury exited the courtroom with the bailiff, who would, as the judge had instructed, "feed you and sleep you." Ted Poston rushed to find a phone so that he could call in a story on the day's proceedings to the news desk at the *New York Post*. In the stairwell he had to run a gauntlet of deputies and other Lake County men armed and ready to provide security. Before he got to a phone, without any warning or cause he got "jostled by a couple of hoodlums," as he put it, and one of them "accidentally" stepped on his eyeglasses. Poston hadn't brought a second pair.

The trial resumed at 9:30 a.m. on Saturday, September 3, and Jesse Hunter had some cleaning up to do. He first called Groveland bootlegger and *bolita* dealer Henry Singleton to the stand. On the night of July 15, Singleton claimed, a young man whom he recognized to be Charles Greenlee showed up at his house, supposedly to buy some numbers for a Cuba game. Singleton was suspicious, he told Hunter. Nearly certain that Greenlee was casing his home in order to come back and rob him, Singleton chased the boy off, and shortly thereafter he himself went out for a drive. That's when he had by chance run into Samuel Shepherd, and Walter Irvin was with him. So it was that Henry Singleton had, in rather a bland narrative, put all three defendants in Groveland in the early evening of July 15. He had also put himself, and the sheriff, back in control of the county's *bolita* business. It was Hunter's next witness who put the now-deceased Ernest Thomas in Groveland on the fifteenth. His mother, Ethel Thomas, who had been in the lockup during the days preceding the trial and had no doubt had time to contemplate the future of her business, the Blue Flame, had decided to cooperate with the sheriff and state attorney. She testified that her son had gone to a party in town that evening.

Proceeding toward the close of the prosecution's case, Hunter introduced the state's last piece of evidence: a July 1949 almanac, by which he showed the jury that the moon had risen at 10:36 p.m. on the fifteenth day of the month and argued that, therefore, the sky was bright enough for Willie and Norma Padgett to easily identify their attackers. Akerman objected on the grounds that the evidence was irrelevant, since the almanac indicated only that the moon rose at 10:36 p.m. in St. Louis, Missouri. The defense might have enjoyed the moment if the judge, whittling at a cedar stick, had not responded, "Objection is overruled."

So confident of his case was Hunter by this point that he abstained from calling his remaining witnesses. "I see no purpose in introducing them," he said. "Therefore, the State rests." Futch called a recess until 1:30

p.m. that afternoon, and Williams and Akerman decided they'd try to clear their heads and review their strategy in the Florida air.

Just outside the courtroom, the defense attorneys, exhausted by work and nerves, encountered an overly friendly clerk, who asked, "Well, Mr. Williams, how do you like the way the trial is going?" The ill-timed question received an unconsidered reply. "It's the worst framed-up case I have ever seen in my years of practice!" Williams snapped.

Williams later elaborated on the frame. "It was like a story," he said. "Like a Hollywood story. They had it down pat. They had Irvin's shoe prints. Imagine making a cast at the scene of the crime. That only happens in movies. You know, of course [they] could make a cast. They had taken his shoes when they arrested him. They had the handkerchief that belonged to either Irvin or Shepherd which they claimed they had tied over their license plate to hide their license plate. Come on. That is too pat. They had the tire mark. Of course, they had the tire mark. They had the car. They made the tire mark and they made it so you have this country jury impressed by all of this high falutin' FBI type evidence. . . . So, we were up against what appeared to be a firm case . . . that I knew or suspected had been totally manufactured. . . . What were you going to do?"

They were going to put the Groveland Boys on the stand. They had no other choice.

Williams and Akerman took their seats at the defense table. The iron gate behind Judge Futch's desk clanged, the door swung open, and their clients, escorted by deputies, shuffled in. Samuel Shepherd seated himself next to Williams; his brother James and his mother were sitting, attentive, in the balcony. Williams recalled the father, the snakebites on Henry Shepherd's legs, and the sweat, the toil, he dedicated to draining that swampland in Bay Lake so he could plant fields all his own and build a life for himself and his family away from the citrus groves; his son Samuel had gone off to war, come back, found some trouble, and now the father had lost his house and farm, and his boy was looking at the electric chair and . . . Williams was looking into Samuel Shepherd's eyes, telling him that Mr. Akerman was going to call him to the box, ask him some questions, and that Samuel should tell the court plain what happened that night.

When Williams had finished with his instructions, Shepherd turned to him and earnestly offered an instruction of his own. "Mr. Williams," he said, "when the trial is over, be careful."

More words followed, most of them lost by the dazed attorney after he'd heard Shepherd say that someone was "going to get that nigger lawyer."

Where did he hear that? Williams needed to know.

"Willis McCall," Shepherd told him. "Said he was going to get that nigger lawyer."

Williams spotted McCall across the court, and he saw the monster in the man who, behind the badge of sheriff, had "murdered blacks" in Lake County. Williams had heard the stories, like that of the *bolita* dealer's widow who'd collected a sum of money on her husband's insurance policies—money that McCall claimed was owed to him. He went so far as to have the woman arrested, and when she still refused to pay McCall the alleged debt, she fell to her death from the fourth-floor window of the county jail. Williams himself had seen evidence of the beatings on the bodies of his clients, had seen the bloodstained sheets and the blood on the floor in the cells. By the sheriff's doings as much as anyone's in the state attorney's case, in a matter of hours three black men would be convicted by the court and almost surely sentenced to death.

Judge Futch brought the court to order. Akerman called Samuel Shepherd to the witness box, and Shepherd recounted less plainly than discursively what happened in the course of his night out with Walter Irvin: a narrative about a broken car, a stop for gas, drinking beers in Eatonville, the drive home to get some sleep. Hunter, confident of the state's case, did not bother to cross-examine Shepherd, or Irvin, whose testimony corresponded with Shepherd's, though he spared the court the side stories.

Charles Greenlee was called last. Seated in the box, the look on his face suggesting perpetual shock, the "tall, gangly, overgrown country kid," who to Williams seemed to be "just this side of illiterate," adjusted his posture and, with a glance toward Akerman, waited for the questions to begin. As far as Williams could tell, the boy "did not know what the hell was happening to him," but he'd barely begun his testimony when Williams found himself, literally, on the edge of his seat. In a naive, country-bumbling way, with a childlike attention to detail as amusing as it was engaging, Greenlee recounted the events of his first-ever weekend in Groveland. His "melodious Southern drawl" at once countered and heightened the suspense and danger as well as the gallows humor in his narrative, which frequently elicited appreciative laughter from the benches and the gallery. His guileless, animated delivery prompted Akerman to allow the boy simply to tell "the truth"—because, as Charles reminded his attorney, "if you just tell the good white folks the truth and make them understand, then everything will be all right"—rather than to lead him through his testimony with questions.

When Charles's narrative brought him to the Groveland jail, with him still not knowing that the Bay Lake men had suspected him of being one of Norma Padgett's rapists, he recalled (as the trial transcripts record):

*I said to myself, "What's coming off here?" And then the man what put me in jail, he came and went in the office, there. I guess it was an office. It was a door. And men kept going in the office and coming out. Kept going in and coming out. Kept going in and coming out. Directly an old fellow come in there. I don't know who he was. He about the size of Mr. Hunter, and looked like him but I don't think it was. I don't think he was as old as Mr. Hunter. He say, "Nigger, you sitting up here and telling a lie like that," say, "I ought to go get my shotgun and put you through this hole and shoot you." I say, "What about, Mister?" He say, "You know what I'm talking about." Well, he walked on off. Because, I said to myself, "Something must be wrong around here, somewhere." I know I hadn't done nothing.*

Greenlee testified that he'd never before known or seen his codefendants Shepherd and Irvin until he met them in jail. Furthermore, he said, he had not seen the inside of any car that night, which he had spent at the train depot getting bitten by mosquitoes while waiting for Ernest Thomas to come back for him. Instead, the police had thrown him in jail for loitering and possession of a gun. It was the next morning that he began to be afraid, because more and more men were gathering outside the jail and he heard someone say the men outside were going to kill him. He begged one of his jailers to "hurry up and take me away from here, somewhere, I don't care where," and he was told that some police would soon come to move him to a safer jail.

*So I was sitting up there waiting for the cars, and soon a 48 black Chevrolet pulled up in front of the cell and mens started crowding back around in there. One fellow say, "If you'll lay the keys down, I'll go in there and get him." Another fellow say, "If you'll just tell me that I can have him if I get him." And people kept talking, questioning and telling what they would do if they had me. One fellow drug a big knife in there about this long. Said to me, "Stand up to the door." I told him, say, "Mister, I ain't done nothing and me standing up to the door wouldn't make sense if you want to joog me with that big old knife." So he said, "All right." But say, "You'll get it*

*first and last anyhow, you little black so-and-so." So I sat back down
on the bed. Well, I was about to cry, because I didn't know what was
happening, all of these people around there going to kill me, and I
didn't have no money and Santa Fe was a hundred miles from there
and that's a long ways of walking and I didn't have no money.*

"Would you have been hanging around down there in Groveland if you
had done something like that, Charlie?" Akerman asked.

"Me? If I'd even thought something like that had happened, I would
have been on my way back to Santa Fe or somewhere."

The defense rested.

Once again, the prosecution chose not to cross-examine. Akerman and
Hunter discussed a short break to prepare for closing arguments and Judge
Futch called a recess until 4 p.m. Outside the courtroom, Williams bumped
into "the white lady with the bebop glasses," Mabel Norris Reese, again.
The trial wasn't over yet, but Reese couldn't resist commenting on the
sixteen-year-old's performance in the witness box.

"Charlie Greenlee's such a good actor," she called out. Williams was
stunned. Here was a boy on trial for his life. He'd just told a packed courtroom that a train had killed his baby sister and his mother cried so much he
had to leave home. Deputies had nearly beaten him to death a few weeks
ago and he'd been in jail ever since. And now his aged father, "eyes filled
with grief," was forced to sit by his son each day in court and watch him
being led away in handcuffs.

"When are you going to put him on Broadway, Franklin?"

It was always "Franklin" with Mabel. Never "Mr. Williams." The lawyer had had enough.

"You know what your problem is," Williams sneered. "You've got a
business here, and you're trying to out-cracker the crackers."

Mabel was taken aback by yet another unpleasant exchange with the
New York lawyer. That night she would drive back to her office and begin
typing her coverage of the trial, sarcastically comparing the NAACP's
defense to nothing more than fictitious theater. Under the headline "At
Long Last, the Groveland Story Is Put into Production," Mabel lauded
"Star Greenlee" and noted that the boy "brought in the finale as would
Negro singer Paul Robeson emphasize the crescendo of a song," so much so
that he "would have made a Broadway critic cut the rope of racial prejudice
to give him a rave notice in his column."

Ted Poston followed Jesse Hunter out of the courtroom, and couldn't get Norma Padgett out of his mind. "Except for the slender, petulant blonde's own testimony," Poston noted, "there was not one bit of evidence placed in the record of the three-day trial at Tavares to support her story that four Negroes raped her successively on the back seat of a 1946 Mercury car in the early morning hours of July 16." Poston had heard she'd been examined by a doctor, yet no doctor was called to testify. Approaching Hunter, Poston asked why.

"Not necessary," Hunter snapped. "She said she was raped, didn't she?"

"Mr. Hunter didn't want to embarrass Mrs. Padgett by bringing out all those details," an assistant prosecutor added.

Poston noted that the state did not produce any evidence of "possible stains, spots or any other evidence which must have accompanied a four-way rape in the same corner of the car's back seat." One spectator even said so much to Poston while they were in the "Colored" men's room on the courthouse floor.

"If that white lady was raped like she said, then it was the cleanest rape in Lake County or the cleanest one anywhere."

Heading back into court, Poston spotted *bolita* dealer and witness for the prosecution Henry Singleton, "bowing and cringing behind a deputy sheriff—more frightened even then of the vengeance of his own people. . . ." He even overheard the deputy discussing Greenlee's testimony in the corridor. "Too bad that Greenlee nigger got mixed up in this. You know, he's the kind of nigger you like. It's a shame Miss Padgett had already said he was there."

When court resumed, Jesse Hunter was eager to finish off the defendants. He told Judge Futch, "I won't take very long, Your Honor," then leaned into the jury box and assured the jurors that whatever questions they might have about who was where and at what time, they should remember that "a lot can happen with a good fast car and vicious men." He informed the jury that "no human being ever went through such a terrible night as this girl did," then reminded them that the defense did not call any witnesses to prove Shepherd and Irvin were in Orlando that night "because those two men were not in Orlando that terrible night—they were out on the road to Center Hill raping this woman!"

Akerman rose to counter with a reasonable-doubt argument, claiming that the prosecution's time line defied logic. Greenlee had been apprehended twenty miles away at the same time that Norma Padgett would have been attacked. Without Charles Greenlee on the scene, there was no gun. Akerman closed by telling the jury that in most cases he'd tried, criminals fled after a crime of this nature. Yet these three defendants did nothing of the sort after the alleged crime.

Williams didn't think the jury would be out very long. Earlier in the trial, they had requested to see the inside of the car where Padgett was alleged to have been raped. Williams had held out some hope that perhaps they were considering exactly how this "grim game of 'Musical Chairs' could take place" in the small backseat of the car. But Futch declined, stating that the request was "a little out of line." There weren't going to be any surprises, and Futch had kept a tight rein on the trial.

Williams thought Akerman's closing argument was quite good, given the lack of time to prepare this case and the restraints Judge Futch had imposed on them throughout the trial. But Williams's praise of Akerman did not compare to the praise Judge Futch had heaped on Jesse Hunter.

"Jesse," Futch said, shaking the lawyer's hand, "I have never heard a better argument in all my life."

At 7:25 p.m., the twelve white Lake County men were sent out to deliberate and Poston darted down the block to "the one long distance phone booth" in range of the courthouse. He put a call in to the *New York Post* news desk. He was told city editor Jimmy Graham was nervous, pacing the floor like "an expectant father" because he hadn't heard from Poston in hours. Graham had even phoned Governor Warren, hoping to secure some protection for his reporter.

"Keep your shirt on," Poston said. "There's absolutely nothing to worry about. Tell Jimmy the verdict will be in any minute, and I'll be heading for Orlando—40 miles away—later tonight."

Poston wasn't the only person on a phone near the courthouse while the jury was deliberating. William Bogar, Sheriff Willis McCall's fellow Klansman who had been one of the night riders during the rioting in Groveland in July, received a call from another member of the Apopka Klavern at around the same time. The Klansman told Bogar that Sheriff McCall "needed help" to "run the negro lawyers." A bunch of them were getting together to meet in an open space near a house off Route 441 near Lake Ola, where they'd wait for the car.

Word began to spread that the jurors had reached a verdict, and at 9:26 p.m. they took their seats in the jury box and waited for Judge Futch to bring the court to order. Before the verdict was read, Futch warned that there would be "no demonstration, handclapping or anything of that sort," and that all spectators were to remain in the courtroom until the sheriff and his deputies removed the defendants. The judge asked the clerk of courts to read the verdict. Greenlee's eyes followed the paper that was carried and passed from the jury foreman to the clerk.

*We the jury find the defendants guilty. So say we all, By majority recommendation of mercy for Charles Greenlee.*

*Charles A. Blaze Foreman*

Mabel Norris Reese noted, "Hope was gone from the eyes of Shepherd and Irvin. They were looking past the jury as they gazed forward—past them to their journey to the electric chair."

There was no outburst, just silence. Franklin Williams reached back and gripped the hand of Charles Greenlee. "Then a smile—a smile of boyish triumph came over the face of the Negro boy," Mabel wrote. "The play was done. Charles Greenlee had no reason to be acting then. He was accepting the plaudits due any one who kept an audience spellbound."

A recommendation of mercy meant that the sixteen-year-old would likely spend the rest of his life in jail. The defense had no interest in having the jury polled. They needed to move.

A LEX, PSST, ALEX," came a hiss from across the court. It was Judge Futch, informing the two white lawyers for the defense that they could slip out of the courthouse through his private chambers. Akerman quickly requested that sentencing be delayed for three days so that he could file a motion for a new trial. Futch granted the request, seemingly more concerned with getting the lawyers safely out of his courtroom. As Shepherd, Irvin, and Greenlee were taken away in shackles, Akerman and Price retreated behind the judge's desk. Hunter stayed in the courtroom, urging spectators to "go home quietly and not to cause any trouble."

Williams could hear the iron gate clang behind him as the Groveland Boys were led back upstairs by Sheriff Willis McCall. Hunter approached Williams to shake his hand, and Williams wanted Hunter to know one thing, off the record, as he watched the defendants leave the courtroom. Those boys, Williams told him, had been severely beaten by the sheriff and his deputies.

"I don't doubt it at all," Hunter replied.

With nothing more to say, Williams and Hill were escorted by highway patrolmen downstairs and out the back door, where they emerged in the back lot behind the courthouse, right at the spot where McCall had been met by a mob of angry Bay Lake men who demanded to search the jail for Norma Padgett's rapists back in July. It was hot and humid and dark and quiet, and as they made their way to Hill's car, the patrolmen turned and walked in the other direction.

"Aren't you going to escort us to our car?" Williams asked.

"No, my job is over," one cop said. "The trial is finished."

It was the first time Williams had truly felt fear during the case. He'd been intimidated by Willis McCall, but "I was young enough and I guess silly enough not to be afraid of him."

The two lawyers crossed the lawn just as spectators were leaving the court, and they hopped into Hill's 1948 sedan. Hill tried to light a cigarette, but the car's lighter had started smoking. Williams reached over and knocked the lighter to the floor, burning his finger. Somebody had tried to short-circuit the car and "jammed that cigarette lighter in just a few minutes before we got to it." The two had promised to give Ted Poston and Ramona Lowe a ride back to Orlando, and they waited nervously in the car as spectators came their way.

"Boy, nigger boy," said one man with his wife and daughter as he passed by. More and more of them were filing past the car and Williams was past being edgy.

"Now where the hell is Poston and Lowe?" he muttered.

Ted Poston was just coming down from the Jim Crow balcony when he touched Lowe's arm and guided her into a corridor where they almost bumped into Norma Padgett, who clenched her jaw and glared at the Negro reporters. Poston reached the lobby, but he'd lost Lowe in the jostling and "hostile sea of white faces." He took a side exit and with his jacket slung over one shoulder, he heard Horace Hill, idling his car with the lights out, calling his name softly.

"Hurry up and get in," Hill told him.

"Jesus," Poston remarked. "I am scared stiff."

"Where's Ramona?" Williams asked.

Poston opened the door. He had to go back for her, but Hill tried to stop him.

"Don't argue now, Horace," Williams snapped. "Let him go."

"Look, Frank," Hill said. "You're not in New York now. These clay-eating crackers aren't joking. I know. I wasn't born down here for nothing."

Poston raced back across the lawn and into the courthouse, where he spotted the heavyset Lowe talking to James Shepherd. "Come on," he said, leading her back to the car.

"Now you've done it," Hill scolded, telling the reporters that the state patrol's escort was gone.

Even Williams wasn't pleased at having to wait. "They blame *us* for getting Greenlee out of the chair," he said. "You both might have had a chance."

Hill continued to curse Poston and Lowe for their "damfoolishness" until they were able to make it out of Tavares. The traffic was thick until most of the cars peeled north toward Eustis, and they got onto Route 441, where the road opened up. Hill was moving the car along at 60 miles an hour where the road curled south toward Lake Ola. They were finally able to breathe and even managed some gallows humor about Hill having to live down here with these crackers, but the joking came to an abrupt end when they spotted two cars parked on both sides of the highway, facing Orlando. Hill shot past them, but "the two parked cars lighted up" and a third car followed behind.

Hill put the pedal to the floor and was doing 80-plus miles an hour, passing slower-moving traffic, when Williams noticed two cars coming up on them, with lights flashing.

"Jesus Christ," Williams said. "There is somebody behind us."

Ahead, they spotted a man in the road waving a white handkerchief or a cloth, but Hill had no intention of stopping and the man jumped aside as they passed. Williams spotted three cars in pursuit and in the first car, the silhouette of three men in the front seat. The one in the middle, Williams noted, was wearing a cowboy hat—"the kind that Willis McCall wore."

At high speeds, all four cars plowed through a red light.

"Oh, shit," Williams shrieked. "This is it."

Williams had been through a similar and harrowing experience before, when the car he'd been driving in hit a patch of ice and skidded out of control back in his college days at Lincoln. The crash had been so horrific it made the news, but Williams survived. Still, that car had been totaled, and Williams had been going only at half the speed that Hill was doing.

Ramona began sobbing. "Oh, God. It's my fault. I got you into this . . . I should've—"

"Shut up!" Poston yelled.

In silence, the sedan rocketed toward Apopka, with Williams calmly providing updates. "He's picking up, Horace."

Poston had picked up some "second hand make-shift glasses" but was grateful he could see "no further than two feet ahead." Three times the city desk at the *Post* had turned down his request to cover the Little Scottsboro case, but he persisted, and now he was back in one of those moments that had haunted him every time he went south. They were "hurtling forward in a stygian blackness," as Hill cut the lights, "trusting only the light of the Florida moon." He'd reached 90 miles an hour, but he hadn't lost his Klan pursuers, and he ever so slightly zigzagged on the road so they wouldn't shoot the tires. The cars behind them were close enough that they could hear the drivers honking their horns. Coming into lighted downtown Apopka, Hill ran a few red lights and "missed by inches" a pickup truck near a movie house. Williams noted that one of the cars behind nearly crashed, but straightened up, and "one of the crackers was leaning out the front window."

"I guess this is it, then," Williams said. "No cracker would endanger other crackers—not to mention his own life and limb—just to put a scare into a bunch of Negroes. I guess they really intend to take us."

They were still on Route 441, past Apopka and heading south to Orlando, picking up speed again, when Ramona Lowe screamed.

"They're not back there now!"

The Klan cars had peeled off, perhaps unwilling to take the chase any farther. Williams reached for a cigarette, but Hill kept the speed up until he was sure he wasn't being followed. They reached the familiar Wigwam Hotel, with thirty-one large white teepees off South Orange Blossom Trail, which Hill passed before turning left into Parramore, the black section of town, where they stopped in front of a little hotel.

"I have never been so happy to see so many black folks in my life," Williams thought.

Poston was sitting quietly in the back, where they all looked at each other in silence. He was glad his good glasses were broken, he later wrote. "I couldn't see my own shame, which must have been reflected in their eyes."

Hill parked the car and they entered the hotel, only to go right out through the back door and up to the woman's house where Williams was staying. They grabbed a drink and sat for about an hour. Once they'd settled their nerves some, Williams and Hill got back into the car to drive to Akerman's office. "We've got to get to work on that appeal," Williams said.

When they arrived, Akerman and Price were already going over the case files. Williams told them the story of being chased by three cars at 90 miles an hour through Lake and Orange counties.

"Aw, you have got to be kidding," Akerman said.

"For Christ's sake," Williams told him, he wasn't kidding.

# | 12 | ATOM SMASHER

Flat Top, also known as the "death house," at Florida State Prison in Raiford.
(*Courtesy of the State Archives of Florida*)

WILLIS MCCALL HAD decided the time had come for the Groveland Boys to "get right with the Lord." He'd had his deputies drag Walter Irvin and Samuel Shepherd to his office below the Tavares jail. The two rapists would soon be transported back to Florida State Prison in Raiford, this time to death row, where they'd be waiting for their date with the electric chair. Now, though, while he had the chance, McCall wanted to have a little conversation with the two boys. He preferred there be no lawyers present.

McCall pointed toward the wire recorder. He suggested to the boys that the time had come for them to clear their consciences; that it couldn't hurt to make a statement, since they'd soon be heading to the chair anyway. Shepherd and Irvin both refused, both of them stating, as they had in court, that they were innocent. McCall looked them hard in the eyes; neither man flinched. The sheriff had them taken back to their cells. They'd be gone from Lake County quick enough, and the only way they'd be coming back was in a pine box.

With Charles Greenlee, the sheriff played hardball. He pointed to the wire recorder on his desk; he told the boy he wanted a statement. The boy's eyes darted from the recorder to the sheriff to the ceiling, a wall. Was he going to be beaten, he wanted to know, "if he didn't say what the sheriff wanted to hear." McCall fumed. No, he told him, not beaten—killed.

The sixteen-year-old was sufficiently intimidated: "He was going to hand me over to the mob," Charles Greenlee said later. McCall turned on the wire recorder and proceeded to lead the prisoner through a series of simple questions. Convinced that he could avoid trouble if he cooperated, the boy responded with the answers he figured the Big Hat Man wanted to hear. They were nothing like the boy's rambling responses from the witness box, which prompted twelve white men on a jury to spare his life. Life on the chain gang—it galled the sheriff that the boy had gotten off easy.

"You lied on the witness stand?" McCall asked.

"Yes, sir."

"Did you make up that story?"

"Yes, sir."

"Sometimes it's better if you tell the truth about what happened," McCall said. "Who went first?"

"Ernest Thomas, I believe."

"Now, you didn't take a lot of talking into, did you?"

"No, sir," Greenlee replied.

"Why didn't ya'll kill the woman?"

"Well, I begged them not to, they were talking about it."

Seeing an opportunity to embarrass the NAACP with a recorded statement by their defense team's star witness, he asked, "Now, did these lawyers talk to you, did they put you up . . . What did they say to you?"

Greenlee didn't bite. "They just asked us our story. And then they said to don't worry, that they were going to defend us, that they were going to fight for us."

McCall finished with a string of rapid-fire questions: "Now nobody has promised you anything?" "Nobody has offered you, or made any promises to you?" "Nobody's threatened you?" "You're not under any threat of any kind?" "Now you didn't have to say any of this, did you?"

"No, sir." "No, sir." "No, sir." "No, sir." "No, sir," came Greenlee's prompt replies.

Willis McCall was satisfied. His voice became quiet, almost reassuring.

"I just wanted to know for my own curiosity what had really happened there," he said slowly. "I just wanted to know for my own curiosity if you had lied." Then he reached across his desk and switched off the recorder.

Deputies Yates and Campbell led the lanky boy back to the elevator in the Lake County Court House—the elevator that just two months before had taken him down to the basement where he'd been cuffed to an overhead pipe and mercilessly beaten. He'd survived the question-and-answer session with Sheriff McCall without a scratch. The deputies locked him in his cell on the fourth floor. Yates departed with a sneer.

Samuel Shepherd and Walter Irvin watched in silence. The boy sat down. He buried his face in the palms of his hands; his body trembled. He began to cry.

S COTLAND YARD, PLEASE Don't Take Our Yates."
Mabel Norris Reese wrote her own headlines for the *Mount Dora Topic*, and she seemed never to tire of advertising the top-notch detective work of Deputy James Yates. To his forensic analysis of the tire tracks and shoe prints at the crime scene Mabel attributed, in her posttrial coverage, the sentences to death by electrocution that the Whittlin' Judge had so justly delivered to Samuel Shepherd and Walter Irvin. The photo of Deputy Yates standing beside his plaster casts on the front page of the *Topic* was enough to turn Thurgood Marshall's stomach, for the Yates that he saw in the photo was the sadistic deputy who had severely and serially beaten the Groveland Boys.

The only good news that Franklin Williams, on his return to the NAACP office in New York, had to offer to Marshall was that Charles Greenlee had received a life sentence of hard labor: "An unlettered but articulate 16-year-old boy literally talked himself out of Florida's electric chair," as one reporter had written. On all other matters, Judge Futch had ruled uncompromisingly, and unsurprisingly, against the defense. He had not only rejected the motion for a new trial but also made a point of noting for the record both that the attorneys for the defense had had "ample opportunity to prepare" and that Williams and Akerman had "inject[ed] the racial question into the record." Meanwhile, the "vicious," in Williams's judgment, Mabel Norris Reese had filled the pages of the *Mount Dora Topic* with her grossly biased coverage of the trial and its aftermath, which was spiked with quotes by the self-satisfied sheriff Willis McCall, such as his reminder to the residents of Lake County that "the evidence was overwhelming, all three confessed." The reportage galled Marshall no less than it had Williams.

In Williams's absence from New York over the past two months, Marshall had, as usual, been overwhelmed with casework, on top of which had been added the responsibilities attendant to overseeing, along with Roy Wilkins, the day-to-day operations at the NAACP, as Walter White continued to be on leave. In August, Wilkins, as acting secretary, had authorized a three-hundred-dollar annual salary increase for Marshall, but in early September he wrote to Arthur Spingarn, "My feeling is that this is not a sufficient raise" and recommended that the board approve an additional five hundred dollars, which brought Marshall's total annual salary to $8,500.

Of more immediate concern to Marshall, and Williams, was funding to sustain the Groveland Boys case, for, as Williams had told his people in Florida, "that Tavares business is only the first scuffle" and "the real wrestling match is just begun." Yet, to date, the NAACP had pulled in only about fifteen hundred dollars, mostly in individual contributions from poor Florida blacks, whereas the case had already cost more than five thousand dollars, with "far more costly appeals ahead." Roy Wilkins listened sympathetically to Williams's pleas and Ted Poston's stories, and he took the same position as Marshall, who had stated weeks before that the NAACP's resources should be "thrown behind the defense of these boys." Wilkins affirmed, "We'll keep Frank's promise, although it will cost at least twenty thousand dollars more to fight this case up to the Supreme Court. We'll get the money somehow."

"Somehow" was, at least in part, a speaking tour, and Marshall decided to put Franklin Williams back on the fund-raising road, much the way he had when Williams traveled the country with the blinded soldier, Isaac Woodard, a few years earlier.

Stories of prisoners' beatings, abusive interrogations, and legal lynchings in Lake County had gained editorial attention in regional and national newspapers after the Groveland Boys trial, and by mid-September Ted Poston's "Horror in the Sunny South" series had been running daily in the *New York Post*, his story of the ninety-mile-an-hour chase out of Lake County by a "bloodthirsty, motorized mob" having gotten particular, nationwide attention. The time was ripe with possibilities. As Williams noted, "We have provably innocent sons of fine, decent Negro-American families in the old tradition. We have burnings. Mob action . . . A whole community of peace-loving Negro workers scattered . . . lawyer intimidation, etc." And Williams proved Marshall to be right. His tour of the Groveland Boys case—which in his retelling afforded him "all the characteristics of a dime-store novel . . . A perfect frameup"—raised more than $4,600 for the NAACP's legal defense fund.

Franklin Williams, at thirty-one years old, appeared to have unlimited potential. "He may have been the most gifted speaker I've ever heard," LDF associate Jack Greenberg said of him. "His admirers use the term 'silver-tongued,' but even that didn't seem adequate to describe his oratorical skills." To his detractors, Williams was "glib," sometimes brash, and he could certainly raise Mabel Norris Reese's hackles. She'd once suggested that the New York lawyer might benefit from living some while in the gentlemanly South; without courtesy Williams bellowed, "I would *not* live in the South!" Marshall placed his confidence in Williams's silver tongue and sterling intellect, which the young attorney had evidenced abundantly in Florida; so, to Marshall, it only made sense to have Franklin Williams argue the Groveland case before the state appellate court: a necessary step in the appeals process, if a fruitless one, for the NAACP had no real hope of a reversal in the state of Florida.

First, though, the LDF had to decide upon the structure of the Groveland Boys' appeal. With Shepherd and Irvin both facing the electric chair, they would surely join the appeal. Charles Greenlee, however, had been sentenced to life imprisonment on a jury recommendation of mercy. It was therefore entirely possible that he might win his appeal but in the retrial be sentenced to death. Not until 1981 (in an LDF-assisted case) did the Supreme Court rule that such a possibility discouraged appeal and "deterred the assertion of constitutional rights." In essence, then, the Supreme Court interpreted a less-than-death sentence as an "acquittal" by the jury of "whatever was necessary to impose the death sentence" in the first trial, and thus ruled, under the double jeopardy clause of the Fifth Amendment, that an appellant could not subsequently be sentenced to death in a second trial. In 1949, though, a legal misstep in the appellate process could send Charles Greenlee from a work farm to death row.

Williams's own experience in Lake County had convinced him, as he would convince Marshall, that Greenlee's life sentence constituted as much mercy as the callow, sixteen-year-old defendant or his defense could expect. Further, any chance of a second recommendation of mercy would in all likelihood be forfeit, Williams reasoned, when, after two or even three years in prison, before a retrial, an older, perhaps hardened, less ingenuous, eighteen- or nineteen-year-old Charles Greenlee would appear in court. On the basis of this reasoning, Marshall and Williams devised their strategy: They would not include Greenlee's name in the appeal; thus, if they should fail, Greenlee would still escape the electric chair. If, on the other hand, they should succeed in winning acquittals for Shepherd and Irvin, the consummately persuasive Marshall would strive to get the governor to commute Greenlee's sentence. The two attorneys explained to the boy his alternatives, and a week after he'd received his life sentence in Tavares, Charles Greenlee in his own hand wrote a letter in which he stated that he understood fully the choice he was making and that, while he had consulted with lawyers and his family, the decision not to join the appeal was ultimately his. "So if God be with me," he wrote, "I'll pray that he do I will get a pardon if the other boys go free." Shortly thereafter he was shipped off to Florida State Road Department Camp No. 16 in Lake City to begin his sentence of hard labor on a road gang.

Guilty verdicts and death sentences did not, as Mabel Norris Reese had assured her readers, return Lake County to its Edenic bliss. Instead, wave after wave of undesirable publicity had been inundating the county ever since the close of the trial, much to the chagrin of Judge Futch, State Attorney Hunter, and Sheriff McCall. The publication nationally of Ted Poston's *New York Post* story of the dramatic posttrial chase in the *Nation* especially pained Hunter, who preferred to believe that the people of Lake County had allowed the law to take its course. So, in an attempt to discredit Poston, Hunter held a hearing in Tavares, at which he invited highway patrolmen, police, and deputies from across Lake County to testify that they had not seen any cars speeding at ninety miles an hour toward Orlando on the night of the trial; and that they had not seen anyone step on Ted Poston's glasses, either; and that Poston had not complained to any officers about anyone doing so.

McCall remained mostly silent about the chase, but when Poston's series on the Groveland trial earned the reporter a five-hundred-dollar award from the CIO American Newspaper Guild, the press-clipping, image-conscious sheriff was apoplectic. That guild, he railed, was a "damn bunch of Communists," and Poston was but another "part of the Communistic element trying to tear down racial relations; trying to separate the races instead of bringing them together." When Poston won a second prestigious prize for his series, Mabel Norris Reese took up her pen; in a letter to the chairman of the Heywood Broun Award committee she disputed the accuracy of Poston's reporting. The committee was unmoved.

Satisfied though Hunter, Futch, and McCall were that the hearing had sufficiently debunked Poston's story as pure fiction—after all, why would the residents of central Florida choose to believe a communist reporter and lawyer from the North over the police and patrolmen of Lake County?—the FBI was not. The FBI chose to believe Bill Bogar, Exalted Cyclops of the Apopka Klavern of the Ku Klux Klan and key informant for the bureau. Bogar fingered Willis McCall as the party who'd initiated the storied but factual chase, and the FBI report indicated that the Klan had "intended to stop car and severely flog occupants, with instructions to leave state." It also later led to the indictment of four Klansmen by a federal grand jury on perjury charges.

The FBI's investigations into the Groveland Boys case as well as Poston's articles and Williams's detailed reports to the NAACP in New York prompted Marshall again to contact the attorney general's office. In a letter informing the attorney general that a "federal grand jury investigation is warranted" not just into the beatings of the Groveland Boys but also into the actions of deputies James Yates and Leroy Campbell, Captain Herlong of the Florida National Guard, and Flowers Cockcroft, the "leader of an armed band of civilian men" who had terrorized Negro residents and burned their homes, Marshall urgently requested that the attorney general prosecute these individuals. He also offered the NAACP's complete cooperation.

On September 13, Alexander Campbell of the U.S. attorney general's office informed Herbert S. Phillips, the U.S. attorney in Tampa, that "there is substantial evidence . . . that the victims were beaten and tortured as charged and that Yates, [Wesley] Evans, and [Leroy] Campbell played active parts in submitting the victims to the described indignities." Then the strength of Alexander Campbell's convictions wavered. The attorney general's office, he said, would "greatly appreciate" if Phillips would consider whether action against Yates, Evans, and Campbell "would be warranted and desirable," given the "temper of the people in the area" as well as their "fears and apprehensions." In closing, he issued the weakest of directives: "[W]e must consider the need for enforcing the paramount law," Campbell wrote, "so long as such action does not unduly interfere with local processes." Campbell had provided Phillips with the opening he needed.

In his response to the attorney general's office, Phillips stated that, in his opinion, the defendants had "as fair a trial as any persons could have," and that although Yates, Campbell, and Evans "may be guilty of committing a serious and despicable crime," there were "certain matters connected with this case that should be carefully considered before prosecuting the parties for beating the alleged victims." Reluctant to move forward with the case despite the overwhelming evidence proffered by the Justice Department, Phillips stated he "had serious doubt" that a grand jury would indict, but if one did, "it might result in another effort to commit serious violence on the defendants or victims." In other words, any attempt to prosecute Yates, Campbell, and Evans might only incite violent parties to further harm the Groveland Boys, who were in fact rather *fortunate*, Phillips reasoned without irony, to have been beaten when they might have been lynched, the physical torture being "a small matter as compared to what would have happened if the sheriff had not handled the matter as he did." A final point to consider, Phillips wrote, was that although "a strict interpretation of the law" protects prisoners from being coerced into confessing, it was important to remember that "the confessions were not used in evidence."

AS THE 1940S came to a close, Thurgood Marshall and his LDF attorneys were about to enter the most productive and important months of their careers. Cases were mounting. Aside from his work on the Groveland appeal, Marshall was preparing briefs for two cases that for twelve years the LDF had been waiting to bring before the Supreme Court. In addition, Marshall's mentor Charles Hamilton Houston, who'd recently suffered a relapse after a heart attack, asked his former pupil to take over a case involving a black woman who had been denied admission to the University of Maryland's School of Nursing.

Fifteen years before, in 1935, Marshall and Houston together had successfully sued the University of Maryland to open the doors of its law school to black applicant Donald Gaines Murray, and Marshall now set out to convince the judge that the striking similarity between the two cases supported Esther McCready's admission. The defendants, on the other hand, argued dissimilarity, since the Murray case had involved the law school whereas Esther McCready was suing a school of nursing.

"Judge, I agree with that," Marshall apparently conceded. "The law school and the nursing school are different, and I can *prove* it." The judge leaned forward, attentive, curious as to the direction of Marshall's argument. "I can prove it," Marshall continued, "because I went to law school—and I didn't come out a nurse."

It was the kind of line that Marshall's mentor, "Old Iron Shoes," as he was known, would never have uttered in court, but certainly the stroke of wit did not diminish the strength of Marshall's argument. He did his ailing friend and mentor proud. He won the case for the plaintiff, and he didn't even have to file an appeal with the U.S. Supreme Court. The Maryland Court of Appeals ruled in McCready's favor.

The New York office was meanwhile buzzing with activity. Busy "all day and virtually every night at the office," the LDF lawyers—Franklin Williams, Jack Greenberg, and Constance Baker Motley—were getting the education of a lifetime as they worked on briefs not just with Marshall but with academic consultants and top-flight lawyers who were, in Greenberg's words, willing to use their "considerable talents at something other than getting rich": men like Louis H. Pollak, the former law clerk to Supreme Court justice Wiley Rutledge. (His father, Walter Pollak, had worked on the Scottsboro Boys defense.) Space at the NAACP offices in the Willkie Building being limited, Marshall's lawyers were able, by his arrangement with the Association of the Bar of the City of New York, to work at its library in a landmark building not far from the Willkie in midtown Manhattan. After work, Marshall and his LDF team would often gather at the Blue Ribbon, a German restaurant just down the street, to drink "great dark Munich beer on tap" and, in Marshall's case, to eat pigs' knuckles. After the knuckles and beer and conviviality, however, Marshall more often than not would lead them back to the office for another all-nighter.

The work, though, was exciting for both Marshall and his young staff, who could see in the briefs they were filing for the Supreme Court real possibilities of changing the racial face of America. One such case was that of Heman Marion Sweatt, a black mail carrier in Houston, who had been denied admission to the University of Texas Law School in 1946 solely on the basis of his race. Under representation by the NAACP, Sweatt sued the University of Texas on the grounds that in the state of Texas there existed no law school for blacks. Marshall was clear in his intentions: "If we can force the University of Texas to admit Heman Sweatt," he told one reporter, "we can knock down this whole theory of separate but equal accommodations, not only in schools, but in other public endeavors as well." In response to the lawsuit, the University of Texas president, Theophilus Painter, had leased the basement of a petroleum building near the state capitol, dumped a few boxes of textbooks inside, and notified the NAACP that there was now a separate law school for blacks that was "equal to the University of Texas Law School."

When Thurgood Marshall arrived in Austin in May 1947, he was confident that he had found the perfect case to strike a critical blow to legalized segregation. Eager to hear how Marshall would argue his case that a pile of textbooks in a basement did not a law school make, dozens of white University of Texas law school students as well as local NAACP members crowded into the Travis County courtroom. The bailiffs' commands that the white students not sit in the black section were met by recalcitrance, the students refusing to budge unless a black person requested them to move. After the first recess, with blacks and whites sitting shoulder to shoulder in the packed courtroom, the bailiffs gave up trying to enforce segregated seating.

The University of Texas students booed when the dean of their own law school stated under oath that the two law schools were equal, and they booed when he defended segregation as a necessity in order to ensure quality education for whites. Marshall, though, won their applause when his witness, the dean at the University of Pennsylvania Law School, testified that it was absurd to call an institution with one student a law school. Half the show in Marshall's courtroom performance was played to those white students outraged by their university's institutionalized segregation and administrative hypocrisy. It was those same students who founded in Austin the nation's first all-white chapter of the NAACP.

To no one's surprise, Judge Roy Archer—who had laughed out loud in court when he was shown photographs of the new Texas law school for blacks—ruled against Sweatt. So did the Texas Supreme Court on appeal. Marshall, however, had had the foresight to focus the legal debate not on the obvious physical differences between the two facilities, or on the paucity of books or absence of a law library, but rather on the intangible advantages that a "traditional" law school would offer as well as the social and psychological disadvantages of learning in a segregated environment: points that he would argue before the U.S. Supreme Court in 1950.

From the outset of *Sweatt v. Painter*, Marshall's vision had extended beyond the case in the Travis County courtroom, by which he was essentially setting the juristic stage for the U.S. Supreme Court to overrule *Plessy v. Ferguson*, the landmark 1896 decision upholding racial segregation. One reporter observing Marshall in Texas wrote "everyone knows what the score is . . . and those of us who sit in the crowded courtroom day after day realize that we are watching history being made."

At the same time that Marshall and his attorneys were preparing for *Sweatt v. Painter*, they were also filing briefs for another segregation case, *McLaurin v. Oklahoma State Regents*, wherein George McLaurin, who'd already earned his master's degree, had applied to the University of Oklahoma to pursue a doctor of education degree. The state of Oklahoma had never been friendly territory for Marshall and his staff; he'd lost the Lyons murder case there years before, and more recently, in 1946, he'd returned to argue a case on behalf of Ada Sipuel, who had been denied entry into the all-white University of Oklahoma Law School. The Sipuel trial had been nearing its end when the judge had summoned Marshall to his chambers; there the judge had acknowledged the clarity and intelligence both of Marshall's arguments and of his black expert witnesses, all of which had "'opened [the judge's] eyes,' to the wrong of school segregation." Marshall could only briefly savor the moment, for the judge had then returned to the courtroom and ruled against Sipuel and the NAACP attorney.

On that same occasion, but away from the bench, Marshall had had a less satisfying private exchange with the assistant attorney general of Oklahoma, who'd inveighed, "You keep talking about equal justice, equal facilities. We're setting up an atom smasher at the University of Oklahoma. Do you mean that we've got to set up an atom smasher for niggers? Everybody knows that niggers can't study science." A year later, when arguing the Sipuel case on appeal in Oklahoma, Marshall had again run into the distasteful assistant attorney general and again, Marshall recalled, "it was 'nigger' this and 'nigger' that." More surprising, though, had been the assistant attorney general who in 1948 had arrived in Washington, D.C., to argue *Sipuel v. Board of Regents of Univ. of Okla.* before the Supreme Court, especially when, to Marshall's dismay, he'd informed the justices that he was defending segregation only because of his oath of office and that if the Court ruled against him, he would "not only follow the letter, but the spirit of the law." Marshall's shock had ceded to curiosity when, in the lawyers' lounge, he'd asked the attorney "what the hell happened" to him. "My son's been a student at the University of Oklahoma," the attorney had replied. "He's read about this case. He's been berating me about it, including the question whether I really believe in the U.S. Constitution. He convinced me that I was a jackass."

Marshall's argument of *Sipuel* before the Court was observed by the future Supreme Court justice John Paul Stevens, then a law clerk to Associate Justice Wiley Rutledge: "Thurgood was respectful, forceful and persuasive—so persuasive that on the following Monday—only four days after the argument—the Court unanimously ruled in Sipuel's favor."

At the time that Marshall had returned to Oklahoma City to argue *McLaurin v. Oklahoma State Regents*, the Dixiecrats had been stirring up their ranks with forecasts of the perils immanent in any legislation of social equality for Negroes, particularly with their predictions that "there would be intermarriage" if desegregation was enforced in educational institutions. Marshall, however, had managed to stay one step ahead of the South's political powers that be. In Oklahoma, Marshall noted, "we had eight people who had applied and who were eligible to be plaintiffs, but we deliberately picked Professor McLaurin because he was sixty-eight years old and we didn't think he was going to marry or intermarry. . . . They could not bring that one up on us, anyhow."

The state had responded to the suit by admitting McLaurin to the University of Oklahoma's doctoral program in education, but with conditions. For one, McLaurin was forced to sit at a desk in an "anteroom" from which he could only look into the classroom. (Marshall noted that the "anteroom" was merely a "broom closet.") Protest had then prompted the state to amend its ruling—slightly: McLaurin was assigned a special seat in the classroom; it was surrounded by a railing and marked "Reserved for Colored." The absurdity had not been lost on the white students, who'd immediately torn down the original railing and sign, as well as all the new ones that had replaced them, at a cost to the state of more than five thousand dollars.

Jack Greenberg found the McLaurin case to be especially attractive, and provocative, because "it offered the [U.S. Supreme] Court no escape from deciding the issue of segregation." On the other hand, Greenberg thought at the time that "it was dangerous because it allowed no victory on grounds short of overruling *Plessy*, which the Court might be reluctant to do." He, Constance Baker Motley, and Franklin Williams focused their legal savvy and abundant energy on getting the briefs and petitions cast exactly as Marshall wanted them, for *Sweatt* as well as *McLaurin*, since both cases were scheduled to be argued before the Supreme Court on the same day, April 3, 1950. At the printer's shop, the young lawyers stood by the "clattering hot-lead Linotype machines and clanging presses," and as the pages came off the press they edited them and read them aloud to each other to be sure the proofs were Thurgood-perfect. Their vision may have begun to blur by the time the sun started to rise; but not their focus. Or Marshall's. Standing by them, with them, like them, as Greenberg averred, "Thurgood focused on the end of Jim Crow."

Once the briefs for both *Sweatt* and *McLaurin* were filed, Marshall's mentor, Charles Hamilton Houston, did more than offer his former pupil advice. He launched an attack from the flank, by having his solid connections at the Justice Department file amicus briefs with the Supreme Court in support of both *Sweatt* and *McLaurin*, essentially stating, "*Plessy* must go." Marshall himself was meanwhile filling notebooks with case summaries so that he'd have every relevant reference at his fingertips, and he'd composed lists of every question he could imagine the justices might possibly pose. In Washington, in the days leading up to his arguments, he'd regularly take his staff down to Howard University for "dry runs" before a distinguished panel of academics and lawyers, including Houston and his cousin William Hastie. Mostly, they were trying to prepare for any issue that might be raised by the inquisitional associate justice Felix Frankfurter, the former Harvard Law School professor and the reputed intellectual among the justices, who was perceived by Marshall and his team to be a potentially dangerous adversary. Marshall entered the rigorous moot court sessions at Howard "like a boxer going into training," said Jack Greenberg. "Thurgood would limit himself to one glass of wine at dinnertime, usually sherry, and no other alcohol."

On April 3 and 4, with associates Greenberg, Williams, and Motley along for support, the assistant special counsel Robert Carter argued *McLaurin* and Marshall argued *Sweatt*. In just a few sentences Marshall crystallized his argument for the Court. Emotional but reserved, the lawyer stood before the justices and "employed a rhetoric with persuasive force beyond its basic ideas." Marshall said:

> *The rights of Sweatt to attend the University of Texas cannot be conditioned upon the wishes of any group of citizens. It matters not to me whether every single Negro in this country wants segregated schools. It makes no difference whether every white person wants segregated schools. If Sweatt wants to assert his individual, constitutional right, it cannot be conditioned upon the wishes of every other citizen.*

Marshall proved to be so well prepared, and his argument so tightly constructed, that he did not face a single question he hadn't already anticipated in his "training" at Howard. The attorney general of Texas attempted unsuccessfully to counter Marshall's case with the argument that Sweatt's admission to the university would lead to blacks being allowed in public places such as swimming pools and hospitals. "All we ask in the south," he said, "is the opportunity to take care of this matter and work it out [ourselves]."

THE TWO ARDUOUS Supreme Court arguments now behind them, Marshall and his LDF lawyers returned to New York and to their work on the Groveland appeal, which Franklin Williams would be arguing before the Florida Supreme Court with Alex Akerman. Williams, though, was not eager to revisit the orange groves and white crackers of central Florida, for by the spring of 1950 he had developed a taste for arguing segregation cases in the U.S. Supreme Court, cases that, in Williams's view, stood at the forefront of the nation's growing civil rights movement. With the taste came ambition.

One year earlier, Williams had accompanied Marshall to Washington, where as assistant counsel the thirty-one-year-old lawyer had argued *Watts v. Indiana* alongside the NAACP's star attorney, albeit he'd had to persuade a reluctant Marshall—hard-pressed though he was, as he had no one else to argue the case—to allow him the opportunity. "I was the first deputy of Thurgood's to argue a case before the court," Williams noted, and he'd made a memorable debut, as the Court overturned a murder conviction because the defendant's confession to the crime had not been voluntary. Moreover, Williams's performance had caught the eye of Felix Frankfurter, who wrote a note to his clerk, Bill Coleman, during the proceedings: "Bill, take a few minutes off to listen to Franklin Williams (do you know him?)." Coleman replied that Williams was "now Mr. Marshall's assistant" and that he had "studied his law at Howard and comes very highly recommended." Frankfurter crossed out "Howard" on the note and wrote in "Fordham," then added one more word to describe Williams's courtroom comportment: "Excellent!"

Since his arrival at the LDF in 1945, Williams had aligned himself closely with Walter White, who in fact had hired the recent Fordham Law School graduate. The two men also socialized outside the office. "Walter liked me and respected me as a dynamic young guy in the office," Williams recalled, "and Thurgood probably thought I was in league with Walter—and since I did hang out with him, I suppose I was." So it had come as no surprise to Marshall when he learned that Williams's promptings lay behind the memos Walter White had issued regarding the "overfamiliarity and casualness" in the LDF offices that fostered a less productive working environment. Still, Marshall more than tolerated the young attorney's ambition. Indeed, he encouraged it, for Marshall was not a man to be threatened by bright, enterprising minds.

A self-confident manager and a crafty leader, Marshall thrived on the talents of his staff and associates. Even Williams, as critical as he was of Marshall's apparent informality, had to admire the effectiveness of his modus operandi. "He had great success in picking people's brains and manipulating them in the interests of the cause," Williams said of Marshall. "He'd get a lot of outside lawyers together in a room, and he'd be talking and laughing and drinking along with the rest of them and getting everybody relaxed and open, and he'd seem to be having such a good time with them that you wouldn't think he was listening. But after they'd left, there it all was—he'd had the benefit of all their brains, which was his strategy in the first place. Frankly, it was a little embarrassing—until I came to understand what he was up to."

Williams also understood that, and why, Marshall was chary in regard to the cases he was willing to have the NAACP represent, but understanding did not restrain the younger attorney, who had Walter White's influential ear, from criticizing Marshall for being "cautious to a fault in taking thorny cases." Williams, not unlike other attorneys and associates of the NAACP, was eager to pursue civil rights suits more widely, whereas "Thurgood," said Williams, "had to be convinced of victory beyond a reasonable doubt before he said yes." Fewer of the staff and consultants at the NAACP office, however, agreed with Williams than agreed with Marshall, who was reluctant to bring cases to the Supreme Court prematurely "because they might make lasting unfavorable precedents." Still, Marshall felt the debate as to the aims and reach of the NAACP among its executives and the LDF staff was a healthy one, and he did not discourage it. (He was not pleased, though, when the NAACP magazine, the *Crisis*, mistakenly referred to Franklin Williams as "special counsel." Only half jokingly, the special counsel Marshall dashed off a memo to Williams, stating that "all pretenders to the throne may use any . . . exit to the building without picking up any past due salary," and closing with a not-informal "Please acknowledge receipt.")

In the spring of 1950, Williams's staunch ally Walter White still remained on indefinite leave from the NAACP. So Williams really had no choice. As much as he might have wished to continue working out of New York and Washington on groundbreaking civil rights cases, he was packing his bags and heading back to the Sunshine State with its scary, unwelcoming, clay-eating, car-chasing crackers.

# | 13 | IN ANY FIGHT SOME FALL

Curtis Howard. (*Courtesy of Kim Howard Turner*)

FRANKLIN WILLIAMS MADE a gallant attempt to argue to the Florida Supreme Court that Charles Greenlee could not have been involved in the alleged rape of Norma Padgett because, according to the time line established by her own testimony, police had already apprehended Greenlee miles away from the scene. The Florida attorney general, however, offered a simple explanation for any discrepancies in the time line to which the NAACP counsel attached such importance:

> *Mrs. Padgett didn't have any idea how long the four negroes took to rape her. While sexual intercourse can be a prolonged affair in some settings, it is probable that these four negroes, goaded to a sexual frenzy by the prospect of having intercourse with a young white woman, took about as much time as a bull put to a cow in heat. Cover her, a few rapid thrusts, all over, and off again.*

To Williams, who had traveled to Tallahassee with Akerman to make their case before the justices, it was like arguing "in somebody's back yard . . . to a group of men whose tendency would be to reject the fact that in their state there could be such an oppressive atmosphere that these young men could not get a fair trial." The justices were hardly inquisitive, and there wasn't "much of a play back and forth" of the sort that Williams had experienced when arguing in the U.S. Supreme Court.

To no one's surprise, Florida's highest court upheld the Lake County verdict. Still, the justices did grant Shepherd and Irvin a ninety-day stay of execution, which allowed time for an appeal to the higher court. Marshall set Jack Greenberg to work on the briefs with Williams while the office waited anxiously for the *Sweatt* and *McLaurin* decisions. The Groveland Boys waited anxiously in jail.

FOR THURGOOD MARSHALL in 1950, T. S. Eliot was right: April was the cruelest month. By then the FBI had not only completed its investigation into the beatings of the Groveland Boys but had also pressured the U.S. attorney, Herbert Phillips, to file charges against deputies James Yates and Leroy Campbell. Phillips had responded by impaneling, at the courthouse in Ocala, a federal grand jury, before which Shepherd, Irvin, and Greenlee testified as to their physical abuse at the hands of Lake County law enforcement officials. The grand jury returned "no true bill," essentially declaring the defendants Yates and Campbell innocent, and issued in addition a statement praising Sheriff McCall for his protection of the accused men from extreme violence. In a letter to Phillips the Justice Department's assistant attorney general stated that the department was "disturbed and disappointed in the inaction of the grand jury, for we are convinced that the victims were beaten and mistreated as charged."

Marshall was outraged. Phillips had, at the last minute, summoned to Ocala the two physicians at the Raiford state prison who had examined the Groveland Boys, but by the time they'd arrived that afternoon the hearing had already ended. Phillips had not called any of the prison officials or FBI agents who'd interviewed the three prisoners and photographed their quite visible injuries. Furthermore, not to be accused of racial bias, Phillips had made sure that three black men were seated on the grand jury, and that they would hear the words of two upstanding deputies of the law pitted against those of three convicted rapists. It was clear to Marshall and the Justice Department that if Phillips had actually wanted indictments of the two deputies, he could easily have secured them. Instead, Herbert S. Phillips, an avowed segregationist appointed by President Woodrow Wilson in 1913, had left the critical decisions in the process to his friend Jesse Hunter, who had determined, for instance, that they didn't "need any assistance from F.B.I. agents."

IN AUGUST 1949, when the Groveland Boys trial had been about to begin, Charles Hamilton Houston wrote a letter to Assistant Special Counsel Robert Carter. Ordinarily, Houston would have written to Marshall, but he knew that his former student and longtime friend, along with Roy Wilkins, was fully occupied in the administration of the NAACP office in Walter White's absence; nor did Houston want to burden Marshall with the news of his failing health, that "something other than fatigue" was a problem. The letter assured Carter: "These education cases are now tight and sufficiently so that anyone familiar with the course of the decisions should be able to guide the cases through. You and Thurgood can proceed without any fear of crossing any plans I might have."

Houston, who had suffered a heart attack, had moved into the home of his physician, Dr. Edward Mazique, while attempting to regain his strength after what would later be diagnosed as acute coronary thrombosis. He had placed his casework in the hands of his father, William, with whom he'd been working over the last quarter century, but the fifty-four-year-old Charlie Houston really "didn't know how" to stop working, even when bedridden. More worrying than his casework were Houston's concerns for his five-year-old son, Bo, whom Marshall called "Little Charlie."

Houston's constant chest pains had increasingly been taking a physical toll on his body, and he had not wanted his son to witness him withering away but rather "to remember his father as vigorous, impressive and strong." Houston had always felt extraordinarily protective of his young son. Joseph Waddy, Houston's partner at their law firm, recalled an incident in a Washington, D.C., drugstore, where little Bo had climbed up on a counter stool while his father was making his purchases. "Get down from there, you little nigger—you got no business here," the man behind the soda fountain had shouted at the boy, and had so upset the father that "when they got back to the office," Waddy said, "we had to take Charlie into the back room and give him a sedative."

Although both Charlie's wife, Henrietta, and his son had protested his more recent protective impulses, he had kissed them both good-bye as he'd put them on a train to Baton Rouge and the home of Henrietta's sister.

That December Houston was too infirm to shop for Christmas presents; so, to express his appreciation of the attentive Dr. Mazique, Houston gave him one of his prized possessions, a poster of an "open-air Scottsboro protest meeting in Amsterdam"—in the hope that Mazique would one day hand on the poster to Bo. To explain further to Bo the "domestic and international significance" of the landmark case he had worked on twenty years earlier, he recorded the story of the Scottsboro Boys on tape. Since Scottsboro "you have seen . . . the movement of the great masses of the people," said Houston to his son, and therefore "it is necessary to establish the principle of the indivisibility of liberty so that the masses recognize that no matter where liberty is challenged, no matter where oppression lifts its head, it becomes the business of all the masses."

A second heart attack landed Houston in the Freedman's Hospital at Howard University. Despite the setback, and critical as his condition was, Houston was not prepared to have his family come back to Washington. His aunt Clotill was a frequent visitor, however, and together they would read and discuss the lessons in *Peace of Mind*, by Joshua Loth Liebman. Aunt Clotill had given the book to her nephew, and he exacted her promise to pass the book along to Bo, should he not make it out of the hospital.

In the early afternoon of April 22, Mazique was preparing a medication for nausea and his patient was resting in bed when Joseph Waddy stopped in to visit. "Hi, Joe," Houston said softly, as his slightly raised hand slumped to his side. Charles Hamilton Houston had drawn his final breath. Beside his bed lay his copy of *Peace of Mind*. In its pages Houston had written some last words for his son:

> *Tell Bo I did not run out on him but went down fighting that*
> *he might have better and broader opportunities than I had without*
> *prejudice or bias operating against him, and in any fight some fall.*

He had driven a young Thurgood Marshall across the South; he had opened his onetime student's eyes and mind to the inequalities blacks suffered by law. For decades he had been laying the groundwork to overturn the injustices enacted against his race in *Plessy*. He did not live to see the culmination of his labor. The funeral services for Charles Hamilton Houston at Howard University's Rankin Chapel were attended by Supreme Court justices Tom C. Clark and Hugo Black, an official from President Truman's cabinet, numerous civil rights activists, and hundreds of friends and colleagues. Houston's cousin, William Hastie, whom President Truman had nominated to a seat on the U.S. Court of Appeals in 1949, paid homage to a civil rights champion's "unremitting struggle to win for the Negro full status without discrimination." Hastie celebrated a warrior's spirit: "Yet, as we grieve, we cannot forget that he believed, perhaps above all else, in strength; strength to do and to bear what lesser men would regard as impossible or unbearable. He counted nothing, no physical weakness and not even death itself, as an obstacle to the onward sweep of strong men and women in the accomplishment of worthwhile ends. He had a soldier's faith that winning the fight is all that matters; that every battle must be fought until it is won and without pause to take account of those stricken in the fray. He reflected that conviction in a slogan which he gave to his students: 'No tea for the feeble, no crepe for the dead.' I know he would wish all of us to carry on in that spirit."

Marshall was one of Houston's pallbearers. He was also one of the NAACP executives who would ensure that Houston be posthumously awarded the thirty-fifth Spingarn Medal, a tribute that came years too late. "Whatever credit is given him is not enough," Marshall said of his mentor, whose contributions to the cause of civil rights were ultimately immeasurable as he had so willingly and unselfishly toiled behind the scenes while others received credit for the gains. It was Marshall's idea to present the Spingarn Medal to Houston's son at the NAACP's forty-first annual convention, in Boston. In a photograph that appeared in newspapers across the country, Marshall—the trace of a smile barely masking his sorrow—can be seen standing over the shoulder of the boy as little Bo is being handed his father's medal.

Four years earlier, in Cincinnati, Charles Hamilton Houston had presented the Spingarn Medal to Thurgood Marshall. Even then, Marshall had not outstripped his mentor or ceased to follow his lead. Rarely in the two decades before or four years since had Marshall made an important legal decision without consulting Houston, and with his passing Marshall, too, had lost a protector and a champion. The master's mantle had fallen onto the pupil's shoulders. The legal strategy, Houston had told Marshall, was in place; all that was needed was the courage and strength to see it through. As Hastie had so eloquently eulogized him, Houston "guided us through the legal wilderness of second-class citizenship. He was truly the Moses of that journey. He lived to see us close to the promised land . . . closer than even he dared hope. . . ."

&#8766; &#8766;

THE CRUEL APRIL passed, but the spring, as in Eliot's metaphor, had begun to breed lilacs out of the dead land. Just weeks after Houston's death, the U.S. Supreme Court announced its decisions on *Sweatt* and *McLaurin*. In both cases the justices' opinions were unanimous.

Marshall immediately called Heman Sweatt. "We won the big one!" he proclaimed, explaining to the letter carrier that the Court did not find "substantial equality" between the University of Texas Law School and a basement equipped with a pile of textbooks. "Now the state will have to age law schools like good whiskey," Marshall told him.

The *New York Times* opined that the Court's decisions left *Plessy* in "tatters." More privately, some justices on the Supreme Court concluded that *Sweatt* and *McLaurin*, along with *Henderson v. United States*—a railway segregation case that was decided on the same day—had sealed the fate of Jim Crow. The South braced for the inevitable end of segregation in elementary and secondary schools.

In June 1950, then, Marshall was finally again in the mood to celebrate. Once again he was "Thurgood . . . a party man. 'Party' was his middle name," said Constance Baker Motley. And he proved it. He hosted a victory party at the midtown office, where, as young Jack Greenberg remembered, there was "lots of Scotch and bourbon, clouds of cigarette smoke, lots of laughter and noise and bragging, jokes about race and racial banter, and the almost obligatory poker game." Bobbie Branch, the office manager, "an ample woman who resembled Bloody Mary in *South Pacific*," was especially excited after the decisions; she was swaggering around the place and "swearing like a marine," Greenberg recalled. The press was ringing the phones off the hook, and visitors were parading through the office with their congratulations. Nobody wanted to go home.

Of course, Marshall knew that the decisions had not gone so far as to obliterate *Plessy* completely, but he was at last beginning to see the fruits of the seeds Houston had planted after he and Marshall, in 1930, had sat down together to study the findings in the Margold Report. In the twenty years since, they had honed "the tools to destroy all governmentally imposed racial segregation." The work was not done, but it had unquestionably and irrevocably begun. "It will take time. It will take courage and determination," Marshall said, as if to convince himself that he had the fortitude to continue the mission without the man who had envisioned it.

৵ ৵

PERHAPS THE BIGGEST surprise that spring came to Marshall and the LDF lawyers in the form of a three-part exposé that appeared in the *St. Petersburg Times* in early April. Norman Bunin, a twenty-six-year-old copy editor who had closely followed the Groveland case as it had unfolded in Florida, had felt that some of the testimony simply did not add up. To satisfy his own curiosity, he began reading the trial transcripts and trying to piece together exactly what had happened on the night of July 15, 1949. From the outset, it seemed glaringly apparent to Bunin, by virtue of the accounts of several witnesses, that at the time of the alleged rape Charles Greenlee was already in jail. Only Norma Padgett's testimony placed Greenlee at the scene of the supposed crime, and in fact, with a stunning lack of physical evidence, the prosecution had based its case entirely on the word of Norma Padgett and her identification of the alleged assailants in court. Other details in the court records nagged at Bunin, such as the prosecution's list of witnesses, nearly all of whom were never called to testify: Why? Bunin wondered.

The more he wondered the more obsessed Bunin became with the case. Whatever days he could—he had not been officially assigned to the case for the paper—he spent buried in the court records, and on weekends, driving from the Gulf Coast to Lake County, he did the legwork that the defense had not had time to do before the trial. He drove to Eatonville, and back toward Mascotte, then up toward Okahumpka, to the spot where Willie Padgett's car had stalled. He drove to the scene of the alleged rape near the Sumter County line, and then drove back to the Groveland train depot. He jotted down speeds and minutes and distances; he tried to make sense of the prosecution's time line. But it made no sense.

Bunin not only located alibi witnesses that Williams and Akerman had been unable to find, but also tracked down Lawrence Burtoft, the young man who had spoken with Norma Padgett in his father's café the morning after she'd allegedly been kidnapped and raped. Jesse Hunter had interviewed Burtoft on two occasions, and chose not to call him as a witness. Bunin began to understand why; for, by Burtoft's account, Norma had said that her so-called kidnappers, whom she could not identify, had not in any way harmed her. Moreover, she had appeared to Burtoft to be quite calm, despite the fact that, as she'd claimed, her husband might be lying murdered by the side of the road. She had not asked Burtoft to notify the police. All she wanted, she'd said, was a ride home, and "she waited patiently while he [Burtoft] had his breakfast."

One weekend Bunin drove to Bay Lake. A long, looping road took him to the Tyson farmhouse, where he hoped to interview Norma Padgett. His hopes were not in vain: Coy Tyson voiced no objections, perhaps because Bunin was not a reporter for one of those New York papers nor a person connected in some way to the NAACP, or perhaps because his daughter's rapists had been safely tried and convicted. Norma, in a green farm dress, her hair mussed and her bare feet very dirty, scarcely resembled the girl with the blond curls and homemade bolero who had appeared in the courtroom at Tavares. Her story, however, was much the same, although Bunin did note a few discrepancies, most significantly in regard to her state of mind that morning of July 16. Norma told Bunin that she had been "crying profusely and [was] visibly shaken" when she'd spoken with Burtoft about her rape by the four Negroes, and that she had been anxious to find out if her husband was still alive after the black men had beaten him. Her story did not match entirely her testimony in court, and it did not match at all Burtoft's description of her behavior that early Saturday morning. As for her testimony, almost casually Norma mentioned that her daddy hadn't had much confidence about her testifying in court—he'd even bet a man that she'd "mess up" on the witness stand. She also told Bunin that she didn't care for that "nigger lawyer" one bit.

Bunin's three articles, which were printed in the *St. Petersburg Times* with hand-drawn maps of key locations in Lake County to illustrate the facts in the fiction of the prosecution's time line, infuriated Jesse Hunter, who called the stories "a dastardly lying libel on the people of Lake County as a whole." He added that Bunin and the *Times* "are creating, or attempting to create race hatred and discord in Lake County, where relations between whites and coloreds have always been good." Not one to miss an opportunity to attack Senator Claude Pepper—derisively nicknamed "Red" Pepper by his political adversaries, for he favored civil rights and organized labor—Hunter also made political hay of the "libel." He demanded that Pepper, currently in the midst of his heated reelection bid, repudiate the stories because the *Times* "has become recognized as your most ardent supporter and what they publish is considered a part of your campaign."

Bunin's series only confirmed what Franklin Williams had suspected but had neither the time nor the resources to prove: the prosecution had been hiding witnesses and evidence. He shared the articles with Marshall and Greenberg, then filed them away. They could be very useful, if the NAACP's appeal could convince the Supreme Court to overturn the verdict in the Groveland Boys case.

வ் ஸ்

I N MAY 1950, after nearly a year's leave of absence, Walter White, having failed to find another job, decided to return to the NAACP. He was not exactly welcomed back with open arms. While a sizable contingent within the NAACP had, according to Roy Wilkins, "tried to keep him from coming back," board member Eleanor Roosevelt was not one of them. Rallying behind White, she convinced the board that he should be allowed to resume his role as executive secretary, on the condition that he relinquish administrative duties to Wilkins. Franklin Williams appreciated Roosevelt's intervention on behalf of his ally and advocate, through whose influence he hoped to strengthen his position within the LDF.

In White's absence, NAACP membership had declined significantly. The drop-off was attributed in large part to the doubling of the one-dollar annual dues to two dollars, but there were concerns, too, about the growing organizational divide between local branches and the national office because of failures in leadership and coordination. Only a very small percentage of the black population—in 1950, approximately 15 million—contributed financially to the NAACP. To Morehouse College president and civil rights activist Benjamin Mays, such lack of support constituted a "tragedy" and a "calamity": "If we are going to achieve a larger share of freedom we will have to be willing to pay for it," he admonished.

Harry T. Moore had hoped that the publicity generated by the Groveland case could be used to boost membership in Florida, but there, as in most of the states, the NAACP was suffering from a crippling budget deficit and a spiraling decline in membership. Gloster Current, the director of branches, had expressed to Moore his concern over the "deplorable state of Florida branches," which accounted for his decision to dispatch Daniel Byrd, a Louisiana friend of Marshall's, to Florida to meet with the state's branch representatives. Current had also informed Lucille Black, the national membership secretary, that Moore, though certainly well-intentioned, was simply not "doing as much as could be done to revive the work in that State."

While on his speaking tour in Florida to raise money for the Groveland Boys defense, Franklin Williams had, at Current's request, visited some of Moore's urban branches in the state. Having met with representatives in Miami, Tampa, and Jacksonville, Williams had returned to New York with an authoritative report, concluding that Florida's plummeting membership could be attributed directly to Moore's leadership. Although the members in the NAACP branches of all three cities agreed that Moore's voter registration drives were impressive, they roundly criticized his endorsement of candidates through the Progressive Voters League, since it was alienating Democratic and Republican Negroes alike.

No doubt, Moore could read the writing on the wall. Nonetheless, he continued his push for justice and money. By citing unresolved issues in the Groveland case, Moore had lobbied and successfully arranged for a delegation of black leaders to meet with Governor Fuller Warren to discuss a wide range of topics politically crucial to blacks, from police brutality to voting rights. He continued traveling from county to county in Florida, and continued making speeches and raising money to fund LDF appeals in the Groveland case. He continued writing letters to editors of Florida newspapers, among them Mabel Norris Reese, in which he severely criticized Sheriff Willis McCall, State Attorney Jesse Hunter, and Judge Truman Futch. Months after the convictions, Moore was keeping the Groveland Boys case alive in his hope of saving their lives and his job, his mission, his calling. "I plan to touch many more [branches] while this Groveland Case is fresh in their minds," Moore wrote to the New York office.

Harry Moore was not the only one in the employ of the NAACP whose job stood in jeopardy. Jack Greenberg was sitting at his desk on the fourth floor of the NAACP's Manhattan headquarters working on the Groveland writs when Franklin Williams strode straight past him and into Thurgood's office. The door slammed shut. The women in the office braced themselves; they had witnessed the like of it before, a year earlier, when behind a closed door, in a bout of angry shouting, Williams had confronted Marshall about arguing *Watts v. Indiana* before the Supreme Court. Within minutes Greenberg heard "a lot of yelling and screaming and carrying on" about the Groveland Boys appeal. The Supreme Court might be hearing the case soon, and Williams wanted to be assured that he'd argue it in Washington as he did in Tallahassee. Only Marshall was not guaranteeing anything, a response that Williams interpreted as an undeserved vote of no confidence, and the disputation became even more heated. Fed up, restive, Williams wanted and demanded a straight answer. Was the Groveland case his?

Marshall told him no, and Williams exploded with "I won't take it!"

"Well . . . ," Marshall replied, with a glance toward the door to indicate that Williams was free to go.

Williams ignored the gesture, holding his ground, and Marshall laid into him like, Marshall said later, a "Dutch uncle": "Frank, I know what you're shooting at. You're shooting for either my job or Roy Wilkins's, and so far as I'm concerned, you better start shooting for Roy's because you can't take mine. You're not man enough."

Williams stormed out of Marshall's office and into Walter White's.

It wasn't just about Groveland. Thurgood knew that Williams had been complaining to White, before the executive secretary's leave and since his return, that Marshall was "less than bold in his leadership," particularly in the LDF's assault on *Plessy*. White apparently agreed; in 1949, he himself had voiced his displeasure with Marshall's not expressly combative tactics to the civil rights–friendly Judge Julius Waties Waring of South Carolina, before whom Marshall was bringing the school desegregation test case *Briggs v. Elliott*, the first of the five cases that would ultimately constitute *Brown v. Board of Education*. Waring, in turn, had arm-twisted Marshall into filing a more aggressive attack on the state's segregation laws. The confrontation had "made Marshall look either incompetent or craven," in Robert Carter's opinion, when in fact he was "not dragging his feet in this" but merely "struggling to find the right way." More important, in regard to the staff and operations of the LDF, Marshall believed that the source of his embarrassment over *Briggs* lay with Franklin Williams, who had used Walter White to influence Judge Waring.

Once the indignant Williams had detailed his exchange with Marshall about the Groveland case for Walter White, the recently restored executive assured his young colleague that "he didn't have to worry about Thurgood Marshall, that he'd get a job as long as he was secretary."

White's statement of assurance got relayed back to Marshall. As it happened, Williams had stepped out of the office, so Marshall asked the telephone operator to call him the moment Williams returned. Marshall did not have to wait long for the call. He met Williams at the door, and announced, "You're fired."

Again Williams stormed into Walter White's office. It was immediately apparent to White that in his absence power had shifted in the NAACP offices, and it was soon apparent to Williams that his ally and advocate could not make good on his promises. Franklin Williams would indeed have to worry about Thurgood Marshall, and as for that job he'd get as long as White was secretary . . . "Why, I didn't mean that," White told him.

Franklin Williams did get another job. Within weeks he had been named West Coast director and regional counsel for the NAACP in San Francisco. While his transfer to the West Coast might justly have been viewed as a promotion as well, Williams left New York in disappointment, for, he believed, he would probably never again have the opportunity to argue civil rights cases for the LDF in the U.S. Supreme Court. He told Jack Greenberg that his ambition was to one day return to the NAACP as chief, but he less optimistically confided to other friends and associates that "he felt he was being exiled." As it turned out, he would be back much sooner than he'd have expected.

D
URING THE SUMMER of 1950, Marshall decided to proceed more proactively in the Groveland Boys case. Norman Bunin's exposé in the *St. Petersburg Times* had convinced Marshall that Norma Padgett's story held more than she or the court had revealed, and in the event that the U.S. Supreme Court should reverse Lake County's verdict, he preferred to have further investigations into the case completed or at least under way before a date was set for the second trial to begin. To a meeting in New York with representatives from the American Civil Liberties Union, the Baltimore lawyer and national secretary of the Workers Defense League Rowland Watts, and *New Leader* reporter Terence McCarthy, Marshall also invited a friend from Miami, Buck Owens, of the Owens Detective Agency, and a young private investigator, one "Miss L. B. De Forest." Together, they carved out a plan.

Bunin told Marshall that "although most of the whites there [in Lake County] were happy about the conviction, many of them don't believe Norma Padgett's story." Marshall thought, and the others agreed, that it "could prove fruitful" if Miss De Forest could cultivate relationships with some of the Padgetts, "not all of whom are on good terms with Norma." It was agreed, too, that the detective "should try to get on good terms with the people of Groveland itself, especially the police chief [George Mays]," who had demonstrated a willingness to provide information to both McCarthy and the FBI. McCarthy and Watts would also brief Miss De Forest on further leads. She, it was decided, would enter Lake County undercover, as a potential buyer of real estate, and would regularly send reports back to the "realtor" Rowland Watts in New York, "to avoid any possibility of a slip-up." Marshall agreed to payment by the NAACP of a five-hundred-dollar retainer and thirty-five dollars a day, plus expenses, for the investigator's services. The deal was struck. All Miss De Forest needed to do now was pack her bags and hop on a bus for Lake County, and follow a piece of advice from Marshall, the lawyers, and McCarthy. "Keep away from Sheriff McCall," they told her, although "plied with beer, his deputies might do some talking about their part in the case."

స్త్రీ

THURGOOD MARSHALL ASSIGNED Jack Greenberg the task of writing the writ of certiorari asking the Supreme Court to hear the Groveland Boys case, and Greenberg did exactly as he had been taught: he talked first to academics and law professors; then he talked to Bill Hastie. He learned.

Recently, in the appeal of a Texas murder case, *Cassell v. Texas*, the U.S. Supreme Court had reversed the conviction of a black man on the grounds of unconstitutional jury exclusion practices, the commissioners having "chose[n] jurymen only from people with whom they were personally acquainted, and they knew no Negroes who were eligible and available for grand jury service." As the state attorney in Lake County had selected a grand jury in virtually the same manner, Greenberg made the *Cassell* ruling the first point in his petition. Closed though the mind of the Florida Supreme Court might have been to the argument, the U.S. Supreme Court, Greenberg noted, "would not be likely to treat its own precedent so cavalierly."

Further, in studying the court records, Greenberg was pleased to discover that Williams and Akerman had filed the proper motions with the trial judge in a timely fashion. They had also properly raised constitutional objections over the unfair trial atmosphere in Lake County when filing their motion for a change of venue. While Williams and Akerman themselves may have felt that they were being steamrollered by Jesse Hunter and Truman Futch during the proceedings and trial, what Greenberg felt after reviewing the transcripts and affidavits was confidence that the Groveland Boys might very well prevail at the appellate level.

Greenberg's confidence was not misplaced. On November 27, 1950, the U.S. Supreme Court agreed to hear the Groveland Boys case. The young attorney immediately began working on the brief, in which he would include "a number of old English cases from the 1700s on change of venue, because Justice Frankfurter liked English precedents."

EARLY IN THE summer of 1950, at the NAACP's forty-first annual convention, in Boston, Marshall announced to the delegates, "The complete destruction of all segregation is now in sight. . . . We are going to insist on non-segregation in American public education from top to bottom—from law school to kindergarten." To achieve this far-reaching goal in all (then) forty-eight states without unnecessary political distractions, Marshall and the board of the NAACP found it necessary to pass and adopt an anticommunist resolution, which directed the organization's leaders to "eradicate Communists from its branch units." The irony of the resolution was not lost on the NAACP itself; an article in its magazine, the *Crisis*, later pointed out, "It was one of the great ironies of the era that the nation's oldest civil rights organization discriminated against individuals on the basis of their political beliefs and affiliation." Yet, ever since the Scottsboro Boys case in the 1930s, the rift had widened between communists and NAACP executives who believed that the "radicals had been extremely severe and frequently unfair in their attempts to discredit the NAACP."

Marshall took special delight in trumping the political maneuvers of the NAACP's communist wing. At the annual convention in Los Angeles in 1949, the communist faction of the NAACP had put forth a resolution to stop the Marshall Plan, in which General George C. Marshall, after touring postwar Europe, proposed massive U.S. funding to jump-start the European economy and thereby prevent the spread of communism. Misguided in their conviction that the communists had set out to defeat Thurgood Marshall's plans, delegates at the convention were soon protesting the measure: "They're in there, the Commies are fighting, they're trying to get rid of our lawyer!" the offended delegates shouted. "They're voting against the Marshall Plan!" Marshall's plans got passed pretty easily that year.

The next year in Boston, Marshall could again boast, "we socked them good," after an unsuccessful attempt by the communist faction at the convention to weaken the NAACP's leadership by spreading rumors that vastly inflated the salaries of the LDF lawyers and the executive staff—in part with Marshall's collaboration. For Marshall had been on his way to church with some friends when he'd been spotted by a group of communists who'd wanted to know about "all this money that you and Walter and Roy make." Marshall had replied that as Wilkins, he, and White earned all that money, they deserved it, but he had not appeared to be willing to tell the agitators just how much "it" was. Then he'd paused a moment, as if to consider the matter further, and added, with a touch of glee in his mischief, "Of course, I'll tell you. If you're a member of the NAACP, you're entitled to know . . . fifty-five thousand dollars plus expenses." Pressed further as to Walter White's take, Marshall had estimated "around eighty," although he knew that White was drawing only about ten thousand dollars annually, around fifteen hundred more than Marshall himself. When one of Marshall's friends had inquired why he'd tossed out such inflated amounts, Marshall had responded that if any of those guys at the convention quoted those figures, they'd be "hooted off the floor." And "sure enough," Marshall later recalled, "the damn fools did."

The executive staff and majority delegates of the NAACP had in fact socked the communists good on virtually every resolution they'd brought to the convention floor in 1950. They walked out in frustration "and never came back," said Marshall, whose management of the communist issue in Boston earned him an oral commendation from J. Edgar Hoover (the FBI director had "evidently had the meeting monitored"). "The communists brought it on themselves," Walter White told reporters. "We have always kept the door open. But they alienated and infuriated the members by their clumsy efforts to take over the NAACP."

About the same time that the convention in Boston was ending, on June 25, 1950, communist North Korea invaded the Republic of Korea. Thus began the first significant military conflict of the Cold War. In 1948, two years before the outbreak of the Korean War, President Truman had, by executive order, desegregated the armed forces, but the U.S. Army had not been prepared then or since—and certainly not at a time of war—to effectively integrate blacks into daily military life. Racial prejudice and the negative stereotyping of black soldiers—their supposed fear of the dark, for one example—had a particularly demoralizing effect on the largely African-American 24th Infantry Regiment in Korea, in part, it would appear, because the regiment's white leadership blamed its own failures on the black soldiers in the field. When dozens of men from the 24th Infantry Regiment found themselves being court-martialed and convicted for cowardice and desertion, they began requesting NAACP representation. It struck Marshall as strange that the notable 24th, which, despite "staggering casualties," had demonstrated exceptional valor in retaking the city of Yechon on July 20, 1950, had gone from "heroes to cowards, all within a few days."

Marshall decided he would have to get the facts for himself, in Korea, but he almost immediately encountered problems in his attempt to secure military clearance for his travel. Although the FBI approved Marshall's travel plans expeditiously enough, General Douglas MacArthur, commander of the U.S. troops in Korea, cited evidence from the House Committee on Un-American Activities that Thurgood Marshall had belonged to two legal guilds whose members were known to include communists. On that basis, the State Department denied Marshall entry to the Far East. Marshall countered by appealing to President Truman, and the White House pressured MacArthur to withdraw his objections. Marshall arrived in Tokyo on January 14, 1951. He spent weeks there, interviewing blacks who'd been imprisoned at the Tokyo stockade, before proceeding to Korea. There, Marshall had to hunt down the military court's records of the "so-called trials," which he eventually found in a warehouse near Tejon. The transcripts were astonishing. In hearings that lasted mere minutes, men had been sentenced to life imprisonment. One man—Leon Gilbert, a black lieutenant—had even received a death penalty, for being absent in the presence of the enemy: to Marshall's mind, a highly suspect charge, given the testimony of two medical officers that Gilbert had not gone AWOL but had been "in a base hospital."

To track down witnesses, Marshall traveled to the front lines. "There was so much sniper fire that we couldn't even go to the bathroom without a buddy," Marshall recalled, "and then both of us had to take rifles." On one occasion, he was walking with a group of soldiers and his escort, Colonel D. D. Martin, when the sound of a rifle pop and the whish-crack of a bullet overhead sent the men scrambling for their lives into a nearby ditch. "Where are you, Marshall?" the colonel shouted in alarm; in an uncharacteristically small voice came the reply: "Are you kiddin'? I'm under you."

Marshall may have found humor under fire, but he found nothing amusing about the Jim Crow discrimination he witnessed among the armed forces in Korea and Japan. "What happened over there is that they had this big withdrawal, and the records show that that was just [the] damnedest retreat you've ever seen," Marshall said. "They were running, ducking—I mean, it was awful. And they had to stop it. And the only way to stop it was to pick a unit, and court-martial them and make examples of them, and here was this Negro unit. So that's the one they grabbed."

Marshall eventually did meet with General MacArthur, whom he characterized as being "as biased as any person I've run across." Apparently staunch in his conviction that blacks as a race were "inferior," the general had no black soldiers in the honor guard protecting him—had none in his entire headquarters, in fact—"not even in the band," Marshall noted, "and I assume that there are some Negroes who can play instruments." On MacArthur, who failed to follow, or simply ignored, Truman's order to desegregate the troops, Marshall laid the blame for the "ramrod justice" in Korea, even as he reminded the general and his staff that "the United States Air Force took just one day to end segregation. They gave a single order, and the Air Force is now an integrated, American body of men using the best efficiency and skill each man can provide in his country's service."

Ultimately, Marshall managed to have the sentences on many of the black GIs in Korea reduced, and he successfully lobbied President Truman to commute Lieutenant Leon Gilbert's death sentence to time served. In that the courts-martial and convictions of the 24th's black infantrymen so clearly demonstrated racial bias, Marshall was careful to point out that the Korean War was a battle against communism and not a war between the races. "The Red Koreans and Chinese bayoneted black as well as whites," Marshall said, adding that anyone who signed petitions for communists claiming to represent black GIs in Korea were "dupes or dopes."

In some of the GI cases Marshall determined that no injustice had been committed on grounds of race, such as one in which he concluded that the convicted soldier was "just a bad egg and is using the race question as a cover up for his misdoings." With military as with civil cases, Marshall urged his staff to exercise caution in choosing which cases to represent, to look at the person beyond the color. It was a principle Marshall had established early in his legal career at the NAACP, and one he would follow for nearly a quarter century. "My dad told me way back"—way back being when young Thurgood was growing up in Baltimore—"that you can't use race. For example, there's no difference between a white snake and a black snake. They'll both bite." Some lessons you don't forget.

# | 14 | THIS IS A RAPE CASE

*From left to right:* Thurgood Marshall, Jack Greenberg, Franklin Williams, Mr. and Mrs. Alex Akerman, James Nabrit Jr., and Robert Carter, on the steps of the U.S. Supreme Court following the March 9, 1951, argument of the Groveland Boys case. (*Courtesy of* The Crisis *magazine*)

S HE ARRIVED IN Lake County on a Greyhound bus on July 24, 1950. First thing she did, she called the Baptist minister in Leesburg: she'd be needing accommodations for a few days and maybe he could direct her to some parishioners with a room to rent? She found a place, at a home on Main Street, close by the filling station where Curtis Howard was working the night that Willie Padgett showed up after he'd been assaulted, so he'd said, and his wife had been abducted by four black men.

In her mid-twenties, wearing a plain farm dress and lugging the suitcase she'd packed with clothes, stationery, and a Bible, she introduced herself to the woman of the house on Main Street as L. B. De Forest; only that wasn't her real name. She told the woman and everyone else she met in Lake County that she was looking to buy a house with a small orange grove; that wasn't true, either. She'd come to the Bay Lake area foremost to cultivate a relationship with Norma Padgett, and through that acquaintanceship to uncover evidence that might aid the Groveland Boys case should the U.S. Supreme Court overturn Lake County's verdict. Miss De Forest was strongly opposed to capital punishment, and she was also convinced that the Groveland Boys had been victims of institutionalized injustice. Once the young woman's intentions on her visit to Lake County had become clear, Judge Truman Futch would tell reporters that a "Communist agent . . . had been sent into Lake County" and engaged in activities that violated the laws of Florida.

Two nights after her arrival, at a Baptist church service Miss De Forest was introduced to the congregation as "a stranger coming to live among us." She was welcomed warmly: "They seem to have taken me into their hearts and homes," she reported. Some of the younger ladies at the church invited her to join them for a soda at Carney's Drug Store, just across the street from where she was staying. Over vanilla Cokes they discussed possible places Miss De Forest might consider for a permanent residence, and the young stranger feigned surprise when she was told that Lake County had experienced some racial trouble last year. The ladies from the church offered details about "the case" and about the Groveland Boys. One of the ladies noted that "Negroes are o.k.," but if they "step out of their place . . . they'll burn." Another said, "The Northerners spoil them and treat them like *equals*." The woman who'd rented Miss De Forest a room in her house was also eager to talk about the rape of Norma Padgett, who, so she'd heard, had been beaten so savagely she'd been confined to the hospital for two weeks after the attack because "her breasts were lacerated and injured by the teeth of her abductors." Rumor had rewritten the reality of the case.

Over the next few days De Forest had "some success in dodging some of the realtors" keen to show her houses with orange groves in Lake County. She wore a "World Peace" pin of her own design that, she wrote, "interests everyone and is a good cover." Each night in her rented room she composed letters on the progress of her investigation, which she mailed to Rowland Watts of the Workers Defense League in New York. In the coming days, she told him, she hoped to be introduced to some of Norma

Padgett's relatives, so she expected soon to be packing up her stationery, clothes, and Bible and moving to some place in Bay Lake.

O NCE THE L. B. De Forest private investigation had been set up by Thurgood Marshall, Rowland Watts had shared with NAACP lawyers the results of the WDL's own, long-running investigation into the peonage conditions in Lake County. For the WDL, the Groveland Boys case provided an opportunity to focus media attention upon the forced labor practices common in Florida's citrus groves and at the same time to highlight, and hopefully to rectify, a criminal injustice in a death penalty case. Watts's high-level contacts in Florida, all of them sympathetic to the Groveland Boys' cause and willing to aid, if clandestinely, in the investigation, had access to official documents like driver registration records and even police department records. Among Watts's confidential informants was Milton C. Thomas, formerly an editor at the *Orlando Morning Sentinel* and now public relations director for U.S. senator Claude Pepper, sworn political enemy to Jesse Hunter and Willis McCall.

Thomas had had numerous conversations with reporters in central Florida who had been following the Groveland Boys case for their local newspapers but had felt pressured by the Lake County Sheriff's Department not to dig too deeply into the story. Ormond Powers was one of those reporters. He had covered the Groveland Boys trial for the *Orlando Morning Sentinel*, and prior to that he had reported from the scene of the Groveland riots. He'd seemed always to find himself at the side of Sheriff Willis McCall, who had spoon-fed Powers news items like the claim that all three defendants had confessed. Powers had essentially collaborated with McCall, he'd printed the news the sheriff deemed was fit to print, but he'd later come to resent the fact that he had been used by law enforcement in Lake County. One of the stories he had not reported in any depth was that of Curtis Howard, which Powers believed to be one of the keys to the case.

L . B. DE Forest hired a taxi to take her to Burtoft's Café, where Norma Padgett had sought the help of Lawrence Burtoft on the morning of the alleged rape. After speaking with Burtoft's mother about the modern six-room home and three-acre orange grove she was interested in selling, De Forest turned the conversation to the topic of Norma Padgett. "If we were to tell the truth about the case, the true facts," a neighbor of Mrs. Burtoft's said, "it would bust the case wide open, and the boys would have evidence for a new trial." The neighbor, De Forest wrote, "scoffed at the rape theory—said it was false."

Mrs. Burtoft had other neighbors who knew "true facts," too, neighbors who had even signed affidavits as to what they'd witnessed on the morning of July 16, 1949, just outside their Okahumpka home. Clifton and Ethel Twiss were already awake that Saturday morning when, sometime between 6 and 6:30 a.m., they heard a car slow down in front of their house. They heard the motor turn off, and a moment later, when Clifton Twiss "heard the motor start up again," he looked out his window and saw her: a young lady, "quite small and slender," in a light pink dress; she was carrying a white handbag. She did not look disheveled, and she did not seem to be panicked. She walked away from the car, "about 4, 5 or 6 feet away—walking toward Center Hill," and when she got to the fork she simply paced back and forth for about thirty minutes, Twiss stated—he and his wife had taken turns observing her through binoculars. They'd thought she was a hitchhiker, but it seemed funny to them "that a lady would be hitching a ride at 6 o'clock in the morning." The small, dark car had driven past the Twiss house "on the way to Groveland," after the lady had been dropped off; a white man was driving. Both Mr. and Mrs. Twiss had agreed to sign statements about what they'd seen that morning, but they had refused to testify on behalf of the defense: "Wouldn't do to be called 'nigger lover,'" Clifton Twiss said.

One of Rowland Watts's sources had informed him that the initial "police alarm," which had been radioed before Norma was found, may have indicated that the deputies were searching for a Buick. Indeed, when Deputy James Yates showed up at the Groveland jail on the following morning, one of the first questions he asked Charles Greenlee was "Where's that new Buick or old Buick you was in?" Also, the Twisses were later shown pictures of a small, dark Buick, which, they'd said, resembled the car outside their house on the morning of July 16. And Curtis Howard had testified in court that on July 16 he had been driving a '46 Buick. "I know you realize the significance and value of untangling the Buick car and Curtis Howard's activities that night," M. C. Thomas wrote to Watts, who had begun to suspect there was a "probability that [Howard] knew the Padgetts before" that weekend in July.

Watts's suspicions about Curtis Howard were well-grounded. In the days following the alleged rape, Howard had told several people around Lake County that "it was he who had discovered and rescued [Norma

Padgett] as she wandered in the woods." By the time of the trial, however, his story had become more consistent with Norma's account. In court Howard had testified that after Willie Padgett arrived at Dean's filling station in Leesburg and told Howard that Norma had been kidnapped, Howard phoned his uncle, Deputy Leroy Campbell, who appeared at Dean's in a matter of minutes and took Padgett away in his car to investigate. That might have been the end of the story for this average filling-station attendant who placed a helpful call to police, but it wasn't. Around 6:30 a.m., after he was relieved at Dean's, Howard was on his way to Groveland for a cup of coffee when, he'd claimed, he spotted a young blond girl "sitting in the grass" by the side of the road. Howard slowed his car. He knew that his uncle, a deputy sheriff, had set out with Willie Padgett to find his seventeen-year-old wife, who had been kidnapped by four black men a few hours earlier—he'd even told people afterward that on leaving work he'd gone to look for the girl himself—yet, inexplicably, after seeing a young girl (in a torn dress, by Howard's account) sitting in the grass by the side of the road just after sunrise, Curtis Howard did not connect her to Padgett's missing teenage wife. He'd testified that he "didn't pay too much attention" to the girl and kept driving on to Groveland.

At about 7 a.m. Howard arrived at a café in Groveland. There he ran into his uncle and another deputy, James Yates, along with Willie Padgett. They had still not found Norma Padgett, and Curtis Howard still made no mention of the girl he'd seen only minutes before. Instead, at Yates's request, Howard agreed to drive Padgett home; Willie wanted to change his shirt. In the eight-mile ride to Bay Lake they made two stops at the houses of Norma's relatives; Willie would testify that he "thought she might have gotten some way to get home." On one of those stops, Willie's sister-in-law showed Howard a picture of Norma. Only then, it would appear, did Curtis Howard figure that he knew where Norma was.

O RMOND POWERS HAD no problem expounding the flaws in the prosecution's case against the Groveland Boys: the lack of medical evidence; Norma Padgett's reputation and credibility, both dubious; "vagaries in both the husband's and wife's stories"; "a series of marital rifts" that were, Powers said, "substantiated." Powers told the former *Sentinel* editor M. C. Thomas that, in his opinion, "the four boys were all mental superiors to the alleged rape victim and her off-again, on-again spouse."

What Powers could not to his own satisfaction explain were the strange coincidences that brought Curtis Howard into the Groveland story, most notably the fact that Howard had actually "seen the girl not far from the alleged attack scene." Powers speculated that Howard might have a "Dick Tracy complex"—he was frequently observed hanging around the sheriff's office with his uncle, Deputy Leroy Campbell, when not at the filling station—and thus "he apparently started looking for the missing girl on his own hook." What did not make sense to Powers, though, was that Howard would fail to attach any significance to a young blond girl he'd seen by the side of the road at the exact time that he'd set out in his Buick to look for a young blond girl who'd reportedly been abducted by four black men at a roadside.

Rowland Watts compiled a list of "comments on defense in second Groveland trials" should the NAACP be successful before the U.S. Supreme Court. It was clear that Watts gave credence to Mr. and Mrs. Twiss's statements. Watts believed that Curtis Howard had not driven past Norma Padgett on the morning of July 16, 1949, but rather, the young filling-station attendant had driven to that spot and let Norma out of his car by the side of the road. In his comments, under the section heading "Discredit Curtis Howard," Watts listed a series of questions: "Why did he go to Groveland in the morning? Did he stop his car at Okahumpka? How close was Norma to car? Why didn't he stop, get out, and talk to her, knowing that a girl had been abducted in that area? Why didn't he mention fact of having seen girl to Yates and Padgett in café? Try to pin his own activities that night and the probability that he knew the Padgetts before."

O N MARSHALL'S RETURN to the New York office after his travels in Tokyo and Korea, which had overextended his calendar and his energy, he resumed working with his New York office staff on preparation of the Groveland Boys case for the Supreme Court. He had intended to argue the case himself, but his trip to the Far East, and his monthlong absence, made him reconsider his plan. He faced an awkward decision. While Robert Carter was more than capable as a counsel, he was not as especially familiar with the case as Jack Greenberg, who had prepared the brief. Greenberg, on the other hand, lacked Carter's experience, since he had only recently started working at the NAACP offices, and although he had already gained Marshall's confidence, he was not yet ready, in Marshall's opinion, to argue his own Supreme Court case.

In early December, Franklin Williams wrote to Marshall, pleading for the chance to argue before the Supreme Court. "I am sure you can appreciate my having this desire," Williams wrote, adding that it "would be the logical conclusion" of his association with the Groveland case. Marshall, however, was dismissive. "To pull you out of the west coast for a week or two would certainly deprive the Association of your services during that period," he wrote, adding, "I think you will agree that it will be better to leave things as they are."

His point made, Marshall soon realized that he did not have any other real choices. His differences with Williams did not prevent him from acknowledging the younger attorney's notable legal talent, not to mention his unmatched grasp of the Groveland case, and in the winter of 1951 he brought the "exiled" Williams back east to argue *Shepherd v. Florida* before the Supreme Court. Marshall acknowledged that Williams was not merely the best available choice for the job but also probably the best lawyer to handle the arguments, period.

On March 9, Marshall, in a heavy winter overcoat and fedora, arrived on the steps of the U.S. Supreme Court, where he posed for a photo with his LDF team: Jack Greenberg, Franklin Williams, and Robert Carter. Alex Akerman, who had worked with Greenberg on the brief for the appeal, as he himself had presented the case for the Groveland Boys' defense before Judge Truman Futch in Tavares, had traveled up from Florida to see the attorney he had partnered at the original trial, Frank Williams, argue before the nine justices on the Supreme Court. On the trip north, Akerman had run into Reeves Bowen, the assistant attorney general of Florida, against whom he had argued the Groveland case before the Florida Supreme Court. Akerman had wondered why Bowen had decided to come to Washington himself to argue *Shepherd v. Florida*. "Well," Bowen had responded, "I wasn't going to send anybody else up to be slaughtered." For, once the Court had ruled on *Cassell*, Bowen had little doubt as to what the outcome would be in *Shepherd*.

"Oyez! Oyez! Oyez!" the marshal of the court bellowed. "All persons having business before the Honorable, the Supreme Court of the United States, are admonished to draw near and give their attention, for the Court is now sitting. God save the United States and this Honorable Court!"

*Shepherd v. Florida* was called. Robert Carter, who was sharing the case with Williams, approached the podium. The NAACP lawyers were set to argue three specific issues before the Court: jury exclusion, change of venue, and lack of adequate time to prepare a defense. For reasons known only to him, Marshall had assigned the jury issue to Carter. Williams later stated that it "irritated me a little bit that Thurgood gave him that assignment because that was the issue on which I was probably at the time, according to Thurgood, the nation's leading authority." Still, Williams wasn't surprised by the move, as "Thurgood and I did not get along anyhow, not too well."

No sooner had Carter begun to present the jury exclusion argument than, in Williams's words, he "botched it up": Frankfurter immediately interrupted him by citing "five or six other systematic exclusion of jury cases" and asking Carter if the Groveland case proved to be the same as them.

"Yes," Carter answered, but when he attempted to proceed, he was again interrupted, this time by Justice Robert Jackson. He failed to see why Carter needed "to say anything more" rather than simply to quote from Florida's admission that it used a racial proportional system for jury selection.

"Well," Carter asked rhetorically, "what is the point of arguing for them?" With that, he left the podium and sat down.

It was a strange beginning, and awkward. Certainly Williams would have handled the issue differently, but he had been assigned to argue change of venue and lack of time to prepare a defense. And he soon proved himself to be equally capable of producing an awkward moment. Williams opened by "paint[ing] a picture" of the atmosphere in Lake County at the time of the Groveland Boys trial. Oral arguments came easily to the dynamic, eloquent New York lawyer, and since he had experienced firsthand the antagonistic, tension-filled environment he was describing, he effectively accomplished the task of showing that "it was impossible to get a fair and impartial trial" in Lake County. Most important, Williams knew the record "backwards and forward," and the appellate record included all those newspaper stories that he and Akerman had collected: stories of white mobs burning Negro homes in Groveland; articles quoting Sheriff Willis McCall's proclamations to the press, such as his notices that he had obtained confessions from all three defendants. Then, for no reason that was clear to him or Marshall or the justices or anyone else, Williams addressed Frankfurter: "And Mr. Justice Frankfurter, this is a rape case."

Williams cringed at the words he himself had spoken, and not just because Supreme Court protocol required that lawyers, unless they are directly posed a question from the bench, address only the chief justice. "Jesus, I wanted to go through the floor," Williams recalled, "but I was so conscious of the fact that Frankfurter had considered me excellent." Justice Jackson, not resisting the awkwardness of the moment, leaned forward and asked Frankfurter, wryly, "Felix, since when are you an authority on rape?"

Nonetheless, in Greenberg's estimation, Williams argued the case "superbly." In Florida's response to Williams, the assistant attorney general

Reeves Bowen, as he had anticipated, got slaughtered. Bowen had barely uttered his denial of the racial tension that Williams had so dramatically presented on the change of venue issue when Justice Jackson halted him with the proposition that "the hardest thing for you to overcome" is the establishment by Judge Truman Futch of special rules "in anticipation of some kind of violence."

Likewise, Bowen's attempt to defend the jury selection process was stopped short, and he was forced to admit that "a system of racial proportional representation had deliberately been used" to select grand jurors in the Groveland Boys case. His argument crumbled when he justified the jury selection process in Lake County in terms of "the historical background of the South," stating that the county commissioners "just don't think about Negroes as jurors" in the same way that they would not "think of having Negroes on a list for a social function." Justice Harold Burton wondered if there was "anything to prevent" jury commissioners from putting the names of both whites and blacks in a box and "drawing them out by chance." Justice Tom C. Clark marveled that Lake County had never heard of placing the names on a "jury wheel" and allowing spins of the wheel to randomly select the names of prospective jurors. Both justices drew laughs from the spectators and reporters. Bowen absorbed the judicial blows, and Marshall grinned from ear to ear.

Marshall relished any moment in Supreme Court proceedings that forced Southerners to defend their Jim Crow traditions before the country's top legal minds. It almost made up for the constant humiliation he'd had to endure so often in the courtrooms of the South. Except that when the lawyer for the state of Florida walked out of the Supreme Court building at the end of arguments, he would shake hands with his opponents and return safely to his home in the south of the South. No one was going to chase Assistant Attorney General of Florida Reeves Bowen out of the capital at ninety miles per hour, or drag him at gunpoint to a waiting mob along the banks of the Potomac.

Akerman, too, headed back to Florida, and Williams boarded a long flight back to the West Coast. Marshall joined the other LDF attorneys on the train to New York.

# | 15 | YOU HAVE PISSED IN MY WHISKEY

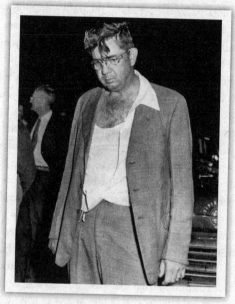

Sheriff Willis McCall. (*Courtesy of
the State Archives of Florida*)

THURGOOD MARSHALL SENT a twelve-word telegram to Dellia
Irvin: "Won new trial for Walter Irvin in Supreme Court of United
States."

On April 9, 1951, exactly one month after they had heard arguments in
*Shepherd v. Florida*, the nine Supreme Court justices handed down a per
curiam decision—that is, a decision authored by the Court as a whole
rather than by a specific judge—and thus were the convictions of Samuel
Shepherd and Walter Irvin overturned.

It had been Robert Carter's argument in regard to Lake County's grand
jury selection process that had afforded the grounds for reversal. Justice

Robert Jackson wrote a concurring opinion, in which he was joined by Felix Frankfurter, scorching the roles that Judge Truman Futch, State Attorney Jesse Hunter, Sheriff Willis McCall, and even Mabel Norris Reese of the *Mount Dora Topic* had played in convictions that "do not meet any civilized conception of due process of law." Justice Jackson pointed to "prejudicial influences outside the courtroom . . . [that] were brought to bear on this jury with such force that the conclusion is inescapable that these defendants were prejudged as guilty, and the trial was but a legal gesture to register a verdict already dictated by the press and the public opinion which it generated." So it was, Jackson opined, that "[t]he only chance these Negroes had of acquittal would have been in the courage and decency of some sturdy and forthright white person of sufficient standing to face and live down the odium among his white neighbors that such a vote, if required, would have brought." In the end, the justice accounted the jury selection issue on which the two convictions were overturned to be of "only theoretical importance." To characterize aptly Florida's handling of the Groveland Boys case required, for Justice Jackson, stronger language than that offered by counsel or by the precedent cited in *Cassell v. Texas*; and in a stinging conclusion, he provided it: "The case presents one of the best examples of one of the worst menaces to American justice. It is on that ground that I would reverse."

With those two sentences Justice Jackson had indicted the legal establishment and law enforcement offices of Lake County. Reporters scurried for comment from county officials. While Judge Truman Futch refused to issue any statement on the Supreme Court's decision, a justice on the Florida Supreme Court allowed that he was "not surprised" by the ruling. Florida attorney general Richard W. Ervin stated that he was "very disappointed" by the decision, but "the thing to do now is to go ahead and re-try the case as quickly as possible and dispose of it." Jesse Hunter was less restrained. For months he had been openly critical of the NAACP's fundraising efforts to "perfect this appeal," efforts for which there was "no reason whatever . . . except to pay their lawyers." Ironically, it had been Hunter's disingenuous attempt to demonstrate lack of bias by handpicking and seating a black man on the Groveland grand jury that had provided the NAACP lawyers and the U.S. Supreme Court the constitutional grounds for reversal. Sidestepping questions about Jackson's blistering concurring opinion, Hunter insisted to the *Pittsburgh Courier* that the case had been overturned on a "technicality." He also noted that he was "very fond of Atty. Franklin H. Williams of the NAACP."

As for the image-obsessed sheriff of Lake County, Willis McCall, he was infuriated by the Supreme Court's decision and his bad press. In a public statement he ranted against the Court's reversal and "subversive influences" like the NAACP and the CIO Newspaper Guild: "The fact that they did not appeal the case of Greenlee along with the other two is an admission of guilt. The fact is that our U.S. Supreme Court let a few minority groups such as the NAACP and their eloquent and sensational lies and the receiving of awards from the CIO Newspaper Guild, such as received by Ted Poston, Negro writer for the *New York Post*, influence them to such a prejudiced extent that they saw fit to reverse one of the fairest and most impartial trials I have ever witnessed. It is shocking to think that our Supreme Court would bow to such subversive influences."

In twenty months McCall's resentment that black reporters and the NAACP had descended on Lake County "to see that justice was done" at the trial of the Groveland Boys had hardly abated, and he sneered at the claims made by the black New York lawyer and the award-winning reporter about being chased out of Lake County after the trial: "They realized they were meddling where they had no business. . . . I informed them that no one had invited them to Florida. That they were not needed here and were only making things more complicated. . . . I suggested they return home or where they could feel safe, that we could handle things here in an orderly manner without the interference and confusion they were causing."

Twenty-two months before, in mid-July, when that angry mob was gathering outside the Tavares jail, Willis McCall had staved off a lynching of the Groveland Boys. Tacitly, he had also made a pact with the men from Bay Lake: that they would allow the rule of law to take its course, but if swift and electric justice did not come to Norma Padgett's rapists as McCall had promised—if the law did not do right—they would restore their white man's justice to Lake County. McCall was now going to have to answer to them, and he was going to have to contend with another black circus, bigger than the one before, making a mockery of lawanorder in his county and a grandstand of the court. He bristled at the thought of another trial. "I have it directly from Sheriff Dave Starr of Orange County that Sheriff McCall is 'sweating blood' over the Supreme Court decision," reporter Ormond Powers told his former editor M. C. Thomas. McCall's "mental attitude . . . is difficult to understand if his hands are clean—which I doubt—knowing something of Florida politics and gambling tieups."

Alex Akerman had contacted McCall by phone after the Groveland Boys trial. Before the lawyer had been able even to state his business, McCall had exploded. In a tirade he had warned Akerman—a "God Damn

Nigger Lover"—not to return to Lake County. Akerman was appalled, and frightened, by the sheriff's vitriol, especially since Shepherd and Irvin were at that point headed to the electric chair and Greenlee to a chain gang. Yet McCall was not boasting or gloating; he was brooding. For months he brooded, collected his press clippings, and added new names to his enemies list. He followed the progress of the Groveland Boys case through the courts; he grimaced at the names: Williams, Akerman, Williams, Marshall, Carter, Jackson, Williams. They'd be back. They'd be back, he'd tell himself, and then he'd say to himself, as he often did, "I don't push easy. Nope. I don't push easy."

T WO DAYS AFTER the Supreme Court decision in *Shepherd v. Florida*, Walter White sent a telegram to Franklin Williams in San Francisco: "Our warm appreciation for the notable part you played in speedy victory won in Supreme Court in Groveland case." That same day in April, President Harry Truman fired General Douglas MacArthur on the grounds that he was "unable to give his whole support to the policies of the U.S. Government." Although Marshall did not pretend that Truman's decision had anything to do with MacArthur's dilatory response to the segregation of black servicemen in the U.S. Army, he was pleased to note that MacArthur's successor, General Matthew Ridgway, "desegregated in about three weeks. Desegregated the whole thing."

Marshall was determined not to be in any way dilatory in the NAACP's response to the *Shepherd v. Florida* decision; he would ensure that the defense in the second trial of the Groveland Boys in Tavares would have adequate time to prepare. With Shepherd and Irvin's arraignment date set by State Attorney Jesse Hunter for August 15, Marshall immediately began putting a defense team in place, and Jack Greenberg immediately volunteered, not just because he felt it was an important case but also because he found it impossible to resist the prospect of a criminal trial in the highly charged racial atmosphere of the South. If "it wasn't very smart," as Greenberg said of his decision—for Franklin Williams's Lake County stories could be worrying—the experience would prove to be as heart-stopping as it was eye-opening.

Alex Akerman had moved to Virginia, and while he would be available for the trial, Marshall still needed an attorney in Florida to work the case: to initiate investigations, to pursue fresh leads (many of them a result of Norman Bunin's exposé in the *St. Petersburg Times*), to file briefs. Paul Perkins proved to be the man. A thirty-two-year-old black lawyer from Orlando who had attended Howard University Law School after serving in the U.S. Army, Perkins seized on the opportunity to work with Thurgood Marshall, even at the meager $3.75 per hour the LDF could afford to pay; he'd grown accustomed to working long hours for small pay or, more commonly among his indigent clients, for "ham or oranges." Deep-voiced, confident, Perkins carried himself taller and larger than his thin, five-foot-five frame, and he shared none of Franklin Williams's compunctions about driving deep into Lake County and knocking on doors. On his trips into Groveland, however, he would take along with him a friend's young son, because, supposedly, some "strange code of ethics" prevented the Ku Klux Klan from accosting a black man in the company of his children.

Part two of the Groveland Boys case began officially on July 6, when Jesse Hunter reindicted Samuel Shepherd and Walter Irvin, who had been transported from Raiford to Tavares by Sheriff Willis McCall and his deputy James Yates. (At the state prison, McCall had observed to the guard, for the benefit of Shepherd and Irvin, "You all haven't electrocuted those niggers yet? When you do, I want to watch them flinch." And Yates had added, "Wish you all would run so that I could shoot the damn hell out of you.") After the reindictment, Hunter assured reporters that the state's case against the defendants was airtight and that the NAACP was just "causing trouble" by employing a legal technicality in an attempt to keep two black men out of the electric chair. Nonetheless, he was going to make certain that this time round "plenty of Negroes" were available for jury service, he said, then added that he'd not mind trying the defendants "before an all-Negro jury."

The Lake County retrial of the Groveland Boys case promised the NAACP a national stage as large as that of the Scottsboro Boys twenty years before, and Thurgood Marshall was determined to take every advantage of it both for the political stature of the NAACP and for the cause of blacks in America. Whereas a "defense by committee" between the NAACP and communist organizations had complicated the Scottsboro Boys case, in the matter of Groveland, the NAACP, convinced of the defendants' innocence from the outset, had not hesitated to take the case, thus preventing the Civil Rights Congress or any other defense groups from encroaching on its juridical territory. With the new trial likely to command the attention of a national event, Marshall recognized that the defense required not only an attorney with estimable credentials and a record of success but also one with extensive public relations experience, a nationwide reputation, and the fortitude to perform unflinchingly on the unfriendly turf of Sheriff Willis

McCall. Marshall liked to say that he had "a big yellow streak running down my back" when traveling in the South. But not inside courtrooms and on courthouse steps: there he'd neither shirk his commitment to protecting the constitutional rights of powerless blacks like Irvin and Shepherd nor shrink from a fight with the Southern white establishment in the shape of a sheriff or a state attorney. By the summer of 1951 Thurgood Marshall had decided that he himself would represent the Groveland defendants, and with him to Lake County he would bring the swagger and confidence of the man who, just after *Brown*, would tell one newspaper publisher, "You can say all you want, but those white crackers are going to get tired of having Negro lawyers beating them every day in court."

In advance of their first trip to Florida, Jack Greenberg asked Marshall if he should reserve separate rooms or a double for the overnight train ride south. "I don't sleep with nobody who don't wear lacy drawers," Marshall informed the eager young lawyer, who later recorded his impressions of their travel aboard a Seaboard Air Line train out of Pennsylvania Station. Although Greenberg had heard Marshall's stories about his own days as a waiter in the dining car on the B&O, he had not expected that the porters would accord Marshall such reverence, and privilege. No matter that "white travelers were not yet accustomed to seeing blacks in dining cars," Marshall received celebrity treatment as well as "treats like the outside cut of the roast beef" from the chef. Waiters kept the bourbon flowing "even in dry states," while Marshall and Greenberg worked on briefs or read trial testimony to each other and took copious notes. They spent the daylight hours in Marshall's room, and at night they'd ride in the front cars for blacks as the train lumbered through the South, past the ramshackle houses huddled in the darkness.

Before he had left for the West Coast, Franklin Williams had briefed both Marshall and Greenberg on the Groveland case. Williams was convinced that no rape had occurred in the early morning hours of July 16, 1949. "Norma Padgett and her husband are very low class people," Williams said, "who live down in this isolated little swamp area not too far from Groveland," an area where Williams had conducted interviews with people who knew the young couple. From them he had gathered that the Padgetts had separated prior to the alleged rape; that because of possible spousal abuse, Norma had gone home to live with her parents. Willie had been trying to mend things between them, so he'd asked Norma out to a square dance. They'd picked up some whiskey at Frisz's Bar and Grill, then headed over to Clermont, where they were drinking and dancing until the hall closed at 1 a.m.

What happened thereafter, in Williams's estimation, was that a very drunk Willie Padgett had tried to have sex with Norma in the car, had maybe even gotten rough with her, and "she gets hysterical and she jumps out of the car and runs away," leaving behind Willie, who's scared that she's going home to "tell the Cracker parents and brothers of hers that he had attempted to rape her." And that, said Williams, would be "the end of him." For it was not uncommon in central Florida for the KKK to act as an enforcer of community morality, with night riders arriving unannounced and ready to mete out punishment at the home of a white man reported to be beating his wife or at the house of a woman who'd been cheating on her husband or drinking and neglecting her children. Klan informants had described to FBI agents a "regulation strap four inches wide and three feet long nailed to a round wooden handle" that had been used on more than a few occasions to correct moral lapses in Lake County. Coy Tyson could easily "put the finger on" Willie Padgett if he were to learn that his daughter Norma was having problems again.

The rape story, Williams firmly believed, was Willie Padgett's idea. His reunion with his wife in the early light of that Saturday morning, when Willie and Curtis Howard, on their drive back to Okahumpka, encountered Norma in Lawrence Burtoft's car, was as unremarkable as Burtoft recounted it because the couple had yet to fix their story. Willie had spoken of kidnapping, rape, and black men to Howard, but Norma had said nothing to young Burtoft that even hinted at violence of any kind. In Williams's surmise, Willie Padgett had run up to his wife and, "out of hearing distance" of Howard and Burtoft, had said to her, "You know, Baby, you just been raped by four niggers. Don't say anything else. This is what I have told him."

Marshall and Greenberg started a list of people to track down and investigate, so as to be able to counter more effectively the prosecution's evidence in the retrial. Locating Lawrence Burtoft was going to be critical to the defense; State Attorney Jesse Hunter had essentially obliterated the young man's bearing on the case, and for an obvious reason—he contradicted Norma Padgett's testimony. Paul Perkins had tracked down some alibi witnesses, including a waitress at Club Eaton, a college girl, who recalled that Shepherd and Irvin had tarried there until at least 2 a.m. A private detective in Miami had recommended to Marshall an expert to evaluate the plaster casts and tire tracks that had roused Franklin Williams's suspicions. The list would grow.

So would the legwork. Once they had gotten settled in Orlando—

Marshall among some willing black families and Greenberg at the San Juan Hotel, because "feelings generated by the Groveland case still ran so high" there was no family willing to risk a Jewish lawyer being spotted at its address—Greenberg and Perkins conducted investigations around Groveland during the day, and at night Marshall and Perkins would join Greenberg at the hotel, which was owned by a friend of Alex Akerman, for strategy meetings. On one of their daytime excursions, Greenberg and Perkins paid a visit to the Irvins, who still lived in Groveland, for unlike the "uppity" Henry Shepherd, who'd deserted the citrus groves for a farm of his own (and been ruined for it), Cleve Irvin knew his black man's place. Their visit revealed that Walter had rented his room in his parents' "unpainted, weather-beaten" home; moreover, the door to the room had a lock on it. Therefore, Greenberg reasoned, the deputies' confiscation of Walter's pants and boots as evidence constituted "an illegal search and seizure," since Dellia Irvin would have had no legal authority to hand over her son's belongings.

As Greenberg traveled around Lake County under "battlefield tension" it struck the young lawyer that residents who were unwilling or afraid to voice their opinions about the Groveland Boys case might respond more readily to the impersonality of a public opinion poll as to whether the defendants could get a fair trial in Lake County. Marshall agreed, and the NAACP was able to hire, at cost, an up-and-coming pollster by the name of Louis Harris, on behalf of the Roper Center for Public Opinion Research at Williams College, to conduct a survey of the Lake County population. Harris soon discovered he had a shadow, and he claimed that ultimately Willis McCall chased him out of town.

Through the summer and into the fall, Greenberg and Marshall traveled by train back and forth between New York and Florida. Steadily they were building a defense for the Groveland Boys, while Perkins continued tirelessly to comb Lake County for potential witnesses. The strategy, put in place by Marshall and Williams in the first Groveland trial, had been to "create an error in the case, so that we could get it reversed on appeal." Once they'd won the appeal, it was the lawyers' hope that with the passage of time, "feelings would have leveled off and you would have a chance": a chance perhaps to prove reasonable doubt in the second trial; or maybe Norma Padgett would have "a change of heart." The lawyers' legwork was beginning to make of chance the possibility of an acquittal. Time at least appeared now to be on their side. As Williams had reminded Greenberg and Marshall months before, "Anything can happen in the interim."

∽ ∾

L. B. DE Forest was having no problems insinuating herself into the daily life of the Lake County communities she visited. She had contacted the ministers at various churches and set up meetings with church members to discuss the abolition of capital punishment. The Baptists and the Methodists were especially supportive of her cause; a Catholic priest, on the other hand, advised her not to waste her time. "Prisons breed criminals," he'd averred, and "no matter how much is done for them, they plan for one thing, escape and freedom. They will kill to free themselves, if they are given the opportunity." She spent several hours with Judge F. R. Brandon of Groveland, who avouched his opposition to "chairs of torture" and entered his signature in her "book" petitioning support of her abolitionist campaign. The judge also offered some personal views on the Groveland Boys case; he "knew one of the boys who were arrested for rape, and thought the punishment too severe," and he deemed the Tysons and Padgetts to be "drinking, shiftless, no-account white trash." A newspaper editor in Leesburg meanwhile agreed to publish her poem "Mother Love." And her "World Peace" pin continued to rouse interest among the county residents. She was making useful connections.

Not everyone was receptive to Miss De Forest's cause. On August 4 in Leesburg, she'd spoken with some of the younger police officers and firemen who had been quite willing to sign her book until the chief of police, Bill Fisher, convinced them that to do so might not be wise. On that same occasion Miss De Forest met the man she'd been warned to stay clear of in Lake County. He was wearing his white Stetson as he lumbered toward her. He looked askance at her peace pin, and her petition. When she voiced her disfavor of capital punishment, enlisting names of abolitionist supporters like Alex Akerman, he growled that Alex Akerman was "no good," and as for her stance on the death penalty, he dissented, " 'An eye for an eye' is the justice I believe in." Then Willis McCall showed her his back and walked away.

More than a few whites that Miss De Forest encountered—Harry McDonald, for one—firmly believed that the Groveland Boys had confessed to rape, as the sheriff had so widely advertised. If De Forest didn't believe it, Harry suggested she visit the state prison in Raiford, where "she could hear it from their own lips." Sure though Harry was, on the night of the rape, he himself, as night watchman at Edge Mercantile, had crossed paths with Charles Greenlee miles away from the crime scene. In Harry's opinion, all four defendants "should have been shot on the spot and not cost the state the expense of a trial."

Curtis Howard signed Miss De Forest's book. When she looked more closely at the signature, however, De Forest discovered that the shifty Howard had written down the name of a coworker, Marvin Smith. And Marvin Smith, it turned out luckily for Miss De Forest, knew "the Padgetts and their friends intimately." Newly wed, Smith and his wife, Marian, the organist at the Baptist church, obliged De Forest with a tour of Groveland. As they drove past the cement shack that had housed the Blue Flame, Mrs. Smith noted that it had been "closed after the rape incident but is now rented to a negro family." Mrs. Smith also noted that Norma and Willie "were acquainted with the four colored boys"—not surprisingly, as Norma came from "poor whites" and "did not bear a very good reputation." Another of Howard's friends and coworkers, Thomas Virgil Ferguson, "had nothing good to say about the Padgetts," either. As De Forest wrote in her report, Ferguson "was disgusted with the Padgetts, and believes they could tell more, if a little pressure were used."

With her peace pin and petition book, L. B. De Forest continued to make her way toward Bay Lake, the clannish swampland in the south of Lake County, an area where she assumed most outsiders felt, and were, unwelcome. Seemingly oblivious to danger, and determined to find Willie Padgett, she boarded a bus in Leesburg on August 2. She got off the bus in Groveland and asked the proprietor at the station where Padgett lived. He suggested she talk to "Ma Padgett," who lived in a house on Main Street. Ma Padgett invited the pleasant young woman in for lunch. De Forest was surprised by the hospitality.

As it happened, a son had borrowed the family car, so Ma Padgett wasn't able to drive her unexpected visitor down to Bay Lake; however, one of her neighbors, a Mrs. Flowers Cockcroft, was willing to help. A short while later, Miss De Forest was traveling over a dirt road with Mrs. Cockcroft and her young children—with the wife and children of the man who, as Terence McCarthy had briefed De Forest, had led the night-riding mob in Groveland—past the scattered bricks and charred remains of Henry Shepherd's home. Mrs. Cockcroft remained silent, her eyes focused on the road before her.

Norma and Willie were not at home. Nearby, Norma's aunt was, and she introduced Miss De Forest to her "very cordial" family and invited her to spend the night. She met Padgetts and Tysons and Tomlinsons, who were also related, and she observed that they "live in a primitive way" in

Bay Lake: "No bathrooms, out-houses a distance from the house; electric lights and oil stoves." On fifty acres of Tyson property were "a horse, cow, hogs, chickens and tractor," as well as a smaller house, owned by Norma's uncle, in which Willie and Norma were living together again. That Betty Lou Tomlinson, Norma's cousin, "talked about the case quite frankly" with the visitor did not sit well with other of the relatives: The Joiners especially "did not like the idea," De Forest wrote. Betty Lou affirmed that the Grove-land Boys had been offered liquor "to repay them" after they'd stopped to help Norma and Willie by the side of the road—an important narrative detail omitted in the trial testimony.

Late in the afternoon of August 2, on her tenth day in Lake County, L. B. De Forest found herself finally face-to-face with Norma Padgett, at a prayer meeting. Norma was holding a newborn boy in her arms. A year after her alleged rape by the Groveland Boys "Norma had just given birth to a white child," De Forest reported, and also noted that Willie "seems fond of his baby." He was now working at a nearby sawmill and "finishing a course in farming." Norma and Willie took a liking to the stranger; they, too, invited her to stay overnight and to go fishing with them the next day. Miss De Forest said yes, twice. In her bag she'd been carrying around a baby gift; an embroidered bib, should she and Norma eventually meet. Norma accepted the bib with a smile.

The friendliness and hospitality emboldened De Forest. She began cir-culating among the parishioners at the prayer meeting of the Bay Lake Mis-sionary Baptist Church. They admired her peace pin; they wondered about her book. She explained that her book was a petition to abolish capital pun-ishment, and the Bay Lake Baptists nodded. They leafed through the pages, surveyed the signatures. De Forest handed one woman her pen. The woman turned to the last page of signatures and penned in her name. The book and pen were passed from one Bay Lake resident to another, from Tysons to Padgetts to Tomlinsons to Joiners. "None of the Padgetts are in favor of capital punishment," De Forest wrote.

Miss De Forest spotted Willie Padgett. He was standing beside Norma, Norma with a baby in her arms. De Forest thought that maybe "they would help to save the two boys from the chair, and shorten the life sentence of the youngest boy, even if . . . they committed the alleged rape." She approached the young couple with a smile on her face, with the pen and book in her hands.

⤙ ⤚

THURGOOD MARSHALL WAS in New York on November 6, the day before preliminary motions were scheduled to begin in Tavares. He was planning to fly into Orlando on the seventh. Perkins, Greenberg, and Alex Akerman, who had returned to Florida for the trial, would deal with the hearings on the motions the defense had filed. Akerman was staying at the San Juan Hotel, as was Greenberg, who had requested a 7 a.m. wake-up call to allow sufficient time for him and Akerman to drive comfortably to the Tavares Court House with Perkins for a 10 a.m. appearance before Judge Futch. The defense had moved for a change of venue and for the disqualification of State Attorney Jesse Hunter as prosecutor on several counts, including the failure of the prosecution to notify defense counsel of witness Lawrence Burtoft, and its dissemination to the press of the defendants' alleged confessions, which would clearly have then become inadmissible as evidence. The probability of success in the removal of Hunter as prosecutor was slim, but the possibility for a change of venue was strong, given the Supreme Court ruling and Justice Robert Jackson's concurring opinion citing the original Lake County trial of the case as "one of the worst menaces to American justice." In another county, at the very least, the Groveland Boys would be relieved of any further court-ordered interactions with their greatest menace of all, Sheriff Willis V. McCall.

Just after sundown on November 6, one hundred fifty miles north of Orlando, Samuel Shepherd and Walter Irvin were expecting soon to be leaving the Flat Top—the windowless, white-concrete maximum-security facility enclosed by a wall inside the Florida State Prison in Raiford—where they'd spent the last two years in their individual cells. The Flat Top, built in 1935, housed only the most violent offenders, and a small room in the middle of the rectangular structure housed the electric chair. It had been used ten times since the two Groveland boys had been incarcerated there. Shepherd and Irvin could at least hope that they would not be facing electrocution now that the Supreme Court had overturned their convictions and Thurgood Marshall was handling their case. Both men were wearing their prison-issue pants with a dark stripe down the side. Shepherd had thrown on a sweatshirt and a baseball cap as well, and Irvin had put on a light jacket for the drive down to Tavares. They waited in their separate cells for the prison transfer that would take them back to Lake County for their hearing in the morning.

That evening a black prisoner in handcuffs had been delivered to Raiford from Lake County by Sheriff Willis McCall and Deputy James Yates. Killing two birds with one stone, they'd dropped off the new inmate and were now picking up the two Groveland boys on death row. They escorted the two prisoners, cuffed together at their wrists, to McCall's brand-new 1951 Oldsmobile 98 with the Rocket V8 engine. McCall ordered both men to sit in the front seat; Irvin entered first. Yates got in the back. Once they had driven outside the main gate, the law officers voiced some thinly veiled threats and made a show of drawing and aiming their pistols. "I am ready now for anything," McCall boasted, but the two prisoners had become so accustomed to the sheriff's ways that "we didn't pay much attention to them," Irvin said.

The sedan smoothly rode the pavement on the long, quiet drive down U.S. 441. It was a cool evening, and McCall had turned on the car's heater. He turned east off 441, toward Weirsdale in Marion County, and at the intersection of Weirsdale and Umatilla roads, he pulled up next to a car at the roadside. It was Yates's car; the deputy had met the sheriff at the intersection for the drive up to Raiford. The deputy asked McCall to wait until he made sure his engine started, and when it did, Yates headed east on County Road 42, which ran through the Florida scrub and longleaf pines of Ocala National Forest. McCall followed slowly behind. Several miles on, both cars turned south on County Road 450, a little-traveled, unlit clay road. It wasn't the quickest route to the Lake County jail, Irvin knew, and he knew, too, he'd get nowhere asking McCall questions. They had crossed into Lake County; they were not far from Umatilla and Willis McCall's house in Eustis. The sheriff knew the back roads well.

Over the radio, McCall told Yates, "Go on ahead." Yates answered okay, and the two prisoners watched the taillights of the deputy's car flicker as it sped away and, taking a curve, disappeared. McCall hit his siren briefly, then began to rattle the steering wheel.

"Something is wrong with my left front tire," the sheriff said as he pulled off to the side of the road. He reached under his seat for a large metal flashlight with a red band around it and got out of the car. After checking the tires on all sides, he slid back into the driver's seat and continued down the same dark road. Yates was nowhere to be seen. The Oldsmobile had gone maybe two miles when McCall rattled the wheel again, and again he stopped the car and got out. He kicked the right front tire.

The door of the sedan swung open. "You sons of bitches," McCall said, "get out and get this tire fixed." Samuel Shepherd set one foot down on the sandy soil. As he stepped into the dark Florida night, behind him, cuffed to him at the wrist, his friend Walter Irvin stumbled out of the car. The sheriff stepped back from the door. He drew his gun from his holster.

᳅᳅

THURGOOD MARSHALL WAS sleeping soundly at 409 Edgecombe Avenue when the telephone awoke him early in the November morning. It was Alex Akerman, calling from the San Juan Hotel in Orlando.

"Well," he told Marshall, "we don't have any more case, because you don't have any more defendants." Half awake, Marshall struggled to grasp what Akerman was telling him. "They were killed tonight by the sheriff," Akerman said.

The phone rang at 7 a.m. in Jack Greenberg's room at the San Juan. Roused from his sleep as he'd requested, he picked up that morning's *Orlando Morning Sentinel*, which had as usual been slid under the door. He was jolted awake by the headline splashed across the front page:

### Lake County Sheriff Shoots Two Negroes

Willis McCall standing before his Oldsmobile 98. Samuel Shepherd (*facedown*) is dead, and Walter Irvin is critically wounded. (*Courtesy of the State Archives of Florida*)

Greenberg tried to focus on what he was reading. Smaller headlines jumped out at him: "Officer Kills Suspect in Attack Case." "Pair Enroute to Hearing Try Escape." The name Sheriff Willis McCall was everywhere on the page. McCall had shot the Groveland boys. Shepherd was dead. Irvin was in the hospital, critically wounded. Tried to escape?

Walter Irvin (*right*) survived being shot by Sheriff Willis McCall.
(*Courtesy of the State Archives of Florida*)

None of it made sense to him. Greenberg got on the phone immediately to confirm that the paper had gotten the story right. Yes, Shepherd was dead, but Irvin had survived the shooting. Akerman had already called the FBI's Miami office, saying he "wanted to furnish information with regard to a murder." Thurgood Marshall would arrive in Orlando later in the day. Perkins rushed off a telegram to Governor Fuller Warren to request an immediate investigation into the "killing of Samuel Shepherd and mortal wounding of Walter Irvin by Sheriff Willis McCall." The three lawyers sped off to Waterman Memorial Hospital in Eustis, where Irvin lay in critical condition.

Greenberg, Akerman, and Perkins, as the attorneys for Walter Irvin, were granted permission to speak with their client in the company of a doctor and a nurse. They had barely glimpsed Irvin—in a white hospital gown, his head propped up on two pillows, strips of adhesive tape that ran diagonally from below his left jaw across his nose to the corner of his right eye, a red rubber nasogastric feeding tube inserted through his nose and ending in his stomach—when they were intercepted by a burly man with "the build of a blocking back" and a shoulder holster and pistol "draped over his

250 pound frame." Akerman had stepped toward Irvin's bedside as he'd asked his client to tell him "exactly what happened. Just tell the truth as you've always done," but before Irvin had been able even to attempt a reply, the burly man ordered the three lawyers out of the room: "You might as well go away because I ain't going to let you in."

Greenberg had heard enough of Franklin Williams's hair-raising stories about the hulking, sadistic deputy James Yates to know whom they were confronting. Akerman explained to the deputy that they were visiting by permission of the patient's doctors, and he cited specific language from Florida Statute 901.24 allowing an attorney to meet with his client, in private if so desired. The statute did not convince Yates to grant the lawyers access to their client; instead he made them wait in the hall while he disappeared into another room. On his return, Yates apprised the lawyers that they'd have to receive written permission from Judge Truman Futch in order to get past the deputy's 250-pound blockade. "I have orders not to let anyone talk to this boy," Yates said.

He had gotten his orders from Willis McCall, who himself had been admitted into the hospital. In a room down the hallway from the man he had shot, he was, according to the doctors, "suffering shock and a heart condition." Akerman attempted to reach Judge Futch, while, as Greenberg noted, "Yates kept us under surveillance from a hospital window." When reporters began arriving at Waterman Memorial Hospital, the lawyers could tell them only that Deputy Yates was refusing to allow them access to their client. Akerman elaborated: they would see Irvin "when the law gives us our rights," although he was convinced that McCall "is still in control of Irvin and all his activities, and it is my opinion that the only reasonable inference that can be drawn from McCall's activities is that as long as he can prevent it, he will not permit Irvin to tell his attorneys the facts leading up to the killing of Shepherd and the wounding of Irvin." It was obvious to the lawyers that McCall and Yates were hoping Irvin would die from his wounds before he had the chance to give a statement.

Hours passed, and still no word from Truman Futch. With Irvin totally under the guard of Deputy Yates and the insidious Sheriff McCall in a room down the hall, the lawyers' unease over their client, already critically wounded by the man responsible for his safe transfer to Tavares, continued to grow. When they voiced their concern to hospital officials, one doctor, outraged at the presumption of the sheriff's department, simply stormed past the unacknowledged, startled Yates to check on Irvin's condition. And two FBI agents flashing shields and identification managed to intimidate a flustered Yates out of his post while they proceeded, unbeknownst to the lawyers and the reporters, to interview Irvin for forty-five minutes, until an attending nurse intervened because the patient "appeared to be in pain." Shortly thereafter rumors were circulating around the hospital that Irvin had told an "entirely different story" of the events that led to Shepherd's death and his own injuries.

Willis McCall, meanwhile, had barricaded himself in his room with Assistant State Attorney A. P. "Sam" Buie, the former University of Florida football standout who had aided Jesse Hunter in the prosecution of the Groveland Boys, as well as McCall's old friend Judge W. Troy Hall, who also happened to be in charge of the coroner's inquest into the manner of Shepherd's death. Together they had worked on McCall's statement detailing the events of the previous evening, so that by the time the FBI agents Wayne Swinney and Clyde Aderhold arrived at the sheriff's bedside, he was ready to talk. With their notebooks in hand, the agents followed McCall through his tale of the prison transfer that landed him as well as Irvin in the hospital and Samuel Shepherd in the morgue.

McCall, Yates, and the two prisoners had left Raiford in the early evening, the sheriff avowed. McCall had dropped off Yates at his car in Weirsdale, and he had then followed the deputy across the Ocklawaha River Bridge. He'd lost sight of Yates's taillights where the clay road curved. About the same time, he'd begun to feel a strain on the steering wheel, and when he pulled the car over, he noticed that the tire was "half way down." So he had radioed Yates and told him to send someone from the Gulf service station in Umatilla to fix his flat. Right then, McCall said, Samuel Shepherd spoke up about having to relieve himself.

"He said, 'I will piss in my britches if you don't let me out.' I said, 'All right damn it get out and get it over with.' Those were my exact words, and I opened the door, and they both got out of the car, and just as they stepped out of the car, and just as Shepherd was straightening up from getting off the seat, he hit at me with a flashlight and yelled to Irvin to 'get his gun' and he hit me with the flashlight."

The agents were busy scribbling. McCall continued: "At that time one of the boys, I don't know which one, grabbed me by the shirt . . . grabbed me by the hair of the head and had hold of my shirt and my hair, and then I grabbed for my gun and got to it before either one of them did and started shooting it. I just had to do it, it was either me or them and I beat them to my gun." The sheriff had emptied his gun; then, with Shepherd and Irvin lying in a ditch, McCall had made another radio call to Yates. "The niggers tried to jump me!" he'd screamed. "I had to shoot them!"

The sheriff reenacted parts of the shooting for the agents. He showed them his torn shirt, his broken eyeglasses, the powder burns on his coat. He answered their questions. He also told them that he was not willing to give a signed statement at this time but added that he "might possibly furnish a statement at a later time."

Deputy James Yates, who told the FBI agents that "he knew nothing of the shooting," since it was all over by the time he'd gotten back to the sheriff's car, also declined to make a statement. He said that for now he "would rather think over the matter" and would consider "furnishing a statement to the Bureau at a later date."

To McCall's dismay, agents Swinney and Aderhold continued poking around the hospital; they talked to physicians, nurses, and the administrative staff. In succeeding days they visited the scene of the shooting, took samples of McCall's hair, examined the sheriff's automobile, and attended Samuel Shepherd's autopsy. They were able to verify some important facts and to establish a chain of events that did not seem to be in dispute.

The agents learned, too, that within an hour of the shooting numerous automobiles had converged at the scene, many of them carrying friends of the sheriff. Among the first to arrive was Spencer Rynearson from the Gulf service station, who, despite the fact that the bodies of two black men were lying next to the car, had been instructed by McCall to change the tire. He had thrown the flat in the back of the sheriff's Oldsmobile; in one of the grooves he'd noticed the nail that had punctured the tire. Yates had interrupted a city council meeting with news of the shooting, and McCall's Umatilla friends, the town's mayor, and members of both the city council and local Kiwanis Club had soon shown up at the roadside, along with police. State Attorney Jesse Hunter had arrived about the same time as Marie Bolles, the editor of *Eustis Lake Region News*, who'd promptly begun photographing the disheveled McCall at the scene: He's standing alongside his car, his rumpled, torn shirt hanging over his belt, a cut on his temple plainly visible; two bodies are splayed awkwardly in the grassy ditch behind him, the head of one resting on the thigh of the other; blood everywhere.

"Marie, it's just one of those things. I hate it that it happened," McCall had said to his neighbor as she, with Hunter beside her, had moved in closer to photograph the two dead prisoners. That was when Hunter "saw one of them move." Reuben Hatcher, the jailer at Tavares, had confirmed that one of the Negroes was indeed still breathing, and on Yates's car radio he'd contacted Waterman Memorial Hospital. There would be a delay; a Jim Crow car was being dispatched from the Dabney Funeral Home in Leesburg because the hospital ambulance could not be used to transport blacks. In the meantime, Walter Irvin, groaning and writhing in pain, lay unattended. Concern centered on Sheriff McCall's injuries.

Stetson Kennedy, a Jacksonville native and frequent contributor to many liberal and black newspapers, observed Jesse Hunter eyeing McCall suspiciously at the scene of the shooting that night. The sheriff was hovering around his Oldsmobile, where his trademark ten-gallon Stetson sat crumpled on the hood; his hair mussed up, his broken glasses perched on his nose, a trickle of blood on his temple yet to be wiped away, he appeared to be in a daze. His hangdog look of exhaustion and remorse won him no sympathy from the state attorney, whom the sheriff could barely look in the eye. Hunter shifted his gaze from McCall back to Walter Irvin, now curled on the ground with his knees bent and his open mouth gasping for breath. Turning again, leaning in toward McCall, the prosecutor believed himself to be out of anyone's earshot when, displeased, he spat, "You have pissed in my whiskey."

McCall was vocal in expressing concern for the black man while the small crowd of maybe thirty people waited for the ambulances to arrive. "One of them has a pulse—a good pulse," McCall said. "I hope he makes it." At the same time, McCall's boyhood friend, the judge and county coroner W. Troy Hall, was charged with conducting the inquest. In the glare of the headlights from the dozen and more cars that had gathered on the clay road, Hall had hastily assembled a jury of six "friends of Sheriff Willis V. McCall," including Marie Bolles.

Once the ambulances had arrived, both McCall and Irvin had been taken to Waterman Memorial, just six miles away in Eustis. Irvin, who had been given an injection of Demerol, had arrived in "extreme shock," unconscious and unable to answer any questions. Examination had indicated "gurgling" and "sucking" sounds emanating from two bullet wounds to his upper body and another to his neck. Doctors had removed a "lead pistol ball" from his right shoulder. They had noted that, aside from "extreme shock from hemorrhage," Irvin's mental status was normal, and within hours he'd become "oriented as to time, person and place and willing and apparently able to answer questions readily."

The next morning at the hospital, McCall and Yates, though able, were not willing to take any questions from the press. Speaking on behalf of the sheriff, Judge Hall addressed the reporters who had gathered at Waterman Memorial, and as if he were confirming the results of his own coroner's inquest—he reported that he himself had seen "a batch of the sheriff's hair" in Irvin's hand—he delivered essentially the same statement he'd worked out with McCall the night before in the sheriff's hospital room. Some in the press corps were beginning to wonder how a county official acting as the sheriff's spokesman in regard to the shooting was also going to be able to conduct an impartial inquest into the shooting victim's death.

McCall was willing to pose for a press photograph in his hospital bed. He was wearing dark, polka-dotted pajamas; behind him stood his wife, Doris, and son Malcolm while his younger son, Donnie, sat on the bed. "I'm just happy to be here with my arm around this boy," McCall told the photographer from the *Orlando Morning Sentinel*. As the newspapermen were shuffling out of the room, the sheriff, no doubt anticipating the news items he'd be obsessively clipping over the next few days, halted them with some parting words. "I expect I'll get a lot of criticism for this," McCall said, "but I'd rather be criticized than dead."

Walter Irvin's family tried to visit him that morning as well. Desperate to see their son before he slipped into a coma or died like his friend Samuel Shepherd from gunshot wounds, Cleve and Dellia Irvin had arrived early at Waterman Memorial only to be denied visitation rights by Deputy James Yates at the door to Walter's room. They had no recourse, it seemed, especially since the NAACP lawyers had left the hospital to meet Thurgood Marshall at the airport, and Cleve Irvin was scared and confused, subject to rules and procedures he had long given up trying to understand. Rights were what white people told him to do; he knew no law beyond that. So he would not even think to question the authority of Deputy Yates. Instead, with his wife he turned and walked away.

He was spotted in the corridor by the British reporter Terence McCarthy, who had covered the rioting in Groveland for the *New Leader* in 1949. The two men spoke, and Cleve, his anxiety reducing his voice to a whisper, for he did not want Dellia to hear, implored, "Please give me a truthful answer. . . . If my boy has to appear to give evidence against Mr. McCall, do you think they will kill us? Will they kill my other children? Should I take them away from here? You know, we didn't move like Mr. Shepherd [Samuel's father, Henry] did—because they didn't tell me, like they told him, that we weren't to come back to live here [after the rioting]. Do you think it's safe for us here now?" As much as McCarthy wanted to assure Cleve Irvin that he and his family would be safe, especially now that Thurgood Marshall was coming, the reporter remained silent. "To Mr. Irvin's questions," he knew, "there could be no truthful answer."

One man did manage to visit with Walter Irvin that morning. He was feeling the weight of his years; his health wasn't good, and it would soon take a turn for the worse. He hadn't much stomach for what he had witnessed on the dark road near Umatilla not twelve hours before. "Visibly shaken," he had watched the performance of Lake County's sheriff: McCall stumbling around his car, feigning concern for Irvin, telling everyone how blessed he was to survive. Till then, either the sheriff hadn't known Irvin was alive or, worse, he'd known and hadn't wanted anyone there to attend to the injured man before he died. One thing was certain, something wasn't right.

Doubt and suspicion had followed the old man home, and he'd telephoned his friend Mabel Norris Reese. "Guess what. McCall's shot those niggers," he'd said, and Reese, aghast, unable to speak, had simply let the old man tell his story while she took notes. "Mabel," he'd said, "I don't believe those boys attacked the sheriff at all. I think it was deliberate." He'd said what he'd concluded.

So, the next morning, his step slow but his direction sure, the old man was walking down a brightly lit hallway of Waterman Memorial Hospital. One hand tucked into his red suspenders, he smiled warmly back at the nurses—everybody knew him. At the doorway to Walter Irvin's room he offered Deputy James Yates a firm nod of his head, but he did not break his deliberate pace. He paused at the side of Irvin's bed; he'd gotten what he wanted, a private moment. He surveyed the room, made sure it was the two of them alone. He leaned forward, looked Walter directly in the eyes. Then, in a whisper, Jesse Hunter began to speak.

# |16| IT'S A FUNNY THING

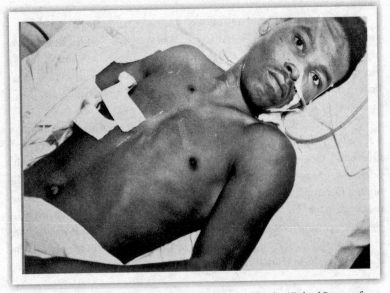

Walter Irvin at Waterman Memorial Hospital, Eustis, Florida. (*Federal Bureau of Investigation*)

T HIS IS WHAT human rights means in the United States! This is the American way of life," shouted Soviet foreign minister Andrei Vishinsky from a podium at the United Nations to Security Council members and the world. He was brandishing a copy of the *New York Post* trumpeting, in an extra edition, the latest shocking news to come out of Lake County about the Groveland Boys shooting. "I think some people should look after their own business before sticking their noses into other people's business," Vishinsky scoffed.

☙ ❧

O N NOVEMBER 7, 1951, the Groveland Boys case again exploded onto the front pages of newspapers around the country. Locally, the *St. Petersburg Times* bannered "Lake Rape Case Negro Shot, Killed" across the top of its front page, and the following day, an editorial stated that "the shooting of the Groveland defendants was inexcusable" and called the incident a "terrible black eye" for Florida justice. Reporters like Stetson Kennedy, who was covering the story for the *Nation*, were pouring into Lake County, many of them checking into the Fountain Inn in Eustis.

Amid the firestorm of publicity across the nation and even abroad over the killing of Samuel Shepherd and shooting of Walter Irvin, Thurgood Marshall landed at the airport in Orlando, where he was met by attorneys Alex Akerman, Jack Greenberg, and Paul Perkins. When they arrived at Waterman Memorial Hospital, awaiting them was a throng of journalists eager for comment from "Mr. Civil Rights." Marshall's presence amplified the importance of the recent events in Lake County, for sure; yet, comfortable though the NAACP's most public figure was with the press, he cut the reporters short. His first order of business that day was to talk to his client, Walter Irvin.

About the same time, special investigator Jefferson Jennings Elliott had pulled into the hospital parking lot in his 1950 Ford coupe, which comprised a "primitive mobile crime lab outfitted with kits for identifying semen, blood, and fingerprints; paraffin for detecting recent gun firings; portable lights for illuminating crime scenes; and a complete autopsy kit." Elliott had been sent to Eustis by Governor Fuller Warren's office to "check all angles" in McCall's shooting of the prisoners—and to "let the chips fall where they may." Heavy-jowled, with a big belly that hung over his belt and a large fedora tipped awkwardly on his head, Elliott might have walked out of a hard-boiled detective novel. Adjusting his round, horn-rimmed glasses, he told the reporters, "Well, boys, I'm here, but that's all I can say."

Hoping to keep within Lake County's jurisdiction any inquiries into the fatal shooting, Willis McCall had asked Judge Futch to have a "court-appointed elisor" investigate the death of Samuel Shepherd, but Futch had declined, stating, "the Governor said he wouldn't recognize such a person." Instead Elliott would be conducting the investigation; so, on Wednesday, November 7, with a court stenographer in tow, the governor's man was leading Marshall, Akerman, Greenberg, Perkins, Mabel Norris Reese, seven other members of the press, and a "special nurse" into Irvin's hospital room.

The feeding tube was still taped to the patient's face; Irvin was weak but lucid. The room grew very quiet in anticipation of the rumored "entirely different story" from Sheriff McCall's version of events. Alan Hamlin, the court reporter, steadied his stenographic machine. Marshall stood by Irvin's side. J. J. Elliott had his notebook and pen ready. Greenberg, Perkins, and Akerman had heard the rumors, too, but they knew no more than anyone else what specifics might make their client's story "entirely different." Also, as Reese would report, "This was the first time Marshall saw Irvin, so there could be no coaching."

"No one's going to hurt you," Alex Akerman said softly to Irvin before he began the questioning. From the outset it was evident that despite the trauma Irvin had suffered, he was sustaining no memory loss. His voice was breathy, strained, but his responses were crisp, and he delivered his answers without mental hesitation. He described being taken out of Raiford at night; he recalled being handcuffed and told to sit in the front seat. He remembered that Sheriff McCall had let Yates out of the car at Weirsdale and had then followed the deputy, now in his own car, down a clay road while talking to him on the radio. Up to that point Irvin's account of the prison transfer mirrored McCall's, but after Yates had driven out of sight, when the sheriff was rattling the wheel and claiming something was wrong with the tire, Irvin's version diverged. McCall had gotten out of the car to check the tire, but, in Irvin's account, McCall hadn't then radioed Yates about contacting the Gulf service station as the sheriff had stated.

Instead, in Irvin's telling, the sheriff had leaned in at the open door and yelled at the two prisoners, "You sons of bitches, get out and get this tire fixed." The problem was, Irvin "did not see any tires in the back, but we had to obey, because he was the Sheriff, and so we went to get out, and [Shepherd] he taken his foot and put it out of the car, and was getting out, and I can't say just how quick it was, but he shot him, and it was quick enough, and he turned, the Sheriff did, and he had a pistol and shot him right quick and then right quick he shot me, shot me right here [indicating right upper chest] and he come on and when he shot me, he grabbed me somewhere by my clothes, and snatched me . . . he snatched both of us and that threw both of us on the ground, and then I did not say anything."

"Were you still in the car when he shot you?" Akerman asked.

"I was just getting out," Irvin said, "but the bullet knocked me into the car, and then he snatched me out."

Irvin paused. The silence in the hospital room hung heavy. You could hear the scribbling of pens on notebook paper. The stenograph clicked, stopped. Without prompting Irvin continued.

"I didn't say nothing, so . . . after he snatched me, he shot me again, in the shoulder, and still I didn't say anything all the time, and I knew that I was not dead."

Irvin recounted that McCall had run around the car to get to the radio. He'd called the deputy sheriff. "I heard him say 'I got rid of them, killed the sons of bitches' but I still did not say anything. . . . I heard him say 'Pull around here right quick . . . these sons of bitches tried to jump on me and I have done a damn good job of it.' I wondered what he meant by that, because we hadn't done that . . . and then in about five or ten minutes Deputy Yates was there."

Irvin—twice wounded but still conscious, though unable to move in any case because he was cuffed to Shepherd—had no other choice: he lay quiet and pretended to be dead. Samuel's hand was pressed next to his, the two Groveland boys linked together . . . only Sammy was gone. McCall's first shot had put a hole in Shepherd's chest; the shot that followed right after, lodged now in the frontal lobe of his brain, had severed his spinal column. McCall's next two bullets had torn through Irvin's chest and side. McCall had then returned to Shepherd, lying on the ground, and shot a .38-caliber round straight through his heart.

Irvin lay quiet. He saw the headlights come from the direction of Umatilla. They lit the rear end of the sheriff's Olds before they dimmed. Deputy Yates got out of the car. He and the sheriff exchanged a few words. The deputy had a flashlight; he shone it down on the two prisoners lying in the ditch. Irvin closed his eyes, but he could sense the spot of light crossing his face, back and forth, from eye to eye, light, then dark, then light only, for a long moment, hurting his eye. He could feel the blood seeping from his nose, his mouth, in the light; he tried to hold his breath, to keep himself lying quiet, in the light pointed down on him. He couldn't stop the awful pounding of his heart when he heard the deputy's voice call back to the sheriff, "This nigger is not dead. We better kill this son of a bitch."

The hospital room itself might have gasped at that. Marshall's eyes met Greenberg's, then Perkins's and Akerman's; the horror was worse than any that Irvin's lawyers had imagined.

Irvin resumed, picturing himself lying on the ground and looking up at the deputy standing over him with a pistol in his hand, and without a sound watching the deputy lean down over him and slowly aim the gun. "The Deputy Sheriff then pointed the pistol on me and pulled the trigger, snapped the trigger, and the gun did not shoot, and so he took it back around to the car lights, and looked in it and shined the light in it, and then something they said was about letting it stay cocked, and so he turned it on me again and pulled it, and that time it fired, and went through here [indicating it went through neck] and then I began to bleed and bleed, out of my nose."

"Is that Deputy Yates you say?" Akerman asked, stunned.

"Yes, sir," Irvin replied, his voice fading. He paused to catch his breath. "He shot me the third time, but I managed to pull through OK cause I did not say anything, and did not let them know that I was not dead, and after all the people came, there was lots of people came there, and some of them predicted that I was not dead. . . . I heard some remarks that 'he ought to have been dead long ago.'"

Realizing that Irvin's story would be headlined on the front page of virtually every newspaper in America the following day, the lawyers strove to get as much testimony from Irvin as possible before doctors stepped in and called a halt to the proceedings. "I know you are tired," Akerman said, "but there is just one or two questions. Had you tried to jump him? The Sheriff?"

"No, sir," Irvin answered.

Marshall leaned in. "Where was his gun?" he asked. "Did he carry it on the right hand side next to you?"

"Carried it on his left," Irwin said.

"Did you ever try to escape that night?" Marshall asked.

"No, sir, never."

"And you were in the front seat of the car?"

"Yes," Irwin said. "He put us both on the front seat."

Perkins took a turn: "Walter, did you have good hopes of coming out of this thing alright?"

"Yes, sir," Irvin said, "I sure did, for I sure did have high hopes of coming out alright, and why would I try to escape, didn't have no reason to."

Akerman punctuated the hospital room press conference with a few final, terse questions to ensure that the reporters held the most salient facts of the shooting in their minds when they left to file their stories.

"How many times did the sheriff shoot you?"

"Two times," Irvin told him.

"How many times did Deputy Sheriff Yates shoot you?"

"One time."

"You were shot three times?"

"Yes, sir."

At that point the nurse closed the interview. Alan Hamlin folded up his stenograph. Marshall requested that Elliott have Irvin removed immediately from Sheriff Willis McCall's custody; Elliott replied that such action lay beyond his authority but that he would relay the request to the governor. Flanked by Greenberg and Perkins, Marshall proceeded downstairs to the hospital entrance, where, he knew, the reporters were expecting him to make a statement. As Irvin was still going to stand trial if he survived the shooting, Marshall felt it necessary to assume an attitude of unruffled rationality so that the recent conduct of the renegade sheriff would seem all the more extreme by contrast.

"We sincerely hope the good people of Lake County will insist that the action so obviously indicated by the sworn statement of Walter Lee Irvin will be taken immediately," Marshall announced, and when asked if the NAACP lawyers would press for murder charges against Willis McCall, he replied, "The good people of Lake County should have time to take action, but if they don't the NAACP will."

Stetson Kennedy rushed off to get further comments from hospital staff. Mabel Norris Reese called State Attorney Jesse Hunter to relate to him the details of Irvin's statement. Other reporters stuck to the NAACP team, conspicuous among them Marshall's New York friend Evelyn "Big East" Cunningham, also known as the "Lynching Editor," who was covering the events in Eustis on behalf of the *Pittsburgh Courier*. "Colored men who are accused of raping white women don't have a chance in this part of the world," she wrote. "Walter Irvin's chances found a thin string to hang on Saturday when Lake County finally woke up and began to believe that maybe he was innocent after all."

One reporter tracked down James Yates at his home in Mount Dora. The deputy appeared to be caught off guard when asked to comment on Irvin's claim that it was Yates, not the sheriff, who had fired the intended kill shot into Irvin's neck. "It's a funny thing," Yates stammered, adding, "no comment at this time."

Hunter, who "was visibly shaken" by what he had witnessed on Tuesday night, had, "since the shooting, virtually run out on Sheriff McCall," one reporter observed. "This is the worst thing that ever happened in Lake County," Hunter said. "It will ruin the county."

The FBI agents returned to their district bureau to type up their notes and file their reports. In confidential report MM 44-267 the following notation would appear: "IRVIN agreeable to lie detector test. Sheriff McCALL and Deputy YATES do not desire to take lie detector test, McCALL claims sees no reason to take test as he has told truth."

☙ ❧

BACK AT THE San Juan Hotel, the lawyers worked on strategy. Greenberg amended a motion for a change of venue, citing the attempted murder of Walter Irvin by the sheriff and his deputy as a reason that Irvin could not get a fair trial in Lake County. Marshall, meanwhile, telegraphed the Justice Department; he wanted McCall and Yates to be found in contempt of court for defying the U.S. Supreme Court "and the laws of this country." Marshall also contacted Roy Wilkins and Walter White in New York, to have them instruct all NAACP branches that as of now the Groveland Boys case was their top priority. Marshall wanted Walter Irvin's story to be recounted in every black church on the upcoming Sunday; he wanted protests staged at the local level everywhere across America. In response, Wilkins set up a plan whereby every NAACP branch would arrange a "Groveland Memorial Protest Meeting" and engage in an organized letter-writing campaign in newspapers and on the radio to draw attention to the nature of Southern justice. "We must leave no stone unturned to see to it that the entire Nation learns the facts about this cold-blooded murder of a boy in shackles," Wilkins informed NAACP officials. "We must bring every possible pressure to bear to the end that these legal lynchers are brought to justice. If we fail in this, our whole struggle for human rights will be in jeopardy." Very soon—from labor unions, from churches and synagogues, from veterans committees and fraternal organizations, from individual outraged citizens across the country—Governor Fuller Warren's office in Tallahassee would be inundated with letters and telegrams condemning Sheriff McCall's brutality.

Marshall also sent a telegram to his old friend Harry T. Moore: the one man in Florida with the tenacity and fortitude to bring pressure to bear on the men in Lake County who were not only responsible for the injustices in the Groveland Boys case but also determined "to whitewash the whole affair." Moore, in fact, had already wired Governor Warren to urge an investigation into the sheriff's shooting of the two Groveland boys; and for years, with no success but with perseverance nonetheless, Moore had been pressing the governor's office to launch an investigation into lynching in Florida. Marshall wanted Moore beside him in the Groveland Boys fight for justice, no matter the precariousness of Moore's position in the NAACP. The national office, and more particularly Gloster Current—in Marshall's view, a good company man with an eye only for budgets and membership rolls—had been building a case against Moore's management and leadership in Florida's branches, but

Marshall, by virtue of his own experience in the South, knew more particularly the hostile conditions that dedicated men like Moore had to endure continually in the regions they represented. "There isn't a threat known to men that they do not receive," Marshall said. "They're never out from under pressure. I don't think I could take it for a week. The possibility of violent death for them and their families is something they've learned to live with like a man learns to sleep with a sore arm." For Marshall, Moore was one of the heroes. In the telegram Marshall asked if Moore could meet with him on Friday, November 9, in Orlando. Moore said yes.

On November 8, newspapers across the country published Walter Irvin's version of the shooting outside Umatilla, with Irvin's claim that Deputy Yates had fired the intended coup de grâce capturing most of the headlines, none of them as sensational as the *New York Post*'s: "Blood Lust of Sheriff and Aide Bared, Florida Anger Grows in Negro Killing." The *Post* ran the headline large and provocatively on its front page, with a story by Jay Nelson Tuck, who'd found himself, like Ted Poston before him, reporting an event of even more moment than the trial he'd been sent to cover—it described law enforcement officials who were "ducking, weaving and scattering for cover today." The Associated Press picked up Marie Bolles's images of the bloodied Groveland boys lying by the roadside, as well as a portrait of Deputy James Yates, which one paper published above the caption "It's a funny thing."

State Attorney Jesse Hunter was reported to have spoken on November 8 with Governor Fuller Warren, who reportedly agreed with Hunter's recommendation that Sheriff McCall either be suspended or be ordered to resign temporarily from office. News of the meeting apparently effected a remarkable improvement in Sheriff McCall's physical condition, as he checked himself out of the hospital and then drove two and a half hours north to Jacksonville, to a hotel, for a secret meeting with Fuller Warren. In November 1951 Warren was in the midst of a statewide barnstorming tour, replete with stump speeches and country music jamborees, in an attempt to recapture some of the magic that had swept him into office in 1948. Or at least, to rehabilitate his reputation. Illegal gambling scandals had put Warren in the investigative crosshairs of his longtime nemesis, Senator Estes Kefauver. The nationally televised Kefauver hearings on organized crime in 1950 not only had exposed the involvement of numerous Florida law enforcement officials in widespread corruption, by which they raked in payoffs from illegal numbers and *bolita* games, but also had aired allegations that Warren's gubernatorial campaign had been heavily financed by prominent figures in organized crime. Kefauver had invited Warren to Miami to testify, but Warren had refused. Then, in 1951, resolutions calling for Warren's impeachment had been introduced in the Florida House of Representatives, so the governor was now fighting for his political life. It took Willis McCall not much more than an hour to convince the former Klansman and governor that he might want to reconsider the wisdom of a suspension or temporary resignation for the sheriff. That done, Sheriff McCall headed back to Eustis, where he had set up another late-night, closed-door session, this time with Warren's special investigator, J. J. Elliott, at a Lake County hotel. Again, no doubt by extortionist means, McCall got results, and Elliott got a singular role in the imminent coroner's inquest.

Early on Friday, a young FBI informant was riding the road to Tavares with several Klansmen, among them Eddie Jackson, the Exalted Cyclops of the Orlando Klan. Jackson wanted to run a plan by Willis McCall, and if the sheriff okayed it, the Klan would be able to "break you in right," Jackson told the young, supposed prospective Klansman. They'd arranged to meet the sheriff in the men's room of the courthouse. There Jackson explained that he'd come to Lake County with "a couple of the boys" to do a bit of a favor and to initiate a new member into the Klan. Jackson then put it more bluntly: they'd come "to kill Alex Akerman." To the Klansman's disappointment, McCall rejected the idea summarily. "No, I'm in the clear on this case," the sheriff told Jackson, "and I don't want you to do it, it would only cause trouble."

McCall had not said anything about them not scaring Akerman, though. So the Klansmen drove to Eustis and parked their car across the street from Waterman Memorial Hospital, where they waited for Akerman to arrive for a visit with his client. Only Akerman didn't—he was working in Orlando that particular day—so Jackson and his men turned their attention to other potential targets, like that Negro who was "a big SOB in the NAACP."

I T WASN'T LIKE Harry T. Moore at all, Marshall thought. Not only had Moore failed to show up for their Friday meeting in Orlando, but he'd failed even to notify Marshall that he'd not be there.

Over the past twelve months the pressure on Moore from the NAACP's director of branches, Gloster Current, had been intensifying. A year earlier, the New Orleans field secretary and former Harlem Globe-trotter Dan Byrd had been dispatched to the Florida State Conference in Tampa with instructions to do a "hatchet job" on Moore, although, when the delegates' votes were counted, Moore had managed to hold his position as executive secretary in Florida. In only two weeks, however, the regional director for the Southeast, Ruby Hurley, along with Walter White, would be attending, at Current's behest, the 1951 annual state conference in Daytona Beach, and Hurley's reputation was stellar: she "always delivered the votes." In the past, Marshall had kept himself distant from Current's branch business, as Moore surely knew. Still, Robert Carter and other of the NAACP lawyers were "wondering if Moore hadn't gotten cold feet" when he failed to show up for the November 9 meeting, albeit Marshall had made it clear to him that he wanted to discuss the Groveland case.

By November, too, the cumulative stress of the Groveland Boys trial and appeals and the now-thwarted retrial, from July 1949 nearly to the end of 1951, was beginning to wear on the normally self-possessed Moore. His commitment to a rectification of the injustices suffered by Shepherd, Irvin, and Greenlee had become hazardous. A citrus grower in Moore's hometown of Mims had opined to an NAACP official that Moore's "neck ought to be broken." Also, recently letters had been threatening Moore with injury, or worse, for his work on behalf of the Groveland Boys; he had taken to carrying the letters on his person in the event that harm came to him. He had confided to one NAACP leader that he was now "afraid to travel in the daytime." His fears were not unjustified; later that winter, on returning with his wife, Harriette, to their house in Mims for the weekend, he found the door lock broken, their home ransacked, and his shotgun stolen.

Nevertheless, despite the threats, and in the face of his fear, Moore had continued—indeed, had increased—his efforts in the Groveland Boys' cause. He organized mass meetings and protests; he delivered speeches. He helped the Shepherd family retrieve Samuel's body, with the assurance that the local branch of the NAACP would cover the cost of their son's funeral. He seized every twist and turn in the Groveland case as an opportunity to write letters to newspaper editors like Mabel Norris Reese, who was finding it more difficult to defend the injustices of law enforcement in Lake County. He remained Sheriff Willis V. McCall's most vocal critic. He also continued to support and complement the efforts of Thurgood Marshall and the LDF in Lake County, no matter that, for whatever reason or misunderstanding, he had failed to appear at that meeting in Orlando on November 9.

Late in the evening of November 9, Judge W. Troy Hall began the official proceedings for his coroner's inquest with a viewing of Samuel Shepherd's body by the jury in the company of special investigator Elliott, the state attorney Jesse Hunter, McCall, Yates, and members of the press as well as a nurse and a court reporter. On Saturday morning, November 10, the inquest resumed at Waterman Memorial Hospital, where Irvin's attending physician, Dr. Rabun Williams, was scheduled to, but did not, testify, the judge having determined the doctor's testimony to be unnecessary. The jury, press, and county officials proceeded with Judge Hall and J. J. Elliott to Walter Irvin's room, where they heard the same story he'd told to his lawyers and members of the press on Thursday. Both Hall, as coroner, and Elliott questioned Irvin at length, but his recitation of the events of November 6 did not vary in any detail from his previous account. After forty minutes of testimony, Irvin tired; he was wheeled from his room to the waiting ambulance that delivered him to the prison hospital at Raiford.

The inquest next moved to the roadside near Umatilla, where, in the view of Judge Hall, an attempted escape, not an unprovoked murder, took place. Hall led his friend Willis through the presumably evidence-based version of events. In the trunk of McCall's Oldsmobile lay a tire, the tire that another of the sheriff's friends, Spencer Rynearson, had changed shortly before most of the witnesses had arrived on the scene Tuesday night; lodged in one of the "grooves between the tread design" of the tire was, as Hall pointed out to the jury and the press, a box nail. Hall then addressed McCall: "I will ask you to examine this nail here in the tire and ask you to state whether or not it appears to have been worn by contact with the pavement." After claiming that he'd never noticed the nail until "someone pointed it out to him," the sheriff answered, "Yes, it is worn, it looks as if it had been in the tire while the tire was being run on; of course, it is a little rusty now."

Mabel Norris Reese, who had heard Walter Irvin describe twice, and quite believably, what had occurred at the roadside on the night of the prison transfer, was not convinced by the physical evidence: "The nail on the tire was so obviously planted that it made you sick that people would stand there, look at it and believe it."

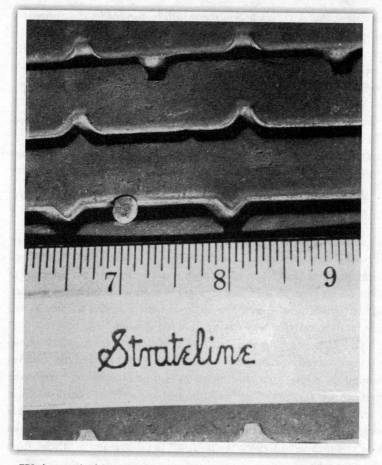

FBI photograph of the nail in Sheriff Willis McCall's tire. (*Federal Bureau of Investigation*)

Hall then had McCall lead a walk-through of the roadside incident. Noticing that the ground was dug up where Shepherd and Irvin had been lying after being shot, Hall asked, "Was this ground dug up in this manner at that time?" McCall said no, as he surveyed the three square feet of overturned sand and clay, and explained, "The F.B.I. has been sifting it, trying to find the bullets." One bullet in particular—the bullet, still unaccounted for, that had passed through Irvin's neck—posed a significant challenge to the credibility of McCall's and Yates's rendering of the prisoners' daring attempt to escape. According to the sheriff, he had fired the six rounds in his gun at the same time as he had backed away from the two prisoners when they'd attacked him. By Walter Irvin's account, however, the last shot had been fired by Deputy Yates, when he had stood over Irvin, who was lying faceup on the ground, and had aimed the gun straight down. The bullet, which had struck mostly soft tissue and muscle as it had cleanly penetrated Irvin's neck, would probably never be found if, as McCall claimed, the prisoner had been advancing toward him when the sheriff had fired his last shot. If, on the other hand, Irvin had already fallen to the ground when the bullet coursed through his neck, it might well have been found in that three-foot-square patch of sand and clay.

The jury reconvened at the Community Building in Umatilla. Hall extracted, or coaxed, a few more details of the shooting from McCall— what caliber revolver he'd carried, what time Yates arrived, whom the sheriff spoke with over the radio—and then produced a series of witnesses, including Umatilla's mayor and a town councilman, who had appeared at the roadside in the dead of Tuesday night in order to establish that the sheriff had fired in self-defense: from first to last, every witness testified he had seen strands of McCall's hair clutched in Irvin's hand.

The coroner having constructed a case of self-defense and the judge having essentially exculpated the self-defender, Hall allowed the sheriff to remind the jurors, press, and spectators that he himself had acted as the protector of the Groveland Boys: he had on previous occasions safely transported Shepherd and Irvin between Tavares and Raiford, and in July 1949 he had even hidden them at his home in Eustis "until I got permission to put them in Raiford the first time in order to protect them" from an angry mob.

"You did that to protect their lives, is that correct?" Hall asked.

"Yes, I did," McCall answered. "If I was going to do something like they have said that I have done, I would have done it long ago. I just want to say that I am very thankful that I am still here instead of in my grave today."

"Now, Sheriff," Hall asked, "did you or one of your deputies make a special trip to the blood bank in Orlando on Tuesday night in order to get whole blood from them for the treatment of the prisoner?"

"Yes," McCall replied, "one of my deputies did. And I also signed a release for his operation, because no member of his family was here to do it, and so I signed a release for the doctors to operate."

Stetson Kennedy, in his coverage of the inquest, observed that McCall was treated as a "guest of honor" whom neither the judge nor the jury would dare to question on any point that might give credence to Irvin's accusations. Nor did Governor Warren's special investigator Jefferson J. Elliott, as it turned out. His bearing authoritative and his manner persuasive, Elliott presented himself as a man of science for whom evidence comprised not the ambiguities of eyewitness accounts or the contradictions of oral testimony but rather the objectivity of forensics: the kind of evidence that he detected in his state-of-the-art mobile crime lab; the kind of evidence that did not lie. Evidence like the powder burns on the coat of Sheriff Willis V. McCall. "I believe that this is the most important piece of evidence that we have before this jury," Elliott announced solemnly to the jury as he noted the location of the powder burns on the left arm of the coat, thus indicating that the sheriff's left arm was raised at the time of the shooting, not pointing down, and thus supporting McCall's claim that he was "trying to fight somebody off or hold somebody off . . . which indicates to me some sort of struggle that was going on at the time of the shooting. He certainly was not target shooting." Thus was the hearing closed.

The jurors needed little more than half an hour to find that Samuel Shepherd's death was "justified by reason of the fact that Willis V. McCall was at that time acting in line of duty and in defense of his own life." McCall was cleared of any wrongdoing.

On Monday, November 12, Judge Truman Futch issued a statement of the court. Contrary to his previous determination, he had decided not to impanel a grand jury in regard to the shooting death of Samuel Shepherd. "At that time," Futch wrote, "I did not know that the Coroner's jury could or would be able to conclude its work; nor did I know how thorough its work might be. Usually the work of a Coroner's jury is perfunctory and superficial, but in this instance, I am of the opinion that the Honorable J. W. Hunter as State Attorney and the Honorable W. Troy Hall, Jr., as County Judge and ex officio coroner, together with members of the Coroner's jury, have done a thorough job insofar as any criminal liability of any one is concerned in connection with the death of the prisoner Samuel Shepherd. . . . There is now no need for a grand jury in Lake County, Florida, and none will be impaneled at this time."

The Honorable J. W. Hunter, however, had not entirely willingly associated himself with the inquiry into Samuel Shepherd's death. After the coroner's inquest, he issued his own cryptic statement, on which he later refused to elaborate, that he had participated in the investigation "only as I have been directed to do by [Judge Hall]." Hunter's unease with the verdict in Hall's inquest and with Futch's decision not to impanel a grand jury almost certainly stemmed from information that had not reached the coroner's jury on November 10 and would be withheld from the public record by virtue of Judge Futch's action on November 12.

On Sunday, November 11, FBI agent Robert Wall contacted both the state attorney Jesse Hunter and Judge Hall to apprise them that the FBI had located a bullet "directly beneath a blood spot where victim Irvin was lying after the shooting incidents." The agents had "dug a hole about ten inches deep" and with their fingers had sifted through the "sandy loam-type soil," in which they'd found a .38-caliber bullet. The FBI believed that the single slug buried in the sand directly below the position of Irvin's neck had traveled at a slight angle straight downward into the sand. Lab tests would later reveal that the bullet's high-speed passage through the sand had obliterated any markings that might identify conclusively the specific gun from which it had been fired.

For Hunter, the new evidence was conclusive enough to confirm his suspicions that Sheriff Willis McCall and Deputy James Yates had in essence committed murder, especially in light of other information that the FBI had been sharing with Hunter over the past two days. Walter Irvin had told the two FBI agents who'd invaded his hospital room that after Yates had shot him, he had watched the deputy and the sheriff as they'd huddled in the glare from the headlights of McCall's Oldsmobile 98: The sheriff "reached up and grabbed his shirt with his hand and tore it," and Irvin "heard him tell Mr. Yates, we got to make it look like they tried to escape." Jesse Hunter knew Willis McCall; he knew there was more fact than fiction in tales like those relating how the orange groves of Lake County were "fertilized with niggers that Willis McCall had killed"—if need be, with Deputy James Yates at his side. Jesse Hunter didn't like piss in his whiskey.

At their private get-together that Sunday, Agent Wall had offered to make the FBI evidence available to Hunter and Hall "for probable use before the Grand Jury." When Hall had subsequently advised Truman Futch that the FBI had located the missing, last bullet, the two judges came to the decision, quickly, that there was "no need for a grand jury." The last bullet need never be mentioned, in or outside a county courtroom, since the FBI would not be releasing its report to any other party. Disgruntled by the judges' decision in regard to the grand jury, Hunter wished to dissociate himself from all the proceedings of the past few days. He did not appreciate having his good name used in a whitewash.

The FBI found this bullet buried in soil directly beneath Walter Irvin's "blood spot." (*Federal Bureau of Investigation*)

At Hunter's urging, Governor Fuller Warren had been prepared to suspend Willis McCall or force him into temporary retirement on November 8, but by the next day the governor had changed his mind, with some help from the sheriff himself at their private nighttime meeting in a Jacksonville hotel. Apparently Warren had decided that his administration could weather another civil rights scandal better than it could bear further allegations of impeachable offenses that linked the governor to the interests of organized crime. The former might prove to be embarrassing to the author of *How to Win in Politics*, but the latter would be ruinous to his political future. By mid-November Warren's office had again been flooded with letters and telegrams and editorials in local and national newspapers demanding that he intervene in the latest miscarriage of justice by Lake County officials in the Groveland Boys case. Governor Fuller Warren issued a statement through his assistant that he was "out of the city at the present time on a statewide speaking tour." Aside from that, he had no comment.

Lake County newspapers viewed the decisions of the coroner's jury and of Judge Truman Futch regarding a grand jury as a "complete vindication" of their sheriff: his shooting of Shepherd and Irvin had been justified as self-defense, and he would not face any investigation of possible charges against him by a grand jury. Northern and urban newspapers around the country, meanwhile, were reporting a whitewash operation not only at the county level but also at the highest reaches of Florida's state government. Impugning everyone from Sheriff McCall to Governor Warren, editorials in the national press decried the lack of outrage over the lawlessness and "fantastic savagery" in "Florida's Jungle." No one was more incensed than Thurgood Marshall.

"Irvin's story was so convincing," Marshall said, "that all who heard it are certain that he and Shepherd were the victims of a deliberate cold-blooded plan to murder both of them before the retrial ordered by the Supreme Court." Marshall fired off an angry telegram to Fuller Warren, in which he first chided the governor for meeting with Willis McCall the night before the start of the coroner's inquest, then reproved the fact that "after this conference your representative J. J. Elliott testified in defense of McCall. All this fits directly into new pattern which has replaced old type of lynching. You still have an opportunity to demonstrate whether or not the state of Florida believes in fair play and justice." Marshall requested that Warren replace both McCall and Elliott. "The answer is in your hands," he wrote.

Marshall's harshest indictment fell on Willis McCall. In an interview with columnist Arnold DeMille for the *Chicago Defender*, Marshall asserted, "This is the worst case of injustice and whitewashing I have come across in my career. There is no question in my mind or in the minds of others who heard Walter Lee Irvin's statement that he and Samuel Shepherd were deliberately shot by Sheriff Willis B. McCall last Tuesday. The bullet hole in [Irvin's] neck reminded him with every breath and every word that he, too, could have been dead and might yet die. Any man in that condition is certainly not apt to lie. In listening to Irvin tell what happened you got the impression that he still wondered why the Lord had spared his life." Marshall then raised the obvious questions that the coroner's inquest did not: "Was it necessary to shoot two men, handcuffed together, three times in 'self defense'? Why would not the body of the dead man have prevented Irvin, who was handcuffed to him, from running or doing anything else? Why did Sheriff McCall have only himself to guard two persons charged with capital offense on a road late at night? If Sheriff McCall was that brave, why would he have to shoot them six times? The last, and final question, is: If Sheriff McCall was shooting to defend himself, how could the bullets be so well placed, that none of them went wild?"

Willis McCall didn't collect and clip only local newspapers. He also culled less flattering notices of his achievements in office from black newspapers like the *Chicago Defender* and the *Pittsburgh Courier*, which allied themselves editorially to the civil rights platform of the NAACP—an organization led by men who, in McCall's estimation, "are no good at all." The reversal of the verdict in the Groveland Boys case, argued by NAACP lawyers before the U.S. Supreme Court, McCall took personally, as an affront to his stature as an officer of the law in Lake County. The fact of the reversal and the prospect of the retrial had fueled further the sheriff's resentment of the NAACP, twenty-eight months of it toward Franklin Williams, and his indignation at Thurgood Marshall, who was now slandering him in the Northern black press as a caricature of the Southern white racist sheriff. Not that reporters like Jay Nelson Tuck hadn't recognized McCall's bigotry with no help at all from the NAACP. In a *New York Post* article, Tuck expressed abhorrence at the "sheer, filthy offensiveness of it when Sheriff McCall tells a public inquest that he opened his car window in the rain 'because the nigger smell got too strong.'" McCall preferred to present himself as a man who spoke the truth frankly, and if people couldn't handle the facts of it, the fault was not his. "I don't think there is any question about it that the white race is a superior race to the black race," McCall once said. "I believe that's a proven fact. In their native country, they're still eating each other. We don't do that."

Willis V. McCall may have been vindicated in Lake County, and he had dodged state criminal charges in the shooting death of Samuel Shepherd. Still, the need to set the record straight in the court of public opinion—to gain vindication by all—obsessed McCall. He had work yet to do, and he knew just how to do it, too.

Flyer announcing Thurgood Marshall's appearance in Miami, Florida. (*Library of Congress, Prints & Photographs Division, Visual Materials from the NAACP Records*)

ANOTHER JOB DONE, special investigator J. J. Elliott allowed himself a moment of self-satisfaction as he headed back to his room at the

Fountain Inn in Eustis. He had been doing well by Governor Fuller War-ren. After Senator Estes Kefauver's hearings had exposed the statewide cor-ruption in Florida on live television in 1950, Elliott had gotten some payback for Governor Warren in Washington, D.C., where he'd uncovered "crap games, after-hour whiskey sales, and prostitution flourishing right under Kefauver's nose."

With an armful of newspapers headlining McCall's exoneration, Elliott was fiddling with the key to his room when Stetson Kennedy spotted him, and joined the special investigator for a chat. After making some small talk with Elliott about bass fishing, Kennedy decided, on a hunch, to "play the ace up my sleeve": from his wallet he pulled a "Klan Kard."

An activist and folklorist as well as a journalist, Kennedy had traveled across Florida with Zora Neale Hurston during the Great Depression, when the two of them had collaborated on a WPA Florida Writers' Project chron-icling the sights and sounds of American folk life in turpentine camps, on railroad gangs, in soup kitchens, and the like. In the mid-1940s, Kennedy had infiltrated the Ku Klux Klan in Georgia as part of his research for pub-lications that sensationally exposed the organization's activities and inner workings, its arcane rituals and "secret codewords," to a fascinated public. In a 1947 letter, Georgia governor Ellis Arnall had credited Kennedy with uncovering evidence that "has facilitated Georgia's prosecution of the Ku Klux Klan." In 1951, he had not yet published *I Rode with the Ku Klux Klan*, a book that would have more clearly revealed his identity to Elliott. Kennedy handed the Klan Kard to the special investigator.

"Well, well!" Elliott said. "I see you know Mr. A-y-a-k [code for "Are you a Klansman?"] . . ."

"Sure do," Kennedy answered, "and Mr. A-k-a-i ["A Klansman am I"], too."

In reply, by Kennedy's account, Elliott disclosed that he was a member of the East Point Klavern in Atlanta, and after a quick exchange in which he and Kennedy shared the names of people they both knew, Elliott "opened up immediately" to the reporter about the Groveland Boys case.

"On the basis of that Kard you just showed me," Elliott said, "I don't mind telling you that when those niggers were first delivered to the state pen they'd had the hell beaten out of them." Elliott remarked, too, that Raiford officials "were so afraid somebody might try to pin the beatings on them," they'd had the Groveland Boys photographed as soon as they'd arrived.

The conversation was interrupted when a fellow reporter showed up, and Kennedy excused himself, wanting to avoid any chance of his under-cover work arising as a topic for discussion. He left with what he thought was a major scoop, although by then the FBI had already documented that the deputies Yates and Campbell had beaten the Groveland Boys. The other, perhaps bigger story was that Jefferson J. Elliott had admitted to being a member of the KKK: a detail that, to Kennedy's mind, might point to a conspiracy on the part of the governor, himself a former Klansman, and his special investigator to whitewash a cold-blooded murder by Sheriff Willis McCall.

Stetson Kennedy didn't even stop to pack a toothbrush or his clothes. Bent on flying direct to Washington, he hopped a bus to Orlando and got to the airport, where he found himself short of cash to pay for the passage to D.C.—but not so short he couldn't buy some bar bourbon, which he spilled down the front of his shirt so that he was smelling, if not entirely looking, like a common drunk. He telephoned Thurgood Marshall, now back at his office in New York. He offered the NAACP a deal: in exchange for a plane ticket to D.C., Kennedy would provide them with information about J. J. Elliott that directly affected the Groveland Boys case. "Red hot information," Kennedy said, so hot he "had to get out of town in a hurry."

"What kind of information?" Marshall asked.

"Can't tell you over the phone," Kennedy answered. "Don't know who's listening. Can you meet me at the airport in Washington at 11:30 tonight?"

Kennedy also hinted to Marshall that he was looking "for further funds to continue further investigation." Prepared to deal with only one proposition at a time, Marshall agreed to make arrangements for Kennedy's airline ticket.

"If the information he has can stand up," Marshall told the *Defender*'s Arnold DeMille, who was listening in, "it'll be a heck of a good story and will mean a lot to the case. Let's go down and meet the guy. Maybe he does have something."

Marshall booked flights for both himself and DeMille, and at 11:30 p.m. on November 11, he arrived in Washington from New York. He checked into Hotel 2400, where he waited in his room with DeMille; a local NAACP attorney, Frank Reeves; and a special agent from the FBI.

The FBI was unimpressed by Kennedy's information, whereas Kennedy was "completely surprised" by theirs: that a grand jury had already declined to indict Yates and Campbell on charges related to the beatings of the Groveland Boys. To better represent in his work the treatment of the Grove-land Boys by the Lake County Sheriff's Department, Kennedy suggested that the FBI provide him with their internal reports. Further, Kennedy outlined for the FBI agent the nature of the investigation that would be required to effect a reopening of grand jury proceedings; he also indicated that the agents assigned to the investigation should not be from or currently located in the South, as the agents who had worked on the case, he believed, had shown "prejudice to negroes."

The FBI agent immediately challenged Kennedy. He wanted names, he wanted dates, he wanted instances, he wanted specifics to support claims of agent prejudice. Kennedy hedged; he required time to consult his files. Still, the FBI would persist; on Kennedy's return to his home in Jacksonville, the bureau would daily contact him by phone to demand from him the specific information that he had supposedly placed in his files: to either "put-up or shut-up." The bureau's internal reports on the meeting with Kennedy in Washington, D.C., would include the directive that if Kennedy failed to provide specifics, agents should "back him down completely on these allegations." The reports would also make note of the writer's leftist connections, supported by quotes from interviews with Kennedy's associates who described him as "the most dangerous Communist in the State of Florida." After reviewing the reports, J. Edgar Hoover would write across the bottom, "I would waste no more time on Kennedy. He is just a phony."

On a call to the FBI the morning after the meeting, Marshall admitted that "it looked like Kennedy had swindled the NAACP into paying his transportation from Florida to Washington," for in the exchange the NAACP had gained no new information vital to the Groveland case. While Kennedy's communist affiliations hardly bore upon the case, they did provide Marshall, in his dismissal of the writer's presumed scoops, with the opportunity to affect solidarity with the FBI. As always, Marshall expressed his appreciation for the bureau's efforts as well as "the thoroughness of the investigation [the FBI was] conducting." In return, he was thanked "for his appreciation of confidence in the work of this Bureau and was assured that the Bureau is only too willing to receive any information from him at any time." Once again, Hoover and Marshall performed their private rites of cooperation.

DeMille told Marshall he didn't want to touch the story about Elliott being in the Klan, as it "could result in the nicest, fattest liable [*sic*] law suit" sure to have "yours truly pounding the streets looking for a new job." However dismissive of Kennedy's import Marshall may have been with the FBI, he did put the information regarding Elliott to use in a telegram he sent to Fuller Warren. While Marshall did not refer explicitly to Elliott's possible affiliation with the Klan, he did imply to Warren that the governor knew exactly what outcome the special investigator would effect on his mission in Lake County, and to whose particular advantage that outcome would be. Also, Kennedy's firm belief, however vaguely supported, that FBI agents in the South were "prejudiced in Civil Rights investigations" was very much in line with Marshall's own thinking. (Marshall himself had walked into the same trap with Hoover, who had demanded agents' names and specific incidents that Marshall likewise had failed to provide.) Moreover, for all the FBI's efforts to marginalize Stetson Kennedy as a communist and dismiss him as a phony, his reporting on the Groveland Boys case had been consistent with the news stories being published at the same time in Northern papers. Finally, his claim connecting Jefferson J. Elliott to the Ku Klux Klan was one that even the FBI had acknowledged to be "entirely possible," given that Elliott was "formerly on the Investigative Staff of Governor [Eugene] Talmadge of Georgia," an admitted KKK flogger and racial demagogue who presided over a "Klan-ridden regime." The FBI had questioned both Warren and Elliott in this regard, and both had denied that Elliott was a Klansman. "Sometime later," however, according to FBI notes, Elliott allowed that he was a Klansman, describing his membership as being "part of my job."

T HE HEARINGS IN the retrial of the now one Groveland boy for the rape of Norma Padgett had been postponed for thirty days because of the shootings. Walter Irvin was meanwhile recovering from his wounds at Raiford. Jack Greenberg had amended the change of venue motion. Thurgood Marshall was preparing to return to Lake County, where a curious item had just appeared in local newspapers. That Judge Truman Futch, on December 4, 1951, had signed a confidential order instructing Sheriff Willis McCall to (again) transport Walter Irvin from Raiford State Prison to Tavares for the change of venue hearing had evidently been leaked to the press by the incensed state attorney Jesse Hunter. Apparently even McCall's friend Judge W. Troy Hall thought it a bad idea, as he had contacted the FBI to explore the possibility of enlisting a bureau agent to accompany the sheriff as an escort. Marshall contemplated the news piece with incredulity. No matter that Governor Warren had ignored every protest Marshall had wired to him in regard to the catastrophic prison transfer a month earlier, in dismay Marshall pleaded in yet another telegram: "In the name of human decency and justice we urgently request that you replace Sheriff McCall and have Irvin transported by State officials other than McCall. We further urge that you take all of the necessary steps to assure that Irvin will not be killed or wounded on this trip."

Hunter's alarm spared Walter Irvin the experience of another two-hour car ride with the man who had shot him not a month before; Irvin was transferred by the state highway patrol. Willis McCall paid a visit to Raiford, nonetheless. To date, McCall had escaped indictment on criminal charges by the state in the roadside shootings near Umatilla, but the sheriff was fully aware that the FBI had located the telltale sixth bullet buried in the sand where Irvin had fallen. So McCall had located a tale-teller of his own: Merlin James Leiby, a twenty-four-year-old white prisoner on death row at Raiford. The sheriff's trip to Raiford proved to be fruitful. Leiby, the "doomed murderer" who had been scheduled to die in the electric chair within days, instead was issued a stay of execution by Governor Warren. The governor had thus broken his monthlong silence on the Groveland Boys case, and he had done so on the basis of a written request by the sheriff of Lake County. McCall's letter reported that prior to the transfer of the prisoners Shepherd and Irvin from Raiford to Tavares by the sheriff and the deputy Yates, Merlin James Leiby had overheard his fellow inmates on death row "planning to escape." McCall then made his point: "I believe that testimony from him [Leiby] in person would have great bearing in case the prejudiced groups in New York bring enough pressure to bear in Washington for the Justice Department to place this case before a Federal Grand Jury."

Leiby soon found himself telling his tale to two FBI agents. The night before the transfer, Leiby told them, he'd overheard Samuel Shepherd say to another inmate, "I'll be thinking of you when I'm out there drinking that Calvert Reserve whiskey and juking on Wednesday night." And on the night of the transfer itself, according to Leiby, as Shepherd was leaving his cell, he told another inmate, "Well boys I'll be a free man tonight." On further investigation, the agents learned that another inmate, Robert Cecil Bell, had overheard a conversation as well. In his statement, Bell claimed that he'd heard two prison employees—"free people," in prison argot—discussing how Leiby could likely escape his date with the electric chair if he had been fortunate enough to have heard Shepherd and Irvin planning their getaway. According to Bell, when one of the two prison guards asked, "Why don't you suggest it to Leiby?" the other replied, "It's already been taken care of." In the end, the FBI found that for every inmate who believed Leiby's story there was another who corroborated Bell's statement that the prison employees had planted the idea for the story in the mind of the doomed inmate. The

FBI concluded that "no action appears to be warranted." While the NAACP scoffed at still another of McCall's efforts to whitewash his shootings—with Walter White noting that in his experience with jailhouse stool pigeons, "it is not the practice" for white prisoners to be housed anywhere near enough to black inmates so as to be able to overhear their conversations—McCall's effort did result in press coverage of the governor's stay of execution and in the sort of publicity the sheriff sought in his endeavor to stave off federal charges. It also bought Merlin James Leiby time, until, one year later, the state of Florida pulled the switch on him at Flat Top.

ON THE WEEKEND of November 23, the Florida State Conference of NAACP Branches held its eleventh annual meeting in Daytona Beach, the city in which all of Harry T. Moore's family had received their bachelor's degrees, at Bethune-Cookman College. Harry had actually been the last; he had been awarded his degree only a few months earlier. For most of those few months Harry had been contemplating his options. The college degree provided him with some professional insurance, in the not unlikely event that he should be ousted as an executive secretary by the NAACP: a prospect that he was still not able to fully acknowledge. He could have opted to resign, or he could have chosen to work out some alternative position with the national office. Instead he was doing what he always did. He had chosen to come to Daytona Beach and fight.

The first resolution on the agenda concerned the Groveland case, with a call for Governor Fuller Warren to "remove Sheriff Willis B. McCall forthwith from office" that might have been drafted by the letter-writing, speechifying Moore himself. It was overwhelmingly approved in a floor vote, unlike resolution 5, which met with more resistance than Harry might have expected and a lot more than Gloster Current and Ruby Hurley had anticipated. The national branches director and Southeast regional director, it turned out, could not deliver the votes, and the resolution to abolish the position of Florida's paid executive secretary stalled on the floor. It proved to be no victory for Moore, either. Rather than engage in a protracted battle that might cripple the NAACP branches in Florida, Moore agreed to a compromise by which he would receive over time all back pay due to him—more than $2,600—on the condition that he would continue with the NAACP as an unpaid "state coordinator."

Moore left Daytona disillusioned. Current and Hurley "came in and took over," Moore complained, making "this meeting . . . about the worst we ever had." He returned home frustrated, in large part because his problems with Current and Hurley stemmed from his inability to raise more money in Florida. He told his mother, Rosa Moore, that "he could not understand why the colored people in Florida did not take more interest in NAACP work," why they could not see that investing time or energy or two dollars annual dues in the NAACP was investing in a better future for themselves and their children. Change was coming, but it would be coming sooner with more support from the black community. As Marshall would often remind the NAACP staff and field workers, "the easy part of the job is fighting the white folks."

Again, Moore considered options. He would have some income from the NAACP and from his back pay (one could be cynical about that); also, Harriette's position in the Palm Beach County school system was secure. They owned their house in Mims, and they were no longer financially supporting their daughters, as Peaches was teaching at a school in Ocala and Evangeline was working for the U.S. Department of Labor in Washington. Harry himself had received a good offer to teach, starting in February if he was interested, and he'd also thought he might go back to school for his master's degree. But again, with or without back pay, as secretary or coordinator, Harry knew he was, as always, in it to the end of the civil rights fight.

In the weeks before the annual meeting in Daytona, a wave of racial violence had swept through the state of Florida. The year had begun with isolated beatings of blacks by the Klan, but the violence had intensified in March when a Winter Garden man was flogged and then shot to death. In April the violence had escalated. To the state senate's passage of an "anti-mask" bill, which banned the wearing of hoods as well as unauthorized cross burnings, the Klan responded with a rash of "hit and run" cross burnings up and down the state. That spring, too, in an attempt to unite various Klan factions in common cause, Bill Hendrix, by day a plumbing contractor in Tallahassee and otherwise the Grand Dragon of the Southern Knights of the Ku Klux Klan, had declared a war on "hate groups," most notably the NAACP and B'nai B'rith. In Miami, bombings had laid waste to a Jewish community center and a black apartment complex; dynamite had been discovered, but had failed to detonate, at both a Hebrew school and a Catholic church. In the rubble of another bombed Jewish site had been planted a cross bearing "anti-Semitic and anti-Negro slogans" as well as Nazi and KKK symbols. "The Jew has already ruined the northern cities and wishes to invade the South," read one letter that had arrived at the governor's office. "They are teaching communism to the colored people, and inciting rioting through them." By autumn, violence by dynamite had spread to central Florida. The Klan had flattened the Creamette Frozen Custard Stand in Orlando because the owner had refused to dedicate a separate service window for blacks. Before the year's end the "Florida Terror," as it was dubbed by the press, had resulted in a dozen disastrous bombings and numerous failed attempts to destroy racial and religious-based sites: the *Saturday Evening Post* designated 1951 as "the worst year of minority outrages in the history of Florida or probably any other state in recent times."

For Harry Moore, all the outrages of white supremacy in Florida were epitomized by one case and one man. On a weekend in December, after the Daytona conference and before the Christmas break at Harriette's school, Moore sat down at his desk in the Mims house, where he rolled a piece of stationery into his typewriter—still fretful over his treatment by the NAACP, he chose the Progressive Voters League of Florida letterhead—and with "Dear Governor" he began. Heatedly his fingers hit the keys, no matter that the lengthy, indignant letter would be stuck by some assistant to the governor into the Harry T. Moore file, already thick with unanswered correspondence and telegrams regarding Sheriff Willis McCall and the case of the Groveland Boys. Two decades of experience, twenty years of exasperation in the battle for civil rights in Florida informed Moore's wrath over the Groveland case, in which the state was now complicit with the sheriff in murder. McCall's rounds of fire, beyond killing one black man and seriously wounding another, were, Moore wrote, "still echoing around the world." So he had questions for Governor Warren, questions that had to be asked again even though he had been asking them of Florida governors for twenty years, with no reply. "Is it true that in Florida the word of a Negro means nothing when weighed against that of a white person?" Who will be there for black families chased from their homes by the bomb-throwing Klan? Who will stand up for young Willie James Howard, murdered in front of his father for sending a white girl a Christmas card? Who will demand justice when a white man rapes a young black girl and is only levied a fine in court? By the time he finished writing his letter, he knew who. Harry T. Moore.

Lately he had taken to carrying a pistol. "I'll take a few of them with me if it comes to that," Moore told his two daughters and loyal wife.

MARSHALL GATHERED HIS legal staff in New York to discuss another fund-raising tour. He thought "the best person would be someone from Shepherd's family," but he also had practical concerns. "Shepherd's father can't go because you never can keep him sober," Marshall told them.

Greenberg chimed in, "We really ought to call the Civil Rights Congress and find out how they raised money." But Wilkins quashed that idea. "We do not have the same kind of discipline as the Communists do. The people in our branches will never work as hard."

"Some of the tactics are what we should use," Marshall said. "We ought to get the most horrible pictures printed and out to the public." He finally decided to send out "eight thousand letters to higher income bracket people," adding, "We can say that Shepherd is dead and we paid for his funeral so that we have cared for the dead. But we must now care for the living."

WALTER IRVIN, WITH handcuffs around both wrists, emerged from a state highway patrol car at the county courthouse in Tavares, where pretrial hearings in the Groveland Boys case were beginning on December 6. Thurgood Marshall and Jack Greenberg both winced at the sight of him, for the defendants in the second trial had been reduced to one. "As matters now stand," Marshall told reporters, "two colored men have already lost their lives as a result of this charge of attack of a white woman; one being killed by a sheriff's posse and one by Sheriff McCall. Another is serving a life sentence. The fourth, Walter Irvin, although shot twice in the chest and once in the neck, must still stand trial and face the threat of the electric chair. This is typical Southern Justice."

However ambiguous Jesse Hunter's own feelings about the sheriff of Lake County may have been, the state attorney was not about to rein in his fervor in the prosecution of Walter Irvin for the rape of Norma Padgett. First off, Hunter moved that Marshall and Greenberg not be admitted as counsel for the defendant, on the grounds that the NAACP had been responsible for the publication of "vicious, slanderous and libelous matter" in regard to the case. Hunter introduced fund-raising materials that the Florida Committee of 100 had circulated nearly two years earlier, which included Ted Poston's Groveland Boys article, "The Story of Florida's Legal Lynching," and he then contended that the committee, under the aegis of the NAACP, had set out to "stir up scandalous and libelous matter and material against the good people of Lake County, Florida." Marshall countered that he was a lawyer representing a client, Walter Irvin, and that the committee "has nothing whatsoever to do with my office." He had also experienced his first sting of the hostility that had unsettled Franklin Williams in this same courtroom.

Still, Marshall had come to Florida prepared. The defense moved to disqualify Jesse Hunter, not because they held any hope that Judge Truman Futch would so move but because they wanted to have Hunter's actions vis-à-vis Lawrence Burtoft, the first person known to have spoken with Norma Padgett after the rape, entered on the record. They called the state attorney to the stand.

Akerman asked, "Did you interview him [Lawrence Burtoft] as a prospective witness in this case?"

"Yes, I did, but I am not going to tell you what he told me," Hunter answered; "he is your witness and you can find out from him."

Challenging Hunter, the defense pointed out that in an interview with the reporter from the *St. Petersburg Times*, Burtoft claimed he had told Hunter that Norma Padgett had said she wasn't hurt and had said she could not identify her abductors.

"That statement is entirely false," Hunter barked in his gravelly voice. "He made no such statement to me at any time, and I am not going into what he did tell me. . . . You can prove it by Mr. Burtoft, not by me."

"Mr. Burtoft is out of the province of this court, he is in the armed forces of the United States, in North Carolina," Akerman noted.

"Well, you will have to go further than that before you ever get him back here to make any such statement as that, because he never made the statement," Hunter replied.

Now that Hunter had been fully engaged in battle with the defense, he'd resorted to old, tried-and-true tactics. He dodged and he denied, for of course he had not had Burtoft testify under oath in the first trial, for the same reason he had not called Dr. Geoffrey Binneveld as a witness: in neither instance would the testimony have supported the prosecution's case. Hunter also doled. As if he had never heard the Supreme Court's admonishment in regard to the doling out of disinformation to the press before the first trial, Hunter was telling reporters that the FBI had concluded that all six bullets had been fired from the same gun, when, in fact, the FBI had informed the state attorney that the sixth bullet could not be positively connected to McCall's gun.

On the motion for change of venue, despite Jesse Hunter's argument that "this whole thing has been in the hands of a bunch of radicals . . . and it is directed to the men who came in here from out of the state to create race hatred," Judge Truman Futch had little choice but to rule in favor of the defense. While the judge wanted a speedy conviction no less than Hunter did, Futch recognized that he had been clearly mandated by the U.S. Supreme Court to move the trial out of Lake County. Not that the ruling would prove to be an advantage to the defense.

Marion County shared Lake County's northwest border and its demographics. Its sheriff had also been recently involved in a shooting with a sixteen-year-old black youth, much to the consternation of Thurgood Marshall and the defense. For in this case the black youth, who had been picked up by Sheriff Edward Porter Jr. for questioning in the theft of a coat from a men's store, had first attacked the sheriff with an ice pick, then shot Porter several times with his own gun. Sheriff Porter's death was a clarion call to the people of Marion County; law and order had to be upheld at all costs, particularly in the face of unruly blacks. In December 1951 no other county in Florida could have been more predisposed to sympathy for a sheriff who claimed that two black prisoners had attacked him in his car.

Marshall had hoped that Judge Futch would move the retrial to a more urban setting like Miami or Jacksonville, and thereby remove himself from any further proceedings in the Groveland Boys case. Instead Futch chose a venue within the Fifth Judicial District, where he could preside in the retrial. He postponed hearings until mid-January. That done, he "took the first step toward a legal lynching of Walter Lee Irvin," as one newspaper reported: the judge barred Thurgood Marshall and Jack Greenberg from defending Walter Irvin, on the grounds that they "stirred up trouble in the community." The decision was made, Futch said, and as Hunter had earlier argued, "because they represent the NAACP" and not the client.

H ARRY T. MOORE drove his blue Ford down "the Great Black Way" of Second Avenue, past the Lyric Theater and the brightly lit nightclubs and dance halls, into the heart of Overtown—or "Colored Town," or the "Harlem of the South," as the bustling, self-sustaining neighborhood on the other side of the tracks from downtown Miami was more commonly known. It was a world away from the rural communities of North Florida with their whitewashed community centers and tidy churches where Harry would try to raise a few more dollars for the NAACP. In Overtown, the churches were the centers of the community, vibrant, essential to the social and spiritual life of Miami's black population. Moore parked his sedan not far from the Mount Zion Baptist Church. He relished the energy in the early evening air as he walked toward the imposing Mediterranean Revival building. He had expected the scores of stylishly dressed blacks who were filing into the church; he had not expected the police.

Heavily armed, watchful, up and down the sidewalk, policemen were patrolling the streets outside the church. While Miami had seen a rash of violence over the past year, for the most part the bombings had been hit-and-run, the intention being to destroy property, usually unoccupied churches and synagogues, not to assault people. No doubt, though, the mass meeting of December 13 at Mount Zion Baptist Church—its topic widely advertised as "The Truth About Groveland," its purpose to raise money for the Groveland Boys defense—was proving to be provocative: anonymous telephone threats stated the church would be bombed that night when the featured speaker, Thurgood Marshall, took the pulpit. Immediately upon learning of the threat, Mount Zion's pastor, the Reverend Edward T. Graham, had notified a member of the City Commission, and shortly thereafter Miami's chief of police—who "believed that the threat came from someone interested in the Groveland case since it was on that case that Mr. Marshall was to speak"—had promised the church, and Marshall, protection. Two weeks earlier, on a similar NAACP fund-raising occasion, Thurgood Marshall had spoken about Groveland at the Siloam Presbyterian Church in Brooklyn, New York; he had not needed a band of police guards to shield him and sweep him safely into the church.

At Mount Zion, armed guards surrounded the pulpit. Several white citizens were seated on the speakers' platform with Marshall, and whites also filled the first few rows in the church. Thunderous applause greeted Marshall when he rose to speak; the police inside the church shuffled nervously. Moore had never heard Marshall argue a case before the Supreme Court, where, as Jack Greenberg observed, he assumed a courtroom style that was "ordinary, conversational, and undramatic." Mount Zion Baptist Church was not a courtroom, and Moore watched mostly in awe as Marshall—fiery, impassioned, defiant—abandoned his lawyerly measures for preacher-like stylings in a slightly exaggerated Southern drawl. "In a mass meeting," Greenberg said, "he could bring an audience to its feet, clapping and stomping." And that night in Overtown he did.

Moore marveled at Marshall's power in the pulpit. Riveting his audience, eliciting gasps of horror and murmurs of sorrow, he unfolded the story of the Groveland Boys and summoned plaints of outrage in response to the questions that punctuated his tale: the same questions that Moore had been posing in his letters to Governor Warren over the past two and a half years.

"Why did McCall have to remove the prisoners at night?" Marshall's voice boomed, and when the rumble of discontent in the pews began to subside, he roused the audience again: "Why did he have to travel on an isolated road instead of the main highway?" And again: "And why didn't he have a deputy sheriff with him in the car with the prisoners?"

It was murder, Marshall was telling them, a lynching by law enforcement that had been subsequently whitewashed by Lake County officials and the court into an act of self-defense. But he was telling them, too, that the Miami NAACP was standing proud and firm against this travesty of justice, and with their financial support, their contributions tonight, they—the good people of Miami, undeterred by threats and violence—would help Thurgood Marshall and the Legal Defense Fund fight Lake County.

Over the crescendo of noise and enthusiasm, Marshall's voice rose. He had a threat of his own to deliver: a message for Judge Truman Futch and anyone else who thought Thurgood Marshall was going to decamp or desert the Groveland case simply because a judge in Lake County had decided to bar him from defending Walter Irvin. "They can keep me from the courts of Florida," Marshall shouted. "But there is no man alive or to be born who can prevent me from arguing the Groveland case before the U.S. Supreme Court!"

The crowd roared its approval. For Harry T. Moore, it had been a remarkable event to witness. In his two decades of NAACP travels, he had heard his share of inspirational civil rights sermons with their biblical analogues of long desert journeys and parting seas, but Marshall's vision was grounded in constitutional law and he drew the lineaments of his hope from his personal experience, from battles won and strategies mastered, from the efforts he shared with like-minded men and women determined not to see the future repeat the past. The Mount Zion Baptist parishioners reached deep into their pockets that night—their contributions exceeded a thousand dollars—with the highest single donations coming "from some of these white people in the audience." One of the white men in attendance was Caxton Doggett, a minister from Rader Memorial Methodist Church in Miami, who later wrote to Marshall, "I was glad of the chance to hear you the other night in Miami. You are a very fine speaker. If you weren't a lawyer, you would make a good preacher. . . . After hearing you, I decided to join the NAACP. . . . You are doing great work, and I want you to know that I am one of an increasing number of southern white men who have the highest respect for your professional ability and your integrity of character."

In common cause they found community and communion: this was why Moore had dedicated two decades of his life to the NAACP. He didn't have Thurgood Marshall's background in law, or Dan Byrd's charisma, or Franklin Williams's eloquence. He hadn't the stomach for Gloster Current's cold-eyed practicality. What he lacked in magnetism, though, he made up for in persistence and determination, and his commitment to his people in their struggle for justice and equality he would match with anyone's. By the end of the hour in Mount Zion Baptist Church, with the clapping and stomping resounding in his head, and his heart stirred by Marshall's words, Moore had reaffirmed his commitment to the cause. He remembered other words, too: ten years ago, when he'd fought at Marshall's side in the Florida salary equalization lawsuits on behalf of black teachers, Marshall had said, "This is not a single battle, but rather a real war in which we will lose some battles and win others." In the war for the Groveland Boys, Moore was ready for the next battle.

He was driving north on U.S. 1. In two hours, he'd be back in Riviera Beach, where he and Harriette rented rooms during the school year. Classes would soon be ending for the holidays at Lake Park Colored School, and they would be returning to their house in Mims. Harriette's brother, George Simms, a master sergeant in the army, would be home on leave from Korea, and with him and their daughters, Peaches and Evangeline, they would be celebrating not only Christmas but also their twenty-fifth wedding anniversary. He was looking forward to Mims, his family, the celebrations, the new year. He stopped, as he usually did on his drives up the coast, at a small grocery store in Melbourne; he'd gotten to know the owner over the years. They got to talking about the Groveland Boys case, and the man expressed concern for his friend's safety. He wondered if maybe Harry wasn't "going too far" in his work for the NAACP. "I'm going to keep doing it," Moore replied in his understated way, "even if it costs me my life. Jesus Christ lost his life doing what he thought was right. And I believe the Lord intended for me to do this work for the colored race. I may live to be a ripe old age or I may be killed tomorrow, or next month, or perhaps never, but I intend to do this until the day I die."

(*Federal Bureau of Investigation*)

AT NINE O'CLOCK on Christmas night of 1951, a dense ground fog had begun to settle in the orange groves of Mims. Harry T. Moore cranked the engine of his sedan. The Moores—Harry; his mother, Rosa; his wife, Harriette; and their daughter Peaches—had enjoyed a quiet holiday dinner with family and friends at the house of Harriette's brother, Arnold Simms. Moore edged his car slowly onto Old Dixie Highway, the headlights no help in the fog. Still, in a few minutes, he'd driven the short distance, several hundred yards, home.

The Ford parked, Harry helped his seventy-one-year-old mother out of the car and walked her to the house; Harriette and Peaches trailed behind.

Harry lingered for a moment, alone, on the porch, in the fog, his thoughts lost in the surreal atmosphere of the night. Across the grove another man stood quiet, too, in the fog, beneath an orange tree, his eyes trained on a vague, diffuse glow.

The light inside the house seemed all the brighter when Harry joined his family in the living room. The day had tired Harriette, but before she went to bed, her husband insisted, they had more than Christmas to celebrate. It was their twenty-fifth wedding anniversary, after all; they should at least have some cake.

Rosa laid a fruitcake on the oak dining table. Harry was about to cut the first slice when Harriette gently placed her hand over his—they shared a smile, as if posing for a wedding portrait—and together they ceremoniously pressed the knife into the cake. After the cake, when Harriette did retire, Harry sat with his mother at the table as he reminisced about his wedding (a modest affair in the home of a doctor in Cocoa, with only a handful of people in attendance), his youth, his wife, their little girls. Shortly after 10 p.m. Rosa, too, retired; as she headed to the guest room at the back of the house, she reminded Harry to send Peaches to bed and turn off the lights.

Peaches had fallen asleep on the settee in the living room. Harry nudged her awake, and with some comic books in hand, she said good night. Harry turned off the lights behind her.

Rosa was drifting toward sleep when she heard the footsteps. "Is that you, Harry?" she asked. As he ducked into the bathroom, Harry answered her: "Yes, Mamma, that's me."

The house was nearly dark. Peaches had given up reading for sleeping by the time Harry had lain down beside his wife. He switched off the bedroom light. No hazy glow hovered any longer in the fog outside. The man waiting beneath the orange tree had a moment to brace himself and steady his hands for the task. It was 10:20 p.m.

The force of the blast split the house at its seams. It lifted the chimney into the air. It blew out every window; it splintered the front porch. It shredded the floorboards in Harry and Harriette's bedroom, and propelled the back of a chair through the ceiling into the attic. The explosion roused the town of Titusville four miles away.

Only the chimney settled back down in place at the Moores' house in Mims. Jolted by the blast, Peaches had screamed out for her mother, to no response, and then for her grandmother. Groggy, disoriented, Rosa stepped into the room.

"Grandma, are you hurt?" Peaches asked.

"No, are you?"

"No," Peaches answered.

Then Rosa heard the groans. She and Peaches made their way to the Moores' bedroom at the front of the house. Peaches fiddled with the switch of a lamp in the dining room; it worked, and in its light, she and her grandmother could barely make out, in the rubble of the bedroom, on the floor, under the debris, the figures of Harry and Harriette. Their bedspring and mattress had been cast up against the wall.

"Evangeline . . . Evangeline . . ." Harriette was mumbling repeatedly: Evangeline who in two days was planning to join her family for further celebrations in Mims.

When Rosa first stepped into the room her foot sank into the floorboard just inside the door. She and Peaches managed between them to pull a bookcase off Harriette, but they lacked the physical strength to deal with the bodies and all the debris. Rosa sent Peaches outside to call to her uncles for help.

"George! Arnold! Help!" Peaches screamed into the fog, at the Simms house a few hundred yards down the road. "George!"

In minutes they had arrived. The porch, shattered into bits, evidenced the effects of a powerful bomb: dynamite, or nitroglycerin. Whatever it was, Harriette's two brothers were expecting nothing good when they entered the ruin of a home.

Peaches was sobbing, hysterical. "Something has happened to Daddy!" she cried, and the two men rushed to rescue the two bodies from the wreckage of a bedroom.

Once they had lodged Harriette in the front seat of George's roomy Buick sedan with her sisters-in-law Ernestine and Mabel, and Harry in the back with his mother, they sped as much as the fog allowed toward the Fernald-Laughton Memorial Hospital in Sanford, thirty miles away. The silence in the car was taut, broken only by Harriette's faint cries for Evangeline or a worriedly whispered "Harry." He was fading fast. With his head cradled against her shoulder, Rosa tried to comfort him, a boy in his pajamas, her son Harry in his pain. He "groaned several times."

When finally they cleared the fog, George aggressively stepped on the gas. He was worrying over his decision to drive Harry and Harriette to the hospital in Sanford, but he was certain a Jim Crow ambulance would not have responded quickly to a call from Mims on Christmas night. They had just reached the hospital when George heard Harry's gargled moan. And Rosa's stifled cry: Harry's head had dropped down onto his mother's lap; blood was seeping from his mouth onto her clothes and into the Buick's upholstery.

Fernald-Laughton Memorial was not a modern medical facility. A mansion in a residential neighborhood of Sanford that had been converted into a hospital, it had a limited staff: only one nurse and no doctors were on duty that Christmas night when George Simms carried his brother-in-law to a stretcher in the emergency room. The nurse telephoned Dr. George Starke, one of but a few black physicians in the area. Anxious, impatient, Simms, who had seen enough combat injuries in Korea to know that severe damage to the lungs and other internal organs characterized primary blast injuries, considered his brother-in-law's chances, as it was not uncommon for victims to initially survive an explosion before taking a fatal turn for the worst. And still Dr. Starke hadn't arrived at the hospital.

The master sergeant in Simms sent him back to his car. He himself would bring Dr. Starke to the hospital, but his path crossed Starke's in the Florida night. About the same time that Simms arrived at Starke's residence, the doctor was entering the emergency room at Fernald-Laughton. And by the time Simms had raced back to the hospital, Dr. Starke was shaking his head as he stared down at the man on the stretcher. "Cerebral hemorrhage, internal hemorrhages and shock," the doctor was saying to Simms. His words could explain cause but could not alter effect: Harry T. Moore was dead.

"Yes, Mamma, that's me" were the last words Harry T. Moore was ever heard to speak. Minutes later, in his pajamas, he'd peeled back the covers and, as he had for twenty-five years, settled into bed beside his wife, already asleep . . . and in an instant Moore's work was done. His words dissolved into a groan. There would be no more speeches to his people, no more letters to the editor, no more telegrams to the governor, no more words. It was what they wanted, the men behind the man shrouded in the fog beneath the orange tree: no more words. The last words Moore was known to write he had typed in his impassioned letter of December 2 to Governor Fuller Warren, in which he implored the governor to hold Sheriff Willis McCall responsible for the cold-blooded murder of Samuel Shepherd, and the last of the questions he posed in that letter would resonate in the press worldwide in the days ahead.

> *We seek no special favors; but certainly we have a right to expect justice and equal protection of the laws even for the humblest Negro. Shall we be disappointed again?*
>
> *Respectfully yours,*
> *Harry T. Moore*

❧ ⚘

THE CONDENSATION LAY thick over the Moores' orange grove when Brevard County sheriff Bill Williams turned up at the scene of the blast with deputies and a bloodhound. Within hours FBI agents had arrived as well. Investigators combed through the wreckage; they photographed footprints in the grove; they gathered Moore's paperwork, which had been scattered everywhere by the explosion. By the time the morning sun had burned off what remained of the fog, mourners had begun to congregate in front of the Moores' cordoned-off house. They'd number more than a thousand by day's end, and many of them had traveled on foot. They'd all known Harry T. Moore, either through voter registration drives or by his NAACP work. They talked; they conjectured; they wondered why anyone would want to harm the nigh-saintly Mr. Moore. Deputy Clyde Bates attended to the "general talk," and the consensus, he said, linked the killing of Harry Moore to the Groveland case.

At one point, while mourners paid their respects to Moore before a makeshift shrine—a stack of shattered planks that had been the front porch—a young black boy, who had crawled under the house, was beating the underside of the first floor with a stick. He caught the eye, or ear, of Special Agent Robert Nischwitz of the FBI, who asked the boy what he was doing under there. "Trying to scare the rats away" was the boy's reply, in which Nischwitz found an apt metaphor for the situation in Mims. "Certain" that the Klan was responsible for the blast when he had arrived at the scene, the agent noted that Klansmen, too, "were all over the place, like rats." Like rats, they'd have to be beaten out of hiding.

Harriette Moore, meanwhile, remained in shock at Fernald-Laughton. She had begun to regain the strength to talk, but Dr. Starke worried that she might not survive the severe internal injuries she had suffered. The next week would be crucial; the doctor gave her a fifty-fifty chance of recovery. When Harriette was informed that her husband was dead, however, her mood darkened. She let go of hope. "There isn't much left to fight back for," she told a reporter from the *Orlando Sentinel*. "My home is wrecked. My children are grown up. They don't need me. Others can carry on." Asked her thoughts as to who might have committed the bombing, Harriette replied, "I have a couple of ideas who might have done it, but when people do those kinds of things they have someone else do it."

On the morning after the blast, the *New York Times* ran a front-page story, "Bombing Kills Negro Leader," that stated plainly what many

Floridians—and perhaps Harriette Moore—thought when it linked Harry Moore's murder to Willis McCall in its lead paragraph:

> *MIMS, FLA., Dec. 26—A Negro crusader who led a campaign to prosecute a white Sheriff for shooting two handcuffed Negroes was killed last night and his wife was seriously injured by a bomb blast beneath their bedroom. Harry T. Moore, 46 years old, . . . was the third Negro to die in the state by violence believed resulting from the 1949 Groveland rape case.*

The *Washington Post* made the link between the killing and the sheriff even plainer in an editorial titled "Terror in Florida," which stated, "When state officers flout the law, it can be scarcely surprising that the lynch spirit should spread."

Harry T. Moore became the first civil rights leader to be assassinated in the United States when he was killed on Christmas night in 1951. Shortly after the bombing Eleanor Roosevelt warned, "That kind of violent incident will be spread all over every country in the world, and the harm it will do us among the people of the world is untold." Indeed, stories in newspapers as far off as Asia and Africa reported the "violent incident," and editorials in the world's most influential newspapers condemned it.

Moore's killing unsettled Thurgood Marshall profoundly. In his travels across the South his hosts always attended to his safety in his comings and goings to court, on his social visits, and even in his sleep. Although in conversation he generally downplayed the danger and his fear, so as not to worry his family and associates, in a statement he made in 1951 he admitted to the terror he felt every time he set foot in the hostile environment of the South. "I can testify," he said, "there's times when you're scared to death. But you can't admit it; you just have to lie like hell to yourself. Otherwise, you'll start looking under the bed at night." Marshall could empathetically imagine, then, the hostility, the menace—the "pressure"—that locals like Harry Moore bore on a daily basis, year in and year out, as they continued bravely, despite "the possibility of violent death," the campaign for the civil rights of blacks in the Jim Crow South. The governor's office was flooded with thousands of letters and telegrams demanding action on behalf of the Moores, but the telegram that Governor Warren received from Thurgood Marshall struck a more somber note, reminding the governor that the Moores were "representatives of the finest type of citizens of your state" and that "unless they can be secure from lawlessness no one in Florida is safe from destruction."

Governor Warren was aggrieved by the press response to the Moore assassination. Editorials nationwide advertised "Terrorism in Florida," which led to organized efforts calling for boycotts of citrus and tourism. One op-ed page asked, "Notice Negro Blood on Your Grapefruit?" Another criticized the wife of New York's mayor Vincent Impellitteri for vacationing in Florida: "It's a pat on the back to the Klan murderers." And a heavily circulated Associated Press story with the headline "Terrorists Kill by Night; Shadow of Violence Drifts Across Sunny Vacationland" was exactly the kind of national publicity the state of Florida and Fuller Warren did not need.

Under the threat of drastic economic repercussions in Florida's tourist and citrus industries, Warren could not simply ignore the Moore affair—and thereby tacitly exempt the KKK, especially as the Klan was now perceived by the press and the public to be running unrestrained by any governance in the state. Warren thus offered a six-thousand-dollar reward for information leading to the "arrest and conviction of the dynamiters," and he promised a full investigation into Moore's murder, as "his assassins must be caught and punished." In addition, Warren announced, he was sending his special investigator, J. J. Elliott, to Mims.

Elliott, in his turn, declared that he would personally attend Moore's funeral service, where he would be "acting as a human shield to guarantee the church's safety." He indicated, too, that he would be willing to "ride with the family to see that nothing happens, if they want me to." The offer came with a boast: "I am the second best pistol shot in the state." Also, when Walter White announced that he was traveling to Florida "to see what can be done to stop the reign of terror," Elliott proffered his services as an armed personal escort.

As the day of Moore's funeral approached, the public outcry grew. So did the reaction to it, with black-owned homes and social clubs becoming targets for bombings throughout the South. Mostly, though, the nation's attention was fixed on Florida and the increasingly high-profile case of the civil rights leader who was slain in the twelfth of that state's bombings in 1951. The *New York Times* continued its daily coverage of news related to Moore's assassination. It reported, for instance, that Donald Harrington, a minister of the Community Church of New York in midtown Manhattan, had offered a prayer for Florida residents "in their moment of degradation and humiliation"—a moment that had shamed not only Florida but all of America in the estimation of foreign nations: "Our whole country stands blackened and discredited in the eyes of the world because of Florida's failure to protect the lives and liberties of all her citizens." Harrington continued, "I am ashamed of Florida. I am ashamed of the white race. . . . I am ashamed of all the churches of Florida and elsewhere that have turned their eyes away from what has been going on in Lake County for these past years, and passed by on the other side while their fellow-Americans of a darker skin were being denied the most basic American and human rights and privileges. I weep for my country's sacred honor."

The NAACP, which had forced Moore from his executive position in Florida only weeks earlier, was now calling on President Truman for "fast, resolute action" inasmuch as "the killer of Harry T. Moore is the assassin of the democratic ideal." On December 28, as announced, Walter White arrived in Florida. At the hospital in Sanford he presented a check in the amount of $250 to Harriette Moore, with the pledge that all the money owed to Harry Moore by the NAACP—the $2,600-plus in back pay—would be paid in full. In fact, in the coming weeks the NAACP would raise many thousands of dollars on the back of Moore's death, and White realized he could not afford the public relations debacle that would surely result if donors should become aware of the NAACP's ill treatment of its "democratic ideal" in the months before his murder.

With J. J. Elliott indeed as his escort, White visited the Moore house in Mims. There, for the press, he praised the FBI's investigation into the fatal bombing. "Everything was being done that could be done," he told reporters, and he noted that U.S. attorney general J. Howard McGrath had told him "a dozen FBI agents [were] loose on the bombing," because J. Edgar Hoover "has never been so disturbed over a case." White finished the day at a mass meeting in Orlando, where reporters, echoing recent comments made by Governor Warren, suggested to White that communists might have been responsible for Moore's death. White sneered as he replied, "I'm sure as I can be that Sheriff McCall is not a Communist."

Walter White left Florida two days later, as Moore's funeral was being postponed in the hope that Harriette might soon recover sufficiently to attend. White's flight home was hastily arranged, and unpublicized. Although there had been no threats on the NAACP leader's life during his stay in Florida, tensions had been running high throughout his visit. A police spokesman in Orlando owned to reporters that it was "a relief to know that he's gone."

Against Dr. Starke's wishes, Harriette Moore visited her husband's body at Burton's Funeral Parlor. Weeping uncontrollably, she reached out to hold her Harry one last time. She did not make it to the funeral. On the morning of the service her blood pressure dropped precipitously and the doctor forbade her to leave the hospital.

Early that morning, too, George Simms and J. J. Elliott arrived at St. James Missionary Baptist Church. Wearing mechanics' jumpsuits and armed with flashlights, the master sergeant and the special investigator crawled under the church to search for hidden explosives. They found nothing. They then inspected the church interior wall to wall, pew by pew. Satisfied that the church was secure, they allowed the service to proceed.

More than six hundred people attended the funeral of Harry T. Moore on New Year's Day of 1952, most of them in the yard outside the small church. Evangeline and Peaches took their places beside their grandmother, Rosa Moore, in the front pew, and to the strains of "Rock of Ages," played on a phonograph, their father's plain casket adorned with a wilting floral arrangement was borne up the aisle to the pulpit. Among the mourners were representatives from the Civil Rights Congress who circulated a petition—some of it written by Stetson Kennedy—accusing the U.S. government of black genocide. A dozen men and women eulogized Moore, and from New York Walter White issued a statement on behalf of the NAACP's national office.

Following the service, mourners joined the mile-long procession from the church and along Old Dixie Highway to LaGrange Cemetery. Solemn-faced, in dark suits and Sunday dresses, they gathered near a cluster of live oaks cloaked in Spanish moss, at the segregated section of plots for blacks. A final prayer was spoken to take the soul of Harry T. Moore beyond the grave into which his body was lowered. The casket sank slowly, then paused, obstructed in its progress, as had been Harry Moore in his life's work. Peaches and Evangeline gazed helplessly down at the wilted flowers atop the casket—they'd had to have the flowers brought in from Miami because local florists refused to deliver arrangements to Negro funerals—until, finally dislodged, the casket continued its descent.

The next day Harriette Moore continued hers. J. J. Elliott and a state attorney rushed to her hospital bedside in the hope of getting a final statement, but the fading widow of Harry T. Moore was adamant. She would not speak a word to them "even if they had a pistol on them." Harriette Vyda Simms Moore passed away on January 3. Her two grieving daughters braved the burial of a beloved parent for the second time within a week.

Thurgood Marshall was out on the NAACP circuit, delivering addresses at memorial services for Harry T. Moore and his wife. At Mount Olivet Baptist Church in Harlem, where two thousand people packed the pews,

Marshall shared the speakers' platform with the likes of Jackie Robinson as well as Walter White, who announced that the NAACP was considering a nationwide work stoppage if Florida failed to bring the parties responsible for Moore's death to justice—even so, White continued to express his confidence in the FBI. Marshall's more fiery rhetoric, however, was not at all likely to please J. Edgar Hoover. Indeed, Marshall assumed a style that recalled the protests against lynching that he and his friend Moore had organized in Florida's postwar forties, except that now he protested not with but on behalf of his friend. "You can pick up a newspaper or tune in on your radio set any time and learn where the FBI has out-witted some of the cleverest criminals in the world," Marshall declaimed at Pittsburgh's Central Baptist Church. "Yet when it comes to mob violence against Negroes, all you can get is, 'We're investigating.' It's time we got up off our plush seats and did something about it."

The FBI did continue to investigate the case, as did Fuller Warren's man, J. J. Elliott, but neither made any significant progress in the weeks following the bombing. Tracking down a source for the explosives was next to impossible, for, as FBI special agent Frank Meech noted in his reports, "Getting dynamite all over central Florida was like buying chewing gum." Even more frustrating to the agents, and more obstructive to their investigation, was the interview process, on which the FBI heavily relied. County sheriff departments and known Klan members were hardly forthcoming, and in central Florida the line between law enforcement and the KKK had often been indistinct. By the end of the 1940s it was completely blurred. "We'd go in and talk to someone in law enforcement," Meech reported, "and they'd say, 'what the hell are you investigating that for?' He was only a nigger."

With the intensification of FBI activity after the Moore bombing in Florida creating considerable anxiety in the Klaverns of Lake County, Sheriff Willis V. McCall, despite his denial of any affiliation with the KKK, showed up at a local Klan meeting near Groveland. There, according to Special Agent Meech, he lectured the nervous Klansmen on how to deal with FBI agents and their questions. "We had informants that were already in the Klan," Meech said. "Our informants identified McCall as the man who told Klan members: 'You don't talk to the FBI. Don't tell them anything. Don't even tell them your name.'"

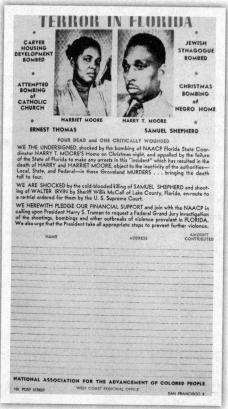

**TERROR IN FLORIDA**

CARVER
HOUSING
DEVELOPMENT
BOMBED

JEWISH
SYNAGOGUE
BOMBED

ATTEMPTED
BOMBING
of
CATHOLIC
CHURCH

CHRISTMAS
BOMBING
of
NEGRO HOME

HARRIET MOORE          HARRY T. MOORE

ERNEST THOMAS                    SAMUEL SHEPHERD

FOUR DEAD and ONE CRITICALLY WOUNDED

WE THE UNDERSIGNED, shocked by the bombing of NAACP Florida State Coordinator HARRY T. MOORE'S Home on Christmas night, and appalled by the failure of the State of Florida to make any arrests in this "incident" which has resulted in the death of HARRY and HARRIET MOORE, object to the inactivity of the authorities—Local, State, and Federal—in these Groveland MURDERS . . . bringing the death toll to four.

WE ARE SHOCKED by the cold-blooded killing of SAMUEL SHEPHERD and shooting of WALTER IRVIN by Sheriff Willis McCall of Lake County, Florida, en-route to a re-trial ordered for them by the U. S. Supreme Court.

WE HEREWITH PLEDGE OUR FINANCIAL SUPPORT and join with the NAACP in calling upon President Harry S. Truman to request a Federal Grand Jury investigation of the shootings, bombings and other outbreaks of violence prevalent in FLORIDA. We also urge that the President take all appropriate steps to prevent further violence.

NAME          ADDRESS          AMOUNT CONTRIBUTED

NATIONAL ASSOCIATION FOR THE ADVANCEMENT OF COLORED PEOPLE
101 POST STREET          WEST COAST REGIONAL OFFICE          SAN FRANCISCO 8

The NAACP raised tens of thousands of dollars in donations for the Groveland defense following the killings of Harry and Harriette Moore. (*Library of Congress, Prints & Photographs Division, Visual Materials from the NAACP Records*)

S PECIAL AGENT WAYNE Swinney of the FBI had been assigned the task of escorting Thurgood Marshall around central Florida. Tensions were still running high after the Moore bombing, and when Marshall had informed the young FBI agent that Eastern Air Lines was "booked solid" and therefore unable to provide a seat for him on a return flight, Swinney had exploded. "I don't care how booked you are," he told the Eastern reservation agent. "You better find a seat for this guy so he can get out of here."

By no means was he underestimating the threat to Marshall in Florida. Swinney, along with nearly two dozen other agents committed to the Moore case "to ensure that the FBI was doing a thorough investigation," had recently been looking into the shootings of Samuel Shepherd and Walter Irvin. In fact, he had just spent three days interviewing Willis McCall and local Klansmen in connection with Groveland and its aftermath, although he had not yet concluded, as he would eventually, that in regard to Harry Moore and his wife, "Klan members and some law enforcement officers were behind these murders." They were also hell-bent on obstructing the FBI, no matter what the case, not to mention hobbling the NAACP. Orange County sheriff Dave Starr, McCall's friend and a known member of the KKK, had, according to Swinney, "continually impeded the FBI's investigation," and the bureau was "worried that physical harm might come to Marshall" when he was in the area.

With Marshall standing beside him, Swinney picked up the phone on the reservation desk and made a couple of calls of his own. Visits to Florida by high-profile NAACP executives like Marshall created security concerns and logistic headaches for FBI agents, who were more familiar than most with the menace the KKK presented. The young agent finally breathed a sigh of relief as he watched Marshall climb the steps and board the plane headed back to New York.

I N EARLY FEBRUARY 1952, Jack Greenberg boarded a train for Orlando. He was traveling with a representative from the Elmo Roper research firm and Arnold DeMille, a columnist for the *Chicago Defender.* They were joined in Alexandria, Virginia, by Alex Akerman. While Greenberg was understandably preoccupied with the upcoming resumption of hearings in the retrial of Walter Irvin, Akerman's thoughts kept drifting back to the first trial, when he and Franklin Williams were defending three Groveland boys as much against the white justice of Lake County as in a case of rape. He tried to prepare his traveling companions for the hazards that awaited them in Willis McCall country. Greenberg had of course heard Williams's unsettling tales, and he'd had some firsthand experience of the law according to

Hunter and Futch, so the discussions between the two defense attorneys tended frequently to favor gallows humor, as DeMille noted when, after one exchange about the county thugs on both sides of the law, Akerman turned to Greenberg and asked, "How you want your body shipped back?"

They arrived in Orlando on the afternoon of Saturday, February 9, which gave them more than a full day to prepare for the hearings that were scheduled to begin at the Marion County courthouse on Monday. Jack Greenberg checked into the downtown San Juan Hotel.

About the same time that Greenberg was settling in at his hotel room, Grand Dragon Bill Hendrix was riling up his troops at a rally in Orlando. Alarmed at the progress of the NAACP in general, and more particularly of Thurgood Marshall, in the fight against Jim Crow, Hendrix had formed, by his claim, an "American Confederate Army" of ninety-seven cohorts in thirty-one states, all of them prepared to bear arms in the event that the Supreme Court outlawed segregation. At the rally that evening, Hendrix's "rebel army" voted in support of three measures in its avowed purpose to forestall justice for all:

1. denounce the NAACP and Anti-Defamation League as "hate groups";
2. retain the hood, robe, and mask as official uniform; and
3. keep the fiery cross as a religious symbol.

"Florida must have a few lynchings if its law enforcement officers don't enforce 100 percent segregation in the state," Hendrix reportedly proclaimed, after marching his army through the downtown streets of Orlando.

Greenberg heard it before he saw it. A terrific roar arose at nightfall: engines revving, horns honking, the din of male voices. In the streets beneath his window Greenberg counted "at least 25 cars" circling the San Juan Hotel as he witnessed the procession of Klansmen in full regalia, "with confederate flags flying, some carrying blazing torches," and for months Greenberg's sleep would be haunted by the "white-hooded, sheeted figure [who] sat on the outsized hood of a Nash Ambassador, waving as it drove by." Only seven years before, Greenberg had been among the first landing of U.S. forces that stormed Iwo Jima in 1945, and aboard ship he had battled Japanese kamikaze attack planes in Okinawa Harbor: "It was frightening, it was exciting. . . . There wasn't any point in being afraid," had said the twenty-year-old Greenberg, who then had an "unthinking belief in his own immortality." At twenty-seven, the survivor of one of the deadliest battles America fought in the Pacific campaign of World War II had less faith in his immortality. With the

Klan parading outside his hotel, Greenberg "took the vain precaution of putting a night table against the door" before he tried to sleep.

The site of Hendrix's KKK rally on February 9 had supposedly been "patrolled" by Sheriff Dave Starr and his deputies. Newspapers reported that neither Starr nor his officers had observed any illegal hoods or masks because they were "too busy with traffic accidents." Hendrix, who had recently declared his candidacy for Florida governor, told reporters that he had been "misquoted" with regard to his "few hangings" speech. He was indicted on February 11 for violating postal laws by mailing "libelous and defamatory" postcards to journalists and politicians.

The Klan had dispersed less than an hour before the Florida attorney Paul Perkins and journalist Arnold DeMille met Thurgood Marshall at Orlando's airport. The rally site was quiet when they drove by. "Your boys, the KKKs were here to greet you," DeMille told Thurgood. "But they couldn't wait any longer and left. They'll see you at the trial in Ocala."

On the morning of February 11, Marshall and his team of lawyers were chauffeured the eighty miles to Ocala, and to their jaw-dropping surprise, the car was a "beautiful shiny Cadillac." They'd arranged for a car, but Marshall would have preferred not to alight at Marion County's Court House in a late-model hearse.

Built in 1907, the Marion County Court House, a stately building with a facade of Indiana limestone, commanded Ocala's Public Square. Reporters were waiting outside when Marshall arrived. They wondered what Marshall had thought of the Klan's "rip-roaring welcome parade" for him, but he dismissively replied, "We're going to trial." More pertinently they wondered how Marshall planned to deal with Judge Truman Futch, who had barred the NAACP lawyers from representing the defendant, on the grounds that they "stirred up trouble in the community." Marshall's response was terse. "The charge is without foundation in facts," he said, and stated that he'd be filing a motion in court: "If the motion is denied, I will appeal and keep appealing until I reach the Supreme Court, if necessary." Marshall hinted, too, that a "sensational new trial element" would be introduced, but when he was pressed by reporters for more details, as he knew he would be, he gave them only one word, and a wry smile. "Witness," he said. And walked on.

As the retrial had been moved to Marion County, Walter Irvin had at least escaped the custody of Sheriff Willis McCall. He had not escaped the painful reminders of their November encounter, however. "My shoulder worries me frequently," he told reporters at the courthouse in Ocala, "and my hand is numb and I get a buzz through my body when I move. For two weeks I begged them to let me see a doctor and when I did I got two pills supposed to be for my nerves. Once they took me to the hospital at Eustis and the doc there says I have a bullet in me near my kidney."

Except for the time he had been hospitalized in Eustis and at the prison, Irvin had spent the last thirty-one months in the death house at Raiford. He complained to reporters that the guards wouldn't give him anything to read, and they "blew up when they heard I was getting a new trial. . . . Sammy was getting *Life* and *Time* and used to let me read them, but they gave out and lately there's been nothing. I get nothing unless somebody arranged to send the magazine to me, and nobody has."

Reporters commented on the thin mustache that Irvin had apparently been permitted to grow since his last appearance before the press. "The captain of the prison say he going to make me shave it off after this trial," said Irvin, "like he must be expecting me back." Irvin's irony prompted a reporter to ask if, then, he was innocent. Irvin seemed to be momentarily stunned by the question, perhaps because to him that had never been a question. Still, he answered it. "Am I innocent? . . . Sure I'm innocent."

C OURT WILL COME to order. No smoking!"
From the balcony down, the courtroom went quiet. Like the balcony in the Lake County Court House, this one seated blacks, and it was "packed to the ceiling." Blacks had "come from all directions with their paper bags." At the midday break they'd gather outside the courthouse and talk together over their bag lunches, for the segregated eateries of downtown Ocala allowed them "no other place to go."

The first order of business for the defense was to petition Judge Futch to rule, contrary to his prior decision, that the NAACP attorneys Marshall and Greenberg be permitted to represent Walter Irvin. Marshall approached the bench with confidence; he doubted that Judge Futch would risk the possibility of another reversal at the Supreme Court were the defendant denied the legal representation of his choice in a capital case. Marshall was also secretly hoping that the feature story in the current issue of *Collier's* magazine, which named him "our greatest civil liberties lawyer," might win him some measure of respect, even in a Southern court. Earlier in his career, when Marshall had been arguing a motion before a Louisiana judge who was "no friend," the opposing counsel had asked the court for more time in order to check the accuracy of Marshall's citations. In open court, the judge had declared, "You don't have to worry about that. If Mr. Marshall puts his signature on it, you don't have to check it." Marshall owed that to Charlie Houston's influence.

Evidently State Attorney Jesse Hunter did not subscribe to *Collier's*. He rose from his chair and was prepared to fight the defense motion. Futch, however, had reconsidered; he allowed the motion, and the two NAACP attorneys resumed as counsel for the defendant. Not unexpectedly, Futch denied the defense motion to disqualify Hunter.

The defense next, and again, raised the change of venue issue. Marshall argued that the results from the Elmo Roper poll, which the NAACP had commissioned, showed clearly that the majority of Marion County residents believed that Walter Irvin could not receive a fair trial in Ocala. Marshall had confidence in the value of qualified, credentialed witnesses whose academic research and statistical analysis could be employed to illustrate systematic discrimination against blacks. Thus, in the school segregation case *Briggs v. Elliott*, he had used the testimony of Dr. Kenneth Clark, who had studied children's reactions to the "good" and "bad" qualities of black and white dolls, to bolster his argument that black children were stigmatized by being educated in segregated schools. In the hearings preceding Irvin's retrial, Marshall called to the stand the Roper poll research executive, formerly a professor of sociology at Cornell University, and led him through a detailed explanation of the survey he had conducted. The survey showed that "not one of 518 whites questioned here in Marion County thinks Irvin is innocent. One percent were found to believe he may not be guilty," testified the Roper executive. Moreover, his research indicated that the farther away Florida's trial venues were from Lake and Marion counties, the more likely they were to "place the trial in a more neutral atmosphere."

Throughout the testimony Hunter mostly lounged in the empty jury box, "chewed occasionally on his teeth and gums," and affected disinterest. In his cross-examination he disparaged the research and ridiculed the witness. "How much did they pay you?" Hunter asked the executive, who quoted seven thousand dollars as the cost of the survey.

"Now, as a matter of fact, your firm predicted the elections of 1948, is that not correct?" Hunter inquired, referring to the famously inaccurate front-page headline "Dewey Defeats Truman" that the *Chicago Daily Tribune*, in its eagerness to go to press early, had run on the basis of polls.

"Yes it did," the researcher admitted, but any amusement elicited in the court was unintentional, because he added, "We predicted it wrong, but we did predict it." Once the laughter in the courtroom had died down, no one doubted that Hunter's objection to use of the survey would be supported by the bench.

Hunter proceeded to counter the defense claim that Marion County's prejudice disallowed the possibility of a fair trial for Walter Irvin, by calling his own witnesses, among them L. R. Hampton, a sixty-three-year-old black dentist. He was stirring. He extolled the love and respect that blacks and whites alike accorded each other in Marion County; he declared Judge Futch to be "one of the best friends of me and my race I have ever known." He praised a county that historically had produced a Negro city council-man and a Negro county treasurer, and he expressed concern that the retrial of the Groveland Boys case in Ocala might harm the "good feeling that has existed all of these years" between the races.

"Now, Dr. Hampton," Marshall asked, as he began his cross-examination, "when were these Negroes Mayors and City Commissioners, like you have testified about?"

"Well," Dr. Hampton replied, "it's so far back that I can hardly remember."

"About how far back was it?"

"Well, it was something like sixty years ago."

"Then what you mean to say," Marshall said, "is that there were Negroes who held those kind of offices back immediately after the Civil War, don't you?"

"Well, it was a long time ago."

Marshall's final question for Dr. Hampton addressed the more imme-diate issue of jury selection and composition. "Would you have considered it proper to have Negroes on the jury?"

"Well," the dentist answered, "I don't know whether they were intel-lectually equipped enough to be on the juries."

Another of Hunter's black witnesses stated, "I would put this county up against Jerusalem itself, and this is where I am going to stay until I die." His sentiments were echoed by a sixty-four-year-old retired black man who had likewise spent his entire life in the county. Still, in his entire lifetime, as he admitted to Marshall under cross-examination, he had never before been inside a courtroom because he had never been called for jury duty.

Marshall then asked, "You are head of the American Legion here, aren't you?"

"Yes, I am."

"Are there any white members of your American Legion post?"

"No, sir, there aren't, we have our own post," the man answered. "We are all colored people, we have our own post to ourselves, because that is the way we want it." Marshall's lips were pursed, but he allowed Hunter's witness to keep talking.

"It could be the other way if we wanted to, I think," the man stammered. "The only reason is we have one to ourselves like we have always wanted to have, and I am head of our post, and . . . what else do you want to know about it?"

"That is all," Marshall said, and turned his back to the witness.

A "gentleman of the frock," who, in the balcony, had attended to the testimonies of the elderly black men on Hunter's witness list, remarked to a reporter, "Such folks I'd take great pleasure and dignity in sprinkling the dust over their remains."

Judge Truman Futch needed maybe five seconds to rule on Hunter's objection to the admissibility of the Elmo Roper survey. "The objection is sustained," Futch said. "The affidavit and the report is rejected."

Marshall was crushed, not only by the expenditure of seven thousand dollars for naught but also by the man-hours his team had spent in processing the research into evidence. Sheriff Willis McCall had run Roper researcher Louis Harris out of Lake County, and now Judge Futch had disposed of the research itself.

During the lunch recess Marshall and the defense team assessed the damage. To their disadvantage, the trial was going forward in Marion County. It was a loss, for sure, but, as Akerman reminded Marshall, they could not reasonably expect very many wins, either with objections or in evidentiary rulings, with Judge Futch presiding. He and Hunter performed effectively as a team, and once the court had seated a jury mostly of the state's choosing, a verdict against Irvin was almost assured. So, the best strategy for the defense was, as in the first trial, to establish on the record every possible grounds for reversal and wait for the court to err.

In the hallway, before returning to the courtroom, Marshall was taking note of the numerous state troopers and deputies posted around the courthouse when the portly Jefferson J. Elliott came bounding toward him. Marshall had of course not forgotten Elliott's role in the coroner's inquest, and whitewash, following the shooting of the Groveland defendants, or Stetson Kennedy's claim that the governor's special investigator was a Klansman.

"I'm here at the wish of the governor," Elliott told Marshall as the two shook hands. Then, leaning in conspiratorially toward the NAACP special counsel, Elliott warned, "First thing is, you look out." He had gotten Marshall's attention.

"You'll see each guy that's got this kind of a pin." Elliott showed Marshall the pin in question, and explained, "They're trying to get you."

"Who?" Marshall asked. "Willis McCall?"

Elliott paused before he answered, his voice low. "No, the deputy is going to get you."

Marshall allowed himself a moment to absorb Elliott's words. Four murders linked to Lake County law enforcement had already been committed since the Groveland Boys case had begun, not to mention the occurrences of death threats, beatings, a bombing, posses, and a high-speed car chase. Marshall did not doubt that his life might be in danger, and he could see that the governor might find it politically inconvenient if "our greatest civil rights lawyer" were to be assassinated in Florida. He had no reason not to take the special investigator's warning seriously.

"So go toward them, but not from them," Elliott advised. Marshall expressed his appreciation for the words of caution.

"Second," Elliott said, after he'd walked Marshall out of anyone's earshot, "the judge and the governor have been on the telephone" and a deal, approved by Fuller Warren, was on the table: if Irvin were to plead guilty, the governor would ensure that the defendant would receive a life sentence.

"Well," Marshall said, "I can't decide that. Irvin will have to decide it." Elliott agreed.

To Marshall and Greenberg—in light of their own dispiriting assessment of the defense's chances given the venue, the judge, and the state attorney in the case—a deal that guaranteed to spare Irvin's life sounded like a good one. It was also exactly the "cautious" kind of approach that disgusted Franklin Williams. "It shocked me," Williams later commented, that Marshall had even considered such a deal. "I would never have discussed it with them. It struck me whether Thurgood himself was not sure whether they were innocent or guilty. I would never have told them that. I would have said, 'No way you will plead guilty. We will fight this thing to the end.'"

Marshall, in fact, was beyond cautious. He was fearful. Just one year before, the Martinsville Seven had eaten their last meals at the Virginia State Penitentiary. The NAACP had won the battle against the Civil Rights Congress—and Marshall against his communist adversary, William Patterson—to appeal the case of the seven young black men who had been convicted of raping a white woman. The win left nothing to be savored; every appeal had failed. On February 2, 1951, the first four of the Martinsville Seven were executed at fifteen-minute intervals in Virginia state's electric chair. The remaining three were electrocuted over the next forty-eight hours. Marshall had no doubt that as sure as the state of Virginia had killed seven men on a rape conviction, and as sure as Willis McCall had shot dead the alleged rapist Ernest Thomas and convicted rapist Samuel Shepherd before they'd had a chance to explore all the legal avenues open to them, the state of Florida would sentence Walter Irvin to death. Franklin Williams might indeed be shocked by Thurgood's willingness to place the deal before Irvin and his family, but Marshall had lost too many clients to the electric chair to deny a defendant, even one who clearly was not guilty, the rare opportunity to spare his life with a guilty plea.

Marshall and Greenberg discussed Elliott's proposition further with Akerman and Perkins, and the four lawyers decided to take up the matter with Jesse Hunter. The state attorney confirmed both that the deal was legitimate and that Truman Futch was prepared to honor it. Marshall sent for Irvin's family.

Present at the courthouse were Irvin's brother-in-law, James Shepherd (Samuel's brother), and his mother, Dellia, "a heavy woman in a dark dress, green scarf and run-down brown shoes," who had hitchhiked the sixty miles from Groveland to Ocala that morning. As much to them as to Walter, Marshall explained the governor's offer, which, he noted, had been acknowledged and agreed to by the prosecutor and trial judge. The room fell silent.

Then: "Well, you got the case reversed once," Irvin said.

"Yeah, but eventually they can't find that . . . " Marshall let his voice trail off. "Odds are," he resumed, "that they'll convict you. And Futch the judge, he sure as hell will give you the death penalty, so it's up to you."

The decision was Irvin's, but both Marshall and Greenberg "clearly implied that [they] hoped he'd accept the deal," because "something might turn up someday to win his freedom."

Irvin set his eyes on Marshall, then his mother. He considered the back of his hand. "Well," he said, "I guess I've got to make up my mind."

He drew his mother and James over to the side of the room. The three of them spoke in hushed tones. Greenberg and Marshall remained silent. It wasn't much more than a minute before Irvin, then his mother and James, turned to face Marshall.

"I guess this is the only way out," Irvin said.

Marshall shrugged. "Well, it's up to you."

"What do I have to do?"

"Nothing. Just stand up there and when they say, 'Are you guilty or not guilty,' you say, I'm guilty." To clarify, to make certain that Irvin knew exactly what his guilty plea would mean, Marshall added, "That you raped that woman."

"That I raped that whore?" Irvin was shaking his head. "I didn't. And I'm not going to say so." He had made his decision.

Dellia Irvin was holding her chin high. Marshall recalled how she, too, could have lied—in the first trial, on the witness stand—and tried to save her son's life by testifying that Walter had come home that fateful July night at 2 a.m. Instead she'd stated that he'd come home but she didn't know the time.

"Won't say it on myself," Irvin insisted. Marshall and Greenberg tried to impress upon their client and his family that they were not going to win this trial in Marion County; they also emphasized that there were no guarantees at the Supreme Court. But Walter Irvin was adamant. He would not admit to rape. They'd have to say that for him, he told his lawyers, who pointed out that the judge would accept a guilty plea only from the defendant's own lips.

Greenberg was dumbfounded by the decision of the steadfast, young defendant "who wouldn't confess after brutal beatings, and who wouldn't die after having been shot three times." Marshall, too, was at a loss for words, though in that moment he knew "damn well that man was innocent."

Irvin reiterated, "I'll take a life sentence right now because that's better than the chair, but if I have to say I had anything to do with that lady I'm not going to do it. I'm not guilty."

Clutching a well-worn Bible, Dellia Irvin gave her son a hug. "All right, now," she comforted the boy in him, and told him he'd be back home with her soon.

After the recess the defense attorneys returned with Irvin to their table in the courtroom. To Marshall, menace seemed to hover in the atmosphere of the room, perhaps because his gaze had fallen on Willis McCall. A bear of a man, he stood tall in his cowboy boots; one hand was resting on the butt of his holstered gun, the gun he'd used to shoot down two of the Groveland boys—and maybe to fire a few of the slugs in Ernest Thomas, too. Marshall's eyes had drifted to the sullen, dull-faced presence of Willie Padgett among some spectators when, with a loud crash, Jesse Hunter's chair broke under him and landed the state attorney, sprawling, on the floor.

It was Hunter's galluses that captured Marshall's eye. Red galluses. Like the ones Herman Talmadge of Georgia wore to honor his father, the former governor Eugene Talmadge. Four years earlier, Herman had honored his father's racial prejudices as well. In his own gubernatorial campaign Herman made fame out of hate with his signal, one-word stump speeches. He'd stand on a stage, tug on his red suspenders, and shout "Nigger!" over and over until he'd whipped the crowd into a frenzy. "You tell 'em, Hummon," his redneck constituents would holler back, their tobacco juice spattering their "red Talmadge neckties." An epithet and suspenders won young Herman Talmadge the 1948 special election decisively. If segregation and white supremacy wanted a symbol in the South, it was found in red galluses.

Hunter got resettled in another chair, and Judge Futch took his seat on the bench, where he had laid out sticks for his whittling. With the permission of Futch, if not of the court attendant, Arnold DeMille snapped a photo of the Whittlin' Judge, who asked the *Chicago Defender* columnist if he might "see it when it was made up."

The last pretrial motion to be heard concerned the admission of Walter Irvin's pants as evidence, which the defense was challenging on the grounds that Deputy James Yates had entered the Irvins' house on the morning following the alleged rape and had collected the evidence—the pants Walter had been wearing the night before—without a search warrant.

Attorney Paul Perkins asked the defense witness Dellia Irvin who arrived at her house on the morning of July 16, 1949, and she replied, "Well, this Deputy Sheriff, he came up to the house and said that he 'came for that little black nigger boy's clothes.'"

Perkins established that the "boy" was her son, Walter, and then asked, "What did you give him?"

"Well, I gave him a pair of brown trousers and a pair of brown shoes, and a white colored shirt."

"Now, Dellia, were you afraid?"

"Yes, sir, I was because he was the law."

Dellia had asked Yates the likely date of the trial, and, as she told Perkins, the deputy had barked at her that "there might not be any damned trial."

The defense argued that because Walter Irvin paid rent to his parents for a bedroom with a lock on its door, Dellia Irvin was not obliged by law to enter her son's private room to gather evidence for a deputy without a search warrant. Further, they argued, Dellia Irvin had not voluntarily surrendered her son's pants to the deputy but rather had been intimidated into doing so by Yates when he stepped into her house. Not until 1961 would the Supreme Court rule, in *Mapp v. Ohio*, that evidence obtained in an illegal search was inadmissible in state courts.

Judge Futch closed the day's proceedings with Dellia Irvin's testimony, but it was no surprise to Marshall the next morning, when court resumed on Tuesday, February 12, at 9:30 a.m., that Futch, in his first order of business, allowed Walter Irvin's pants into evidence. That was not the worst of it for the defense. Marshall had also learned that Irvin's alibi witness—Carol Alexander, the waitress who remembered seeing Irvin and Shepherd at Club Eaton until two or three o'clock in the morning—had not returned to Florida for the trial, despite the fact that she was willing to testify and had already accepted travel expense money. Instead, she remained at Clark University in Atlanta. Her family was unconvinced that the NAACP could guarantee her safety. Of even more concern to Marshall was the possibility that his surprise witness, Lawrence Burtoft, might not get back to Florida in time to testify. He was in the army, at Fort Jackson in South Carolina. The defense's witness list was in worse shape now than it had been two and a half years earlier, in September 1949, when Irvin was convicted in the Lake County trial.

Jury selection was no better, either. Of the seven blacks on the panel, four were disqualified because they did not believe in capital punishment. (One of them, Hunter confided to Marshall, was the "best colored man on the panel. Sorry he was excused"—and to his defense team, Marshall confided, "If he says the boy is good then we don't want him.") With the state's peremptory challenges Hunter disposed of the remaining three blacks. Walter Irvin's fate would be decided by twelve white Marion County men, and again Marshall was hardly surprised. He might have been flattered by a comment made by Jesse Hunter after the jury had been sworn in; pointing at Thurgood Marshall, the state attorney said to a guest of the court, "An ingenious man. Knows more law than any man in the United States." Hunter liked to take down a proper adversary.

With trial testimony about to begin, spectators packed the courtroom, blacks upstairs in the balcony, whites downstairs on the main floor. Reporters crowded the press area: Jay Nelson Tuck from the *New York Post*, Richard H. Parke of the *New York Times*, Richard Carter with the *New York Compass*. Carter, who had recently won the prestigious Polk Award for outstanding metropolitan reporting, had been researching a feature story on Groveland in 1949 when he discovered Ernest Thomas's attempt to tap into the Lake County *bolita* rackets, which raised the possibility that Thomas's death had nothing to do with Norma Padgett. Also covering the trial were the Associated Press and the *Saturday Evening Post* as well as, of course, reporters from the Florida papers, including Ormond Powers of the *Orlando Sentinel* and

Mabel Norris Reese of the *Mount Dora Topic*. A separate press table accommodated black journalists covering the trial, such as Robert M. Ratcliffe from the *Pittsburgh Courier* and Arnold DeMille of the *Chicago Defender*.

The indictment in the matter of Walter Irvin was read in court, and Jesse Hunter called his first witness. The slight but muscular figure of Willie Padgett trudged to the stand, his face "remarkable," according to one reporter, with teeth "so large that they stretch the mouth into an expression of perpetual agony. His mouth seems most comfortable when he allows it to hang open, and he seems to do most of his breathing through it." Padgett related essentially the same story he'd presented in the first trial. His car was stuck; four blacks happened along and offered to help him but then began roughing him up. He picked up a stick, "hit quite a few licks" on them, until they overpowered him and threw him down on the roadside, near a fence, where he lost consciousness. He came to in time to see their car drive away, apparently with Norma inside. He waited approximately thirty minutes till another car finally appeared; it gave him a push, but he couldn't remember the car's make or model or, for that matter, the driver who'd come to his aid. He then drove close to ten miles, past quiet homes and several storefront businesses that were still open, and even past the police station, to Dean's filling station on the east side of Leesburg.

In cross-examination by Akerman, Padgett acknowledged that he and Norma were not living together in July 1949 and that they had been drinking whiskey the evening of July 15. Akerman noted, too, that Padgett had previously testified that the car driven by Samuel Shepherd and Walter Irvin was a '46 or '48 black Mercury. Later, Padgett claimed the car was "light green." Akerman, however, failed to address some questionable, key details in Padgett's story: After an assault and suspected abduction, why had Padgett passed by a police station and stopped instead at Dean's filling station? How was it that he could identify with such certainty the black men in the Mercury and recall, in detail, their conversations, but could not remember a single detail about the car or the driver and anyone with him who actually got Willie back on the road?

A baby was crying. Jesse Hunter had called his next witness, and Thurgood Marshall turned his head to find the source of the noise. Norma Padgett was passing a three-week-old infant, her second son, to the outstretched hands of her sister or a cousin.

"Dressed for a party," Jack Greenberg thought as Norma smoothed the front of her cotton dress, white with a floral print, and tugged at her "coral-colored cardigan sweater." The two and a half years since Norma had testified in Lake County—when one reporter had wondered, "Why would a 'rape victim' strut and prance and pose like another Victoria Price of Scottsboro notoriety?"—had not been kind to her. Now nineteen, "bone-poor" and living rent-free on her uncle's farm, she was, relatives said, trapped in a marriage to a man who "neglects" her and "spends his wages recklessly." She walked up to the witness stand; she was not strutting or prancing: She "has the bent carriage and the shuffling walk of a woman three times her age," one newspaper reported. Her blond hair, bobbed and curled at the first trial, was hanging lank and lifeless. Her eyes were puffy. Her arms "ricket-thin" and her shoulder blades poking at her tight dress, she raised her right hand and swore to tell the whole truth.

Jesse Hunter treated Norma gently, his voice nearly as soft and low as hers, "which often could not be heard above the sounds of the traffic outside the open windows of the court." So solicitously—so strategically solicitously, the defense lawyers opined—did the state attorney lead his witness through her testimony that any antagonism in cross-examination was bound to seem harsh, even barbaric, by comparison.

Norma's rendering of the roadside encounter did not diverge from Willie's. After the fight, which left Willie unconscious, the story became Norma's own. One of the black men, she said, told the others, "Grab the lady," and the five of them—Ernest Thomas at the wheel, Charles Greenlee in the passenger seat, and Norma sandwiched between Samuel Shepherd and Walter Irvin in the back—drove to "a little ole side road" near the Sumter County line. The car stopped, "and then this nigger by the name of Thomas got in the back seat."

Asked if Thomas did anything to her, Norma replied, "Yes, sir, Thomas he jerked up my dress, and I jerked it back down, and he told me to leave it alone, and pulled it back up, and he made me take off my pants . . . and Thomas raped me first, Thomas did."

"All right," Hunter said, "which one raped you next?"

"Then Irvin raped me next, he was the second one, and I don't know which one was next after that."

"And all four of them raped you out there on that side road?"

"Yes, sir, they did."

Hunter paused, to allow Norma time to elaborate. Yet the fire she had brought to her testimony in the first trial was gone; she neither craved nor basked in the court's attention, as she had in Lake County. She exhibited no anger or shame, but not out of apparent indifference; she seemed simply to be tired and worn down. She hardly called the Groveland Boys niggers anymore.

So Hunter prompted: "Do you mean that they put their private parts into your private parts?"

"Yes, sir, they did."

"All four of them did."

"Yes, sir, they did," said Norma, confirming the taction of private parts. She need not have said anything more. A white Southern reporter whispered to a Northern newsman, "That's all, brother. The next move is up to the U.S. Supreme Court. This Irvin is convicted here and now."

Hunter proceeded to what occurred after the rape, when, Norma said, the black men were trying to decide what to do with her. "One of them said to me, which would I rather do, ride on down the road with them and be killed or get out and walk, and I said that I would get out and walk, so they got me out of the car. . . ." And Norma ran. She hid in the woods, she said, "until almost daylight," then walked to Okahumpka, where she waited until Lawrence Burtoft opened up the café.

Glossing over any words that Norma may have exchanged with Lawrence Burtoft, the state attorney returned to details of the rape. "Now, Norma," Hunter asked, "did you fight those Negroes in that car?"

"No, sir, I didn't."

"Why didn't you fight them?"

"Because I was scared to."

"Did they threaten you?"

"Yes, sir," Norma said.

"In what way?"

"They said if I made any noise or screamed or hollered or tried to do anything, they would shoot me."

"Did they have a gun?"

"Yes, they did."

Frustrated by Norma's reluctance or refusal to forward her story, Hunter led her further. "Now, Norma, you submitted to those Negroes because you were afraid of them?"

"Yes, sir."

"And you say they had a gun and made threats to you?"

"Yes, sir."

"And you say this defendant sitting here in the courtroom is one of those men?"

"Yes, sir."

"That is Walter Irvin?" Hunter practically pleaded.

"Yes, sir."

"Will you point him out to the jury?"

Norma Padgett pointed vaguely in the direction of Walter Irvin. That two of the Groveland Boys were now dead and another was doing hard labor on a chain gang in South Florida no doubt robbed the moment of some of its drama, but Norma's limp gesture held not a lick of the electricity she'd generated when she had risen in the witness box at the Lake County courthouse and with her finger extended had pointed at each defendant in succession.

*"The nigger Shepherd . . . the nigger Irvin . . . the nigger Greenlee."*

Jesse Hunter's case for the prosecution rested almost singly, and strongly, on his certainty that no jury in Lake or Marion counties would ever accept the word of a black man over the testimony of a young blond farm girl who had accused him of rape. So he had Norma accuse her alleged rapist again, then again and again.

"Now, Norma, this is a very important thing," Hunter stated with emphasis. "I want you to tell this court and jury whether or not that is one of the Negro men that raped you that night in the back seat of that automobile."

"Yes, sir, it is."

"Are you sure about that?"

"Yes, sir, I am sure."

"You are positive he is one of the ones who raped you that night."

"Yes, sir," Norma said, and five times more she said she was sure when five times more Hunter asked her, for he wanted to be absolutely sure that the jury was sure that Walter Irvin was one of the four black men who had raped her.

Marshall had decided, and announced, that neither he nor any other black attorney would be cross-examining Norma Padgett before a white, male jury in Marion County. Mabel Norris Reese saw wisdom in the decision. "You had a farmer jury, a white woman had been raped by negroes and this was in their minds," Reese said. "There was no question at all. They weren't considering evidence. They had their eyes fastened on Hunter . . . it would have been suicide for Marshall to get up and argue anything in the jury."

Careful not to display any antagonism toward the state attorney's witness, Akerman had Norma review her account of the events that culminated in Willie's fight with the four black men. Then, barely acknowledging the alleged rape—for the defense strategy was not to question the allegation of the rape but to raise reasonable doubt as to Irvin's involvement in it—Akerman focused on Norma's arrival in Okahumpka, on foot, outside Burtoft's Café. In the first trial, because Hunter had chosen not to call Lawrence Burtoft as a witness, the prosecution's narrative had omitted Norma's conversation with the owners' son in the café. To Akerman, Norma responded that she knew Lawrence Burtoft, the young man who'd let her inside the café, and she testified that she had asked him for a ride to the roadside spot a few miles away where she had left her husband. She could not, however, recall anything further about their conversation, she said.

"What did you tell him?" Akerman asked.

"I don't remember what I told him," Norma replied. "I was crying. I don't remember now what I did tell him."

Not convinced, Akerman tried to probe further. He wanted to establish that Norma had told Burtoft she'd been "taken off by four Negroes": "You did not tell him that?" he asked.

"No, I did not."

"You did not discuss with him whether or not those things happened to you?"

"No, I didn't tell him anything about it, I was just getting him to take me down there," Norma answered.

"That is all," said Akerman, resigned. It was beginning to appear that the only hope for the defense lay with Lawrence Burtoft, if they could get him to court in time to testify.

Of Norma Padgett's moment in the retrial of Walter Irvin, the award-winning journalist Richard Carter wrote, "You watch her on the witness stand. You listen to her story. You note the righteous ferocity with which the prosecution defends that story. You note the timidity with which the defense challenges it. You count the dead . . . Ernest Thomas . . . Sammy Shepherd . . . maybe Walter Irvin . . . and you realize that it's perfectly all right to starve a Southern white woman and deprive her of education and make her old before her time, but by God, no damned outsider is going to dare question the sanctity of her private parts, the incontrovertibility of her spoken word."

The state attorney called Deputy James Yates, and Marshall studied the "gum-chewing husky in a red corduroy jacket": the officer who had tried to bar the NAACP special counsel's hospital visit with his client; the sheriff's man who found it a "funny thing" and offered "no comment" when asked by a reporter if he'd shot Irvin; the law enforcer who had so badly beaten the Groveland Boys that even the FBI pressed for his indictment; the deputy who, special investigator J. J. Elliott warned Marshall, "is going to get you."

As he had in the first trial, Hunter led Yates through his testimony, and as he had before, the deputy stated that the plaster casts he'd made of tire tracks and footprints at the rape scene "exactly" matched the soles of Irvin's shoes and the tread of tires on James Shepherd's Mercury. On cross-examination, again as before, Yates admitted to Akerman that he'd had no formal training in making casts, nor had he made the casts until hours after the alleged rape, by which time Irvin had been arrested and both the shoes and the car had been placed in the sheriff's custody. Asked if he was familiar with the scientific devices used in "protecting the integrity" of the tracks, Yates replied, "No, I don't know what you mean." Furthermore, Yates noted, he had not been able to deal with footprints and tire tracks in a more timely manner because he'd had to attend to "that woman," Norma Padgett, who "was hurt and I had to get her back to the doctor, and I came on out there later, and poured the tire casts."

An irritated state attorney rose for redirect examination. Hunter did not appreciate Akerman's belittlement of the deputy's expertise in crime scene techniques. To rehabilitate his witness in the eyes of the "farmer" jury, Hunter offered some plainspoken down-home common sense as opposed to the highfalutin language of scientific expertise. "Now, Mr. Yates," Hunter began, "did you ever hear of what he calls 'integrity' of those tracks? Did you ever hear of that before?"

"No, sir, I never have," Yates said. "I don't know anything about it."

"You were not looking for integrity of tracks, were you?"

"No, sir."

"You were looking for the tracks, were you not?"

"Yes, sir."

"That was your business, was it not?"

"Yes, sir," Yates agreed.

"And you just looked and saw that those were the same tracks that fitted those shoes, did you not?"

"Yes, sir."

"And as to whether or not those tracks had integrity, you were not interested in that, were you?"

"No, sir," Yates replied.

"And you know those shoes made those tracks, do you not?"

"Yes, sir."

"And that is the old common Florida way of putting it, is it not?"

"Yes, sir."

Then the state attorney introduced Walter Irvin's pants, which Yates had obtained from Dellia Irvin without a warrant not long after he and

Campbell had beaten the man unconscious in jail. Holding up the evidence, Hunter asked, "Now, Mr. Yates, are there any smears on the front of these pants?"

"Yes, sir, there are," Yates said.

"There are smears all down the side?" Hunter asked.

"Yes, sir, there are."

Hunter passed the pants to the jury. Marshall's incredulity at Hunter's country-boy performance about "integrity" for the jurors now yielded to fury. The pants had not only been admitted into evidence by Judge Futch against the motion of the defense but had also been admitted without laboratory examination. Scientific analysis of the evidence—a free service provided by the FBI to local law enforcement—would have almost certainly determined whether or not the stains on Irvin's pants derived from the defendant's "emission of seed," but Hunter had apparently decided, as he had with Norma Padgett's medical examination, not to take the chance that science might not support the prosecution's narrative. Not when he could have the jurors eye the evidence in "the old common Florida way."

Hunter retired to the prosecution's table. For the defense, again, as in the Lake County trial of the Groveland Boys and in the coroner's inquest into Samuel Shepherd's death, even the evidence seemed to be prejudiced and the verdict predetermined. Frustrated, Marshall and Akerman whispered to each other; enough was enough, they decided. Akerman approached Yates.

"Now, Mr. Yates, is it true that the defendant Walter Irvin has accused you and the sheriff of Lake County, Florida, of attempting to murder him?"

Hunter leapt to his feet in objection. Futch sustained.

"May it please the court," Akerman said. "It shows bias on the part of this witness toward the defendant."

Alex Akerman didn't wait for a ruling. He returned to his seat beside Marshall.

# | 20 | A GENIUS HERE BEFORE US

*From left to right:* Paul Perkins, Jack Greenberg, Walter Irvin, and Thurgood Marshall. (© *Bettmann/CORBIS*)

NORMA PADGETT LEFT any strutting to be done in the courtroom to the fourth witness for the prosecution. Tall, dark-haired, and movie-star handsome, the twenty-three-year-old Curtis Howard, wearing "a spread collar and a sharply-cut suit," swaggered with an athlete's confidence to the front of the courtroom. And vowed to tell the whole truth, so help him God. Howard would break his share of vows over the next few years, as countless affairs and sexual indiscretions with young ladies up and down Lake County would land him three times in divorce suits—all three of them with the same wife: his high school sweetheart, and Leesburg High cheerleader, Libby Dean. No question, the sweet-talking Howard did have charm.

With all his charisma and his slightly crooked, mischievous smile,

Howard had come back to Ocala for the trial from Montgomery, Alabama, where he'd been stationed after his enlistment in the army. Three questions into his testimony on Wednesday, February 13, Howard began breaking his vow to tell the whole truth. The Leesburg native told State Attorney Jesse Hunter that he was currently living in Montgomery with his wife, but, in fact, Howard had run out on Libby in 1950, after she became pregnant with twins, and he had left her in Florida when he'd moved to Alabama. He and Libby were presently in the process of getting their first divorce.

As in the first Groveland Boys trial, the state attorney took Howard through the events of the early morning hours on July 16, 1949, and, as before, Howard related that he had been working the overnight shift at Dean's filling station, which was owned by Libby's father, when, at about 2:30 or 3 a.m., Willie Padgett pulled into the station in his 1940 Ford. Willie looked like he'd been hit above the eye; blood had dried on the side of his face. He told Howard he'd had some trouble.

"Just tell what happened," Hunter coached his witness.

"Well, he gave me information that his wife had been raped," said Howard.

Hunter immediately addressed the "mistake" in Howard's response, and the witness corrected himself, saying that the wife had been "kidnapped and carried away" instead of "raped." For, by Willie Padgett's own testimony, he at that point knew only that four black men had abducted his wife, not that they had raped her. It was because of slips like these, which could produce contradictions and inconsistencies in the prosecution's narrative, that Hunter pressed Lake County's law enforcement personnel to allow the FBI only written statements (which Hunter helped prepare) and to refuse the agents any oral interviews. Hunter could not wield the same control over Walter Irvin, who told FBI agents that in the early hours of Saturday morning, July 16, before Norma Padgett had been found, Deputy Yates asked him, "Why did you rape that white woman?" Also, a Florida highway patrolman, who, on that same Saturday morning, had driven Irvin and Shepherd from the Irvins' house to the scene of the alleged robbery and kidnapping, told the FBI that he had heard the two suspects being questioned by deputies Yates and Campbell about the "rape."

In the retrial, as in the first trial, Hunter, of course, took every precaution to forestall any impression that a "story" had been put in place by the prosecution. Still, he could not prevent every slip, especially as he wasn't always working with the quickest of witnesses. Curtis Howard, however, came across as a model citizen who had gone out of his way to help a man in difficulty. Continuing his narrative, Howard recounted for the court how, after finishing his shift at the filling station, he had seen a young girl by the side of the road but had thought nothing of it, and had driven on to Groveland, where, as it had happened, he had run into Yates and Campbell, as well as Willie Padgett. He had then driven Padgett to Bay Lake, so he could change his shirt, and it wasn't until Willie's sister showed a picture of Norma to Howard that he had connected Willie's missing wife with the girl he'd seen in the roadside grass back in Okahumpka.

"Did you tell them that you thought the woman you saw was his wife?" Hunter asked.

"Well, I told them that I thought I knew where she was," Howard said, "and so we went and got in my car and went back down there to the intersection, and she was in another car with another boy by the time we got there, and I supposed that it was someone that she had gotten from that dining hall or dancing place." Howard did not refer to "another boy" by name, nor did he give any indication that he'd recognized the "someone" with Norma. Yet they were not strangers, Howard and Lawrence Burtoft. They had been classmates at Leesburg High, where they had played together on the baseball and football teams.

Hunter asked what happened next with Norma. Akerman objected on the grounds of hearsay. Futch overruled. Howard responded: "Well, I asked her if she was hurt in any way, and she said that her legs were hurt and bleeding, and said that her clothes were torn, and she was all messed up and dirty, and I asked her if the men did anything to her, and she said that 'all four of them attacked me,' and she described what had happened from that time."

"What was the condition of her clothes?" Hunter asked.

"Well, they were torn and messed up, and as I remember it, some of her underclothes were hanging down beneath her dress, and her dress was torn."

As one reporter observed of Howard during his testimony, he was "as smooth as Willie is bucolic." Leroy Campbell's nephew was also providing Jesse Hunter with splendid testimony for the state's case in the event that Lawrence Burtoft should take the witness stand for the defense.

Hunter excused the witness, and in what was surely the missed opportunity of the trial, Alex Akerman declined to cross-examine. The state rested its case. Curtis Howard returned therewith to Alabama.

The first trial might have won Curtis Howard some commendation in the communities of Lake County; in his own household, at least, he might have been seen as a hero of sorts. But he wasn't. The Groveland case was never mentioned in the Howards' home, and shortly after the trial Curtis and Libby's marriage began to crumble into divorce. First married at the age of twenty, Curtis and Libby would remarry and divorce two more times, but at no time in the wobbly course of their relationship would they speak of the role that Curtis Howard played in the conviction of Norma Padgett's alleged rapists. Kim Howard, Curtis and Libby's daughter, would remember the contention in the household over her father's carousing and womanizing and lying but nothing of Curtis Howard's testimony about the girl in the roadside grass when he appeared in the most illustrious trial to take place in central Florida.

"My mother was a saint to put up with him," Kim Howard said, for Libby was fully aware that her husband was committing serial adultery. "There were just so many young girls that he would go off with. He was indiscriminate, and so charming and charismatic that there was no end to the girls. He couldn't stop. My parents' second divorce involved my father getting our babysitter pregnant." Her father was also an unapologetic racist, Kim Howard claimed: "He and Uncle Leroy were very close. He would do anything for him." So, when for the first time she learned about the Groveland Boys trial, Kim Howard said, "My first thought was, 'Curt, what did you do now? What did you get yourself mixed up in?' My father didn't drive past Norma Padgett. He wasn't stupid. Knowing my father, he had something to do with that girl. He'd gotten himself mixed up in something. If he was really a hero, and my mother believed it, we would have heard about it."

T WELVE YEARS EARLIER, in the case of the black butler Joseph Spell, who stood accused of raping socialite Eleanor Strubing, Marshall had refused a plea offer from prosecutors and elected to go forward with a trial because he believed that in Connecticut a white woman's claim of rape would not, by force of cultural necessity, be accepted as unassailable fact. Marshall correctly gauged the jury's disinclination to convict on the basis of race and won an acquittal for Joseph Spell. No less correctly Marshall concluded it could never happen in central Florida.

In declining to cross-examine Curtis Howard, the defense was passing up the chance perhaps to lay bare the very heart of the Groveland Boys case. But because this was an interracial rape case in the South, the defense team had to tread lightly. As one reporter noted, "The absence of medical proof . . . could only be alluded to in passing." That Norma and Willie, having shared a pint of whiskey, were no doubt drunk, that they had not been living together, or that Willie had passed a number of houses and even a police station after his wife's alleged abduction "could only be hinted at in the most discreet and obscure terms." Another reporter covering the trial had wondered if Norma might have concocted the rape story to "extricate herself from an embarrassing or compromising position" or if the story had been invented "to extricate husband, wife and third party from the trouble that might attend disclosure of a fight which involved the eternal triangle." No matter how "demonstrably true" any such scenarios might prove to be, none of them, the reporter wrote, could "be entered as evidence in a Southern trial of this kind." The defense dared not to question in any way either the purity of the Flower of Southern Womanhood, however indelicately she might be represented by Norma Lee Padgett, or her probity in the "contention that she [had] been ravished" by four savage blacks. Should the defense dare to tread upon a white Southern woman's honor, not only would the jury fail to acquit a black man of a rape charge, but they would also most surely deliver him a death sentence. So the only practicable strategy for the defense in the Groveland Boys case was to raise reasonable doubt by showing that the state of Florida had arrested the wrong men.

Marshall had to scramble to bring Lawrence Burtoft to Ocala. He had minister S. Ralph Harlow, a member of the Committee of 100, write to Burtoft in Fort Jackson, South Carolina: "We need you very much if that trial is to be fair. . . . This boy's life is at stake and the honor of Florida is at stake. Only a fair trial can free Florida from a blot that can never be cleaned. You can do much to make that trial fair. I pray that you may have the courage, the sense of justice, the spirit of Christ, to bear witness to the truth."

The testimony of Lawrence Burtoft, which outright challenged the truth of Norma Padgett's tale, was indeed "as far as the defense dared to go." Burtoft had been flown to Ocala from Fort Jackson, South Carolina, on a plane chartered by the NAACP. Still in his uniform, he took the stand as the first witness for the defense. The Okahumpka native testified that on the morning of July 16, when Norma Padgett showed up at his father's café (the local "dining hall or dancing place," as Curtis Howard identified it), she told Burtoft that her husband had been "hit over the head and she thought maybe that he had been killed." She also said that she had been kidnapped by four Negroes but made no mention of being raped.

"Did she make any statement to you as to her ability to identify those men?" Akerman asked for the defense.

"She told me that she could not identify them, that one was light, and one was extremely dark and that's all she knew about them," Burtoft replied.

Burtoft was the only defense witness who worried Hunter, because the state attorney knew that the testimony of the café owner's son would not corroborate the story that the state's witnesses were spinning. Hunter's aim in cross-examination, then, was to destroy Burtoft's credibility as a witness.

"Are you prejudiced against the state of Florida?" Hunter asked.

"No, sir, I am not prejudiced against anybody."

Despite Akerman's objections, which Futch overruled, Hunter implied that Burtoft was in "bad standing" with the sheriff's department of Lake County: an implication that the soldier calmly denied. Hunter then insinuated that Burtoft had changed his story since his interview with the state attorney two and a half years back, shortly after the alleged rape: "Didn't you tell me the first time when I talked to you about this case that you had heard a woman pass by your place in an automobile screaming for help that night?"

"No, I didn't," Burtoft said emphatically. "I don't even know when they went by."

"Didn't you tell me you heard a woman screaming for help going by your place?"

"No, sir, I did, I did not hear anything of the kind, and I don't know where you got any such information as that."

Hunter pressed harder. He told Burtoft that he had decided not to call the Okahumpka boy as a witness for the state in the first trial because he knew the boy's testimony was not true, and he repeated what he had said to Burtoft in their 1949 interview, that "we were not going to use any liars in that trial," so as to ask, "You don't remember me telling you that?"

"No, I don't," Burtoft answered, unwavering. "You did not say that. You cannot fool me. I know what you said."

Hunter then addressed again Burtoft's supposed prejudice by suggesting that he "was trying to get even" with the state of Florida for its occasioning of a rift within the Burtoft family. At this point, as at any number of others in the state attorney's cross-examination, Marshall and Akerman could have objected, but they were thus far pleased, and surprised, by the equanimity Burtoft was displaying in response to Hunter's questions. And Burtoft remained unrattled by Hunter's suggestion, even though young Lawrence, according to one reporter, had struggled with the fact that there was "at least one Ku Klux Klan member in the Burtoft circle" and that "regional tradition" might dictate adverse actions against his father's business if Lawrence were to testify for the defense of a black man charged with a white woman's rape. Charlotte Burtoft, Lawrence's mother, had a "genuine fear of reprisals from some of the extremists around Groveland" were her son to testify. Her other children did not want Lawrence to return. But Mrs. Burtoft also believed that Walter Irvin was innocent, and she supported her son's desire to tell the truth under oath. Lawrence had discussed his concerns at length with his family, who had ultimately "wanted him to let his conscience be his guide"—whereupon he had applied to the Pentagon for a special pass so that he could travel to Ocala and testify.

Hunter proceeded to Burtoft's testimony, which he strove to discredit. "Now, as a matter of fact, Mr. Burtoft, that girl was hurt when you saw her, was she not?"

"No, she was not hurt," Burtoft answered.

"And you took your own time about getting a car, did you not?"

"Well, I was not going to carry her on my back," Burtoft noted. "The car was up at the house."

"Was there any reason why she would put any confidence in you?"

"I didn't ask. It was not my place to ask her. I just asked her if she thought she would recognize them, and she told me she didn't think she could," Burtoft said. "She just told me the rest of her story voluntarily, and she just told me that she had been kidnapped by four Negroes, and I asked her if she thought she could identify them, and she said no."

"You did not think that amounted to anything?" Hunter asked.

"Well, I helped her."

"Don't you think you would be helping her more if you told the truth for once in your life?" Hunter shouted with vehemence. To this, Akerman did object. And Judge Futch did not pause in his whittling to overrule; in sustaining the state's objections and overruling those of the defense the judge could not be faulted for inconsistency.

Hunter continued to grill Burtoft, but after forty-five minutes the state attorney had proved to be unable to shake the young man in his testimony. One last time Hunter implied that Burtoft's account of Norma Padgett's presence at Burtoft's Café early that Saturday morning in July was tantamount to a lie, but Burtoft stood firm. He recalled for the attorney a particular conversation the two of them had shared: "I have told you once before," Burtoft said, "that she looked to be in pretty calm condition for her husband to be lying down dead beside the road, and you told me . . . that she was not the type of girl to be showing her emotions." Hunter dismissed the witness.

For all his attempts to diminish Burtoft's credibility, Hunter knew better than most that the defense's surprise witness had not been fiddling with the truth. Under oath, Norma Padgett had denied telling Burtoft that she'd been taken away by four black men at gunpoint, and had denied telling him even that her husband had been in a fight with four Negroes. By her account, she had persuaded Lawrence Burtoft, with no explanation, to drive her to a random spot "down there" by the side of the road where her husband had been. It was preposterous. Furthermore, it was contrary to her own written statement to the FBI—a statement that Hunter himself had helped to prepare only days after the alleged rape—in which Norma avowed that she had shown up at the Burtofts' place and "reported to a man who runs a store there what had happened to me." Fortunately for the state's case, the proof of Norma Padgett's perjury lay buried in an FBI file, which was not in 1949 and would not in 1952 be introduced as evidence in the trial of the Groveland Boys, or boy. The U.S. attorney's office had quashed subpoenas served by the defense to have FBI agents testify, citing the "confidential nature of the FBI's investigation."

The testimony of Lawrence Burtoft had, without qualification, been brave, given that his parents not only resided but also owned and operated a business in the county run by Sheriff Willis McCall. Before the retrial, McCall had made it clear to Burtoft that because of his military commitment he did not have to accept a subpoena. Yet Burtoft had returned to Florida, and done so for one reason alone: "To tell what I knew." In Justice Robert Jackson's opinion concurring with the Supreme Court decision to reverse the verdict in the Groveland Boys case he addressed the issue of justice beyond the "theoretical importance" of jury selection, for in light of the "prejudicial influence" in the court before and during the trial, he wrote, "The only chance these Negroes had of acquittal would have been in the courage and decency of some sturdy and forthright white person of sufficient standing to face and live down the odium among his white neighbors that such a vote, if required, would have brought." Though not a juror, such a "white person" was Lawrence Burtoft, and in his testimony as a witness lay perhaps Walter Irvin's "only chance."

In the September 1949 trial, when Walter Irvin had last sat in the witness box, he had been able to share the experience silently, in a look or a glance across the courtroom at the defense table, with his best friend, Samuel Shepherd. They had grown up together in Groveland; as kids they'd played together; in their teens they'd picked citrus together. On the same day, at the same time, they had enlisted in the army, and they'd served together in the same outfit in the Philippines. The last moment that the two of them shared with each other they were, as they had long been, inseparable: joined in spirit, if also linked hand to hand by steel cuffs as they took bullets not from some enemy lurking in an Asian forest, but from two Lake County law enforcement officers. Since then and before, Irvin had presented his version of the events on the roadside outside Okahumpka countless times: to a grand jury, a trial jury, a coroner's jury; to FBI agents, to newspaper reporters, to doctors—to white people. And none of them, it seemed to Irvin, had believed him, or if they had, they hadn't cared, and their indifference was going to cost him his life. Walter Irvin glanced across the courtroom; he knew the look he saw in the eyes of the men in the jury box, the look that saw a guilty black man sitting on the witness stand. They'd wanted to lynch him at the jail or on the road, and they had settled for a conviction and the electric chair. They'd accept no less this time round. Those eyes meant business.

Irvin was fighting for his life, but he had no ammunition beyond the truth that he had recited all those times before. Akerman guided him through his testimony, and again he denied that he had kidnapped and raped Norma Padgett. He denied, too, that the stains on the legs of the pants in evidence had been present when he had taken them off on the morning of July 16. Akerman then turned the witness over to the state attorney. Hunter's cross-examination focused largely upon where Irvin was on that Friday night in July, so as to place him at the scene of the crime squarely in the time frame of the state's narrative. The fact that the defense had been unable to produce any alibi witnesses allowed Hunter the opportunity to plot Irvin's movements in the state's story more freely. Irvin's denials in regard to the kidnapping and raping of Norma Padgett concerned Hunter little. Even without the state's evidence to put Irvin at the scene— the tire tracks, the footprints, the stained pants—the decision for the jury would still come down to Norma's word against the Negro's. He had no doubt which way the scales of justice would tilt on that.

The last witness for the defense landed the bombshell that Marshall felt their case needed. Between two criminal trials, the appeals, and a Supreme Court case in the matter of Groveland Boys, the NAACP had spent nearly fifty thousand dollars on lawyer fees, travel expenses, research polls, and chartered flights. In that, the eight hundred dollars paid to the Miami-based criminologist Herman Bennett was a serious bargain. The defense established his impeccable credentials: thirty years of experience in the field of criminology; stints with the FBI, the Secret Service Division, the Internal Revenue Service, the Federal Bureau of Narcotics, and the

U.S. Navy; consultation on high-profile criminal cases, including the kidnapping of the Lindbergh baby. As an expert witness, Herman Bennett more than adequately fulfilled Thurgood Marshall's expectations. He was no disappointment to Jesse Hunter, either.

The state attorney sized up Bennett quickly. If the defense saw in him an impressively credentialed criminologist whose testimony would call into question the integrity of the state's physical evidence, Jesse Hunter saw an elitist big-city windbag, who might not play too well before a "farmer jury."

So, just after Bennett had begun recounting his visit to the Lake County Court House in Tavares in the company of defense attorney Paul Perkins, where, by virtue of a court order, he was examining the state's plaster casts, Hunter interrupted. "Just a minute, please, are you referring to any casts that are in evidence in this case?" Hunter asked.

Bennett replied, "I am not in a position to answer that question." But Hunter was; he knew that the only casts that had been entered into evidence had been accidentally broken after Deputy Yates's examination of them.

"May it please the court," Hunter objected. "These casts are not in evidence in this case, we have not introduced them in evidence, and even though I would like to hear this tremendously important man—we seem to have a genius here before us, I would like to hear it—I wish to point out that these casts are not in evidence."

Futch of course found the objection good, and it was sustained, to Akerman's disbelief. Futch had earlier disallowed use of the Roper poll research as evidence, and now he was limiting the defense to an examination only of broken plaster casts on the basis of which Deputy Yates had already presented his findings to the jury.

Akerman was livid. "If the court please! The defendant at this time—"

Hunter cut him off. "Just a moment, I am going to withdraw my objection. I want to hear all of this learned testimony from this expert."

It was a calculated risk, but Hunter was odds-on certain that "all of this learned testimony" was going to work in the state's favor. For Akerman, it was a strange turn in the proceedings, and he hadn't seen it coming—nor did he see where it was going. Not without self-importance, and slightly arrogant in his courtroom manner, Akerman resumed his conversation with Bennett, both of them discussing with intelligence scientific protocols in the witness's work worldwide. They might as well have been speaking Polish as far as the farmers and citrus workers on the jury were concerned, and as Hunter and his assistant, Sam Buie, recognized. The state would thus allow the witness for the defense to talk his way expertly into ineffectuality.

Bennett had begun to elaborate on his findings in regard to the stains on Irvin's clothing when Buie broke in. "Will you please let him indicate how long he has been doing that particular phase of this work?" Buie asked. "He is setting himself up to be an expert, and he has only given us a general background."

Akerman relaxed: at last, a civil exchange instead of an objection. "All right, Mr. Bennett," Akerman said. "Will you please explain what you know and what your experience has been in regard to stains on clothing and so forth?"

"Well, the subject of stains on clothing is a scientific question, and is something that can be microscopically and scientifically determined, that is to distinguish between stains, and of course in the field of scientific criminology you have to have a broad general knowledge of every department. There are several different methods in which stains are examined, and the principal and proper manner to examine them in the field of criminology is to examine them by microscope. . . ."

Akerman, apparently taking his cue from the loquacious Bennett, in long-winded fashion posed a question about semen stains, which prompted another of Bennett's erudite elucidations, this one on "certain fluorescent quantities." Again, Buie interrupted. "Name that fluorescent quality and tell what it is!" he demanded.

And gladly Bennett obliged. "Well, it is a fluorescent substance, and when a garment is placed under an ultra-violet ray light, these little articles of fluorescent material will show up under that light; however, I will say this, that that is not a conclusive test, because of the fact that other foreign matter may have gotten into or on the material, or the cloth, and these other foreign materials might exude a fluorescent fire when exposed to the ultra-violet light, but would enable the investigator to localize that portion. . . ." And his disquisition on stains and cottons and textiles and the specifics of chemical analysis comprehensible to criminologists like himself continued on.

Hunter and Buie had dispensed with the formality of objections; they simply interposed into Bennett's testimony their questions and snide requests for reiteration or further explanation. Futch meanwhile whittled, like a substitute teacher tolerating an unruly class. At one point Hunter even meandered among the spectators, and while laughing and "cracking wise to his friends," he heckled the defense from the floor. When Akerman finally realized the state attorney's intent, he demanded that the judge "stop the prosecutor from heckling and laughing." The judge told the witness to "get on with the testimony."

What nearly got lost in the courtroom circus was the criminologist's testimony that the plaster casts made by Deputy James Yates *had been faked*. "After carefully studying these shoes and casts," Bennett concluded that in his opinion "there was no foot in the shoe at the time the impression was made." Whereas a normal footprint would leave a concave impression, Bennett explained, the impression made by an empty shoe or one with a shoe tree inside it would be convex. The impressions in Deputy Yates's casts of Irvin's shoes, Bennett declared, were patently convex.

In cross-examination, for the benefit of the jury, Hunter feigned incredulity at the claim made by the defense's expert witness—and skewed by the state attorney—that all people wear out their shoes the same way, for surely such a proposition must defy good old Florida common sense. To Bennett, he addressed the question: "Then it is your contention that all these twelve gentlemen on the jury wear out the soles of their shoes in exactly the same manner, each one of them?"

"Well, a shoe is never completely [worn] out," Bennett answered, as baffled by Hunter's question as the jurors had been by the criminologist's confoundingly technical answers.

"Do you mean to say that they are worn exactly alike and that all these men walk exactly alike?"

Bennett offered a detailed analysis of shoe construction and weight distribution, from which Hunter wrenched the false conclusion he had been using to sway the jury with his more plainspoken common sense. "Well," he said, "I am going to let the jury be the judges of that fact themselves, as to whether or not they all wear their shoes at the same rate and in the same way." As Hunter had done from the minute that Bennett had so solidly taken the stand, he had again, as Greenberg noted, "ridiculed the testimony."

The state attorney ended his cross-examination by obliging Bennett to reveal his $150-per-day fee. "Then, as a matter of fact," reported Hunter, his voice booming, "you are getting from seven to eight hundred dollars to testify as an expert in this case about this stuff you have testified about?" Bennett answered yes, and with that, Hunter dismissed the witness. "That is all," he said and, with some undisguised disgust, added, "That is enough."

With the day's proceedings ended, Marshall, Perkins, and DeMille repaired to the home of a local family that had agreed to accomodate some of the black reporters and lawyers. Greenberg had moved to a hotel in downtown Ocala where most of the out-of-town whites with an interest in the trial were staying. That evening Greenberg was eating by himself in the hotel dining room when Jesse Hunter asked if he might join the opposing counsel. Unable to "chew anything substantial," Hunter ordered cornbread and milk, which dribbled down his chin onto his shirt as he made desultory small talk—and Greenberg listened patiently to Hunter's tale of a recent trip up north to his nephew's graduation, after which the young people did not want to be seen eating with Uncle Jesse. Mostly, though, the two men ate in silence. Hunter had maybe a spoonful of soppy cornbread left when he looked up from the bowl and for a few seconds considered Greenberg's patient mien before he spoke. "McCall's a brute," he said, then scooped up the last of the cornbread and bade Greenberg good night, leaving the dazed young lawyer with the check.

WHEN TESTIMONY RESUMED on Thursday morning, February 14, the prosecution opened with an unusual maneuver. Sam Buie requested permission to return Walter Irvin to the stand for further cross-examination. To no one's surprise, Akerman objected, reminding counsel that they were in the state's rebuttal.

"We do not insist on it," Buie replied, "we just have one question to ask him, but it is within this court's discretion."

The impropriety of the request did not warrant even the brief second of consideration Futch gave it before ruling, "The objection is good I think and is sustained."

"All right," said Buie, smiling toward the jury as he withdrew, "we don't insist on it. If they don't want him back on the stand, it's all right."

Fuming, Marshall and Akerman requested that Futch excuse the jurors so that they could make a motion. In the absence of the jury, the defense moved for a mistrial on the grounds that under the Constitution a defendant is not required to take the stand and "no comment can be made before the court or the jury as to the failure of the defendant to take the stand": which, Akerman pointed out, the state had just done twice. Futch denied the motion nonetheless. The jury returned, the prosecution resumed.

Bennett's assertion that Deputy James Yates had faked the footprints on the plaster casts had gnawed at Hunter all night. To vouch for Yates's forensic aptitude and thereby validate further the conclusions in his testimony, the state called Leroy Campbell, the former Lake County deputy who was now employed by the police department in the city of Leesburg. Campbell testified that he had been present with Yates the entire time the footprints were being cast in plaster. It was solid evidence, he assured the jury.

Having buttressed Yates's credibility, Hunter set out next to blemish Lawrence Burtoft's character. For that, the state attorney knew whom he could trust. He called Willis V. McCall, sheriff of Lake County, who affirmed only that he was "pretty well acquainted with the people of Lake County," because at that juncture Akerman objected. For reason of being a member of law enforcement, McCall was excused by Futch.

The court proceeded to closing statements, with Sam Buie beginning the arguments for the state. The young attorney first took the jurors through the evening of July 15, 1949, as it had been experienced by seventeen-year-old Norma Padgett: how she had been ravished by four black men but had had the presence of mind to get good looks at all four of them as well as to take note of the car they were driving. "Gentlemen," he told the jury, "in this case the only thing you have to consider is which testimony you are going to believe. Are you going to believe this girl, or are you going to believe that defendant? They are the only two persons living who were present at that thing to know anything about it. . . ."

Buie next addressed, and deprecated, the testimony by "crazy" Herman Bennett in regard to the plaster-cast footprint evidence. "Now, gentlemen, if you believe the testimony from that man from Miami, then please God turn the boy loose," Buie implored. "Turn him loose, that's what you've got to do if you believe that man, turn that boy loose. And no matter what that poor country girl Norma Padgett said to you, if you believe what that man says for God's sake, turn the boy loose. . . . I submit to you gentlemen that the statements that he made is the most asinine statement that I have ever heard before any competent court in the state of Florida, and yet he sits up here and expects you to believe any such junk as that, I tell you gentlemen, that is an insult to your intelligence."

In closing, Buie reminded the jurors that the officers and deputies of Lake County had solemnly sworn to uphold the law. "Now, are all these men liars? Have they any reason whatsoever, under God's name, and has either Yates . . . or Campbell or any of the rest of them any reason to lie? No, gentlemen, I don't believe they would, and I know that you do not believe it either."

Marshall knew that he really had no choice; he would address the jury. "They're probably wondering what that big Negro is sitting at the defense table for," he'd told reporters outside the Ocala court. Inside the courtroom, when he rose, Marshall could sense, as he often did when trying cases in the South, that neither the spectators nor the jurors knew quite what to expect from him. He stood "in a difficult spot," as one reporter observed, for, "if he didn't speak, the jury might regard him as some sort of sinister puller of strings for Akerman," but, "if he did speak, he had to avoid seeming 'uppity' to the white jury." He was of course going to speak, because it wasn't a matter of choice; it was an obligation, not only to his client but also to the community. Blacks had crowded into the balcony in large part to hear and see Mr. Civil Rights, and to witness possibility; and in "that big Negro" the whites on the main floor might see something of the future. He surveyed the jurors. The older men among them looked vaguely stunned, "as if they never knew a Negro could 'stand right up there and talk.'" On the other hand, a young juryman with an "honest face" regarded the special counsel as attentively as he had followed the entire trial. He "seemed to listen with respect" as Marshall delivered his address to the jury.

"Gentlemen of the jury," Marshall began, "if you will bear with me for a moment, I will please explain to you who I am and where I am from. I am Thurgood Marshall, chief counsel for the National Association for the Advancement of Colored People, and I am from Baltimore, Maryland, and am associated in this case as defending counsel, and Mr. Paul Perkins is from Orlando, and he is also associated in this case and is a member of the bar of the state of Florida, and gentlemen, I want to tell you that I think we understand the problem we have here, and insofar as I do understand it, I would like to discuss it with you for a few moments."

Irvin sat erect in his chair, "drumming his fingers together, listening the way a man listens when his life depends on what he's listening to," one newspaper reported. Another noted that off to the side, Willis McCall "listened intently, gritting his teeth."

"Now, in cases of this type," Marshall continued, "we are all of us up against a pretty tough proposition, but the guarantee of a fair and impartial trial to every man accused of crime stands just as securely in this case and cases of this type as it does in every other case. But there are times when violent crimes are committed, when all good Americans are shocked and revolted, and resent such crimes, and criminals of the type who commit such crimes. . . . And when the crime of rape involves a white lady and a colored man, then there is a great amount of ill feeling and ill will against the alleged defendant."

Marshall explained that the Constitution and further statutes appertaining to the rights of individuals as defendants "fill up pages and pages of law books, but they can easily be summed up to this one thing, that every defendant is assured and guaranteed a fair and impartial trial, and is assured and guaranteed equal justice under the law, equally . . . no matter whether or not he is white, black or yellow, and our government is the finest Government in the world . . . and our great United States government is built on that principle . . . and that is the reason that our government has survived through the ages. . . ."

First glorifying the law as being derived from "basic precepts set down by God himself in heaven" and "written lovingly and painstakingly, through the hundreds of years," Marshall then brought law as a divine abstraction into the concrete reality of the Marion County courtroom, where constitutional safeguards continued to protect the rule of courts and the power of juries, as in the matter of the defendant seated before them. "Walter Lee Irvin is charged with the crime of rape and he is now on trial before you gentlemen as his jurymen, and in cases of this kind, I have heard judges make the remark, that cases of this kind are the kind that will try the souls of men." Yet by their tried souls would the soul of Walter Lee Irvin be tried, and by them would his life or death be determined, for, as Marshall reminded them, "when this government was founded, and the old Magna Carta says that the final say of whether a man is to live or die is left solely in the hands of twelve representative fellow men of the area where the case is being tried, and that is why you are here today."

Marshall's objective, however, was less to inspire the jurors with awe at their mission than to appeal to their common sense in its execution. "Now I will tell you that I myself have never been on a jury, but to my mind there are certain things that strike me about the testimony in this case . . . and the thing that struck me the most, and still is in my mind, is this. When they carried Walter Irvin out there to the scene of where this thing is supposed to have happened, and when they were tracking his footsteps there in the ground, and they asked Irvin if those were the shoes he had on the night before, and he told them no. He told them that his shoes he had on the night before were at home. Now, gentlemen, if those were Irvin's footprints out there on that ground, and Irvin knew what a serious charge was hanging over his head, and when Mr. Yates asked him if those shoes he had on the night before, now, remember gentlemen, Walter Irvin is an intelligent young boy. Now he understood what Mr. Yates was charging him with . . . and what did Irvin tell him? He told him, no, that they were at home. . . . Now, gentlemen, it seems to me that if Walter Irvin had been guilty of that crime, when he realized that the shoes that he had on were not fitting in those imprints there on that ground, that any guilty man would have instantly said to Mr. Yates, 'Yes, these are the shoes I had on last night.' He would not have told Mr. Yates that the shoes were at home."

Outmatching the masterly Jesse Hunter in the arena of common sense, Marshall asked the jurors to consider, too, if Irvin's actions the morning after the alleged rape suggested those of a guilty man. "I don't believe that anybody who has just committed such a crime as that would be willing and able to go to work the next morning and to lead a perfectly normal life." Indeed, even in the face of his arrest, he demonstrated no hint of guilt; he was "not even nervous or excited" and "when his mother told him the police were there looking for him, he told her to tell them to come right on in, that he had not done anything."

Marshall reasoned with the jurors in conversational tones; he spoke "patiently, politely, softly, but fluently and with dignity," as one reporter noted. For years Marshall had been honing his approach to all-white juries in courtrooms across the South, and his reasonableness was difficult to resist. "With Marshall, you really got the impression that what he was saying had to be right," a fellow lawyer observed. "That no honest person could really avoid the thrust of what he was arguing. That he really, really believed in this cause. And that made him very effective."

Marshall touched briefly on the matter of Deputy James Yates's plaster casts, or rather on the question that the state had raised as to the bias in Howard Bennett's testimony, for which the reputedly expert witness had been handsomely paid by the defense. Alex Akerman would argue the evidence itself in his closing statement, but what Marshall wished to make clear, he explained to the jurors, was that it was the defense's duty to offer the court the "best evidence we could find" just as it was the state's obligation to present their best evidence. "It is awfully hard to get the best evidence in the world without paying for it," Marshall told them.

To a significant degree, the money expended on expert testimony indicated the importance that the NAACP attached to the Groveland Boys case and to the life of the defendant. Marshall emphasized to the jury "that this is an extremely important case, and it is an extremely important case to Walter Lee Irvin. There is a man's life involved here, his life is at stake, and gentlemen, I urge you, when you are considering this case, and making up your verdict in this case, to keep in the foremost part of your mind this fact. That every man, no matter what his color or race or creed might be, and no matter what the crime that he is charged with, each man in those circumstances is entitled to the fairest treatment that anybody can possibly give him. . . . You are the sole judges of the evidence and the testimony in the case, and it is your responsibility to reach this verdict. . . ." Marshall finished with a nod and "thank you for your patience and attention."

Futch called a recess for lunch. As the jurors were filing out, Jack Greenberg, at the end of the defense table, heard one of them say to another, "Damn, that nigger was good. Sure looks like it'll be close."

THE COLORED WAY

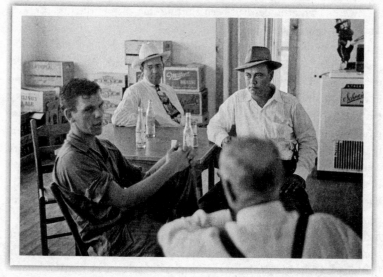

State Attorney Jesse Hunter questions Lawrence Burtoft in July 1949, while Sheriff Willis McCall and Deputy James Yates glare. (*Photo by Wallace Kirkland/Time & Life Pictures/Getty Images*)

B OY, THAT'S A great man," Hunter said, speaking of Marshall.
   Mabel Norris Reese had had ample opportunity to observe the two opposing counsel in court, and in the course of the trial they had seemed to grow quite "buddy-buddy." During breaks in the proceedings, Hunter had on occasion sat down with his coffee at the defense table to engage Marshall in conversation, to make the NAACP lawyer from New York feel more at ease in Marion County. Willis McCall might not have been impressed by Thurgood Marshall's closing argument on behalf of Walter Irvin, but the state attorney from Lake County—"a terrible racist," though he was known to be, according to Reese—unquestionably was.

Reese had detected a change in Hunter's attitudes toward race as well as toward the sheriff ever since the shooting of the two Groveland boys that November night on a dark road near Umatilla: a change that was reflected when Marshall's name came up at a lunch with Hunter during the court recess on the Thursday of the trial, and Reese noted, "You could just see the respect all over [Hunter's] face for that man. It was such a shame they could never have lunch together, but at the time no restaurant in Florida would have permitted it."

Reese's own attitudes had been shifting, too. Before the first trial, she later admitted, she had been "conned into believing that these boys were guilty. . . . In the beginning, I just felt the evidence was there, and I admit I tried them before they'd been given a chance to be tried." After the trial, and the appeals, and the reversal of the verdict by the Supreme Court, which was in essence an indictment of the prejudicial system of justice in Lake County, Hunter had been "his usual blunt self and didn't like it one bit," Reese recalled, and Willis McCall had "raved and raved." Reese also recognized, however, that as a reporter and columnist for the *Mount Dora Topic*, she had collaborated with Lake County's officers of the law and the court. "I was probably prejudicing minds by my pipeline information [from Hunter] without thinking about it too much. I probably needed to be stepped on." The reversal of verdict subjected Reese to criticism along with Hunter and McCall; it also chastened her. Certainly, by the time of the retrial, her hostility toward the NAACP and the LDF lawyers had abated. Early in the proceedings she had suggested to Marshall that he attend a "Lake County NAACP conference" where whites and blacks could air their opinions about the Groveland Boys case and its ramifications. Marshall's answer had surprised her; he said that he would be very pleased to attend "because of its possible good effects upon race relations and the United States' world-wide fight against communist propaganda which seeks to blacken us through our race difficulties." His positive response even prompted Reese to praise Marshall in a letter to J. Edgar Hoover. (Reese's letter requested that the results of the FBI's investigation be released. Hoover replied that the investigations were confidential.)

After Reese's lunch with Hunter, at the end of the recess, she accompanied the state attorney back to the courthouse, where he would be presenting his closing argument that afternoon. In the hallway, just outside the courtroom, they spotted Deputy James Yates. Reese felt Hunter's hold on her elbow tighten; they broke their pace, and he leaned in toward her. "Stay away from that man as far as you can," Hunter whispered. "He just like to hurt people."

Court reconvened. Alex Akerman approached the jury. He argued the evidence, or lack of it, by which the state was attempting to reconvict Walter Irvin. Addressing first the alleged rape itself, he made clear that the defense was questioning not what Norma Padgett had said had happened to her on the night of July 15 but whom she had identified as her assaulters. "We don't say that she was not raped or ravished in that place, but we do say that this defendant knows nothing about it." While Akerman did point out the state's failure to produce medical evidence in support of Norma's ravishment—"I understand she was taken to a medical doctor by the deputy sheriffs, and I submit to you gentlemen that there should have been medical testimony in this case, and none was introduced to show whether or not this young lady was actually raped or ravished"—he kept the jury focused on the issue of identity. As had Marshall before the recess for lunch, Akerman argued after it in terms of the folksy Florida common sense that Jesse Hunter so valued. "Now I think most of you have had the experience of identifying Negroes. I know it is true with me, and I believe it is true with just about every one of you gentlemen, that the first time you see a Negro, you see nothing but a Negro, and if you see him again the next day, you probably would not recognize him as being anything but a Negro, and after he has worked for you say two or three or four or five or six days, then you finally begin to recognize him, and distinguish him as Jim or Joe or Jack or George. But as a matter of fact, if you have never seen a Negro but one time and it was in the dark, on a dark night, such as this alleged case was, then I submit to you gentlemen that you would not be able to recognize him again, so positively as Norma Padgett did."

Akerman then proceeded to the failure on the part of the state to send physical evidence to the FBI for analysis and to its reliance instead on the forensic skills of the less qualified deputy James Yates. Furthermore, Akerman clarified, the defense had paid the expert witness Herman Bennett to analyze the deputy's plaster casts; they had not paid him, as the state had implied, to falsely claim that the evidence had been compromised, or faked. If the defense had indeed been paying Bennett for false testimony, they would have had him testify simply that the plaster-cast footprints did not match the soles of Walter Irvin's shoes. In fact, the prints did match, but the impression was not convex. "Now, we don't want to say, and we do not know, and we do not contend that the Deputy Sheriff put a shoe tree in them, and made a false impression, we don't contend that at all, and we don't contend that Sheriff McCall did it," Akerman maintained. "We are not casting any dispersions [*sic*] or misrepresentations against any persons whatsoever. But we do say this . . . we believe we have proved it. . . ."

State Attorney Jesse Hunter rose. He was not only closing the argument for the prosecution; he was also capping a career in law that had spanned four decades, in which time he had argued no case as controversial or as consequential as the Groveland Boys. He surveyed the packed courtroom; he eyed the press tables, the reporters, many of whom he had known for years. The case, the public, the court, his vanity—they demanded a virtuoso performance. He turned his attention to the gentlemen of the jury.

Hunter started on an accordant note. He agreed, he said, with Marshall's assertion that every man, black or white, was entitled to a fair trial, and as state attorney he had built his career on that principle. "Gentlemen, although I am not trying to brag about it, I wish to tell you that in any case where I sincerely believed that the defendant charged with the crime was innocent . . . there was nothing in the world that I could do but tell the court to dismiss him. I have done that many times. . . . I have never prosecuted a man in my career who I believed to be innocent of the crime with which he was charged. I have never prosecuted a man that I did not think was guilty. Now, gentlemen, I tell you this, I don't want on my soul or my conscience the prosecution of an innocent man, and I am always careful about that thing."

It was Hunter's reprise of the testimony of Lawrence Burtoft under his lengthy cross-examination by the state attorney that brought the proceedings to a momentary standstill. "My friend criticized me for some of the questions I asked Mr. Burtoft," Hunter began, "because I asked him if he did not have it in for the law enforcement agencies of Florida and Lake County, and by a technicality he stopped me from proving it." Hunter was convinced that Willis McCall would have been able to discredit Burtoft had Judge Futch allowed the sheriff to testify.

Akerman shot to his feet. "May it please the court!" he shouted. "We ask that the jury be withdrawn."

"For what purpose?" Futch asked.

"For the purpose of making a motion to the court out of the presence of the jury."

Futch had the jury withdraw. As Akerman and Marshall were approaching the bench, Marshall noticed that Hunter, standing off to the side, was sending hand signals to the jurors as they exited the courtroom. Marshall might have thought that Futch was ringmastering a circus rather than presiding over a trial, except that the judge's attention seemed to be commanded solely by cedar sticks while his longtime friend, the state attorney, committed one improper offense after another. Futch did pause in his whittlin' to deny Akerman's motion for a mistrial on grounds of the state's "technicality" remark. Then he denied the defense request that the remark be stricken from the record. Then he had the jury brought back.

Hunter resumed. He recalled for the jury the testimony of Herman Bennett, "who sat here and told you for over thirty minutes what a wonderful man he was. It was awfully funny to me. He struck me as being afraid that Hoover was going to call him up to take over Hoover's job." Having subjected the criminologist's testimony again to ridicule, Hunter elevated the reputation of James Yates by personally vouching for the deputy sheriff's honesty, so that he, the state attorney, could not "believe that you gentlemen for one instant believe that any man in a responsible position like that, of a deputy sheriff, would try in any way to fake tracks on anybody. I don't believe that you gentlemen believe that any such foolishness took place."

Hunter tightened his bond with the jurymen by offering them a joke, in dialect, about "two colored men walking down the street," and after that bit of cracker humor he opened the cracker soul of the case. "Here is this young girl, Norma Padgett," Hunter said. "You saw her here on the stand. She was an honest old cracker girl, born and raised up in Lake County, Florida. She was a poor honest girl and had never even probably been out of Lake County and had never been in any trouble in her life. . . . She was just an old common Florida country girl, and came from an old common Florida family, and I ask you which are you going to believe?"

As he described the rape, one reporter observed, he "whooped and hollered, waved his arms and then crooned as to a babe in arms." That his voice was strained by a cold and he was battling laryngitis seemed only to heighten the alarm he infused into his depiction. "Now, gentlemen, she sat there in that car being held prisoner, and she told you that she was afraid. She was afraid for her life, and oh, my God, why should she not be? . . . A woman's chastity is the greatest thing on earth to her, and nothing in the world compares to it." So it was that the crime committed in the car that night was a violation not just of Norma Lee Padgett but also of Southern womanhood, and so, too, the jurors' verdict would be punishing the accused for a crime against not one woman but all women, against their own wives and daughters. "You have a right to sit on this jury for the protection of your womenfolk, and I would like to tell you this example, on one historical occasion, there was a good woman, from a good family, on the eve of her wedding, and she was caught in the back yard and savagely raped, and she walked over to the edge of the cliff and hurled herself into eternity, rather than sacrifice that which to her was dearer than life itself. That, gentlemen, was her chastity. Now, gentlemen, Norma Padgett, this simple country girl, chose to live, and she has suffered the greatest tragedy that can befall any woman, and she will suffer for it for the rest of her life. She has lived to tell the story, and don't you gentlemen forget that that thing, that horrible thing, will never be erased from her mind."

Hunter paused to catch his breath. His rhetoric hung in the air: "savagely," "greatest tragedy," "protection of your women-folk"—he was sparing the jury no drama, or fear. After a moment, Hunter drew himself up and moved in closer to the jury. A downcast look crossed his face. He was solemn. His voice sank lower. "Now, gentlemen, I am about to conclude my argument to you in this case. I have tried to do a good job. That is my sacred duty. Gentlemen, I have been seriously ill, and this is probably the last capital case I will try in this county. . . . I have been stricken with what may be a fatal disease."

His words were lost on no one in the courtroom. Mabel Norris Reese, Thurgood Marshall, the defense team, Sam Buie, everyone's ears pricked up. For a second Judge Futch even forsook his cedar sticks.

"Gentlemen, I don't want to do any man, whether he be black, white, or colored, an injustice, and I have come to the realization that I may soon have to meet the Almighty, and I don't want to meet the Almighty with any innocent blood on my soul. Gentlemen, I don't believe that I will ever do so, but I do want to leave this county in such condition, that you and your wives and your daughters and your sisters and your sweethearts can walk and ride the streets of this county and this state in perfect safety, as you should do. I want to leave this county and this state in such a condition that no bunch of men can come in and snatch up your wife or your daughter and carry her out in the woods and rape her."

Marshall had lost count (though Greenberg had not) of Hunter's instances of prosecutorial misconduct in his closing argument, but his revelation of a "fatal disease" was clearly a ploy to gain jurors' sympathies and, again, grounds for a mistrial (another for Greenberg to record in the event of an appeal). Still, the defense did not object, as Hunter was wrapping up his summation, and the judge would surely have overruled in any case.

Testimony and arguments had been completed. Walter Irvin did not meet his gaze as the special counsel reminded him, as Marshall had been reminded by the state attorney, that the governor's plea offer was "open up until the case went to the jury." Once the jury withdrew for its deliberation, though, the defendant's last chance to ensure himself a life sentence rather than the death penalty, in the event of his conviction, would be forfeit. And again, Marshall reminded Irvin that he would in all likelihood be facing the electric chair.

Stoic, staring into the distance beyond the defense table, Irvin had listened to his counsel. His silence was heavy. Then his eyes met Marshall's. "I didn't do it," Irvin said, and said he would not plead guilty to what he didn't do. Marshall nodded, and clasped the resolute Irvin's shoulder.

Judge Truman Futch charged the jury. As the twelve white men exited the courtroom, the NAACP attorney approached the bench, where the judge, his everyday brown tropical business suit dappled with cedar shavings, remained slumped in his swivel chair. He wore a Masonic signet ring; so did Marshall, and earlier in the trial the judge and the lawyer had compared their rings and amicably shared some of their experiences in Freemasonry. At the moment, however, Marshall was feeling neither cordial nor fraternal. He was livid with Jesse Hunter.

"Judge Futch, I'm quite serious about this," Marshall said. "I'm going to make him lose. Every one of those jurors has got a Shriner's pin, did you notice that?"

"Sure, I noticed it," Futch replied.

"Did you also notice that the state's attorney, three different times gave the Masonic distress signal to that jury?"

"Yeah," Futch said, "as a matter of fact, it was four."

"Well, I'm going to make an objection," Marshall told him.

"I wouldn't do it," Futch answered.

"Why not?"

"There's nothing racial about that," Futch said. "He does it all the time whether you're white, black, or green. He gives the distress signal all the time."

Greenberg, Akerman, and Perkins felt no better about the prospects for the defendant than did Marshall. The whole trial, it seemed, had proceeded by the ordainment of the state, which apparently enjoyed the grace of Judge Futch. Predetermined though the verdict appeared to be, Marshall had Akerman request that the court submit additional instructions to the jury, urging that deliberations not be influenced by public sentiment and that the testimony of Norma Padgett be "rigidly scrutinized," since there were no other witnesses to the alleged act. Futch refused.

Marshall retreated to the hallway for a cigarette. He kept a wary eye out for Deputy Yates; he had no inclination to be chased out of Marion County by a band of Klan riders after the verdict—not in a hearse, anyway. The Marion County Sheriff's Department was well represented at the court-house, but even in their Stetsons, with their guns holstered on their hips, they projected none of the menace of their Lake County counterparts.

A white man sidled over to Marshall. "How long's the jury going to be out?" he asked.

"Damned if I know," Marshall said. "I can't tell."

Both men puffed on their cigarettes in silence, the white man staring down the corridor. "I can tell," he said.

Marshall waited for an explanation. The man was pleased to offer one. "You see that man over there just lit up a cigar?"

Marshall spotted him, said yeah, and the man remarked, it seemed to Marshall, with undue confidence, "When he's finished that cigar, the jury will come back."

Marshall furrowed his brow. "What the hell you talking about?" the lawyer asked.

When the man pointed out that the cigar smoker was a juror, Marshall recognized him, as well as a second juryman who appeared and also lit up a cigar.

"They're not gonna waste that cigar," the man told Marshall. "They're going to finish the cigar before they come in."

Marshall observed the two jurors. He detected no nervousness in their gestures, no tension in their body language, as they casually smoked their cigars. It was not a good sign. Marshall would have preferred to be seeing them uneasy, on edge, ready to skip the courthouse as soon as they had, con-trary to popular demand, acquitted Walter Irvin. Instead, the two jurymen looked as if they might have been passing time outside a barbershop on a lazy Saturday afternoon. Not a good sign at all. Marshall lit another cigarette.

The cigar smoke billowed around the heads of the two jurors. A few more minutes ticked slowly by. Then, one juror stamped out his cigar; he lingered for a moment, and with a nod to his companion, he disappeared from the hallway. With no apparent urgency, the second juror followed. Marshall butted his cigarette.

He was just stepping toward the courtroom when word came out that the jury had reached a verdict, after one hour and twenty-three minutes of deliberation. Marshall's team gathered at the defense table. Walter Irvin was brought back from his cell. His family along with the black spectators, curious and hopeful, packed themselves into the balcony. The main floor buzzed. The press corps waited, alert. Jesse Hunter took a seat next to Sam Buie at the prosecutor's table. Judge Futch returned to the bench.

A cigarette in his hand, Judge Futch addressed the spectators. "Now when the jury gives its verdict, I don't want a man to move in this room until the sheriff takes the defendant out."

*And what happens if he's not guilty?* Marshall thought. The conclusion appeared to be foregone.

Just before 4 p.m., the twelve jurors filed into the courtroom, their eyes giving nothing away. The room settled into a hush. The verdict was read.

"We the jury find the defendant guilty." There was no recommendation of mercy.

Irvin betrayed no emotion. He sat, unmoving, except for the twitch of muscle in the hollows of his cheeks. Walter's mother swallowed her wail as she broke down in tears. Around her in the Jim Crow gallery sobs accompanied Dellia Irvin's grief.

Marion County sheriff Don McLeod patted Irvin on the shoulder. "Like a man stunned," the defendant stepped before Judge Futch for sentencing. His senses numb, he barely heard the words that would echo inside his head for months: " . . . electrocuted until you are dead and may God have mercy on your soul."

Immediately, Marshall made a motion for a mistrial on the basis of Hunter's prosecutorial misfeasance in his summation before the jury. Futch denied the motion, and borrowing a pen, after fumbling in his pockets in an unsuccessful attempt to find one, he sealed Irvin's doom with his signature. Reporters raced to telephones and their typewriters. The jury was dismissed, and Walter Irvin, again in handcuffs, was escorted by Sheriff McLeod, in a suit and fedora, from the courtroom to a waiting patrol car.

Richard Carter, reporter for the *Compass*, lingered at the courthouse. He wanted to get some quotes from the prosecutor, but he settled for Sam Buie, whom he asked for a clarification of a remark made by the state attorney in his closing argument. Addressing a point raised by the defense as to why Walter Irvin, if he were guilty, had not simply fled after raping Norma Padgett, Hunter had scoffed at the logic and told the jurors what he knew they'd know, "Don't you know that is the *colored* way of thinking?" Buie explained to the inquisitive reporter that Hunter had in fact meant to use the word *criminal*, not *colored*. Carter, who had that very day been named the 1951 recipient of the George Polk Award, given to "the reporter who was faithful to the best tenets of his profession even at the risk of life itself," was not convinced. He would later write, "Could this be another of the 'rape' cases which Southern authorities have been known to whomp up as an afterthought in order to keep the Negro in his 'place'?"

Once Carter had walked out of earshot, Assistant State Attorney Sam Buie asked some other reporters who were standing close by, "Say, is that Carter a nigger? He's got awful curly hair. You sure he's no nigger?"

Dellia Irvin caught up with Thurgood Marshall as he was leaving the courtroom. Tears formed ragged trails down her cheeks. "She had the most impressive face I've ever seen on a woman," Marshall said later. "Real high cheekbones and a whole lot of red in that black. A whole lot of red, and a lot of Indian. And she just had these piercing eyes. . . ."

"Lawyer, don't you let my boy die, you understand that?" Dellia Irvin enjoined him. "She said it four times," Marshall recalled. "Don't you let my boy die. I could hardly go to sleep. I could see this face, and boy, it really . . ."

Overcome himself, Marshall took the inconsolable woman into his arms; her body was trembling. "Don't worry, honey." Marshall tried to comfort her. "With the faith of our people and the grace of God, we'll be back." Tears welling in his eyes, too, Marshall assured her, "We're going to stick by you. . . . We are going to keep on fighting."

On Monday he would be filing a motion for a new trial in Tavares, Marshall told the reporters outside the courthouse, before he climbed into the hearse. With Paul Perkins, Arnold DeMille of the *Defender*, Robert Ratcliffe of the *Courier*, and Milton "Buddy" Lonesome of the *Baltimore Afro-American*, he rode to the small hotel in Parramore, where some of the black news correspondents picked up their luggage, and then dashed on to the airport in Orlando.

Mabel Norris Reese was waiting in the courthouse lobby. The sun was beginning to set, and she had a long drive back to Lake County, but something had to be said. What, she wasn't sure, but something, even though she knew that he was ill. So she was waiting, and when she saw him ambling toward her, all the words she sought got lost in tears. Jesse Hunter gently clasped her arm; he tried to console her, suggested they might get something to eat.

"Get away," Reese said, pulling her arm away from him.

The vehemence, restrained but unexpected, left Hunter aghast.

"How could you do that?" she asked him, tears spilling from her eyes.

Hunter swallowed. "I just had to," he said.

Reese shook her head, unable even to look at him.

"It was my duty," he said, his hoarse voice failing him. "As a prosecutor."

# |22| A PLACE IN THE SUN

LeRoy Collins is sworn in as Florida's governor on January 4, 1955. (*Courtesy of the State Archives of Florida*)

I DON'T SEE HOW in the name of God anybody could subject that boy to any more inhuman punishment. Florida is a bad place to live," observed *Baltimore Afro-American* reporter Buddy Lonesome, dumbstruck by the cruelty he had witnessed both at Irvin's trial and outside the courtroom. He was sitting next to Marshall, scribbling down notes for the next day's paper, as their hired car sped toward the Orlando airport on Thursday night, February 14.

The verdict made front-page news across the country on February 15.

The reporters who'd covered the trial had hardly been surprised that Walter Irvin was found guilty; that Lake County justice had not been tempered by mercy, however, did confound many of them. Newspapers shouted outrage in boldface type, but even less inflammatory headlines noted the want of clemency, like that of Friday's *New York Times*, which read: "All-White Jury in 3-Day Retrial of '49 Groveland Rape Case Fails to Urge Mercy." The national press expressed its expectation that in view of the beatings and shooting that Irvin had endured, Judge Truman Futch might exhibit some restraint, even in the absence of a recommendation from the jury, and sentence the retried and reconvicted Groveland boy to life imprisonment.

Local newspapers praised the "tranquillity" of the trial atmosphere in Marion County, but editorials in the North's leftist and black presses were unforgiving of white justice in central Florida. "Brutal and cynical white supremacy Florida has again announced its intentions of smearing the Constitution and the Bill of Rights with the blood of a Negro," declared an editorial in the left-wing *Daily Worker*. "A lynch court presided over by a lynch judge has gone through a lynch trial of the 24-year-old Walter Lee Irvin before an all-white citizenry, 99 percent of which believed the defendant guilty. This court differed only in form from a white-supremacist mob. Instead of the savage whoops, there were the prejudiced appeals of Prosecutor Jesse Hunter." The newspaper called on citizens to swamp Governor Fuller Warren's office "with demands for a pardon to Irvin" and to protest the court's action with work stoppages and demonstrations. The editorial noted, too, that "not one of the more than 14 bombings in Florida has produced a defendant."

After the "lynch trial" in Ocala, Walter Irvin had been returned by the Marion County sheriff to Raiford, and to death row. A *New York Post* reporter interviewed Irvin at the state prison, where he again wore the gray coveralls issued to condemned prisoners. Irvin admitted to no regrets for having refused the plea deal proposed by the governor. "I'm not sorry, not even now," he said. "Naturally, I would rather have a life sentence than the electric chair, but I thought it wouldn't be right for me to plead guilty when I'm not guilty." The decision had been his alone, he told the reporter—"my attorneys didn't tell me what to do. They left it up to me"—although he did ask them "why the state made that offer. They didn't know. They knew the case had lots of publicity and maybe that was why." Irvin himself "thought the state probably thought I was innocent. I was happy about that, but I told my attorneys I didn't think it would be fair to plead guilty. I would have been telling a lie on myself." Even though, as Marshall had told him, he might be free in eight to ten years, barring bad behavior, if he accepted the deal, and despite the fact that, if he didn't, his attorneys "couldn't make me a definite promise about what would happen," Irvin hadn't needed time to think about it. "I knew I was taking a chance," he told the *Post* reporter, "but if I had gotten justice like I should have . . ." Irvin's voice faded. He did not complete the thought, but before he was led back to his cell, he added, "What can I say? I'm not guilty. And I still believe I have a chance." That chance did not materialize for weeks, for months, as he waited for word from the NAACP.

By March 6, Florida law enforcement had made little progress in the investigation into the murders of Harry T. Moore and his wife, but in New York City the "NAACP's Great Night" benefit to honor them was drawing fifteen thousand people into Madison Square Garden. Cohosted by Lena Horne and Oscar Hammerstein II, the gala featured some of the greatest names in the 1950s entertainment industry, among them Henry Fonda, Harry Belafonte, Tallulah Bankhead, Ed Sullivan, and Jimmy Durante as well as the NAACP's own great Thurgood Marshall. Among the performances in the program were a dramatic sketch, "Toll the Liberty Bell," which included a piece celebrating Moore's life, and "The Ballad of Harry Moore," a poem written by Langston Hughes and set to music by Sammy Heyward. During the intermission, with charisma and rhetoric, Franklin Williams, who had been flown in from the West Coast for the occasion, made a dramatic appeal for funds. The show raised more than fifty thousand dollars for the NAACP. Later in the year, Rosa Moore accepted the 1952 Spingarn Medal, which was being awarded posthumously to her son, Harry.

March 1952 also took Thurgood Marshall back to the South, this time to Clarendon County in South Carolina, where he was continuing the battle against school segregation in *Briggs v. Elliott*. The case—built upon the fact that public spending on the education of white children totaled four times the amount allocated to blacks—had already been argued by Marshall in the U.S. Supreme Court, where it had been vacated and remanded to a three-judge panel in federal district court in South Carolina. It was progressing much the way Charlie Houston had said it would, and the possibility of public school integration in the South was moving closer to becoming a reality. Marshall, as Houston's disciple and successor in the education cases that would ultimately constitute *Brown v. Board*, was feeling pressure from within his own ranks and, more negatively, from his opponents. For Clarendon County afforded Marshall no escape from the atmosphere of menace he had experienced the month before in the counties of central Florida. In the postwar forties in the Clarendon County court-house, the NAACP had tried unsuccessfully to prevent the state of South Carolina from executing George Stinney Jr., a ninety-pound fourteen-year-old boy convicted of murder. Rushed to the electric chair within months of his conviction, Stinney became the youngest person ever to be executed in the United States in the twentieth century. Racist sentiment had scarcely abated by 1952; at the end of the *Briggs* proceedings in the same county courthouse Marshall was delivered a stern warning by one of the opposing white lawyers: "If you show your black ass in Clarendon County ever again, you're a dead man."

In April, the executive board of the NAACP appointed Marshall head of the Legal Defense Fund, and the position of special counsel became director-counsel. With the change in Marshall's title came a change in status for the LDF, which was established as a subsidiary corporation; so Walter White was no longer Thurgood Marshall's boss. In the summer the LDF moved into its own offices three blocks away from NAACP headquarters in midtown Manhattan. The Times Square building offered the LDF lawyers more space, if also a seedy foyer and gated elevator that reeked of urine. The building apparently did not provide much security; on more than one occasion, the staff found themselves without typewriters, as with little difficulty burglars could scale the fire escapes and pry open the windows under the cover of night.

Despite its tax-exempt status, the LDF was always short on funds. As Marshall said, "We could only move when we had the money," and to raise money, the lawyers frequently went on the road on speaking tours. Jack Greenberg attributed the success of this funding program largely to Marshall's "charisma," which the director-counsel wedded to the charity of the audiences at the LDF speaking engagements. Greenberg himself delivered between ten and twenty fund-raising speeches every month in the two years leading up to *Brown* in 1954, and Marshall did more. Apparent to them, as they prepared the appeals on behalf of Walter Irvin, was the especial "fund-raising and organizing potential" of the Groveland case. The story of Walter Irvin and the Groveland Boys riveted audiences across the country. On one occasion, in Richmond, Virginia, Greenberg simply read the statement given by Irvin from his hospital bed after he'd been shot by Sheriff McCall and his deputy; it was punctuated by gasps and sobs among the fifteen hundred people in the audience. That Greenberg had to ad-lib when he realized a page was missing from the text hardly mattered. The audience was in every way generous. Ultimately, the Groveland Boys story accounted for the

LDF's recovery of a thirty-nine-thousand-dollar shortfall, but not from the usual wealthy donors like Marshall Field III or from the significant annual donations that Thurgood was able to garner from associations like the black Masonic order, the Prince Hall Masons. Rather, it was collected from "black people of no great means" moved by a tale of cumulative injustice and heroic perseverance.

Throughout the summer and fall of 1952, legal setbacks would continue to impede LDF progress on Walter Irvin's case; his situation would become more desperate. Marshall had counted more than twenty errors in the prosecution of the second Groveland trial, and he had retained Alex Akerman and Paul Perkins to handle the appeals. Marshall and his team of lawyers had decided first to ask an established, well-connected Jacksonville lawyer to file an amicus, or friend-of-the-court, petition to explore the legality of procedure when a law enforcement officer kills a witness for a defendant in a capital case. In November 1952, the Florida Supreme Court denied the petition. Greenberg continued preparing the appeals while at the same time writing the first draft of the *Brown* brief.

After the Thanksgiving weekend, Marshall checked into Washington's Statler Hotel; it was the first time that he had visited the nation's capital and not been required by law to stay in Jim Crow accommodations. He turned his suite into a war room in advance of his sixteenth appearance before the Supreme Court. Over the next ten days the most prominent black lawyers in the nation would be marching in and out of Marshall's suite as they helped him prepare for battle in *Briggs v. Elliott*. He was edgy, irritable; he had been for months. "He's aged so in the past five years," his wife, Buster, had noted around the time he was working on the retrial in the Groveland Boys case. "His disposition's changed—he's nervous now where he used to be calm. This work is taking its toll of him. You know, it's a discouraging job he's set himself." William Hastie, who had hosted the Marshalls in the Virgin Islands when Thurgood was recovering from his mysterious "Virus X" in 1946, noticed that the lawyer, once again, appeared to be exhausted "beyond the limits of the human anatomy."

On December 9, Marshall argued *Briggs v. Elliott* before the U.S. Supreme Court. Near the end of his argument—to Greenberg's surprise, for in Florida he had seen Jesse Hunter use the same ploy—Marshall flashed the secret Masonic distress signal to his fellow Mason, Justice Robert Jackson, who responded in kind. Marshall returned to his seat with a grin.

That same December day, in South Florida, regarding the Carver Village bombings in Miami, a federal grand jury indicted three Ku Klux Klan members for lying under oath to both the FBI and the grand jury. Having previously also indicted seven Klansmen for perjury in the matter of the high-speed chase that ran two NAACP lawyers and two black reporters out of Lake County, the FBI claimed to be making progress against KKK violence in Florida. The murders of Harry T. Moore and his wife, however, remained unsolved.

The months had passed into another year for Walter Irvin on death row. Depressed as he was for a want of reading material and a radio in his cell, he still believed in the chance that lay with Thurgood Marshall working on his appeal. Fellow inmates on death row meanwhile continued to take their last walk down the corridor to the electric chair. In June 1953, as Marshall had expected, the Florida Supreme Court reaffirmed the Marion County verdict of February 14, 1952. While the justices cited several of Judge Futch's lax rulings on prosecutor Jesse Hunter's "irregular" and "improper" remarks, they deemed them to be essentially harmless errors; they thus did not find them significant enough to warrant reversal. One month later, Paul Perkins argued before the Florida Supreme Court for a stay of execution, and that, too, was denied, although the state court did grant the defense a ninety-day stay in which to appeal to the U.S. Supreme Court.

The defense team in New York was otherwise swamped that summer. The justices of the U.S. Supreme Court were requiring more clarity in the five school segregation cases now included in *Brown v. Board*, and had ordered all five of them to be reargued in terms of the authors' intent in drafting the equal protection clause in the Fourteenth Amendment, so as to determine whether the abolishment of segregation in public schools fell under the powers of Congress or indeed of any federal agency. To build the case, Marshall enlisted more than two hundred lawyers and historians nationwide. He traveled up, down, and across the country to consult with them in marathon conferences, and when he returned to New York, where he met in seminar-style discussions with his LDF team of lawyers, prominent associates, and scholarly experts, he strove to keep the out-of-town attorneys and historians abreast of developments by telephone and telegraph. No one on Marshall's legal staff took a vacation day that summer, or fall; secretaries not only worked double shifts but worked them six and seven days a week—everyone in the LDF offices was busy making history. Marshall himself seemed never to leave his desk. Disheveled, his tie loosened and top shirt buttons undone, a cigarette dangling from his lips, he might suggest, come the middle of the night, "Why don't we take a fifteen minute break." So the scholar John Hope Franklin, then of Howard University, remembered on one occasion when they had worked into the hours of the early morning, except that Franklin had left Marshall to his fifteen minutes in the office while he stole back to his room at the Algonquin Hotel and slept through what was left of the night. He found Marshall still at his desk the next morning.

Marshall was relying upon historians like John Hope Franklin and C. Vann Woodward of Johns Hopkins University to address the Supreme Court's concerns about desegregation and congressional powers by placing the rationale for *Brown* convincingly in a social and political context. The task, Marshall repeatedly reminded the historians, who were sometimes given to academic speculation regarding possible Court opinions, was solely to "present a case so persuasive that the Court would be compelled to rule in our favor." To that end, Marshall had his LDF team introduce research from psychologist Kenneth Clark's study of the effects of segregation on the mental attitudes of black children, as in his "doll test," into the *Brown v. Board of Education* brief and summation. (Clark's research confirmed what Marshall had himself concluded from conversations with black children, as when he'd ask boys what they wanted to be when they grew up and—heartbreakingly, to Marshall—even the brightest among them would reply, "I'm going to be a good butler" or "I hope I might be able to get in the post office.") For months Marshall's team worked and reworked the *Brown* brief. They incorporated the results of their legal research with those of the historians' examination of political and social issues germane to the case; they supported arguments with sociological data and the evidence of Clark's psychological studies. They produced, in 235 pages, a manifesto for equality, its language, depth, and persuasiveness exceeding all expectations, said Franklin. Another historian noted, "It deserves a place in the literature of advocacy."

Hours before day dawned on December 7, 1953, blacks were lining up outside the Supreme Court in the hope of witnessing history being made. The morning had broken cold when Thurgood Marshall arrived with his wife and mother, Buster and Norma, who were escorted to their reserved seats. Marshall sat in the well of the court. Before oral arguments began, he glanced over the team of NAACP lawyers who for months, for years, had worked assiduously on the five education cases in *Brown v. Board of Education*, and: "I realized there wasn't a single one of them who hadn't been touched by Charlie Houston. Either taught by him, or friendly with him, or guided in their careers by him. Every one of them, including me." To Charlie Houston, his mentor and friend, Marshall might have dedicated this day—their day—in court.

For three days Marshall and his lawyers argued *Brown*; they were not expecting a decision until the spring. In January 1954, however, they did have word from the Supreme Court regarding another matter: Walter Irvin's appeal had been denied; the Court had declined to hear the Groveland case. Jack Greenberg had thought the illegal search and seizure of Irvin's pants and shoes might have supported a reversal of the verdict (it would have seven years later, when the Court determined that a defendant could not be convicted by illegally obtained evidence), had not Dellia Irvin testified that she had retrieved the evidence in question and given it to Deputy James Yates. Greenberg filed a petition for rehearing the Groveland case, which the Court also denied. Irvin's lawyers had no further judicial recourse to pursue. They could only focus now on staying the date of Walter Irvin's execution.

The Supreme Court, Marshall knew better than most, could be wildly unpredictable, especially in criminal cases. He had argued thirty-two cases before the Court, and though he had lost only three decisions over his career, two of them had been death penalty cases. The third had been the 1944 *Lyons v. Oklahoma* case, in which the black sharecropper W. D. Lyons confessed to murder after being repeatedly beaten and then presented with a pan of the infant victim's charred bones. Marshall had prepared the brief for the case with William Hastie, and Marshall himself had established the precedent regarding coerced confessions in criminal trials four years earlier, when he had argued *Chambers v. Florida* before the Supreme Court. He had every reason to believe he stood on solid ground for a reversal. Yet the Court had upheld Lyons's conviction. There was speculation that Justice William O. Douglas, who had till then consistently voted to reverse in coerced confession cases, might have cast his vote to let the conviction stand because it was possible that he might be chosen to be Franklin D. Roosevelt's vice presidential running mate and he wanted, therefore, not to offend the Southern wing of the Democratic Party. Or, as the Supreme Court had done in cases before *Lyons*, it might have upheld the Oklahoma court's decision to credit the state for the progress it had made in the conduct of criminal trials involving race. After all, the defendant had not been rushed to trial, he had not been sentenced to death, and he had certainly been represented by competent counsel. Nonetheless, Marshall found the Court's decision to be wrongheaded. Over the next decade, he continued to pressure the state for Lyons's early parole. He also corresponded with Lyons in prison and sent Lyons money from his own wallet.

On May 17, 1954, the Supreme Court announced its unanimous decision in the most important civil rights case of the twentieth century. The Court had found, just as Charles Hamilton Houston and Thurgood Marshall had observed on their tour of the South twenty years earlier, that "separate educational facilities are inherently unequal." State laws that established separate public schools for blacks and whites were thus ruled unconstitutional, in violation of the equal protection clause in the Fourteenth Amendment.

The ruling was just cause for celebration in the LDF's New York offices. Champagne flowed. The staff was boisterous; the din and laughter were thunderous. Marshall playfully chided Walter White for taking the credit for the abolishment of segregation in public schools. The party moved on to the Blue Ribbon, where lawyers and staff and consultants toasted each other and Marshall with dark beer as they shared platters of pigs' knuckles with their director-counsel. Thurgood's wife did not attend—she'd been ill and sometimes bedridden the past few months with chest pains and a persistent viral infection in the lungs—and in the early morning hours, when the party was breaking up, more than one of Marshall's colleagues noticed that he had left the Blue Ribbon with Cecilia Suyat, Gloster Current's secretary. "Thurgood was very discreet about his affairs," said John Aubrey Davis, an academic researcher who had worked on *Brown*. "There was never an example of it except at the victory celebration. He was leaving with Cissy. . . . That was the first time I'd ever seen any indication that she wasn't just another worker there."

The victory was not celebrated in the South. The *Brown* ruling triggered a resurgence of Ku Klux Klan activity and White Citizens' Council activism, whereby "respectable citizens" joined together to exert economic pressures against local individuals and organizations that either supported desegregation or did not openly oppose it. In Lake County, an editorial by Mabel Norris Reese praising Thurgood Marshall and the Supreme Court's decision was not inconsequential. The opposition planted a burning cross on her front lawn, smeared "KKK" in red paint across her office windows, and poisoned the family dog with strychnine.

Ironically, for all the briefs that the LDF lawyers had filed on the Groveland case over the past five years and for all the appearances Marshall had made in the Supreme Court as well as in Florida county courthouses in the attempt of the NAACP to save the life of Walter Irvin, it was Marshall's *Brown* victory in Washington that incidentally set in motion a sequence of events in Florida, which, as it happened, gave the Groveland boy his best chance of escaping the electric chair. For the *Brown* decision infuriated

Willis McCall, both in itself and all the more because the case's celebrated, winning lawyers were the very same who had descended on Lake County and had as much as called its sheriff a cold-blooded murderer. Not that he'd allow them to intimidate him, or their Supreme Court decision to determine how he would maintain law and order in his domain.

Streams were going dry and farms to ruin in the South Carolina drought of 1954, so in the spring Allan Platt decided to move his family south, to Mount Dora in Lake County, Florida, where his brother helped him find work picking oranges. He and his wife, Laura, enrolled their five children in the white public school, only to discover they were not white enough. The school did not ignore the complaints of parents expressing concerns that the brown-skinned Platt children might be Negroes; instead, the principal reported the complaints to the county sheriff. So it happened that Sheriff Willis McCall, accompanied by the school principal, paid a visit to the Platts' residence, where he conducted his own anthropological investigation. He lined the five children up against the wall, and peering down over his glasses, one by one, he studied them. "You know, he favors a nigger," he decided, thus dispensing with seventeen-year-old Denzell; as for thirteen-year-old Laura Belle, "I don't like the shape of that one's nose"— and in as many minutes as children he determined that all five children were indeed Negroes. Despite Allan Platt's claims to Irish and American Indian descent, and unconvinced by birth certificates as well as a marriage license which designated the Platts as "white," McCall ordered the children to be kept out of school, pending further investigation. Platt's objections fell on deaf ears. If there was one thing Willis McCall could do, he bragged, it was identify both "Black Angus cattle and mulattoes."

"The sheriff is the law here," school officials responded when the Platts protested the sheriff's dictum. So, too, Mabel Norris Reese reported in a series of articles that would ultimately earn her a Pulitzer Prize nomination and continuing coverage in *Time* magazine. Taking up the Platts' cause, Reese also renewed her old feud with Sheriff McCall. "If the children never see the inside of another school, they will not go to a Negro school," Allan Platt told Reese. For his family had no association with blacks; they had attended only white churches, and his grandfather had fought for the Confederacy in the Civil War. Furthermore, the Platts were legally designated as "white," though some documents indicated, too, a Croatan Indian ancestry—which, McCall was quick to point out, was defined by Webster's dictionary as a line of "people of mixed Indian, white and Negro ancestry." McCall spouted, and Reese's articles spurred sixty-five pupils at the Mount

Dora school to sign a petition stating that the Platt children's "right to an education has been taken away because of the opinions and prejudice of one man." The next day, when school opened, the children found a chalk line running down the middle of the sidewalk; one side was marked "White People," the other "Nigger Lovers." One child who had signed the petition was stoned with pebbles. A deputy meanwhile visited the Platts with a message from the sheriff's office "that if they weren't out by that night, their house would be burned down."

In the summer of 1954, the outspoken Willis V. McCall was named a director of the National Association for the Advancement of White People, which devoted itself primarily to the advocacy of racial segregation. At a rally in Delaware organized by NAAWP founder Bryant Bowles, the sheriff from Lake County was introduced to a crowd of five thousand segregationists as an "expert" in race relations and "a man who knows how to handle Negroes." Decrying the *Brown* decision, McCall urged everyone in attendance to "go to it" in their opposition to integration. On his return to Lake County he told one newspaper, "I for one, am going to do all I can to forestall such a movement. I am one who, instead of sitting around grumbling about these agitators, goes into action. We need more action and not so much wishie-washie grumbling."

News of the sheriff's call for "action" soon reached Thurgood Marshall in New York, and immediately the NAACP fired off a telegram to Florida's acting governor, Charley Johns, requesting that he remove McCall from office. Johns responded by telling reporters that McCall's speech was "ill-advised" but adding that "I have no grounds to remove him." The partners may have changed, but for fifteen years the dance Marshall had been stepping with Florida governors had remained the same, and they were still stepping on his toes. Only Charley Johns stomped. Johns had become Florida's acting governor when Dan McCarty died suddenly of a heart attack in September 1953, and Johns had since lost in the Democratic primary to LeRoy Collins, who was running unopposed in the 1954 special election. On November 1, the eve of that election, the acting governor, the "hog and hominy" segregationist from North Florida, with two months more to serve, attended to what for him was a more pressing matter of business. He signed the death warrant of Walter Irvin. The execution was set for Monday morning, November 8.

The NAACP at once petitioned the Florida Supreme Court for a stay of execution in light of "new evidence," specifically that Dr. Geoffrey Binneveld, the physician who had examined Norma Padgett after the alleged rape, would have testified, had he been called as a witness, that Padgett "had not been" assaulted. Florida assistant attorney general Reeves Bowen scoffed at the request; he accused the NAACP of sitting idly by "till the last tick of the clock" before bringing the appeal to Tallahassee. The court refused to grant a stay.

Thurgood Marshall had no other options; he knew what he had to do. He'd done it before, stopped an execution at a last, heart-in-the-throat moment. Except that he had been unable to locate Chief Justice Fred Vinson anywhere—not at home or at any of his haunts around Washington. Then he got a tip: a room number at the Statler Hilton, two blocks from the White House. He busted in. The chief justice was playing cards, Vinson v. Truman.

"How did you find me?" Vinson asked.

"I can't tell you," Marshall said, sliding the brief toward the justice.

Vinson's eyes skimmed the pages; time mattered. He waved the brief at Marshall. "Can you vouch for this being true?"

"Yes, sir. I wrote it," Marshall replied.

President Truman watched in silence. Marshall waited, his breath held. Vinson lowered the brief to the table; he picked up his pen.

"I'll tell you one thing, if you've got guts enough to break in on this, I've got guts enough to sign it," said Vinson, passing the brief back to Marshall.

It was late in the evening, Saturday, November 6, three years to the day since Walter Irvin had been lying in a ditch with a gun pressed at his neck—*"This nigger is not dead"*—not yet—but in less than two days he would be taking his last walk, down the corridor of Flat Top to Florida's Old Sparky, unless . . .

Marshall managed to track down Justice Hugo Black, who submitted the signed brief to the Court at a conference of justices. The last-minute stay gave Marshall twelve days to prepare for the meeting of the Supreme Court on November 20, when the justices would again decide whether or not to grant a review of Irvin's conviction. In the forty-five days between then and January 4, when Governor-elect LeRoy Collins took office, Marshall had no doubt that Governor Charley Johns would deliver Irvin to the electric chair the first chance he got. Nor did Marshall doubt that if he could somehow stretch out the judicial process until Johns had vacated the statehouse in Tallahassee, the likelihood that he could rescue Irvin from execution would increase significantly.

An affable man at forty-five, the Tallahassee lawyer LeRoy Collins came from "Old Florida," and like most Southern politicians, he condemned the

*Brown* decision. Even though Marshall did not yet know what to expect from Collins, he knew too well where Johns stood. On November 20, Marshall made a fourth appeal to the U.S. Supreme Court, which agreed to review Irvin's conviction. Florida had thirty days to reply, at which time the Court would decide whether to hear the case for argument and opinion. Marshall had reset the clock ticking off the time between Irvin and the electric chair. Better yet, he had gotten Charley Johns's hand off the switch.

Another clock was ticking at 409 Edgecombe. Buster came home from the hospital for Thanksgiving. She and the doctors had kept the bad news from Thurgood, but time now was short. The chest pains, the virus: it was cancer. Remorseful, reproaching himself for the constant travel, the cases, the endless hours at the LDF offices, the indiscretions, Marshall took a leave of absence from the NAACP. He barricaded himself in the apartment, and at Buster's bedside, attentive and tender, Thurgood spent the final weeks in the quarter century of their marriage: a marriage that may have years ago lost its intimacy but that had never wanted for love. Suffering with her, as if he could suffer for her, Thurgood pined. His body seemed to be mirroring hers. "He had become cadaverous," Jack Greenberg observed on one of Marshall's rare visits at the office. In midwinter, on February 11, 1955, her forty-fourth birthday, Vivian "Buster" Burey left Marshall. It had been nearly ten years ago that she had traveled with Thurgood to the Virgin Islands when he was recuperating from his mysterious illness. Marshall had not taken a vacation since. The NAACP sent him on a cruise, all expenses paid, and Marshall—"morose and unhappy . . . in very bad shape," as Greenberg noted—sailed sadly off to Mexico.

UNLIKE ANY OTHER state in the Deep South, Florida was undergoing a large-scale, transformative demographic shift in the mid-fifties. From the end of World War II until LeRoy Collins took office in January 1955, industrial activity in the United States had increased by nearly 11 percent; in Florida it was up more than 50 percent. During Collins's first year as governor, more than five million tourists would visit the Sunshine State, and from 1950 to 1960 Florida's population would grow by almost 80 percent. The state was enjoying an economic boom that stood, as Collins said, on "three sturdy legs. Tourism. Industry. Agriculture."

At Collins's inauguration on January 4, thousands gathered at Capital Park in Tallahassee to hear the address of the newly sworn-in thirty-third governor of Florida. Conservative politicians shifted uncomfortably in their seats under the bright sun when Collins adopted a combative tone and promised that the days of a "ward-heeling, back-scratching, self-promoting political system" were over. "Government, too, must have qualities of the spirit," Collins told the crowd. "Truth and justice and fairness and unselfish service are some of these. Without these qualities there is no worthwhile leadership, and we grapple and grope in a moral wilderness."

Marshall took notice. He made sure that a new host of letters and telegrams, thousands of them, brought the case of Walter Irvin to the new governor's attention when he took up his post. Marshall had also enlisted Tom Harris, the executive editor of the *St. Petersburg Times*, in the cause. The *Times*'s coverage of the original Groveland Boys trial had drawn the ire of Willis McCall for having the gall to question the evidence against the defendants, and once again the newspaper began publishing articles and editorials questioning procedures and protocol in the court. *Times* reporters who had worked diligently on the case, the paper noted, "were never convinced of the guilt of the four defendants" and indeed believed that the defense had shown more than enough reasonable doubt. Thus, the *Times* argued, the situation now called for "compassion and calm judgment," and in the event that the courts should in time discover the four defendants not to have been guilty of rape, the best way to ensure justice would be to commute Irvin's sentence to life imprisonment.

One week after LeRoy Collins took office, the U.S. Supreme Court declined Marshall's fourth appeal on behalf of Walter Lee Irvin. Among the letters that continued to pour into the governor's office in support of Irvin were two letters from the prosecution in the case. A letter from Sam Buie, the assistant state attorney, urged the governor, now that he was free to issue a death warrant, to "get rid of this case once and for all." It was not the first time Buie had attempted to influence the case outside the courtroom. In November 1951, only weeks after McCall had shot the two Groveland boys, Buie had a shocking story to tell, and he chose a high-ranking NAACP officer in Ocala to tell it to. Jesse Hunter, Buie told the officer, was so livid with Marshall after the lawyer attempted to disqualify him from prosecuting the second Groveland Boys trial that Hunter entered into a conspiracy with Willis McCall to kill Samuel Shepherd and Walter Irvin. It was Hunter's pride, Buie said of his boss, that "caused him to plot this killing with McCall."

Marshall was immediately notified of the alleged conspiracy and saw right through Buie's ploy. He suspected that by tipping off the NAACP, Buie was doing the bidding of his friend Willis McCall, who was "trying to drag Hunter into this killing." Marshall was convinced that Hunter was not involved in such a plot because by that time, Hunter had himself, through Mabel Norris Reese, been keeping the NAACP informed on the FBI's investigation into McCall's shooting of the Groveland Boys.

Unlike Sam Buie, State Attorney Jesse Hunter made no argument for speedy execution. Hunter's letter to Collins focused instead on the chaos that had erupted in Lake County, with the KKK and members of the National Association for the Advancement of White People breaking into targeted homes and threatening the occupants while their mobs huddled menacingly outside the door, all under the permissive eye of Sheriff Willis McCall.

Hunter's health had worsened since the last Groveland trial. Still, leukemia had not taken the battle entirely out of him. It was Mabel Norris Reese who reported to her seventy-five-year-old friend the recent plight of Allan Platt. While Platt and his family had managed to resist the bullying of Sheriff McCall and his deputy's threat of arson, their landlady had not. A visit from the sheriff had convinced her to evict the Platts, out of concern, as she told Platt, that the "house might catch fire." Hunter decided that Sheriff McCall was "out of control," and on behalf of the Platts, the former prosecutor sued the Lake County School Board. On his own money he traveled to South Carolina to obtain documents necessary to support the Platts' claims, and in court, demanding that the board produce evidence to prove conclusively that the Platt children had Negro blood, he left the school board's unsupported and insupportable case in shreds. "Much as I hate it," said the judge, Truman Futch, he had no choice but to rule in favor of the Platts, who in October 1955 won the right to return to the white public school. "The Lord be praised," said Allan Platt, near tears. "I knew it couldn't be any other way."

The verdict did not please Sheriff McCall any more than did Jesse Hunter's apparently blossoming friendship with the "Communist" reporter for the *Mount Dora Topic*. "I have no comment to make whatsoever," McCall told reporters. "Absolutely no comment." He did have a comment for Allan Platt, though, a few days later when a band of "night-riding terrorists" firebombed the Platts' home. McCall's investigation turned up footprints at the scene that, the sheriff informed Platt, could have been made by some high school boys who "didn't want to go to school with burrheads." McCall then placed the blame for all harassment, threats, and violence aimed at the Platts, not to mention the embarrassment brought upon the Lake County School Board, on Platt himself, as he had instigated the whole series of events by contacting Mabel Norris Reese. "I've got more justice from Mrs. Reese than I have from you," Platt told the sheriff.

Again the Platt family had been forced from their home, and the children from their school; eventually they were invited to enroll in a private school in Mount Dora. Jesse Hunter publicly and strongly criticized McCall not only for failing to protect the Platts but also for telling reporters that the Lake County Sheriff's Department had no cause or intent to protect them. The former prosecutor also, and again, contacted Governor Collins. "Disturbed" by reports like Hunter's, the governor issued a statement: "Lawlessness of this kind in Lake County has just got to stop. Not only are the rights of the individuals involved but the good name of this fine county and of the state is put in jeopardy." Sheriff McCall remained undeterred. At a meeting of the Lions Club not long after the firebombing of the Platts' house, he announced, "In my book, they're still mulattoes. This only proves that there are some people who will stoop to integrate our schools."

In New York Marshall had been following the press coverage of the Platt case, and he took particular interest in the coverage by Mabel Norris Reese. That Reese had once called for honor to be avenged in the rape of Norma Padgett and declared Lake County a racial paradise, and that she had lost all regard for the sheriff of that county, attested to the human capacity to change. No longer able, after the sheriff's shooting of the two Groveland defendants, to turn a blind eye to the racism and white supremacy in her own backyard, she had tipped off the NAACP about the last bullet found in the sand, and she had since kept the New York office informed, through intermediaries, of what she learned further about the case from Jesse Hunter. Hunter himself, it appeared, had begun to rethink the entire Groveland Boys matter, "due chiefly to the influence of Thurgood Marshall," according to Reese. Hunter may have even begun to regret the "sacred duty" that compelled him, a man stricken with a fatal disease, to win his last capital case in Lake County at the cost of Walter Irvin's life.

IN HIS FIRST year as governor, LeRoy Collins took countless "Florida selling" trips to New York, where he chased manufacturing deals, the construction of atomic energy plants, and insurance company relocations. He was, as *Time* magazine observed, "an indefatigable salesman of his state boom." The last thing Collins wanted to see, then, was a New York newspaper headline asking, "Notice Negro Blood on Your Grapefruit?" Not only would bad press cost the state a tremendous loss in agricultural and manufacturing dollars; it would also stem the flow of money from Northern tourists and winter residents, whose seasonal migrations had prompted a boom in housing and construction. Neither an advertisement nor an asset for the Sunshine State were trigger-happy sheriffs and bomb-planting, torch-wielding mobs in white robes and hoods.

With letter-writing campaigns and newspaper stories rekindling interest in the Groveland Boys case and the plight of Walter Irvin, Thurgood Marshall turned to a friend, a former president of the NAACP's Legal Defense Fund, Allan Knight Chalmers, for additional purchase. A highly respected white minister who had chaired the Scottsboro Defense Committee in the 1930s, for seventeen years Chalmers had negotiated tirelessly with the state of Alabama until all nine defendants had gained their freedom. At the time of the first Groveland Boys trial, Chalmers had participated in the investigation into the case by the Committee of 100, and he had come away convinced that the defendants were innocent. In 1955, when Marshall contacted him in regard to the fate of Walter Irvin, Chalmers was teaching at Boston University, where he was mentoring a young student named Martin Luther King Jr. In Chalmers, Marshall saw the kind of man by whom LeRoy Collins might be persuaded to favorably address Walter Irvin's situation, as Collins appeared to be a man moved by words and ideas. Moreover, Chalmers's 1951 book, *They Shall Be Free*, struck chords that Collins had also touched upon in his inaugural address, as in Chalmers's call for "effective action" in what Collins would name a "moral wilderness":

> *There are enough staid people in the world holding things as they are. We need no more of them. What we need is people caught by the truth that no one is free when anyone is bound. That is not an easy idea to have get a hold on you. It has to be applied person by person, not just in the pious generalities of the resolutions good people pass when they gather for a moment and separate without effective action.*

Marshall's request produced a letter to clergymen in which Chalmers called for their support of clemency in the case of Walter Irvin: what Chalmers described as a "desperate situation." In the letter, too, he cited a Florida newspaper that, in the same day's edition, covered Irvin's impending date with death in one article and in another reported that a thirty-year-old white man had been fined a hundred dollars in the rape of a fourteen-year-old black girl. The coincidence hardly spoke to the "truth and justice and fairness" Collins espoused in his inaugural address.

The governor did act upon the case, if without fanfare or even an inside-page notice in the newspaper. Shortly after taking office, Collins initiated a secret investigation into the Groveland Boys case by his personal friend Bill Harris, a Tallahassee lawyer. What Collins wanted was an objective, detailed, fact-based report; so, to obviate any social or political fallout for either Harris or the governor's office, Collins assured Harris, who would be acting only in an advisory capacity, without a fee, that the report would not be made public. A thorough review of the evidence and the testimony left Harris unconvinced that the Padgetts had been able to positively identify the Groveland boys. More apparent was the failure of the state to utilize procedures available for valid scientific analysis of the pants stains, footprints, and tire tracks that "could have nailed this case down and removed any reasonable doubt." At issue, too, was the lack of any medical evidence to support the rape charges. Harris more than doubted the validity of the prosecution's time line; he rejected it, for how could the gun in Charles Greenlee's possession have been used in the crime when Greenlee was already in custody nearly twenty miles away from the scene of the alleged rape? Neither did Harris accept the findings of the coroner's jury, which concluded that Sheriff Willis McCall was justified in the shooting of Samuel Shepherd and Walter Irvin. In his report Harris stated that the shooting was "in its best light an act of gross and willful negligence, and in its possible interpretation an act of criminal negligence."

Seeded further by the likes of Chalmers and the Committee of 100, the storm of letters and telegrams to the governor's office did not abate. Clergymen pleaded for clemency. Tourists vowed never to spend another penny in the Sunshine State. Florida residents expressed shame at the sanctioned inhumanity of Irvin's case. But other voices decried any attempt by committees or agencies or associations to alter the status quo either in Florida or in the case of Walter Irvin. In a letter to Governor Collins from U.S. Attorney Herbert Phillips, who had angered the U.S. Justice Department and the FBI in 1950 when he failed to take action, despite "substantial evidence . . . that the victims were beaten and tortured" by members of the Lake County Sheriff's Department, the avowed segregationist—Phillips bristled at the mere mention of Thurgood Marshall's name—wrote: "Since I am your personal friend and desire that the NAACP shall not prove itself more powerful than our courts . . . I see no reason why the leaders of the NAACP and those who follow their leadership should expect you . . . [to be] setting aside the verdict of guilt of two juries, the judgment and sentence of the Circuit Judge, the two decisions of the Supreme Court of Florida, and the decision of the U.S. Supreme Court, upholding and affirming the death sentence imposed on Irvin."

Inhumanity, shame, virulence, segregationism—none of it aligned with the governor's personal vision for his state. Within months of each other, LeRoy Collins and Thurgood Marshall appeared on the cover of *Time* magazine in 1955, but the two men had more in common than political celebrity. Collins, who stood among the first of the "New South" politicians, and Marshall, who was emerging as the architect of a new America, both championed the cause of racial justice, no matter its political inexpediency, and both men would become leading, outspoken opponents of the death penalty in the United States. Marshall would later say, "In recognizing the humanity of our fellow beings, we pay ourselves the highest tribute." More bluntly, Collins would declare the death penalty to be "Florida's gutter of shame." He might have said the same of the racial injustices that had for too long defined the social tenor of the conservative Old South, although in his gubernatorial campaign he himself had opposed desegregation. "I realized we had to change," Collins said after he had read those letters and telegrams, for without change he could not achieve the new Florida that he had envisioned in his inaugural address: a Florida that could "offer to the people of the world the finest investment on earth—a place in the sun."

Memorable among the thousands of letters, and moving as well as suasive, was one that Collins received from Jesse Hunter. The prosecutor of the Groveland Boys related how he and Thurgood Marshall had reached an agreement whereby Irvin would receive a life sentence in exchange for a guilty plead, but subsequently, after a lengthy conference, Marshall had informed the state attorney that the defendant insisted he was innocent and refused to plead otherwise. Hunter then recounted for the governor the details of the private meeting he'd had three months before the retrial, on the morning of November 7, 1951, when he had slipped past Deputy James Yates at Waterman Memorial Hospital and stepped into the guarded room. In the hospital bed, barely conscious, with a red tube taped to his face, lay Walter Irvin, the defendant he had already once sent to the electric chair and the man whom Hunter had noticed was still alive the night before. The man's chances of recovery were uncertain, as Hunter had suspected—that was why he had driven to the hospital at the crack of dawn. The two men briefly discussed Irvin's condition, and Irvin told the prosecutor he believed that he was going to die. Hunter sensed an opportunity: "Confess to the rape," he whispered, promising Irvin that anything he said would be confidential and not ever be used against him. "For my satisfaction alone," Hunter added. And waited, until: "No . . . I'm not guilty," Irvin rasped.

To Collins, Hunter's intent in the letter was clear. After his bedside conversation with Irvin, the ailing state attorney had confided to Mabel Norris Reese that he had doubts concerning Irvin's guilt. Yet the prosecutor in him would not allow him to quit on the case and the chance of a second conviction. Now, seventy-six years old, leukemic, his health failing, the former prosecutor was striving to clear his conscience, to do what was right—to persuade Governor LeRoy Collins to commute Walter Irvin's death sentence.

Hunter's intent was clear to Willis McCall as well, and it rankled the sheriff even more than the Supreme Court's reversal of the first Groveland Boys verdict. After meeting with the governor, McCall sent Collins a letter of his own, in which he tried to explain away the former prosecutor's change of heart as "a demonstration of senility . . . greatly influenced by a radical female editor who in the opinion of many citizens in this county has pink leaning in her editorials."

In the letter McCall argued further, with a parting shot at Thurgood Marshall and his New York lawyers, that commutation of Irvin's sentence to life "would only be a victory for NAACP who has set out to destroy the authority of our courts, as it is an undisputable fact that they are the ones behind this movement. Should they accomplish this goal, it would mean one thing. That all a Negro criminal would need to do would be to pick out some innocent helpless white woman as a target to satisfy his ravishing sexual desires, keep his mouth shut, proclaim his innocence and let NAACP furnish the money and lawyers to beat the rap. Governor, at this time I have great confidence in you as a deep thinking man, I am praying that you will see fit to let the verdict of the Court stand and keep our great State safe for our fair womanhood. This obligation we owe to our children." The sheriff's argument might have persuaded Collins's predecessors, Fuller Warren and Charley Johns, but the New South governor had no ear for still more racially motivated cries for blood and vengeance. Collins was persuaded more soundly by Bill Harris's less biased report, which by the way showed Willis McCall's fingerprints to be all over the Groveland Boys case. From the start, McCall had wanted the four Groveland boys dead, and he had proved himself ready to execute them himself if the state of Florida hadn't the stomach for it.

Mabel Norris Reese had no stomach for it, or for the renegade sheriff of Lake County. Neither did Jesse Hunter any longer. Eventually in the matter of Groveland, and in the Platt case, both Reese and Hunter had stood up to McCall at the risk of their families and their property, as had Harry T. Moore, whose protests of injustice had cost him and his wife their lives. Like Collins himself, Reese and Hunter had been willfully blind to the issues of race in Florida, and Collins, like them, had "realized we had to change."

Governor Collins was close to his decision on the Irvin matter when, on September 21, 1955, a petition came across his desk. It came bound in a well-traveled book that apparently had made its way around Lake County about five years before, when a young woman had circulated it. A poet, an activist, a supporter of world peace, an opponent of capital punishment (and a private investigator with the Owens Detective Agency in Miami)— she'd roused some curiosity and no alarm. No one knew quite what to make of her, with her peace pin and her farm dresses. She was friendly enough, a harmless sort of girl and maybe a little naïve, and she seemed to know the Bible. She talked a lot about justice and the death penalty. She was collecting signatures in her book, "to abolish capital punishment." She'd gotten hundreds of them—it wasn't many, she knew—no matter that people like Willis McCall tried to shoo her away. Most people, though, listened to what she had to say. Simple people, hardworking farmers and housewives, they invited her into their weatherworn shacks scattered around the Bay Lake swampland; they offered her meals and a place to stay. They might feel strongly against the blacks, but they firmly believed, and said so, that capital punishment was wrong. God-fearing country Baptists, they knew that by their deeds and tenets they, too, would be judged someday. The girl believed that every signature was important, that each could make a difference, and that collectively the signatures could change a mind or bestow mercy or realize a truth that people had not yet dared to speak: the pen was a mighty instrument.

The book lay open on the governor's desk. It had come to Collins from the well-known Reverend Ben F. Wyland, the leader of a group of fifty churches in the state of Florida. Idly the governor flipped through the pages of the petition as he pondered whether to spare the life of Walter Irvin. A signature caught his eye. There, on the page before him, among the hundreds of Lake County residents declaring in the strokes of a pen their opposition to capital punishment, he read: "Norma Tyson Padgett."

**HEAR MR. "CIVIL RIGHTS"**

Meet the man who beat Jim Crow in the United States Supreme Court . . . "and the walls came tumbling down!"

**THURGOOD MARSHALL**
Esquire
Special NAACP Counsel—New York City

**MASS MEETING**
**OAKLAND ARENA**
**SUNDAY, MAY 22, 3 P.M.**
**— ADMISSION FREE —**
Sponsored by: West Coast Region
National Association for the Advancement of Colored People
(NAACP)

*(Library of Congress, Prints & Photographs Division,·Visual Materials from the NAACP Records)*

THE STATE," Governor LeRoy Collins said, "did not walk that extra mile—did not establish the guilt of Walter Lee Irvin in an absolute and conclusive manner." Collins's decision to commute Irvin's sentence, he told reporters, had been weighted heavily by a letter from former state attorney Jesse Hunter, which had reinforced the governor's own feelings about the case. He explained, "My conscience told me it was a bad case, badly handled, badly tried and now, on this bad performance, I was asked to take a man's life. My conscience would not let me do it." On the basis of Hunter's letter and the findings in Bill Harris's investigation, not to discount the presence of Norma Lee Padgett's signature on a petition proposing the abolition of capital punishment, Collins had led the State Pardon Board to a unanimous approval of the Groveland boy's "long-pending plea for clemency."

Probably in an effort to offset the inevitable political consequences of his decision, Collins, who had that week been featured on the cover of *Time*, also impugned the NAACP for its involvement in the case, which was "prompted by the bare fact that the defendant is a colored man rather than by careful evaluation of the circumstances of his guilt or innocence." The censure infuriated Thurgood Marshall, however pleased he may have been by the action taken by the governor and the pardon board to end the long battle for Walter Irvin's life. In response, Marshall declared that Collins's commutation in fact vindicated the NAACP's position that Irvin had been "the victim of a gross miscarriage of justice." Marshall also, in turn, reproached the governor, whose "every statement" regarding the NAACP had been "completely in error," for following "the pattern of other southern officials in using the NAACP as the whipping boy for the repeated injustices against Negroes in the south." Had the NAACP not intervened, Marshall asserted, all four Groveland boys would be dead, and Collins "would not have had to request the pardon board to commute Irvin's sentence." One thing Marshall had to concede, however, was that, as one newspaper stated, "it took far more political courage [for Collins] to spare the life of this Negro than it would have taken to let him go to the electric chair."

For Walter Irvin, the play of politics in the commutation was superseded by gratitude and relief, and hope. "I want you to know that, as long as I live I must, and I will, with all sincere, look to you as my earthly god," Irvin wrote to Governor Collins. "Now that my health is failing, I do hope and pray that I will be able to go free someday because I feel, as I have, and I did for a lifetime, live a clean and law abiding life, Sir!"

Lake County did not take the news of Irvin's commutation well. Judge Truman Futch presided over a grand jury called to investigate the State Pardon Board's action on the grounds that Collins had been influenced by "Communist pressure tactics." The judge did allow, though, that the governor may have been "the innocent victim of a clever deception," apparently implemented by a communist agent. For, Futch claimed, "startling documents"—like a petition protesting capital punishment, it would appear—had come into his possession to prove that "at least one person suspected of being a Communist agent had been sent into Lake County" and that efforts "to gather information on this case . . . have transgressed both the law of God and man." Sheriff McCall enlisted two of the signatories to the petition, Norma Padgett and her aunt, to testify before the grand jury that any signature of theirs on any petition had to have been obtained by a "ruse," as they had not knowingly ever signed any such document. The governor refused to testify. Being "accountable only to his conscience," Collins stated that he would not participate in any secret grand jury proceedings, although he was perfectly willing, he said, to answer any questions "in the Cabinet room with the press and public present."

Truman Futch's special and unprecedented grand jury investigation elicited negative editorial comment from Mabel Norris Reese in the *Mount Dora Topic.* Her protest won her, first, the load of dead fish that was dumped into her front yard. Second came the hand grenade that was tossed at her house; the explosion was heard five miles away, but fortunately neither she nor her family was home at the time. Sheriff McCall was "investigating."

In the end, the Lake County grand jury found that Collins and the State Pardon Board had acted within their legal rights to commute Irvin's sentence. The jury did, however, rebuke the "smearing of the good people of Lake County and its law enforcement officers" by Tom Harris of the *St. Petersburg Times* as well as Reverend Ben F. Wyland's "obtaining and circulating a petition seeking clemency for Irvin." Wyland had also written to Collins, stating that both Norma and Willie had signed the petition at a time "when feelings ran high," and emphasizing the "victim's" compassion. "If this woman who suffered most could show mercy and forgive her enemies surely we could follow such a worthy example."

No fan of the governor, Sheriff McCall was not satisfied by the outcome of the grand jury's investigation, not with his friend Fuller Warren planning another run at the governorship in the next election. So McCall hatched a plan to embarrass the sitting governor outside the grand jury room, and again he enlisted the aid of Norma Padgett. At a Washington's Birthday parade in McCall's hometown of Eustis, just as Collins was leaving the Grandview Hotel, two Lake County deputies escorted a "neatly dressed" and not so forgiving Norma Padgett over to him, and in front of hundreds of parade-goers, she accosted the governor, screaming, "You're the one who let out the nigger that raped me! How would you have felt if that had been your wife or daughter?"

꽃 ꃌ

H IS BODY ILL, betraying him, but his conscience finally clear, Jesse Hunter lived long enough to see Irvin's sentence commuted. He passed away in February 1956.

I N MARCH 1960 Deputy James Yates found himself in strangely familiar circumstances. A middle-aged white woman claimed she had been raped in the city of Fruitland Park. She was fuzzy as to details of the crime, except that maybe one of her attackers was in his forties or fifties, and the other was about seventeen years old. So Yates picked up two black citrus workers, no matter that they were in their early twenties, and after they confessed to the crime under interrogation, the deputy confiscated their shoes. The victim, who had been ruled incompetent by the court and committed to a mental institution shortly after the attack, did not take the stand for the prosecution. The alleged rapists were convicted and sentenced to die in the electric chair, almost solely on the basis of footprint evidence.

The NAACP got involved, and this time got lucky. A week before the scheduled execution of the two men, Noel Griffin, one of McCall's deputies who had worked on the Fruitland Park rape case, disclosed to a Florida NAACP lawyer that the defendants had been framed by the Lake County Sheriff's Department. According to Griffin, Deputy Yates had used the defendants' confiscated shoes to make plaster casts of their footprints not at the crime scene but in another deputy's backyard. Griffin's allegations were confirmed by the FBI, whose analysis showed the soil mixed in the plaster casts to be consistent with that of the deputy's backyard. Furthermore, the FBI concluded—as had Thurgood Marshall's expert witness, Herman Bennett, in the Groveland rape case ten years before—that when the defendants' footprints had supposedly been left, their feet had not been in their shoes. The fact of the falsified evidence enabled the NAACP to rescue both men from electrocution; a federal judge overturned their convictions.

In December 1962, the two deputies, James Yates and his accomplice, were suspended and indicted by an Orange County grand jury on charges of perjury and conspiracy. Convictions would have carried life sentences for both, if James Yates and his deputy accomplice had ever made it to court, but the case was so long delayed that the statute of limitations expired. Both deputies were reinstated by Willis McCall, with back pay.

☙ ❧

Fuller Warren's special investigator J. J. Elliott was off by twelve years when he forecast that McCall's shooting of Shepherd and Irvin would guarantee the sheriff three more terms in office. In fact, McCall served seven consecutive terms as sheriff of Lake County. In his twenty-eight-year tenure, on various charges of misconduct, McCall was the subject of dozens of investigations. Not a single charge stuck. The sheriff's personal reign of terror ended in 1972, when he was indicted and suspended from office by Governor Reubin Askew: the sixty-two-year-old McCall had kicked to death a mentally retarded black prisoner in his cell. Although McCall was acquitted of the charges, the time he'd spent defending himself in court had prevented him from campaigning effectively enough to win that year's election. Still, he was only barely defeated in his bid for an eighth consecutive term.

Willis McCall's name surfaced often in the ongoing FBI investigation into the murder of Harry T. Moore and his wife. For four decades and more McCall denied any involvement or knowledge. Not long before his death in 1994, he avouched, "I never hurt anyone . . . or killed anyone who didn't deserve killing." The FBI ultimately laid responsibility for the bombing in Mims on the KKK and named four likely suspects, two of whom, Earl Brooklyn and Tillman "Curly" Belvin, belonged to the Apopka Klavern, as did McCall, and both men had participated, according to FBI informants, in the Groveland riots. Seven KKK members were indicted for perjury in regard to their whereabouts that Christmas night when Moore was murdered. Frank Meech, an FBI agent who investigated the Moore killings, was critical of the Department of Justice for having the seven "indictments quashed for the 'Tranquility of the South.'"

The case remains unsolved, though not for want of Stetson Kennedy's efforts. In the sixty years since the explosion beneath that modest wooden house in an orange grove, Kennedy never stopped trying to solve the murder of Harry T. Moore. He filed Freedom of Information Act requests to access FBI cases files, he hunted down witnesses, he continued to pressure Florida attorneys general and the state's governors for action, and he lived to see the Moore case reopened three times: in 1978, 1991, and 2005. Stetson Kennedy died in Florida in 2011 at the age of ninety-four.

In the eight years Charles Greenlee had been serving at Belle Glade State Prison Farm, he'd been a model inmate. He had worked his way off a chain gang and onto a road construction crew. He liked his new responsibilities; he enjoyed having more freedom. So much so that one day in 1957 he simply walked away from the work farm, and eighty miles to the north, in Fort Pierce, he found a job and in six weeks had settled into a "model life." That's when he was apprehended, and returned to Belle Glade. In July 1960 Greenlee was awarded parole. He married, raised a family, and built a successful heating and cooling maintenance business in Tennessee, where he lives today.

Norma and Willie Padgett's marriage did not last; they finalized their divorce in July 1958. Norma remarried, but is now a widow living in Georgia.

Miss L. B. De Forest . . . vanished.

In 1961 Jack Greenberg succeeded his mentor as the LDF's director-counsel at the NAACP when President John F. Kennedy appointed Thurgood Marshall to the U.S. Court of Appeals for the Second Circuit. Greenberg is the former dean of Columbia College and is currently the Alphonse Fletcher Jr. Professor of Law at Columbia Law School in New York.

Franklin Williams was appointed by the Kennedy administration in 1961 to assist Sargent Shriver in organizing the Peace Corps. President Lyndon Johnson later appointed him ambassador to Ghana, but not before first consulting his friend Thurgood Marshall. "I would put Frank there without any hesitation," Marshall told the president. In 1985, Williams returned to Florida to give an interview on the Groveland Boys case for the University of Florida's Oral History Project. When the talk turned to Sheriff Willis McCall, Williams bristled. "This man is a, is a vicious killer," Williams stammered. "Is he still alive?" he asked, and was answered yes. "I would not doubt," Williams averred, "if he knew I were here today speaking. I would not doubt that he would come and try to kill me. I do not want to cross him." Franklin Williams died in New York in 1990.

Mabel Norris Reese shared Williams's opinions of Willis McCall. Her fears fueled by dead fish and hand grenades, she left Lake County shortly after Governor Collins commuted Walter Irvin's sentence. She divorced and remarried, and Mabel Norris Chesley, who counted Martin Luther King Jr. and other prominent black activists among her friends, committed herself as a reporter and columnist for the *Daytona Beach Morning Journal* to the advancement of the civil rights movement in Florida. She wrote regularly to Walter Irvin, and took occasion to visit him, throughout the years that he remained in prison at Raiford.

January 1968 brought Walter Irvin his parole, with the stipulation that he not return to Lake County. Now forty, he had spent nearly half his life in prison. In Miami, where he lived with his sister Henrietta, he found work in construction, even with his impaired health, and tried to lead something like what people called a normal life. In February 1969, Irvin received permission from his parole officer to attend the funeral of an uncle in Lake County. He had been back in Willis McCall country for but a few hours when friends and relatives found him apparently sleeping in a car after the drive north; but he wasn't sleeping. Walter Irvin was dead.

Mabel Norris Chesley was suspicious. She did not doubt the depth of Willis McCall's resolve to visit his county justice upon the Groveland boy, especially as he had failed to do so on that dark country road eighteen years before. The Lake County Sheriff's Department report on Walter Irvin's death stated that the forty-one-year-old black male had died of natural causes. A *St. Petersburg Times* reporter told Mabel that he had tried to speak to the doctor who'd pronounced Irvin dead. The doctor had hung up on him.

E NCLOSED WITH THE letter to Justice Thurgood Marshall was the newspaper article by Mabel Norris Chesley on Walter Irvin's death in Groveland, reportedly of natural causes. Marshall had by then been a sitting associate justice on the U.S. Supreme Court for about a year and a half, and Walter Irvin had been free on parole four months less than that. For eighteen years Irvin had been imprisoned at Raiford, but Marshall had at least been able to keep his promise to Dellia Irvin—he'd kept her boy out of the electric chair.

The day before the letter arrived, Marshall had voted with his fellow justices at the Court to overturn a conviction of another sort, in *Brandenburg v. Ohio*. Ku Klux Klan leader Clarence Brandenburg's speech against "dirty niggers" and "Jews" at a Klan rally had been captured vividly on film, on which evidence he'd been charged with advocating violence, convicted in a state court, and sentenced to ten years in prison. In a unanimous decision, the Supreme Court had ruled that on First Amendment grounds the government could not punish abstract inflammatory speech. The Constitution was the Constitution, and Justice Marshall did not struggle with his vote.

For a quarter century the younger Thurgood Marshall had fought in lower courts and argued in the highest one for constitutional rights, though not ever for white supremacists. At the NAACP the special counsel had championed politically disenfranchised and socially oppressed—and like Irvin, falsely accused—blacks in Oklahoma, Georgia, Alabama, Florida.

The train rides south, the stifling courtrooms with their Jim Crow balconies, the vanes of fans rotating slowly overhead, the iron gates clanging, black men in shackles, men like Irvin, with bumps on their heads, welts on their arms, as they shamble shoeless to the defense table—with an article and a letter and a name, Walter Irvin, the past comes back: a sheriff and his deputies share a joke and a laugh with the judge as they turn their squinty eyes toward the no-good NAACP lawyers from up north.

It all changed—and in his way, with the Groveland Boys, Marshall had helped to change it. "There is very little truth to the old refrain that one cannot legislate equality," Marshall posited in a 1966 White House conference on civil rights. "Laws not only provide concrete benefits, they can even change the hearts of men—some men, anyhow—for good or evil." In Groveland, Mabel Norris Reese had come round. So had Jesse Hunter. Governor LeRoy Collins had done the right thing. Maybe, too, that young juror with an honest face, the one who'd been listening so intently to Marshall's summation at the retrial in Ocala, had fixed his mind on a different kind of future for the South. Marshall's civil cases, the long battles for voting rights and school desegregation, unquestionably effected lasting social changes, but the criminal cases more immediately brought justice. They "did the most immediate good, because they saved people's lives," Marshall said.

Mabel's article did more than stir Thurgood's memories. He picked up the phone, and just as he had done twenty years before, when the Groveland Boys story and the name Walter Irvin first crossed his desk at the NAACP in New York, he called the director of the FBI. From J. Edgar Hoover he learned that at the present time, no, the bureau was not conducting an investigation into Irvin's death, presumably of natural causes, but the director would have all the materials relevant to the case delivered straightaway to the Civil Rights Division of the U.S. Department of Justice. Marshall thanked the director and hung up the phone. Willis McCall would soon be hearing from Hoover's men, again.

Natural causes. There was room enough in that conclusion for reasonable doubt. When it came to the sheriff whom Marshall had long referred to as "the sonofabitch," nothing would surprise him, least of all the murder of a Groveland boy.

Marshall set aside Mabel's article on Walter Irvin's death for his files. Before he clipped the letter to it, he read the carefully handwritten words again. They were dated March 7, 1969.

*My dear Mr. Justice,*

*Enclosed please find clipping which I believe needs checking.*

*I have thought of this poor man often over the years. I was shocked to read this over my morning coffee.*

*McCall is a disgrace to the law of this wonderful country of ours.*

*I have lived in Holly Hill, Florida for 18 years. I am Catholic, I am white, married and have a son 16 years of age.*

*I am proud of you.*

*Sincerely,*
*Mrs. Ruth N. Starr*

# | ACKNOWLEDGMENTS |

MY MOST SINCERE thanks go to Jack Greenberg, the Legal Defense Fund attorney who served as Thurgood Marshall's right-hand man throughout the Groveland Boys case. Professor Greenberg's assistance was invaluable to me, as he patiently explained, clarified, and otherwise pointed me in the right direction with regard to the many questions I had in the research and writing of this book. I could not be more appreciative of his generosity, candor, and willingness to help me tell this story.

I am eternally grateful and forever indebted to Ted Wells, Jeffrey Robinson, and Debo Adegbile at the NAACP Legal Defense and Educational Fund for all that they did to arrange my access to the LDF files. Adrienne Cannon in the Manuscript Division at the Library of Congress was instrumental in this process, too, and I'm thankful for her help and guidance along the way.

There were a great many people who were kind enough to spend time talking to me; sharing notes, memories, clippings, photographs, and records; and helping me to better understand this story, this time in American history, and Thurgood Marshall. In particular I would like to thank Cecilia "Cissy" Marshall, Evangeline Moore, the late Stetson Kennedy, Vernon Jordan, the late Norman Bunin, Gloria Samuels, Kim Howard Turner, Gary Corsair, Ben Green, Mark Tushnet, Daniel Richman, Alexander Tureaud, Rachel Emanuel, Isaac Flores, Susan C. McCarthy, Caxton Doggett, Ernest Hekkanen, Robin Bridges, Kathleen Eckelt, and Marvin

Dunn. I count each and every one of these conversations as a gift, and I am most thankful for their kindness and their generosity. I was also fortunate to speak with several people who, for various reasons, have asked me not to identify them. But their insights and contributions to this story were important, and I'm thankful they were willing to share a painful part of the past with me.

This book benefits tremendously from the research and counsel of the brilliant Matthew J. Boylan of the ASK NYPL division of the New York Public Library, who is in a category all by himself, and an indispensable source on history, political science, law, and journalism, to name but a few.

Early versions of my manuscript were turned over to a number of trusted friends who were charitable enough to read and offer valuable advice and encouragement. Karen Abbott lent her sharp eyes and well-honed storytelling instincts, and Jim Wohl his astute judgment and big-picture sensibilities. Both brought their sense of humor (in the margins and comments) to the most grinding of work—the rewrites. Carlo DeVito is, as always, an optimistic force of nature, spurring me on whenever I got stuck (often), while attorney extraordinaire Tom Burka was always there with the answers to my strange and perplexing legal questions. Betsy West gave me sage journalistic advice, and Anita Kimberly Sower and Dorothy King were trusty researchers who helped me track down material across the country. Boyd Murphree, archivist at the State Archives of Florida, and William Lefevre at the Walter P. Reuther Library at Wayne State University helped me get my hands on files and information that were essential to this book, and Judi Mackey came through for me in a very big way. I'm also grateful to the staffs of the National Archives, the Library of Congress, the University of South Florida Libraries Special Collections, the Schomburg Center for Research in Black Culture, the Moorland Spingarn Research Center, Howard University, the Rare Books and Manuscript Library, Butler Library, Columbia University, and the New York Public Library.

I don't know what I would do without the discerning Peter Skutches in my corner, looking over my manuscript. Patient, reassuring, and indefatigable, he's a godsend of a friend and a devil with a green pencil.

I'm grateful to my longtime friend Joe Hamilla and his family (Cheryl, Hanna, and Jonathan), who were kind enough to put me up, and put up with me, over several research trips to Lake County, as well as to Janet, Jack, and Chase Wohl for their Southern hospitality. And to another long-time friend, Tom Schmidt, whose good company and comfortable couch kept me well rested during my stays in Washington, D.C., despite all the caffeinated beverages. For love and support, profound gratitude to the upstate Kings, Ed, Janette, Emily, Eileen, and Jimmy, as well as Dorothy King, Mary Jane Miles, and the ever-present Poppy.

Special thanks to my former editor, Julia Cheiffetz, whose passion for this story from the very beginning was inspiring, and to Gail Winston, my current editor, who enthusiastically took over the reins of this book and expertly guided it to completion. I couldn't be more grateful for Gail's composure and calm assurances on an entirely smooth transition. Also at Harper, Maya Ziv and Katie Salisbury were immensely helpful and efficient, Tom Pitoniak was ever alert and meticulous, and Melanie Jones showed great diligence in her legal read of the manuscript.

I'm extraordinarily lucky to have Farley Chase as my agent—always encouraging, clearheaded, and sharp as they come. It's a pleasure to acknowledge my respect and admiration for him.

Finally, there are only a few words that matter for the three girls who matter most, Lorna, Maddie, and Liv. I love you.

# | A NOTE ON SOURCES |

There were many excellent works that were especially valuable in my research into the life of Thurgood Marshall. Jack Greenberg's *Crusaders in the Courts* (1994) is highly engaging, and provided an indispensable firsthand account of his years spent working for Thurgood Marshall and the Legal Defense Fund. I made considerable use of Juan Williams's authoritative biography, *Thurgood Marshall, American Revolutionary* (1998), in my research. Williams did an extraordinary amount of legwork, and his interviews with Marshall helped shed a bright light on the life and career of the civil rights lawyer.

Carl Rowan's *Dream Makers, Dream Breakers: The World of Justice Thurgood Marshall* (1993), Mark Tushnet's *Making Civil Rights Law* (1994), and Richard Kluger's *Simple Justice* (1975) were also exceptionally useful in helping me put the pieces of Thurgood Marshall's life together. There were two other books that were most valuable companions to have at my side. Gary Corsair's exhaustively researched book, *The Groveland Four* (2004), was most helpful, and anyone interested in learning more about the Groveland Boys would be well served to read Corsair's thorough account of the case. And Ben Green's *Before His Time: The Untold Story of Harry T. Moore, America's First Civil Rights Martyr* (1999) is an engrossing and highly readable biography of Moore that deservedly spotlights one of the forgotten heroes of the pre–civil rights movement.

Helpful to me in its own way was *An Autobiography of Willis V. McCall,*

*Sheriff of Lake County*, published by Willis V. McCall, a copy of which I received from the University of Florida Libraries, P. K. Yonge Library of Florida History.

The majority of the research for this book was compiled from the vast and unredacted Groveland FBI case files, which were released to me following my filing of a Freedom of Information Act request. These files had been sealed for sixty years, and their content provided an abundance of rich material and interviews that were essential to my understanding of the case. When former Florida attorney general Charlie Crist released the results of the state's investigation into the murder of Harry and Harriette Moore in 2006, the FBI files from that case revealed further interviews and bureau reports relating to the Groveland case and the Ku Klux Klan that were most enlightening.

I relied heavily on the personal papers of Franklin Williams at the Schomburg Center for Research in Black Culture, as well as the papers of the NAACP and the papers of Thurgood Marshall, both at the Library of Congress. The Workers Defense League Collection at the Walter P. Reuther Library at Wayne State University provided much insight into the relationship between the NAACP and the WDL, and was where I discovered the journal entries of Miss L. B. De Forest.

Gaining access to the NAACP's Legal Defense Fund files at the Library of Congress was by far the most challenging part of this research, and I continue to be grateful to Ted Wells, Debo Adegbile, and especially Jeffrey Robinson at the LDF, who went above and beyond his call of duty to carefully vet this material so that I would be able to examine it.

# NOTES

## Prologue

**2** **"nigger briefs":** Greenberg, *Crusaders in the Courts*, p. 71.

**2** **"inherent defects":** Remarks of Thurgood Marshall at the Annual Seminar of the San Francisco Patent and Trademark Law Association, Maui, Hawaii, May 6, 1987; commonly referred to as Marshall's "Bicentennial Speech." Thurgood Marshall Papers, Manuscript Division, Library of Congress.

**2** **the Founding Father of the New America:** *Jet*, February 22, 1983. On the naming of the Thurgood Marshall Federal Judiciary Building in 1993, Georgia representative John Lewis praised Marshall, stating, "Supreme Court Justice Thurgood Marshall laid the foundation, in the legal sense, of the modern Civil Rights Movement. I would go far enough to say that he must be considered the founding father of the New America. . . . We would not have made the progress we have made, without the leadership and ability of a man like Thurgood Marshall."

**3** **"I could see my dead body":** Columbia University Oral History Project, Thurgood Marshall with Ed Erwin, Columbia Center for Oral History, Columbia University, Butler Library, New York, NY (hereafter cited as COHP, Marshall).

**3** ***"the nigger Shepherd":*** Samuel Proctor Oral History Project, Franklin Williams, interview by David Colburn and Steve Lawson, University of Florida, Gainesville (hereafter cited as FOHP, Williams).

**4** **"battle fatigue":** Clark, *Toward Humanity and Justice*, p. 107.

**4** **"You know," Marshall said:** Ibid.

**4** **"suicidal crusader":** Rowan, *Dream Makers, Dream Breakers*, p. 7.

**4** **"Thurgood says he needs me,":** Ibid.

**4**  **"There is very little truth"**: Marshall's speech, 1966 White House conference on civil rights, *Thurgood Marshall: Justice for All*, A&E Biography, 2005.

**5**  **It also became the impetus:** Greenberg, *Crusaders in the Courts*, p. 93.

**5**  **"glued together"**: Ball, " 'Thurgood's Coming': Tale of a Hero Lawyer."

**5**  **"Men are needed to sit"**: Clark and Davis, *Thurgood Marshall*, p. 107.

**5**  **"They came in their jalopy"**: Williams, *Thurgood Marshall*, p. 201.

**5**  **"a lawyer that a white man"**: Janis Johnson, "A Tense Time in Tennessee," *Humanities*, Vol. 25, No. 2, March/April 2004, http://www.neh.gov/news/humanities/2004-03/tennessee.

**5**  **"Thurgood's coming"**: The original source of this phrase is unknown, but the phrase "Thurgood's coming," or "the lawyer's coming," has been repeated countless times in stories by Marshall's former Supreme Court clerks and quoted in articles, books, and law journals.

## Chapter 1: Mink Slide

**7**  **"If that son of a bitch"**: Dray, *At the Hands of Persons Unknown*, p. 373.

**8**  **soda fountains:** O'Brien, *The Color of the Law*, p. 66.

**8**  **"spit-spangled"**: Leon A. Ransom to Daisy Lampkin, Library of Congress, Manuscript Division, NAACP Papers, November 14, 1946 (NAACP).

**8**  **"those niggers up there"**: Williams, *Thurgood Marshall*, p. 137.

**8**  **"the first major racial"**: Stephen Smith and Kate Ellis, *American RadioWorks: Thurgood Marshall Before the Court*, http://americanradioworks.publicradio.org/features/marshall/.

**8**  **"Lose your head"**: Greenberg, *Crusaders in the Courts*, p. 41.

**9**  **"law enforcement would"**: *Daily Worker*, November, 20, 1946.

**9**  **"the situation in"**: Walter White to Robert Carter et al., NAACP, June 8, 1946.

**9**  **"no telephone calls"**: Ibid.

**9**  **"create a nation-wide"**: White to Thurgood Marshall, NAACP, June 12, 1946.

**10**  **"broke and bedraggled"**: O'Brien, *The Color of the Law*, p. 224.

**10**  **"You almost started"**: Janis Johnson, "A Tense Time in Tennessee," *Humanities*, Vol. 25, No. 2, March/April 2004, http://www.neh.gov/news/humanities/2004-03/tennessee.html.

**10**  **"terrible summer of 1946"**: White, *A Man Called White*, p. 325.

**11**  **"The Columbia case," he said:** Marshall to Ransom, NAACP, undated.

**11**  **"What you stop"**: Ikerd, *No More Social Lynchings*, p. 14.

**11**  **"Kill the bastards!"**: Minor, *Lynching and Frame-Up in Tennessee*, p. 48.

**11**  **"Stephenson niggers"**: O'Brien, *The Color of the Law*, p. 11.

**12**  **"Let us have them"**: Ibid., p. 12.

**12**  **"We fought for freedom"**: Williams, *Thurgood Marshall*, p. 133.

12 **"blankets over their":** Ibid.

12 **"Uptown, they are":** Ikard, *No More Social Lynchings*, p. 19.

12 **"Here they come!":** O'Brien, *The Color of the Law*, p. 18.

13 **"burn them out":** Ikard, *No More Social Lynchings*, p. 33.

13 **"You black sons":** O'Brien, *The Color of the Law*, p. 24. O'Brien cites the testimony in *State of Tennessee v. William A. Pillow and Lloyd Kennedy,* with Kennedy recalling a patrolman shouting, "You black sons of so and so . . . " I took the liberty of using instead "You black sons of bitches," since the testimony is rife with that expression elsewhere, and Kennedy was no doubt self-censoring in the formal setting of the court.

14 **"blood running in the gutters":** Williams, *American Revolutionary*, p. 134.

14 **"situation is in the":** *Columbia Daily Herald*, February 26, 1946.

14 **"This makes me proud":** Notes on telephone conversations between Ollie Harrington and Walter White from Nashville, TN, NAACP, October 5, 1946.

14 **"shut up":** Ikerd, *No More Social Lynchings*, p. 109.

15 **"something serious":** *Daily Worker*, November 20, 1946.

15 **"wind up in Duck River":** White, *A Man Called White*, p. 314.

15 **"I just sold the last":** Williams, *Thurgood Marshall*, p. 132.

15 **NIGGER READ AND RUN:** NAACP, undated.

15 **"Take care of yourself":** White to Marshall, NAACP, June 12, 1946.

16 **"Thurgood, Looby said":** The dialogue and details in this scene are culled from several sources: COHP, Marshall; Marshall's letter to Assistant Attorney General Theron I. Caudle, December 4, 1946; the "Five Star Final" Radio Broadcast, November 20, 1946, from the NAACP Papers, the script of which Marshall approved; Carl Rowan's *Dream Makers, Dream Breakers*, p. 109; *Daily Worker*, November 20, 1946; and Stephen Smith and Kate Ellis, *American RadioWorks: Thurgood Marshall Before the Court*, http://americanradioworks.publicradio.org/features/marshall/.

17 **"Master Race preachments":** Miscellaneous Columbia, TN, reports, NAACP.

17 **It was under a cedar tree:** The Cordie Cheek incident is largely derived from Minor, *Lynching and Frame-Up in Tennessee*, pp. 31–34.

18 **"the famous Duck River":** Marshall to Caudle, NAACP, December 4, 1946.

19 **"You go over there":** The dialogue and details in this scene are derived from the following sources: COHP, Marshall; Williams, *Thurgood Marshall*, pp. 140–41; *Daily Worker*, November 20, 1946.

20 **"the pattern of all":** *Daily Worker*, November 20, 1946.

20 **"Well, Thurgood":** Rowan, *Dream Makers, Dream Breakers*, p. 109.

20 **"they beat the driver":** Ibid.

20 **"I am certain":** *Daily Worker*, November 20, 1946.

20 **"would never have been":** White, *A Man Called White*, p. 321.

**20** **"Drunken driving?":** The dialogue in this scene was derived from COHP, Marshall.

## Chapter 2: Sugar Hill

**21** **"Nigger boy, what":** Williams, *Thurgood Marshall*, p. 107.

**22** **"So I wrapped":** Kluger, *Simple Justice*, p. 224.

**22** **"One entered the city":** Jackson and Dunbar, *Empire City*, p. 687. Architectural historian Vincent Scully was critical of the 1963 destruction of Pennsylvania Station, noting, "One entered the city like a god. One scuttles in now like a rat."

**22** **"Ride the Surface Way":** Schomburg Center for Research in Black Culture, Photographs and Prints Division, New York Public Library.

**23** **"Put that gun away!":** Janaya Williams, "Jason Moran Takes Fat Waller Back to the Club," NPR Music, May 13, 2011, http://www.npr.org/2011/05/13/136274480/jason-moran-takes-fats-waller-back-to-the-club.

**23** **"We got yellow girls":** Dance, *From My People*, p. 170.

**24** **"was so busy arguing":** Ted Poston, "On Appeal to the Supreme Court," *The Survey*, January 1949.

**24** **"How much is that":** Williams, *Thurgood Marshall*, p. 99.

**25** **"You know how much":** Ibid., p. 100.

**25** **"To Be Demolished":** Schomburg Photographs and Prints Division.

**25** **"perhaps the most modern":** Wald, *Josh White*, p. 48.

**25** **"live on that attractive":** "Down Under in Harlem," *New Republic*, March 27, 1944.

**26** **"father of black American":** "In Sugar Hill, a Street Nurtured Black Talent When the World Wouldn't," *New York Times*, January 22, 2010.

**26** **"that legend, only":** Kurt Thometz, "The Harlem Revue," Jumel Terrace Books, http://harlemrevue.wordpress.com/on-harlems-heights/.

**26** **"talented tenth":** W.E.B. Du Bois, "The Talented Tenth," in *The Negro Problem*.

**26** **"the White House of Harlem":** Aberjhani and West, *Encyclopedia of the Harlem Renaissance*, p. 320.

**26** **At one of White's parties:** Greenberg, *Crusaders in the Courts*, p. 32.

**26** **"NAACP's unofficial":** Clark and Davis, *Thurgood Marshall*, p. 101.

**27** **They called their little group:** Ibid.

**27** **"Buster had a weak":** Williams, *Thurgood Marshall*, p. 163.

**28** **"social capital of Negro America":** *Ebony*, undated article from 1946.

**28** **"Good Luck, Joe.":** Schomburg Photographs and Prints Division.

**28** **"they treated him like":** Wilson, *Meet Me at the Theresa*, p. 104.

**28** **"distinguished service":** NAACP Bulletin, May 1946.

**28**  "cannot be legally": *Crisis*, May 1944.

**29**  "brought about the most": NAACP bulletin, May 1946.

**29**  "Lest you think": White to Marshall, NAACP, May 8, 1946.

**29**  "Oh, yeah": Ibid.

**29**  "very reasonable rates": Marshall to staff, NAACP, June 13, 1946.

**29**  "an award coming": *Crisis*, August 1946.

**30**  "carrying around a fever": Marshall to Ransom, NAACP, undated.

**30**  "callous and inadequate": White, *A Man Called White*, pp. 63–64.

**30**  "Citing red tape": White to Louis T. Wright and Dr. Ernst P. Boss, NAACP, undated, 1946.

**30**  "cancer of the lung": Marshall to George Slaff, NAACP, undated.

**30**  "due solely to the fact": White to Board, NAACP, September 9, 1946.

**31**  "I warned you not": Rowan, *Dream Makers, Dream Breakers*, p. 132.

**31**  "The President only": Ibid.

**31**  "You know," the deliveryman: COHP, Marshall.

**31**  "twenty-pound": Williams, *Thurgood Marshall*, p. 137.

**31**  "Virus X": COHP, Marshall.

**31**  "not more than three": White to Board, NAACP, September 9, 1946.

**31**  "far from out of": White to staff. NAACP, July 12, 1946.

**31**  "Give them the bad news": Ibid.

**32**  "taking it more than easy": Marshall to White, NAACP, October 1, 1946.

**32**  "I will have a difficult job": Ibid.

**32**  "It is doubtful": White, *A Man Called White*, p. 314.

## Chapter 3: Get to Pushin'

**34**  "top Cabinet, military": *St. Petersburg Times*, July 15, 1949.

**34**  "ambitious to become": Ibid.

**34**  "certain secret work": Ibid.

**34**  scattered wooden shacks: *St. Petersburg Times*, April 9, 1950.

**35**  Rumors around town: FOHP, Williams.

**35**  Her reputation around: Unredacted FBI File 44-2722, (Groveland) Boxes 156–157; Unredacted FBI File 44-4055, (Civil Rights, Irvin, Shepherd, Greenlee) Boxes 222–229, National Archives and Records Administration, College Park, MD. This was based on several sources, among them the reports of FBI field agents who interviewed Lake County residents, as well as Groveland Police Chief George Mays, in July and August 1949.

Reporter Ormond Powers of the *Orlando Sentinel* investigated the alleged crime and reported his findings on Padgett's reputation to Milton C. Thomas, who provided a summary of Powers's statements to Rowland Watts. Workers Defense League Records, Wayne State University, Walter P. Reuther Library, Detroit, MI., The Groveland Case 1950-1952, Box 192, (hereafter cited as WDL). Terence McCarthy of the *New Leader* also spoke with Mays, who referred to Padgett as a "bad egg." Also, Corsair, *The Groveland Four*, p. 233.

**35 "get it pushed off":** *State of Florida, Plaintiff, v. Samuel Shepherd, Walter L. Irvin, Charles Greenlee, Ernest E. Thomas, Defendants*, Transcript of Testimony, Florida State Archives, Tallahassee, August–September, 1949. Much of the detail about the Padgetts' movements on the evening of July 15, 1949, was derived from both Willie's and Norma's testimony (*Fl. v. Shepherd*).

**36 "dine-and-dance":** *St. Petersburg Times*, April 9, 1949.

**36 "Haven":** Ibid.

**36 Samuel Shepherd was having:** Likewise, most of Shepherd's and Irvin's movements on the evening of July 15, 1949, are based on both Shepherd's and Irvin's testimony in *Fl. v. Shepherd*.

**37 "a pure Negro town":** Hurston, *Dust Tracks on a Road*, p. 1.

**37 "a city of five lakes":** Hurston, *Mules and Men*, Introduction.

**38 It was long past midnight:** The dialogue in this scene is mostly based on the trial testimony of Norma and Willie Padgett in *Fl. v. Shepherd*. Neither Shepherd nor Irvin testified about encountering the Padgetts in the early morning hours of July 16, 1949. But Franklin Williams (FHOP, Williams) stated that Shepherd and Irvin did stop their car to help the Padgetts. And despite the fact that the Padgetts did not admit to sharing any whiskey with the two black men, Norma's relatives indicated to L. B. De Forest that whiskey was indeed offered to Shepherd and Irvin. WDL.

**38 "Do you think I'm":** Corsair, *The Groveland Four*, p. 190.

## Chapter 4: Nigger in a Pit

**40 Her nickname was "Big East":** *Congressional Record*, Charles B. Rangel, June 25, 1998.

**40 "When Evelyn Cunningham entered":** Ibid.

**41 "I wanted to do hard news":** National Visionary Leadership Project, Oral History Interviews: Evelyn Cunningham, http://www.visionaryproject.org/cunninghamevelyn/.

**41 "I think I did my":** Ibid.

**41 "I said, 'You know'":** Ibid.

**41 "not particularly savory":** Williams, *Thurgood Marshall*, p. 191-92.

**41 "You can't arrest":** Ibid.

**41 "I would like to defend":** Ibid.

**41 "Time to go home":** Ibid.

**41** **"become distant and":** Ibid., p. 191.

**42** **"lanky, brash":** White, *A Man Called White*, p. 154.

**42** **"Amazed at [Marshall's]":** Ibid.

**42** **"You've won":** Williams, *Thurgood Marshall*, p. 59.

**42** **They'd been living:** Ibid., p. 65.

**42** **Having packed Houston's:** James, *Root and Branch*, p. 56.

**43** **"Motion pictures":** McNeil, *Groundwork*, p. 140.

**43** **"Conditions," Marshall wrote:** Williams, *Thurgood Marshall*, p. 60.

**43** **"evil results of discrimination":** McNeil, *Groundwork*, p. 140.

**43** **"A lawyer's either":** Ibid., p. 84.

**44** **"the only executive":** Marshall to White, NAACP, January 21, 1947.

**44** **"answering the telephone":** Ibid.

**44** **some patterns of behavior:** White to Marshall, NAACP, July 17, 1945.

**44** **"unbuttoned office manners":** Sullivan, *Lift Every Voice*, p. 298.

**44** **"You shouldn't beat me":** Clark and Davis, *Thurgood Marshall*, p. 135.

**44** **"He could tell":** Interview, Mildred Roxborough, *Thurgood Marshall: Justice for All*, A&E Biography, 2005.

**45** **"Nigger in a Pit":** Kluger, *Simple Justice*, p. 643.

**45** **Mr. Turgood:** NAACP, May 1949.

**46** **"Mr. Marshall was":** Author interview, Gloria Samuels, November 11, 2010.

**46** **"total lack of formality":** Motley, *Equal Justice Under Law*, p. 58.

**46** **"nobody was hiring":** Constance Baker Motley, "My Personal Debt to Thurgood Marshall," *Yale Law Journal*, Vol. 101, 1991–1992.

**46** **"His mother was a":** National Visionary Project, Oral Histories Interviews, Constance Baker Motley, http://www.visionaryproject.com/motleyconstancebaker/.

**47** **"first feminists":** Yanick Rice Lamb, "Evelyn Cunningham, A Witness to History," *Heart & Soul*, http://www.heartandsoul.com/2010/04/evelyn-cunningham-a-witness-to-history/.

**47** **"a piece of paper":** *Hearings Before the Committee on the Judiciary, United States Senate, One Hundred Third Congress, First Session on the Nomination of Ruth Bader Ginsberg, to Be Associate Justice of the Supreme Court of the United States*, July 20, 21, 22, and 23, 1993. Also, Rowan, *Dream Makers, Dream Breakers*, p. 21.

**47** **"no sense in coming":** Marshall to Loren Miller, NAACP, undated.

**47** **"I do not want to burden you":** Ibid.

**47** **"It has been suggested":** Daniel Byrd to Marshall, NAACP, April 23, 1948.

**48** **Otherwise they'd work:** Author interviews, Alexander Tureaud, Jr., 2009 and 2010.

**48** **"to the types of":** Marshall to staff, NAACP, February 16, 1949.

**48** **limit[ing] ourselves:** Ibid., Perry note on memo.

**48** **"any experienced lawyer":** Marshall to staff, NAACP, undated.

**49** **"harboring an escaped":** Greenberg, *Crusaders in the Courts*, p. 81.

**49** **"not to sign":** Ibid.

**49** **Her son had just:** Ibid., p. 31.

**49** **"no blacks lived":** Ibid., p. 46.

**49** **"one of those enormous":** Ibid., p. 31.

**49** **"pursed lips and":** Ibid.

**50** **"panic-stricken Westchester":** Daniel J. Sharfstein, "Saving the Race," *Legal Affairs*, March/April 2005.

**50** **"the sex stopped":** Ibid.

**50** **"He was supposed to":** Williams, *Thurgood Marshall*, p. 120.

**50** **"thousands of Negro domestics":** *Chicago Defender*, December 12, 1940.

**50** **"to the limit of our":** Sharfstein, "Saving the Race."

**50** **"I'm sure he raped":** Ibid.

**51** **"not only innocent":** Ibid.

**51** **"lust-mad Negro":** Ibid.

**51** **"shame and disgrace":** *Daily Kennebec Journal*, February 1, 1941.

**51** **"resent bitterly this acquittal":** *Kingston Daily Freeman*, February 3, 1941.

**51** **"What a relief!":** Sharfstein, "Saving the Race.".

**51** **"the actual danger":** Cash, *The Mind of the South*, p. 115.

**51** **"had nothing immediately":** Ibid., p.117.

**53** **"There's the bones":** *Oklahoma Black Dispatch*, February 8, 1941.

**53** **"they beat me":** *Lyons v. Oklahoma*, 322 U. S. 596 (1944), Brief on Behalf of Petitioner.

**53** **"extorted by violence":** *Chambers v. Florida*, 309 U. S. 227 (1940), Petitioner's Brief.

**53** **"could never read aloud":** Black and Black, *Mr. Justice and Mrs. Black*, p. 73.

**53** **"Today, as in ages past":** *Chambers v. Florida*, 309 U. S. 227 (1940).

**54** **"We are going to teach":** Tushnet, *Making Civil Rights Law*, p. 52.

**54** **"a Nigger lawyer from":** Marshall to White, NAACP, February 2, 1941.

**54** **"I ain't scared":** Rowan, *Dream Makers, Dream Breakers*, p. 107.

**54** **"I think I remembered":** COHP, Marshall.

**54** **"scared to try the case":** Marshall to White, NAACP, January 29, 1941.

**54-55** **"a certain Negro lawyer"**: Marshall to White, NAACP, January 28, 1941.

**55** **"a gala day"**: Marshall to White, NAACP, January 29, 1941.

**55** **"two nationalities"**: Marshall to White, NAACP, February 2, 1941.

**55** **"the building did not fall"**: Ibid.

**55** **"about doubled"**: Ibid.

**55** **"Oh, yes, you were there"**: *Oklahoma Black Dispatch*, February 8, 1941.

**55** **"Why," he stammered**: Ibid.

**55** **"six or seven hours"**: Marshall to White, NAACP, April 5, 1941.

**56** **"go up to my room"**: *Lyons v. Oklahoma.*

**56** **"six—either six or"**: Ibid.

**56** **"shaking as though"**: *Oklahoma Black Dispatch*, February 8, 1941.

**56** **"Boy, did I like that"**: Marshall to White, NAACP, April 2, 1941.

**56** **"stopped us in the halls"**: Ibid.

**56** **"90% of the white people"**: Ibid.

**56** **"We are in a perfect"**: Ibid.

**57** **"I think we should aim"**: Ibid.

## Chapter 5: Trouble Fixin' to Start

**58** **The motor shut off**: C. C. Twiss affidavit, WDL, April 29, 1951. Clifton Twiss was visited by Rowland Watts of the Workers Defense League, as well as another man, Seymour Miller, and Twiss provided a signed statement as to what he and his wife, Ethel, witnessed on the morning of July 16, 1949. This account is based on Twiss's statement.

**59** **At about 6:45 a.m.**: Statement of Lawrence Burtoft, WDL, April 29, 1951. Burtoft was visited by Rowland Watts and provided a signed statement regarding his meeting with Norma Padgett on the morning of July 16, 1949. I used this statement, as well as Burtoft's statements to reporter Norman Bunin, which appear in Bunin's series in the *St. Petersburg Times* (April 9, 1949). In this scene, I also quote from Burtoft's testimony in *Fl. v. Shepherd.*

**61** **Sheriff Willis McCall was on his**: MM 44-156, FBI. This scene is derived from this FBI file documenting the civil rights and domestic violence investigation into the beatings of Shepherd and Irvin (part of FBI file 44-4055). The FBI interviewed McCall, Hatcher, Yates, Shepherd, and Irvin, and their recollections and quotes are taken from the statements in this report.

**61** **"We're probably too far away"**: Ibid.

**61** **"What's the trouble?"**: Ibid.

**61** **"Boy, I've never"**: Ibid.

**61** **"A white housewife"**: Ibid.

61  **"pretty high feeling"**: Ibid.

62  **"Call Yates and"**: Ibid.

63  **"armed to the gills"**: *St. Petersburg Times*, July 18, 1949.

63  **"Willis, we want"**: "Murmur in the Streets," *Time*, August 1, 1949.

63  **"husky, brash"**: Ibid.

63  **"I can't let you people"**: Flores, *Justice Gone Wrong*, p. 15. Also author interview with Isaac M. Flores, February 9, 2011.

63  **"I may be in sympathy"**: Flores, *Justice Gone Wrong*, p. 15. Also Corsair, *The Groveland Four*, p. 31.

63  **"Look, McCall"**: Flores, *Justice Gone Wrong*, p. 15.

63  **"The prisoners you want"**: Ibid.

63  **From the back:** "Murmur in the Streets."

64  **He had just arrived in town:** MM 44-156, FBI. Also Corsair, *The Groveland Four*, p. 1. The descriptions and quotes by Charles Greenlee are largely derived from his interviews with Franklin Williams in the presence of stenographer Dorothy N. Marshall at Raiford State Prison, which are included in the FBI file MM 44-127 (part of FBI file 44-4055). Greenlee was also interviewed by agents Tobias E. Matthews, Jr., and John L. Quigley on August 8, 1949, as part of FBI file MM 44-156.

64  **In May, Charles's:** Corsair, *The Groveland Four*, pp. 1-2. Also MM 44-156, FBI.

65  **"Is there anywhere"**: MM 44-156, FBI.

65  **"Hold still a minute"**: Corsair, *The Groveland Four*, p. 3. Also MM 44-156, FBI.

65  **Charles said the gun:** MM 44-156, FBI.

65  **"What road camp"**: MM 44-127, FBI.

65  **"work out something"**: MM 44-156, FBI.

66  **"Stand up, nigger"**: Ibid.

66  **"I wasn't in any car"**: Ibid.

66  **"You're lying"**: Ibid.

66  **"what they would do"**: Ibid.

66  **"He's not one"**: Ibid.

66  **"The boys what took"**: MM 44-127, FBI.

66  **"No, sir"**: Ibid.

66  **"Boy, if you don't know it"**: Ibid.

66  **"hurry up and take"**: MM 44-156, FBI.

67  **"might cause some trouble"**: Ibid.

67  **"two colored boys who were"**: Ibid.

67 **"had a big hole":** MM 44-127, FBI.

67 **"Go ahead and try":** Corsair, *The Groveland Four*, p. 2.

67 **"That's the boy":** Ibid., p. 32.

67 **"stout white man":** MM 44-156, FBI.

68 **"You've got families":** Flores, *Justice Gone Wrong*, p. 16.

68 **"Lake County Bride":** *Orlando Sunday Sentinel*, July 17, 1949.

68 **"Sheriff Staves Off":** Flores, *Justice Gone Wrong*, p. 17.

68 **"fast talking" sheriff:** *New York Times*, July 18, 1949.

68 **The *Miami Herald* praised:** *Miami Herald*, July 18, 1949.

69 **"all hell broke loose":** Sullivan, *Lift Every Voice*, p. 372.

69 **"dressed like a tweedy":** Greenberg, *Crusaders in the Courts*, p. 16.

69 **"Has Science Conquered":** *Look*, August, 1949.

69 **"whomever he wished":** Janken, *Walter White*, p. 371.

69 **"within the rail":** Greenberg, *Crusaders in the Courts*, p. 21.

69 **"Now look," Marshall told him:** COHP, Marshall.

69 **"See that fellow":** Greenberg, *Crusaders in the Courts*, p. 21.

70 **"So he won":** COHP, Marshall.

70 **"a sentence that had":** Greenberg, *Crusaders in the Courts*, p. 9.

70 **"crowd out other":** Ibid., p. 102.

70 **"people of the Negro":** *Shelley et ux. v. Kraemer et ux.*, 334 U.S. 1, May 3, 1948.

70 **"the Joe Louis of the courtroom":** Williams, *Thurgood Marshall*, p. 151.

70 **"wanted to lynch Walter":** Greenberg, *Crusaders in the Courts*, p. 18.

## Chapter 6: A Little *Bolita*

73 **"four niggers":** FOHP, Williams.

73 **"sullen, glint-eyed":** "Murmur in the Streets," *Time*, August 1, 1949.

73 **"15 loads of buckshot":** Ibid.

73 **"Boy," Leroy Campbell said:** MM 44-127, FBI.

74 **"Were you one":** MM 44-156, FBI. Dialogue and details from Greenlee's interrogation are mostly derived from the interview he gave to Franklin Williams, which appears in this report.

75 **"directing the traffic":** Corsair, *The Groveland Four*, p. 37.

75 **"Did you rape":** MM 44-156, FBI.

75 **"Better start saying":** Ibid.

75 **"Shoot him in the stomach":** Ibid.

75 **"in the privates":** Ibid.

76 **"heart yellow pine house":** McCall, *Willis V. McCall, Sheriff of Lake County*, p. 11.

76 **"scratch hard childhood":** *Life*, November 17, 1972.

76 **plowing, and chopping:** McCall, *Willis V. McCall, Sheriff of Lake County*, p. 12.

77 **"This Is a Minute Maid Grove":** *New York Daily Compass*, March 1, 1952.

77 **"tough reputation in the groves":** Robinson, *Law and Order, by Any Means Necessary*, p. 16.

77 **"No white people":** *Journal of Forest History*, Vol. 25, 1981, p. 16. (Forest History Society.)

78 **"charm a snake":** *Life*, November 17, 1972.

78 **"the People's Candidate":** Ibid.

78 **"People have confidence":** McCall, *Willis V. McCall, Sheriff of Lake County*, p. 14.

78 **"sell-out in politics":** *Leesberg Commercial*, July 2, 1945.

78 **"King of Slots":** Ibid.

78 **"It looks very much":** Ibid.

78 **"Just as long as you":** McCall, *Willis V. McCall, Sheriff of Lake County*, p. 14.

78 **"cracker mob of Central Florida":** Dickerson, *Remembering Orlando*, p. 38.

79 **"from the back door":** Robinson, *Law and Order, by Any Means Necessary*, p. 21.

79 **"use their good offices":** Kennedy, *Southern Exposure*, p. 58.

79 **"work or fight" laws:** "Unfit Draftees May Be Uniformed Plant Workers," *Daytona Beach Morning Journal*, February 17, 1945.

79 **"prevent loitering":** Gary M. Mormino, "Midas Returns: Miami Goes to War, 1941–1945," *Journal of the Historical Association of Southern Florida*, Vol. 1, No. 57, 1997.

79 **"a ready pool of":** Nieman, "Black Southerners and the Law," p. 53.

79 **"None of your damn jaw":** Jerrell H. Shofner, "The Legacy of Racial Slavery: Free Enterprise and Forced Laobr in Florida in the 1940s," *Journal of Southern History*, Vol. 47, No. 3, August 1981.

80 **"Florida Bail Bond Racket":** Report on Groveland, WDL.

80 **"secured from the stockades":** Ibid.

80 **"without the formality":** Ibid.

80 **"appears to have been to dragoon":** *New Leader*, Augsut 13, 1949.

80 **"a pattern of beating":** FOHP, Williams.

81 **"the return to eight":** McCall, *Willis V. McCall, Sheriff of Lake County*, p. 63.

81 **"Look at his wrists!":** *St. Petersburg Times*, November 28, 1999.

**81** **"communist infiltrated groups":** McCall, *Willis V. McCall, Sheriff of Lake County*, p. 15.

**81** **"I'm Willis McCall":** Transcript of interview with Mabel Norris Chesley, Franklin Hall Williams Papers, Schomburg Center for Research in Black Culture (hereafter cited as FHW Papers, Chesley).

**81** **"this great big hulk":** Ibid.

**81** **"political shenanigans"":** Ibid.

**82** **"Hitler's gestapo technique":** McCall, *Willis V. McCall, Sheriff of Lake County*, p. 63.

**82** **"Now let that be a lesson":** Green, *Before His Time*, p. 80.

**82** **"big 'red scare' trying":** McCall, *Willis V. McCall, Sheriff of Lake County*, p. 18.

**82** **"a giant milestone":** "Landmark: *Smith v. Allwright*," NAACPLDF.org, http://naacpldf.org/case/smith-v-allwright.

**82** **"the greatest one":** COHP, Marshall.

**82** **"a guy had the right":** Williams, *Thurgood Marshall*, p. 112.

**83** **"told the other states":** COHP, Marshall.

**83** **"warning blacks not to vote":** Newton, *The Ku Klux Klan*, p. 384.

**83** **"making no attempt":** Newton, *The Invisible Empire*, p. 117.

## Chapter 7: Wipe This Place Clean

**84** **"Everything was silent":** FHW Papers, Chesley.

**85** **"People would rush inside":** Ibid.

**85** **"Knots of men":** "Mobile Violence: Motorized Mobs in a Florida County," *New South*, Vol. 4, No. 6, August 1949.

**86** **"leaps and bounds":** "The Carter-Klan Documentary Project: Thomas Hamilton," 2006–2007, Center for the Study of the American South at UNC-CH, http://www.carter-klan.org/Hamilton.html.

**86** **"a beachhead in Florida":** Newton, *The Invisible Empire*, p. 114.

**86** **"see blood flow":** *Time*, March 15, 1948.

**86** **"If you come in here":** *Powell v. Alabama*, 287 U.S. 45 (1932).

**87** **With more than five hundred:** *South Lake Press*, June 5, 2009, http://www.southlakepress.com/060509land.

**87** **"colored people their homes":** MM 44-156, FBI.

**87** **"protecting lives":** Ibid.

**87** **"situation was getting out of hand":** Ibid.

**87** **"psychological effect":** Ibid.

**88** **"as if he was a trusty":** Ibid.

**89** **"Three Negroes Confess":** *Ocala Star-Banner,* July 19, 1949.

**89** **"There'll be no lynching":** Corsair, *The Groveland Four,* p. 38.

**89** **"We're not going to":** Ibid.

**89** **"I told her we":** Ibid.

**89** **"Ku Klux Klan was":** "Mobile Violence: Motorized Mobs in a Florida County," *New South,* Vol. 4, No. 6, August 1949.

**90** **"That's old Joe Maxwell's house":** Sally Watt, Free Speech Radio News, January 1, 2002, http://www.archive.org/details/fsrn_20020101.

**90** **"heard a window break":** Ibid.

**90** **"You better not go down there":** Flores, *Justice Gone Wrong,* p. 20.

**90** **"Sons of bitches":** Ibid.

**91** **"You fellas don't":** Ibid., p. 21.

**91** **"We wanna wipe this place clean":** Ibid.

**91** **"Don't go out there":** Ibid.

**91** **As McCall surveyed the crowd:** MM 44-156, FBI.

**91** **Groveland's Curtis Merritt:** Ibid.

**91** **McCall also recognized:** Ibid.

**91** **"was the chief of":** Harry T. Moore Murder Investigation, Florida Attorney General's Office of Civil Rights/Florida Department of Law Enforcement (Moore Report), Exhibit 53. (Hereafter cited as Moore Report.)

**91** **"to tell where":** "Mobile Violence: Motorized Mobs in a Florida County."

**91** **"Why don't you take that peashooter":** Flores, *Justice Gone Wrong,* p. 22.

**92** **"I don't know the names":** Ibid., p. 23.

**92** **"Where is that son of a bitch":** McCall, *Willis V. McCall, Sheriff of Lake County,* p. 21.

**92** **"I'll tell him":** Flores, *Justice Gone Wrong,* p. 23.

**92** **"down the road":** McCall, *Willis V. McCall, Sheriff of Lake County,* p. 21.

**92** **"Go and get more ammunition":** *New Leader,* telegram to Governor Fuller Warren, NAACP, September 14, 1949.

**92** **"miles of clay roads":** *New Leader,* August 13, 1949.

**92** **"Little" Rochelle Hunter:** *Miami Daily News,* July 19, 1949. Also undated clipping, FHW Papers. (Franklin Williams kept a Groveland scrapbook that included many undated clippings from the *Mount Dora Topic,* as well as other newspapers.)

**93** **"he knew all of the ringleaders":** MM 44-156, FBI.

**93** **"terrorizing the negroes":** Ibid.

**93** **"The next time":** "Murmur in the Streets," *Time,* August 1, 1949.

94 **"had all of his life savings"**: MM 44-156, FBI.

95 **"They tell me my chickens and ducks"**: MM 44-127, FBI.

95 **"ravaged ghost"**: *New York Post*, September 2, 1949..

95 **"Negro self-emancipation"**: WDL, Report on Groveland.

95 **"the best preserve cellar"**: *New York Post*, September 2, 1949.

96 **"No nigger has any right"**: FOHP, Williams.

96 **"too damned independent"**: *New Leader*, August 13, 1949.

96 **"uppity nigger"**: Steven F. Lawson, David R. Colburn, and Darryl Paulson, "Groveland: Florida's Little Scottsboro," *Florida Historical Quarterly*, Vol. 65, No. 1, July 1986, p. 3.

96 **"smart nigger"**: FOHP, Williams.

96 **"that somebody put"**: "Groveland: Florida's Little Scottsboro," p. 4.

96 **"three twisted bed frames"**: *New Leader*, August 2, 1949.

96 **"They should never let"**: Ibid.

97 **He arrived at his property:** J. P. Ellis to Franklin Williams, NAACP-LDF, undated, August 1949.

97 **"I keep getting orders"**: MM 44-127, FBI.

97 **"My family is all scattered"**: Ibid.

97 **"They'll get out"**: *New Leader*, August 13, 1949.

97 **"We'll wait and see"**: *Orlando Sentinel*, July 17, 1949.

98 **"If smart lawyers"**: *New Leader*, August 13, 1949.

98 **"offered up as a"**: Ibid.

98 **"Honor Will Be Avenged"**: *Mount Dora Topic*, July 2, 1949.

98 **"any persons bearing arms"**: MM 44-156, FBI.

99 **"too busy trying"**: Ibid.

99 **"would result in"**: Ibid.

99 **"positive action"**: Ibid.

99 **"had agreed to stop"**: Ibid.

## Chapter 8: A Christmas Card

100 **"You can either jump"**: Hobbs, "Hitler Is Here," p. 150.

101 **"Dear Fried"**: Willie James Howard to Cynthia Goff, NAACP, January 1, 1943 [actually 1944].

102 **"the penalty of his crime"**: Hobbs, "Hitler Is Here," p. 150.

102 **"Willie, I cannot do"**: Ibid.

102  **"terribly afraid of something"**: Lula Howard affadavit, NAACP, March 19, 1944.

103  **"rather die"**: Hobbs, "Hitler Is Here," p. 149.

103  **"I am sure you realize"**: Spessard L. Holland to Marshall, NAACP, February 14, 1944.

103  **"the type of material"**: Green, *Before His Time*, p. 49.

104  **"a waste of time"**: Ibid.

104  **"We are forced to wonder"**: Moore to Marshall, NAACP, June 30, 1944.

104  **"The life of a Negro"**: Green, *Before His Time*, p. 50.

104  It was a lesson: Ibid., p. 71.

104  **"Thus a man gets off"**: Ibid.

104  **"Your letters on lynching"**: Current to Moore, NAACP, July 3, 1947.

105  **"south of the South"**: Raymond A. Mohl, "'South of the South?' Jews, Blacks, and the Civil Rights Movement in Miami, 1945–1960, " *Journal of American Ethnic History*, Vol. 18, No. 2, Winter 1999.

105  **"troublemaker and Negro organizer"**: Green, *Before His Time*, p. 61.

105  Moore, however, was not: Author interview with Evangeline Moore, February 8, 2011.

105  Recruiting his teenage daughter: Green, *Before His Time*, p. 65.

106  **"that rich Professor Moore"**: Ibid., p. 246.

107  **"boldy challenge the"**: "A Century of Racial Segregation, 1849–1950," Library of Congress exhibition, "With an Even Hand: *Brown v. Board at Fifty*," http://www.loc.gov/exhibits/brown/brown-segregation.html.

107  **"the law functioned"**: Martin, *Brown v. Board of Education*, p. 14.

107  **"He seems to be a fine sort"**: Green, *Before His Time*, p. 41.

107  **"Thurgood was the savior"**: Ibid., p. 42.

108  **"From 1882 to 1930"**: Wilkerson, *The Warmth of Other Suns*, p. 320.

108  **"a black man had more risk"**: *Gainesville Sun*, September 3, 2005.

108  **"prosecution of mob leaders"**: Green, *Before His Time*, p. 87.

108  **"[l]ynching of negroes"**: Ibid., p. 69.

109  **"hooded hoodlums"**: Newton, *The Invisible Empire*, p. 117.

109  **"as a favor to a friend"**: Ibid.

109  **"Since mob leaders are known"**: Green, *Before His Time*, p. 87.

109  **"Have written him enough"**: Ibid., p. 90.

109  **"sage and trial-trained Jesse Hunter"**: *Mount Dora Topic*, July 2, 1949.

110  **"You don't investigate"**: Wexler, *Fire in a Canebrake*, p. 130.

111  **"The FBI has established"**: Marshall to Clark, NAACP, December 27, 1946.

111 **"I have found from"**: Williams, *Thurgood Marshall*, p. 159.

111 **"rushing pell-mell"**: Fairclough: *Race & Democracy*, p. 116.

111 **"clear-cut, uncontroverted evidence"**: Ibid., p. 117.

111 **"I . . . have no faith"**: Wexler, *Fire in a Canebrake*, p. 191.

112 **In April 1947**: *Crisis*, December 1955.

112 **"with his charming"**: Williams, *Thurgood Marshall*, p. 161.

112 **"Give this matter"**: MM 44-156, FBI.

112 **"Thurgood Marshall of the NAACP"**: Ibid.

112 **"The Association and Hoover"**: Greenberg, *Crusaders in the Courts*, p. 105.

## Chapter 9: Don't Shoot, White Man

114 **"like you see in a western"**: McCall, *Willis V. McCall, Sheriff of Lake County*, p. 23.

114 **"peddling *bolita*"**: *New York Daily Compass*, March 1, 1952.

114 **"a bearded, fantastic Negro"**: *Mount Dora Topic*, FHW Papers, undated clipping.

115 **"had recently bought"**: Ibid.

115 **"cozy arrangement"**: *New York Daily Compass*, March 1, 1952.

115 **"well-entrenched"**: Ibid.

115 **"the law enforcement officers"**: Ibid.

115 **"Things were coming to a head"**: Ibid.

115 **"Thomas was feeling his oats"**: Ibid.

115 **"It was obvious"**: McCall, *Willis V. McCall, Sheriff of Lake County*, p. 22.

115 **"only time in the whole investigation"**: Ibid.

116 **"with some kin folks"**: Coroner's Inquest, MM 44-156, FBI.

116 **"settled down for the night"**: McCall, *Willis V. McCall, Sheriff of Lake County*, p. 22.

116 **"we had not cased"**: Ibid.

116 **"cotton patch and"**: Coroner's Inquest, MM 44-156, FBI.

116 **"cut his breechesb legs off"**: Ibid.

117 **"That is him"**: Ibid.

118 **"so much excitement"**: Ibid.

118 **"Don't shoot, white man"**: Ibid.

118 **"belligerent as the devil"**: *Ocala Star Banner*, July 27, 1949.

118 **"I was across on"**: Coroner's Inquest, MM 44-156, FBI.

118 **"but it was a bunch"**: *Ocala Star Banner*, July 27, 1949.

**118** "above the eyes": Ibid.

**118** "nearly 400 slugs": Corsair, *The Groveland Four*, p. 64.

**118** "there were other holes": Coroner's Inquest, MM 44-156, FBI.

**118** "when this negro": Ibid.

**118** "Sheriff McCall of Lake County": Ibid.

**118** "glaring flaws": C.M.T. to Rowland Watts, WDL, May 8, 1951.

**119** "being told just the things": Ibid.

**119** "have never been answered": Ibid.

**119** "desperate to seal": Ibid.

**119** "definite threat to": Ibid.

**119** "broadly hinted": *New York Daily Compass*, March 1, 1952.

**119** "Thomas was an bright": Ibid.

**119** After the inquest: Flores, *Justice Gone Wrong*, p. 34.

**120** "learning to try cases": Motley, *Equal Justice Under Law*, p. 70.

**121** "that terrible summer": White, *A Man Called White*, p. 325.

**121** Truman "exploded": Michael R. Gardner, "Harry Truman and Civil Rights: Moral Courage and Political Risks," speech at University of Virginia, September 26, 2003, http://www.virginia.edu/uvanewsmakers/newsmakers/gardner.html.

**122** "a good platform person": FOHP, Williams.

**122** "antimob violence fund": Sullivan, *Lift Every Voice*, p. 320.

**122** he declared it "disgraceful": Kluger, *Simple Justice*, p. 298.

**122** "make your hair stand on end": FOHP, Williams.

## Chapter 10: Quite a Hose Wielder

**124** "Don't worry, Mama": Corsair, *The Groveland Four*, p. 16.

**124** "You little son of a bitch": MM 44-156, FBI.

**125** "Get out of the car": MM 44-127, FBI.

**125** "Why did you rape": MM 44-156, FBI.

**125** "Better talk": Ibid.

**125** "Nigger, you the one": Ibid.

**125** "the right ones": Ibid.

**126** "solve your problems": Green, *The Negro Motorist Green Book*, p. 3.

**126** "Now We Can Travel Without Embarrassment": Ibid., p. 81.

**126** "This wanton killing": Marshall to Clark, NAACP, July 27, 1949.

126 **"There is serious doubt"**: Marshall to Warren, NAACP, July 27, 1949.

127 **"My aunt wanted to know"**: Corsair, *The Groveland Four*, p. 72.

127 **"Their heads were a mess"**: FOHP, Williams.

127 **"Where is the guy"**: MM 44-156, FBI.

128 **"They must have beat us"**: MM 44-127, FBI.

128 **"These are not your tracks"**: MM 44-156, FBI.

128 **"Nigger, you are"**: Ibid.

128 **"a lot of motors"**: Ibid.

128 **"They hit me"**: Ibid.

129 **"he would get a thrill"**: Ibid.

129 **"My mouth was bleeding"**: MM 44-127, FBI.

129 **recognized as Wesley Evans**: MM 44-156, FBI.

129 **"quite a hose wielder"**: Ibid.

129 **"They tried to make me say"**: MM 44-127, FBI.

129 **"saved all the beating"**: MM 44-156, FBI.

130 **"right jaw appeared"**: MM 44-127, FBI.

130 **"I was bleeding"**: Ibid.

130 **"a mob was on its way"**: Ibid.

130 **"Where are those"**: Ibid.

130 **"really kicking him then"**: MM 44-156, FBI.

130 **"red and bruised"**: MM 44-127, FBI.

131 **"All of this is true"**: Ibid.

131 **"was going to tell"**: MM 44-156, FBI.

132 **"I have no shoes"**: MM 44-127, FBI.

132 **"Jesus," Greenlee had said**: FOHP, Williams.

132 **"devoted to the Socialist"**: *New Leader*, January/April 2006.

132 **"I been told by"**: MM 44-127.

132 **"Sammy is a good boy"**: Ibid.

133 **"If they had a picture"**: Wormser, *The Rise and Fall of Jim Crow*, p. 166.

133 **"arrogance"**: FOHP, Williams.

133 **"Had been communicated"**: Ibid.

133 **"uppity Nigger"**: "Florida's Little Scottsboro: Groveland," *Crisis*, October 1949.

133 **"McCall knew exactly"**: FOHP, Williams.

134 **"blood was still in their hair"**: Ibid.

134 **"it was seldom"**: Lawson, *To Secure These Rights*, p. 26.

134 **"The resources of the association"**: Corsair, *The Groveland Four*, p. 78.

134 **"entirely innocent"**: Press release, NAACP, August 9, 1949.

134 **advised Harry T. Moore**: Green, *Before His Time*, p. 92.

135 **"to indict the guilty mobsters"**: Moore to Warren, Florida State Archives, July 30, 1949.

135 **"brutally beaten by local officers"**: *Ocala Star Banner*, August 14, 1949.

135 **"duty bound"**: McCall, *Willis V. McCall, Sheriff of Lake County*, p. 20. Also author interview with Isaac Flores, February 9, 2011.

135 **"It's a damn lie"**: *Ocala Star Banner*, August 14, 1949.

136 **"negroes in a yellow convertible"**: FOHP, Williams.

136 **"very distinguished criminal lawyer"**: Ibid.

136 **"You know, Franklin"**: Ibid.

136 **"he would not raise any issue"**: Ibid.

136 **"I can't do this"**: Ibid.

137 **"I was not completely at ease"**: Ibid.

137 **"would give me some"**: Ibid.

137 **"for failing to follow"**: Tushnet, *Making Civil Rights Law*, p. 97.

138 **"You were in rare form"**: Horne to Marshall, NAACP, August 9, 1949.

138 **"it would appear undesirable"**: MM 44-127, FBI.

138 **"full and exhaustive investigation"**: Ibid.

138 **"all of the persons interviewed"**: MM 44-156, FBI.

139 **"a pair of pants"**: Ibid.

139 **"asked them why"**: Ibid.

139 **"population of thirty-six thousand"**: Census of Population and Housing, U.S. Census Bureau, 1950 Census.

140 **"leading citizens"**: MM 44-156, FBI.

140 **"caused by the people"**: Ibid.

140 **"cleared the county"**: *Orlando Sentinel*, December 3, 1997.

140 **"he wouldn't have a building left"**: MM 44-156, FBI.

140 **"watching the City Hall"**: Ibid.

141 **"one man police department"**: Ibid.

141 **"affirmative action"**: Ibid.

141 **"County Sheriffs openly joined":** Moore Report, p. 7.

141 **"I believe the only thing":** Corsair, *The Groveland Four*, p. 35.

142 **"Bay Lake region people":** MM 44-156, FBI.

142 **"They might have got in a fight":** Corsair, *The Groveland Four*, p. 88.

142 **"physician who examined":** MM 44-156, FBI.

143 **"Report of Accident":** Ibid.

143 **"I knew that this would be":** Corsair, *The Groveland Four*, p. 94.

144 **Unable to fulfill:** *Orlando Sentinel*, July 5, 1992.

144 **"one full day of work":** *Mount Dora Topic*, September 1, 1949.

145 **"The University of Scuffletown":** Ibid.

145 **"filled with odds and ends":** Ibid.

145 **"a tin building":** *Mount Dora Topic*, August 25, 1949.

145 **"He was almost a caricature":** FOHP, Williams.

145 **"Where is the third defendant?":** Ibid.

145 **"The dirty bastard":** Williams to Wilkins, NAACP-LDF, August 25, 1949.

146 **"We are not the defendants":** Ibid.

146 **"Well, come on in":** FOHP, Williams.

146 **"It was very clear":** Ibid.

146 **"in shirt sleeves":** Williams to Wilkins, LDF, undated.

146 **"lawless mobs were roaming":** *Fl. v. Shepherd*, Affidavit, p. 78.

146 **"Filed too late":** *Fl. v. Shepherd*, Vol. 1, p. 78.

147 **"by persons purporting":** *Fl. v. Shepherd*, Affidavit, p. 78.

147 **"completely irrelevant":** *Fl. v. Shepherd*, Vol. 1, p. 320.

147 **good faith reasons:** *Fl. v. Shepherd*, Affidavit, p. 44.

147 **"extremely inconvenient":** *Fl. v. Shepherd*, Vol. 1, p. 4.

147 **"Every time" the defendants:** Corsair, *The Groveland Four*, p. 96.

148 **"disgusting an disheartening":** *Fl. v. Shepherd*, Vol. 2, p. 191.

148 **"What are those nigger lawyers":** *Fl. v. Shepherd*, Affidavit, p. 79.

148 **"Nigger lawyers better":** Ibid.

148 **Particularly hard hit:** Barnes, *Florida's Hurricane History*, p. 184.

149 **So it wasn't much of a surprise:** Corsair, *The Groveland Four*, p. 99.

## Chapter 11: Bad Egg

**150** **"If I were asked":** MM 44-156, FBI. Dr. Binneveld's examination of Norma Padgett on the morning of July 16, 1949, was taken from a report made by Agent John L. Quigley on September 2, 1949, from Agent Watson Roper's investigation and interview with the physician. In this report, Quigley noted that when U.S. Attorney Herbert S. Phillips in Tampa learned of the FBI's interview with Binneveld and the examination of Norma Padgett's medical report, Phillips wired FBI offices with instructions to "discontinue investigation in this matter."

**151** **"highly regarded" Dr. Geoffrey Binneveld:** Ibid.

**153** **"Dirty Commie":** Robeson, *The Undiscovered Paul Robeson*, p. 168.

**153** **"Go back to Russia!":** Ibid.

**153** **"We were having enough trouble":** Rise, *The Martinsville Seven*, p. 60.

**153** **"If you were a Negro":** COHP, Marshall.

**153** **"Franklin Williams had":** Greenberg, *Crusaders in the Courts*, p. 101.

**154** **"was to go into":** Thurgood Marshall, "Remarks at a Testimonial Dinner Honoring Raymond Pace Alexander, November 25, 1951," Tushnet, *Thurgood Marshall*, p. 140.

**154** **"giv[ing] foreign governments":** Ibid., p. 140.

**154** **"high-powered petitions":** Ibid.

**154** **"only the movement":** Rise, *The Martinsville Seven*, p. 66.

**155** **"These cases, the Groveland cases":** Marshall to Patterson, LDF, June 9, 1950.

**155** **"Dear Steve":** Marshall to Spingarn, LDF, June 18, 1950.

**155** **"I never believed":** FOHP, Williams.

**155** **"can come up with more ideas":** Presidential Recordings Program, Lyndon Johnson Tapes Transcripts, Monday, January 3, 1966: Thurgood Marshall, Lyndon Johnson, participants, http://whitehousetapes.net/transcript/johnson/wh6606-01-9403.

**156** **"every bit of energy":** FOHP, Williams.

**156** **"to cause constitutional error":** Ibid.

**156** **Jesse Hunter kept it simple:** *Fl. v. Shepherd*, Vol. 2.

**156** **"Jesse Hunter won't have to ask":** *Mount Dora Topic*, September 1, 1949.

**156** **"Honor Will Be Avenged":** *Mount Dora Topic*, July 2, 1949.

**156-57** **"Special Rules of Court":** *Fl. v. Shepherd*, Affadavit, p. 40.

**157** **"agitators or agents":** Ibid.

**157** **"They had deputies":** FOHP, Williams.

**157** **"worst crime in Lake county's history":** *Mount Dora Topic*, September 1, 1949.

**157** **"there is considerable":** *Fl. v. Shepherd*, Vol. 2, p. 78.

**157** **"Supreme Court is the aim":** *Mount Dora Topic*, September 1, 1949.

**157** "to the staunch believers": Ibid.

**158** "when the true story": Ibid.

**158** "damned scared": Hauke, *Ted Poston*, p. 77.

**158** "in the mail car": Ibid., p. 58.

**158** "kick in the pants": Ibid., p. 59.

**158** When Scottsboro: Ibid.

**159** "grown young lady": Ibid., p. 13. This scene is recounted in Hauke's book: Allison Williams, Poston's lifelong friend, recalls conversations she had with Poston about his boyhood sexual encounters with a white woman.

**159** "Horror in the Sunny South": *New York Post*, September 9, 1949.

**159** "seething jealousy": *Chicago Defender*, July 30. 1949.

**160** "I will leave this place": Ibid.

**160** "The theory was": FOHP, Williams.

**160** "generally read from": Moore Report, Exhibit 71.

**160** "greater modicum of security": FOHP, Williams.

**160** "just in case anything happens": *State of Florida v. Walter L. Irvin, Charles Greenlee, and Samuel Shepherd*, Prosecution Report, April 2, 1950, Exhibit 1, FBI 44-2722.

**161** that Norma Padgett was a "bad egg": FBI 44-2722.

**161** "had grown up": Ibid.

**161** "stirred up" the violence: Ibid.

**161** When pressed by Williams: Bertha E. Davis to Goldberg, LDF, August 1, 1949; and July 21, 1949.

**161** "Mrs. Padgett, her husband": FBI 44-2722.

**161** "any traces of": Davis to Goldberg, LDF, August 1. 1949; and July 21, 1949.

**162** "grave doubts": FBI 44-2722.

**162** "considerably affected": Ibid.

**162** "the investigation will result": Ibid.

**162** "Richard Roe and John Doe": Ibid.

**162** "the confidential nature": Corsair, *The Groveland Four*, p. 121.

**162** "those clay eating crackers": FOHP, Williams.

**162** "How would you feel": *Fl. v. Shepherd*, Vol. 3, pp. 398, 322.

**163** "They are not on trial": Ibid., p. 413.

**163** Akerman's other primary concern: *Fl. v. Shepherd*, Vol 2, p. 236.

**163** "in favor of it": *Fl. v. Shepherd*, Vol 3, p. 338.

**163** **"gray haired old handyman"**: Carson et al., *Reporting Civil Rights, Part One*, p. 127.

**163** **"one of the best niggers"**: Ibid.

**163** **"Women Beg for Reserved Seats at Trial"**: *Mount Dora Topic*, August 18, 1949.

**163** **"Through sentiment"**: *Chicago Defender*, September 10, 1949.

**163** **"Bay Lake Crackers"**: Corsair, *The Groveland Four*, p. 132.

**164** **"always intimidated me"**: FOHP, Williams.

**164** **"bare feet making"**: *Mount Dora Topic*, undated clipping, FHW Papers, July 1949.

**164** **Oppressive heat**: FOHP, Williams.

**164** **"of what he might do"**: Ibid.

**164** **"dying declaration"**: Williams to Wilkins, undated letter, LDF, September 1949.

**165** **"promenading"**: Corsair, *The Groveland Four*, p. 127.

**165** **"Undiscovered American Beauties"**: International Center of Photography Blog, *Ladies Home Journal* Prospectus, September 21, 1948, John Morris, Picture Editor, http://icplibrary.wordpress.com/2010/12/14/ladies-home-journal's-undiscovered-american-beauties-provide-potential-bounty-to-photographers'/.

**165** **"rise and point out"**: *Fl. v. Shepherd*, Vol. 4, p. 509.

**166** **"The nigger Shepherd"**: FOHP, Williams. This is Franklin Williams's recollection of the manner in which Norma Padgett identified her alleged attackers, according to the transcripts from FOHP, Williams. According to the trial transcripts, Norma Padgett, in her testimony, repeatedly referred to the defendants (and the deceased Ernest Thomas) as "this (or the) Thomas nigger," "that Shepherd nigger," "the Greenlee nigger," and even "that Shepherd man" at times. Walter Irvin was referred to only as "Irvin" by Padgett.

**166** **"probably the most dramatic moment"**: FOHP, Williams.

**166** **"resentful-eyed"**: *Mount Dora Topic*, September 8, 1949. Also transcript of interview with Mabel Norris Chesley, Franklin Hall Williams Papers, Schomburg Center for Research in Black Culture (FOHP, Chesley).

**166** **"wasn't wearing a watch"**: *Fl. v. Shepherd*, Vol. 4, p. 521.

**166** **"plaster Paris casts"**: Ibid., p. 541.

**166** **"the sheriff has kept me"**: Ibid., p. 542.

**167** **"feed you and sleep you"**: Ibid., p. 552.

**167** **"jostled by a couple of hoodlums"**: *New York Post*, September 9, 1949.

**167** **"Objection is overruled"**: *Fl. v. Shepherd*, Vol. 4, p. 600.

**167** **"I see no purpose"**: Ibid., p. 601.

**168** **"Well, Mr Williams"**: Corsair, *The Groveland Four*, p. 149.

**168** **"It's the worst framed-up case"**: Ibid.

**168** **"It was like a story"**: FOHP, Williams.

**168** **"Mr. Williams," he said:** Ibid.

**169** **"Willis McCall," Shepherd told him:** Ibid.

**169** **"murdered blacks":** Ibid.

**169** **"tall, gangly":** Ibid.

**169** **"if you just tell":** Ted Poston, "The Story of Florida's Legal Lynching," *The Nation*, September 2, 1949.

**170** **"I said to myself":** *Fl. v. Shepherd*, Vol. 4, p. 600.

**170** **"hurry up and take me away":** Ibid., p. 640.

**170** **"So I was sitting":** Ibid., p. 641.

**172** **"Would you have been":** Ibid., p. 644.

**171** **"the white lady":** Irene Holmes to Franklin Williams, LDF, December 12, 1949.

**171** **"Charlie Greenlee's such a good actor":** Green, *Before His Time*, p. 104.

**171** **"eyes filled with grief":** *Mount Dora Topic*, September 8, 1949.

**171** **"When are you going to put him":** FOHP, Williams.

**171** **"You know what your problem is":** Green, *Before His Time*, p. 104.

**171** **"At Long Last":** *Mount Dora Topic*, September 8, 1949.

**172** **"Except for the":** *New York Post*, September 9, 1949.

**172** **"Not necessary":** Ibid.

**172** **"Mr. Hunter didn't want":** Ibid.

**172** **"possible stains":** Ibid.

**172** **"If that white lady":** Ibid.

**172** **"bowing and cringing":** Ibid.

**172** **"I won't take very long":** *Fl. v. Shepherd*, Vol. 4, p. 644.

**172** **"a lot can happen":** Green, *Before His Time*, p. 103.

**172** **"no human being":** Corsair, *The Groveland Four*, p. 165.

**173** **"grim game of 'Musical Chairs'":** *St. Petersburg Times*, April 9, 1950.

**173** **"a little out of line":** Ibid.

**173** **"Jesse," Futch said:** Corsair, *The Groveland Four*, p. 167.

**173** **"the one long distance phone booth":** *New York Post*, September 9, 1949.

**173** **"an expectant father":** *State of Florida v. Walter L. Irvin, Charles Greenlee, and Samuel Shepherd*, Prosecution Report, April 2, 1950, Exhibit 1, FBI 44-2722.

**173** **"Keep your shirt on":** *New York Post*, September 9, 1949.

**173** **that Sheriff McCall "needed help":** Moore Report, Exhibit 53.

**173** **"no demonstration:** *Fl. v. Shepherd*, Vol. 4, p. 654.

174 **"We the jury find"**: *Fl. v. Shepherd*, Affadavit, p. 22.

174 **"Hope was gone from the eyes"**: *Mount Dora Topic*, September 8, 1949.

174 **"Then a smile"**: Ibid.

174 **"Alex, psst, Alex"**: FOHP, Williams. This scene is mostly derived from Franklin Williams's recollections (FOHP, Williams), and from Ted Poston's "Horror in the Sunny South" stories in the *New York Post*.

174 **"go home quietly"**: Ibid.

174 **"I don't doubt"**: Ibid.

175 **"Aren't you going to escort us"**: Ibid.

175 **"jammed that cigarette lighter"**: Ibid.

175 **"hostile sea of white faces"**: *New York Post*, September 9, 1949.

175 **"Hurry up and get in"**: FOHP, Williams.

175 **"Where's Ramona?"**: *New York Post*, September 9, 1949.

176 **"Jesus Christ," Williams said**: FOHP, Williams.

176 **"Oh, God. It's my fault"**: *New York Post*, September 9, 1949.

177 **"I have never been so happy"**: FOHP, Williams.

177 **"I couldn't see my own shame"**: *New York Post*, September 9, 1949.

177 **"Aw, you have got"**: FOHP, Williams.

## Chapter 12: Atom Smasher

179 **"if he didn't say"**: Corsair, *The Groveland Four*, p. 188.

179 **"He was going to handme over"**: Ibid., p. 188.

179 **"You lied on the witness stand?"**: Moore Report, p. 288. This scene is derived from the transcript that Harry T. Moore's biographer, Ben Green, made (July 15, 1992) from Willis McCall's interview of Charles Greenlee. The transcript appears in the Moore Report.

180 **"Scotland Yard"**: *Mount Dora Topic*, undated clipping, FHW Papers, September 1949.

180 **"An unlettered but articulate"**: *New York Post*, September 6, 1949.

180 **"ample opportunity"**: *Fl. v. Shepherd*, Vol. 4, Affadavit, p. 142.

180 **"vicious," in Williams's judgment**: FOHP, Williams.

180 **"the evidence was"**: Corsair, *The Groveland Four*, p. 188.

181 **"My feeling is that"**: Wilkins to Spingarn, NAACP, September 6, 1949.

181 **"that Tavares business"**: *New York Post*, September 6, 1949.

181 **"thrown behind the defense"**: Press release, NAACP, August 1949.

181 **"We'll keep Frank's promise"**: *New York Post*, Septe,ber 6, 1949.

181 **"bloodthirsty, motorized mob"**: *New York Post*, September 9, 1949.

**182** **"all the characteristics":** FOHP, Williams.

**182** **"He may have been":** Greenberg, *Crusaders in the Courts*, p. 32.

**182** **"I would *not* live in the South":** Corsair, *The Groveland Four*, p. 154.

**182** **"deterred the assertion":** Greenberg, *Crusaders in the Courts*, p. 98.

**183** **"So if God be with me":** Corsair, *The Groveland Four*, p. 194.

**183** **"damn bunch of Communists":** Ibid., p. 198.

**184** **The FBI chose:** Moore Report, Exhibit 76.

**184** **"intended to stop car":** Ibid.

**184** **by a federal grand jury:** Marshall to McGrath, 44-2772-43, FBI.

**184** **"there is substantial evidence":** Campbell to Phillips, 144-18-117, FBI, September 13, 1949,

**184** **"as fair a trial":** Phillips to Campbell, MM 44-156, FBI.

**185** **"Judge, I agree":** Kluger, *Simple Justice*, p. 277.

**185-86** **"all day and virtually every night":** Greenberg, *Crusaders in the Courts*, p. 159.

**186** **"considerable talents":** Ibid., p. 160.

**186** **"great dark Munich beer":** Ibid., p. 159.

**186** **"If we can force the University of Texas":** *The Survey*, Vol. 85, 1949, p. 21. (Charity Organization Society of the City of New York, Survey Associates.)

**186** **"equal to the University of Texas Law School":** Lavergne, *Before Brown*, p. 161.

**187** **"everyone knows what the score is":** Unidentified news clipping, NAACP.

**188** **"opened [the judge's] eyes":** Williams, *Thurgood Marshall*, p. 179.

**188** **"You keep talking":** Rowan, *Dream Makers, Dream Breakers*, p. 148.

**188** **"it was 'nigger' this":** Ibid.

**188** **"Thurgood was respectful":** Address by John Paul Stevens, Associate Justice, Supreme Court of the United States, to the American Bar Association, Thurgood Marshall Awards Dinner Honoring Abner Mikva, Hyatt Regency Hotel, Chicago, IL, August 6, 2005.

**188** **"there would be intermarriage":** Kluger, *Simple Justice*, p. 265.

**188** **"We had eight people":** Ibid.

**189** **For one, McLaurin:** Ibid.

**189** **"it offered the":** Greenberg, *Crusaders in the Courts*, p. 71.

**189** **"clattering hot-lead Linotype machines":** Ibid., p. 159.

**189** **"Thurgood focused on":** Ibid., p. 71.

**189** **"*Plessy* must go":** Kluger, *Simple Justice*, p. 276.

**190** **"like a boxer":** Greenberg, *Crusaders in the Courts*, p. 72.

190 **"employed a rhetoric"**: Ibid., p. 76.

190 **"The rights of Sweatt"**: Williams, *Thurgood Marshall*, p. 183.

190 **"All we ask in the south"**: Ibid.

191 **"I was the first deputy"**: FOHP, Williams.

191 **"Bill, take a few minutes"**: Greenberg, *Crusaders in the Courts*, p. 32. Also FOHP, Williams.

191 **"Walter liked me"**: Kluger, *Simple Justice*, p. 271.

191 **"He had great success"**: Ibid.

192 **"cautious to a fault"**: Ibid., p. 272.

192 **"because they might"**: Greenberg, *Crusaders in the Courts*, p. 33.

192 **"special counsel"**: Ibid.

## Chapter 13: In Any Fight Some Fall

193 **"Mrs. Padgett didn't"**: *Fl. v. Shepherd*, Brief of Appellee, p. 44.

194 **"in somebody's back"**: FOHP, Williams.

194 **"disturbed and disappointed"**: MM 44-156, FBI.

195 didn't **"need any assistance"**: FBI 44-2722-90, Phillips to McInerney, April 28, 1950.

195 **"These education cases are"**: James, *Root and Branch*, p. 199.

195 **"didn't know how to stop working"**: McNeil, *Groundwork*, p. 209.

195 **"to remember his father"**: Ibid.

195 **"Get down from there"**: Ibid., p. 187.

196 **"open-air Scottsboro protest meeting"**: Ibid., p. 207.

196 **Since Scottsboro**: Ibid.

196 **"Hi, Joe," Houston said**: Ibid., p. 211.

196 **"Tell Bo I did not"**: Ibid., p. 212.

197 **"unremitting struggle"**: *Crisis*, June 1950.

197 **"Whatever credit"**: Sullivan, *Lift Every Voice*, p. 382.

197 **"guided us through"**: *Crisis*, June 1950.

198 **"We won the big one!"**: Lavergne, *Before Brown*, p. 253.

198 left *Plessy* in **"tatters"**: Tushnet, *Making Civil Rights Law*, p. 147.

198 **"Thurgood . . . a party man"**: Williams, *Thurgood Marshall*, p. 185; Motley, *Equal Justice Under Law*, p. 106.

198 **"lots of Scotch"**: Greenberg, *Crusaders in the Courts*, p. 78.

198 **"the tools to destroy"**: Williams, *Thurgood Marshall*, p. 185.

**199** **"she waited patiently":** *St. Petersburg Times*, April 9, 1950.

**200** **"crying profusely":** Ibid.

**200** **As for her testimony:** Corsair, *The Groveland Four*, pp. 202–203.

**200** **"a dastardly lying libel":** *St. Petersburg Times*, April 13, 1950.

**201** **"tried to keep him":** *Crisis*, June/July 1982.

**201** **To Morehouse College president:** Sullivan, *Lift Every Voice*, p. 373.

**201** **"deplorable state of":** Current to Black, NAACP, undated report.

**202** **"I plan to touch":** Green, *Before His Time*, p. 110.

**202** **"a lot of yelling":** Williams, *Thurgood Marshall*, p. 154.

**202** **"I won't take it!":** COHP, Marshall.

**202** **"Dutch uncle":** Presidential Recordings Program, Lyndon Johnson Tapes Transcripts, Monday, January 3, 1966: Thurgood Marshall, Lyndon Johnson, participants, http://whitehousetapes.net/transcript/johnson/wh6606-01-9403. (Hereafter cited as LBJ tapes.)

**203** **"less than bold":** Kluger, *Simple Justice*, p. 248.

**203** **"made Marshall look":** Ibid., p. 304.

**203** **"not dragging his":** Ibid., p. 305.

**203** **"he didn't have to worry":** COHP, Marshall.

**203** **"You're fired":** Ibid.

**203** **"Why, I didn't mean that":** Ibid.

**204** **"he felt he was being exiled":** Greenberg, *Crusaders in the Courts*, p. 33.

**204** **"although most of the whites":** Reports of Ms. L. B. De Forest, ACLU, Summer 1950.

**204** **"to avoid any possibility":** Watts to Marshall, August 2, 1950, ACLU.

**204** **"Keep away from Sheriff McCall":** Reports of Ms. L. B. De Forest, ACLU, Summer 1950.

**205** **"chose[n] jurymen":** *Cassell v. Texas*, 339 U.S. 282 (1950).

**205** **"would not be likely":** Greenberg, *Crusaders in the Courts*, p. 98.

**205** **"a number of old English cases":** Ibid.

**205** **"The complete destruction":** Lavergne, *Before Brown*, p. 258.

**206** **"eradicate Communists":** *Crisis*, November 1980.

**206** **"They're in there":** COHP, Marshall.

**206** **"we socked them good":** Ibid.

**207** **"The communists brought it on themselves":** Williams, *Thurgood Marshall*, p. 169.

**207** **"staggering casualties":** *Crisis*, May 1951.

**208** **"so-called trials":** COHP, Marshall.

208 **"in a base hospital"**: *Crisis*, May 1951.

208 **"There was so much sniper fire"**: *Life*, November 12, 1965.

208 **"What happened over there"**: COHP, Marshall.

208 **"not even in the band"**: *Pittsburgh Courier*, March 3, 1951.

208 **"the United States Air Force took just one day"**: *Crisis*, May 1951.

209 **"The Red Koreans"**: Ibid.

209 **"just a bad egg"**: Greenberg, *Crusaders in the Courts*, p. 80.

209 **"My dad told me"**: *New York Times*, June 29, 1991.

## Chapter 14: This Is a Rape Case

211 a **"Communist agent"**: *Ocala Star Banner*, March 29, 1956.

211 **"a stranger coming"**: De Forest, WDL. All observations and quotes are from the journal entries of L. B. De Forest, mailed to Rowland Watts during the summer of 1950.

212 **"If we were to tell the truth"**: Ibid.

213 **"heard the motor start up again"**: Twiss affadavit, WDL, April 29, 1951.

213 **"police alarm"**: Thomas to Watts, WDL, undated.

214 **"sitting in the grass"**: *Fl. v. Shepherd*, Vol. 4, p. 578.

214 **"thought she might have gotten"**: MM 44-156, FBI.

214 **"vagaries in both"**: Thomas to Watts, WDL, undated.

215 **"seen the girl"**: Ibid.

215–216 **"I am sure you can appreciate"**: Williams to Marshall, LDF, December 4, 1950.

216 **"To pull you out"**: Marshall to Williams, LDF, December 12, 1950.

216 **"Well," Bowen had responded**: Corsair, *The Groveland Four*, p. 213.

216 **"irritated me a little"**: FOHP, Williams.

217 **"to say anything more"**: *Crisis*, April 1951.

217 **"Well," Carter asked**: FOHP, Williams.

217 argued the case **"superbly"**: Greenberg, *Crusaders in the Courts*, p. 98.

218 **"the hardest thing"**: *Crisis*, April 1951. The reporting and quotes from *Shepherd v. Florida* are derived from this issue of *Crisis*.

## Chapter 15: You Have Pissed in My Whiskey

219 **"Won new trial for Walter Irvin"**: Marshall to Dellia Irvin, LDF, April 10, 1951.

220 **"do not meet any civilized conception"**: *Shepherd v. Irvin*, 341 U.S. 50 (1951).

220 **"not surprised"**: *New York Times*, April 11, 1951.

220 **"very disappointed"**: Ibid.

220 **"perfect this appeal"**: *Orlando Sentinel Star*, November 9, 1949.

220 **Sidestepping questions**: *Pittsburgh Courier*, April 21, 1951.

221 **In a public statement he ranted**: Ibid.

221 **"to see that justice was done"**: McCall, *Willis V. McCall, Sheriff of Lake County*, p. 23.

221 **"I have it directly"**: Watts Report, WDL.

221-22 **a "God Damn Nigger Lover"**: Green, *Before His Time*, p. 134.

222 **"I don't push easy"**: McCall, *Willis V. McCall, Sheriff of Lake County*, p. 14.

222 **"Our warm appreciation"**: White to Williams, NAACP, April 11, 1951.

222 **"unable to give his whole support"**: *St. Petersburg Times*, April 11, 1951.

222 **"desegregated in about three weeks"**: COHP, Marshall.

222 **"it wasn't very smart"**: Author interview, Jack Greenberg, February 10, 2009.

223 **"ham or oranges"**: Corsair, *The Groveland Four*, p. 219.

223 **"strange code of ethics"**: Ibid.

223 **"You all haven't electrocuted"**: *New York Post*, November 8, 1951.

223 **"Wish you all would run"**: Ibid.

223 **"causing trouble"**: Corsair, *The Groveland Four*, p. 223.

223 **"plenty of Negroes"**: Ibid.

224 **"a big yellow streak"**: Greenberg, *Crusaders in the Courts*, p. 31.

224 **"You can say all you want"**: Kluger, *Simple Justice*, p. 750.

224 **"I don't sleep with"**: Greenberg, *Crusaders in the Courts*, p. 133.

224 **"white travelers were not yet accustomed"**: Ibid.

224 **"Norma Padgett and her husband"**: FOHP, Williams.

225 **"regulation strap"**: Moore Report, Exhibit 74.

225 **"put the finger on"**: Ibid.

225 **"out of hearing distance"**: FOHP, Williams.

226 **"feelings generated"**: Greenberg, *Crusaders in the Courts*, p. 134.

226 **"unpainted, weather-beaten"**: Ibid., p. 135.

226 **"an illegal search and seizure"**: Ibid.

226 **"battlefield tension"**: Ibid., p. 134.

226 **"create an error"**: FOHP, Williams.

226 **"Anything can happen":** Ibid.

227 **"Prisons breed criminals":** De Forest, WDL, Watts Report.

231 **"I am ready now":** Corsair, *The Groveland Four*, p. 253.

231 **"Go on ahead":** "Testimony of Walter Irvin," State of Florida, County of Lake, November 8, 1951, George State University Special Collections Department, Stetson Kennedy Papers.

231 **"You sons of bitches," McCall said:** FBI 44-267.

232 **"Well," he told Marshall:** Thurgood Marshall, "Remarks at a Testimonial Dinner Honoring Raymond Pace Alexander, November 25, 1951," Mark V. Tushnet, *Thurgood Marshall: His Speeches, Writings, Arguments, Opinions, and Reminiscences*, p. 140.

232 **"Lake County Sheriff Shoots Two Negores":** *Orlando Sentinel Star*, November 7, 1951.

233 **"wanted to furnish information":** FBI 44-267.

233 **"killing of Samuel Shepherd":** Greenberg to Fuller Warren, NAACP, November 7, 1951.

233 **"the build of a blocking back":** Greenberg, *Crusaders in the Courts*, p. 141.

234 **"exactly what happened":** *New York Post*, November 8, 1951.

234 **"You might as well go away":** *Orlando Morning Sentinel*, November 8, 1951.

234 **"I have orders not to let anyone":** Corsair, *The Groveland Four*, p. 238.

234 **"suffering shock":** *Orlando Evening Star*, November 8, 1951.

234 **"Yates kept us":** Greenberg, *Crusaders in the Courts*, p. 141.

234 **"when the law gives":** *Orlando Evening Star*, November 8, 1951.

235 **"appeared to be in pain":** FBI 44-4055.

235 **"entirely different story":** Corsair, *The Groveland Four*, p. 239.

235 **"half way down":** FBI 44-4055. Willis McCall's version of the shooting is derived from his statement to FBI agents Swinney and Aderhold and transcribed in this report.

235 **"He said, 'I will piss'":** Ibid.

236 **"he knew nothing":** Ibid.

236 **"Marie, it's just":** *Orlando Morning Sentinel*, November 8, 1951.

236 **"saw one of them move":** Stetson Kennedy Papers, Georgia State University, Special Collections Department.

237 **"You have pissed in my whiskey":** Author interview with Stetson Kennedy, December 7, 2009.

237 **"One of them has a pulse":** Green, *Before His Time*, p. 138.

237 **"friends of Sheriff Willis V. McCall":** *New York Post*, November 10, 1951.

237 **"extreme shock":** Lake County Medical Center, report of Dr. R. H. Williams, FBI 44-267.

237 **"a batch of the sheriff's hair":** FBI 44-267.

238 "I'm just happy to be here": *Orlando Morning Sentinel*, November 8, 1951.

238 "I expect I'll get": *Tampa Morning Tribune*, November 9, 1951.

238 "Please give me a truthful answer": *New Leader*, November 19, 1951.

239 "Visibly shaken": *Orlando Morning Sentinel*, November 8, 1951.

239 "Guess what. McCall's": FHW Papers, Chesley.

239 "Mabel," he'd said: Green, *Before His Time*, p. 141.

## Chapter 16: It's a Funny Thing

240 "This is what human rights means": *New York Times*, November 9, 1951.

241 "the shooting of": *St. Peterburg Times*, November 8, 1951.

241 "primitive mobile crime lab": Green, *Before His Time*, p. 141.

241 "check all angles": *New York Times*, November 8, 1951.

241 "Well, boys, I'm here": *Tampa Tribune*, November 9, 1951.

241 "court-appointed elisor": *St. Petersburg Times*, November 8, 1951.

241 and a "special nurse": *Crisis*, December 1951.

242 "This was the first time": FHW Papers, Chesley.

242 "No one's going to hurt you": *Miami Herald*, November 9, 1951. Also Stetson Kennedy Papers, Georgia State University, Special Collections Department. Walter Irvin's version of the shooting is derived from his interview with lawyers at Waterman Memorial Hospital on November 8, 1951.

245 "We sincerely hope the good people": *St. Petersburg Times*, November 9, 1951.

245 "Colored men who are accused": *Pittsburgh Courier*, November 17, 1951.

245 "It's a funny thing": *New York Post*, November 9, 1951.

245 "was visibly shaken": *Orlando Morning Sentinel*, November 8, 1951.

245 "This is the worst thing": Ibid.

245 "IRVIN agreeable": MM 44-267, FBI.

246 "and the laws of this country": Corsair, *The Groveland Four*, p. 283.

246 "We must leave": Wilkins statement, NAACP, November 8, 1951.

246 "to whitewash the whole affair": Marshall to McGrath, NAACP, November 8, 1951.

246 The national office: Author interview, Vernon Jordan, April 14, 2011.

247 "There isn't a threat": *Time*, September 19, 1955.

247 "ducking, weaving and": *New York Post*, November 8, 1951.

247 "It's a funny thing": *New York Post*, November 9, 1951.

248 It took Willis McCall: Corsair, *The Groveland Four*, p. 250.

248 **"to kill Alex Akerman"**: Ibid., p. 249.

248 **"No, I'm in the clear"**: Green, *Before His Time*, p. 251.

248 **"a big SOB in the NAACP"**: Corsair, *The Groveland Four*, p. 250.

249 **"hatchet job"**: Byrd to Lucille Black, NAACP, September 29, 1950.

249 **"always delivered the votes"**: Author interview, Vernon Jordan, April 14, 2011.

249 **"wondering if Moore"**: MM 44-270, FBI.

249 **"neck ought to be broken"**: Green, *Before His Time*, p. 156.

249 **"afraid to travel"**: Ibid.

250 **"grooves between the tread design"**: MM 44-267, FBI.

250 **"I will ask you"**: Ibid.

250 **"The nail on the tire"**: FHW, Chesley.

251 **"Was this ground dug up"**: MM 44-267, FBI.

252 **"until I got permission"**: Ibid.

253 **"guest of honor"**: *Federated Press*, November 19, 1951.

253 **"I believe that this"**: MM 44-267, FBI.

253 **"justified by reason"**: Ibid.

253 **"At that time," Futch wrote:** Ibid., Statement of the Court, Fifth Judicial Circuit, Lake County, Florida, November 12, 1951.

253–54 **"only as I have been directed"**: *St. Petersburg Times*, November 13, 1951.

254 **"directly beneath a blood spot"**: FBI 44-4066-70.

254 **"reached up and grabbed"**: MM 44-267, FBI.

254 **"for probable use"**: FBI 44-4055-15.

254 **"no need for a grand jury"**: MM 44-267, FBI.

255 he was **"out of the city"**: Kennedy Papers.

255 **"complete vindication"**: *New York Post*, November 10, 1951.

256 **"fantastic savagery"**: Ibid.

256 **"Irvin's story was so convincing"**: Corsair, *The Groveland Four*, p. 279.

256 **"after this conference"**: Marshall to Warren, NAACP, November 11, 1951.

256 **"This is the worst case"**: *Chicago Defender*, November 17, 1951.

257 **"are no good at all"**: McCall, *Willis V. McCall, Sheriff of Lake County*, p. 14.

257 **"sheer, filthy offensiveness"**: *New York Post*, November 11, 1951.

257 **"I don't think there is any question"**: McCall, *Willis V. McCall, Sheriff of Lake County*, p. 14.

## Chapter 17: No Man Alive or to Be Born

259 **"crap games, after-hour":** Green, *Before His Time*, p. 149.

259 **"play the ace up my sleeve":** Stetson Kennedy, *The Klan Unmasked*, p. 245.

259 **"has facilitated":** Ibid., p. xiii.

259 **"Well, well!" Elliott said:** Ibid., p. 245. Kennedy's conversation with Elliott, which also appeared in several newspapers, is derived from his account in *The Klan Unmasked*.

260 **Stetson Kennedy didn't even stop:** Ibid., pp. 249–250.

260 **"Red hot information":** *Chicago Defender*, November 24, 1951.

260 **"for further funds":** FBI 44-4055-27. This report details the FBI's interactions with Stetson Kennedy and also contains Hoover's handwritten notation.

261 **"it looked like Kennedy had swindled":** Ibid.

261 **"could result in the nicest":** *Chicago Defender*, November 24, 1951.

262 **"prejudiced in Civil Rights investigations":.** FBI 44-4055-27.

262 **"entirely possible," given:** Ibid.

262 **"Klan-ridden regime":** Newton, *The Invisible Empire*, p. 125.

262 **"Sometime later," however:** Moore Report, p. 134.

266 **"the best person would":** Groveland Case Minutes, LDF, November 13, 1951.

262 **"In the name of human decency":** Marshall to Warren, NAACP, December 5, 1951.

263 **"doomed murderer":** FBI 44-4055-65. Leiby's statement and the FBI investigation at Raiford are derived from this report.

264 **"it is not the practice":** *Jet*, January 17, 1951.

264 **"remove Sheriff Willis B. McCall":** Resolutions: Florida State Conference of NAACP Branches, November 23–35, 1951, Daytona Beach, NAACP.

264 **"came in and took over":** Moore Report, p. 98.

265 **"he could not understand":** Ibid., p. 34.

265 **"the easy part of the job":** Greenberg, *Crusaders in the Courts*, p. 86.

265 **"anti-Semitic and anti-Negro slogans":** Raymond A. Mohl, " 'South of the South?' Jews, Blacks, and the Civil Rights Movement in Miami, 1945–1960, " *Journal of American Ethnic History*, Vol. 18, No. 2, Winter 1999.

265 **"The Jew has already":** Ibid.

266 **"Florida Terror":** *Gainesville Sun*, November 5, 2000.

266 **"the worst year of minority outrages":** "The Truth About the Florida Race Troubles," *Saturday Evening Post*, June 1952.

266 **"still echoing around the world":** Moore to Warren, NAACP, December 2, 1951.

266 **"Is it true that":** Ibid.

266 **"I'll take a few":** Green, *Before His Time*, p. 155.

267 **"We really ought to":** Ibid.

267 **"Some of the tactics":** Ibid.

267 **"As matters now stand":** *Washington Afro-American*, December 4, 1951.

267 **"vicious, slanderous and":** Corsair, *The Groveland Four*, p. 290.

267 **"has nothing whatsover":** Unidentified news clipping, NAACP.

268 **"Did you interview him":** *Fl. v. Samuel Shepherd and Walter Irvin*, Florida State Archives, Application for Removal of Cause, p. 139.

268 **"That statement is entirely false":** Ibid.

268 **"this whole thing has":** *St. Petersburg Times*, December 7, 1951.

269 **"took the first step":** *Daily Worker*, December 7, 1951.

269 **"stirred up trouble":** Columbia University Oral History Project, Jack Greenberg with Kitty Gelhorn, Columbia Center for Oral History, Columbia University, Butler Library, New York, NY (hereafter cited as COHP, Greenberg).

269 **"because they represent the NAACP":** *St. Petersburg Times*, December 7, 1951.

270 **"believed that the threat":** *Pittsburgh Courier*, December 22, 1951.

270 **"ordinary, conversational":** Greenberg, *Crusaders in the Courts*, p. 76.

270 **"In a mass meeting":** Ibid., p. 29.

271 **"Why did McCall have to remove":** *Pittsburgh Courier*, December 22, 1951.

271 **"They can keep me":** Ibid.

271 **"from some of these white people":** Ibid.

271 **"I was glad of the chance":** Doggett to Marshall, LDF, December 15, 1951, and January 1, 1952.

272 **"This is not a single battle":** Tushnet, *The NAACP's Legal Strategy Against Segregated Education, 1925–1950*, p. 95.

272 **"going too far" in his work:** Moore Report, Exhibit 39.

272 **"I'm going to keep doing it":** Green, *Before His Time*, p. 162.

## Chapter 18: All Over the Place, Like Rats

274 **"Is that you, Harry?":** Moore Report, p. 31. The accounts of the evening of December 25, 1951, are derived from various FBI reports, interviews, and witness statements included in this report.

276 **"We seek no special favors":** Moore to Warren, NAACP, December 2, 1951.

277 **"Trying to scare":** Moore Report, p. 315.

277 **"There isn't much left":** *Orlando Sentinel*, December 28, 1951.

277 **"Bombing Kills Negro Leader":** *New York Times*, December 27, 1951.

278 **"When state officers"**: *Washington Post*, December 29, 1951.

278 **"That kind of violent incident"**: *Crisis*, May/June, 1999.

278 **"I can testify"**: *Collier's*, February 23, 1952.

278 **"the possibility of violent death"**: *Jet*, September 29, 1955.

278 **"representatives of the finest type"**: Marshall to Warren, NAACP, December 26, 1951.

279 **"Terrorism in Florida"**: *Crisis*, February 1952.

279 **"Notice Negro Blood on Your Grapefruit?"**: *Ebony*, April 1952.

279 **"It's a pat on the back"**: *Ebony*, November 1975.

279 **"Terrorists Kill by Night"**: *St. Petersburg Times*, December 30, 1951.

279 **"arrest and conviction"**: *St. Petersburg Times*, December 28, 1951.

279 **"acting as a human shield"**: Green, *Before His Time*, p. 183.

279 **"I am the second best pistol shot"**: *Baltimore Afro-American*, January 5, 1952.

279 **"to see what can be done"**: *St. Petersburg Times*, December 28, 1951.

279 **"in their moment of degradation"**: *New York Times*, December 31, 1951.

280 **"fast, resolute action"**: *New York Times*, January 3, 1952.

280 **"Everything was being done"**: *St. Petersburg Times*, December 28, 1951.

280 **"I'm sure as I can be"**: Green, *Before His Time*, p. 184.

280 **"a relief to know"**: *St. Petersburg Times*, December 31, 1951.

280 **Against Dr. Starke's wishes**: Ibid., p. 186.

281 **"even if they had a pistol"**: Green, *Before His Time*, p. 187.

282 **"You can pick up a newspaper"**: *Pittsburgh Courier*, February 2, 1952.

282 **"Getting dynamite"**: Moore Report, p. 123.

282 **"We'd go in and talk"**: Ibid.

282 **"We had informants"**: Ibid.

**Chapter 19: Private Parts**

284 **was "booked solid"**: Moore Report, p. 316.

284 **"I don't care how booked you are"**: Ibid.

284 **"to ensure that the FBI"**: Ibid.

284 **"Klan members and some law enforcement officers"**: Ibid.

285 **"How you want your body shipped back?"**: *Chicago Defender*, February 23, 1952.

285 **"American Confederate Army"**: *Jet*, July 31, 1952.

285 **1. denounce the NAACP**: Ibid.

285 **"Florida must have a few lynchings"**: Ibid.

285 **"at least 25 cars"**: *Pittsburgh Courier*, February 23, 1952.

285 **"with confederate flags flying"**: Greenberg, *Crusaders in the Courts*, p. 141.

285 **"It was frightening, it was exciting"**: COHP, Greenberg.

286 **"took the vain precaution"**: Greenberg, *Crusaders in the Courts*, p. 141.

286 **"too busy with traffic accidents"**: *Fort Pierce News Tribune*, February 12, 1952.

286 **"misquoted" with regard**: *St. Petersburg Times*, February 17, 1952.

286 **"libelous and defamatory" postcards**: *Lubbock Evening Journal*, February 13, 1952.

286 **"Your boys, the KKKs"**: *Chicago Defender*, February 23, 1952.

286 **"beautiful shiny Cadillac"**: Ibid.

286 **"rip-roaring welcome parade"**: *Pittsburgh Courier*, February 23, 1952.

286 **"stirred up trouble in the community"**: *Atlanta Daily World*, February 10, 1952.

286 **"My shoulder worries me"**: *New York Daily Compass*, February 13, 1952.

287 **"packed to the ceiling"**: *Chicago Defender*, February 23, 1952.

287 **"our greatest civil liberties lawyer"**: *Collier's*, February 23, 1952.

287 **a Louisiana judge who was "no friend"**: COHP, Marshall.

288 **"You don't have to worry"**: Ibid.

288 **"not one of the 518 whites"**: *New York Daily Compass*, February 12, 1952.

288 **"place the trial"**: Greenberg, *Crusaders in the Courts*, p. 143.

288 **"chewed occasionally"**: *New York Daily Compass*, February 12, 1952.

288 **"How much did they pay you?"**: *Fl. v. Irvin*, p. 24.

288 **"Now, as a matter of fact"**: Ibid., p. 29.

289 **"one of the best friends"**: Ibid., p. 93.

289 **"I would put this county"**: Ibid., p. 105.

290 **"gentleman of the frock"**: *Chicago Defender*, February 23, 1952.

290 **"The objection is sustained"**: *Fl. v. Irvin*, p. 57.

290 **"I'm here at the wish of the government"**: Juan Williams interview with Thurgood Marshall, http://www.thurgoodmarshall.com/interviews/early_naacp.htm. This scene between Marshall and J. J. Elliott is derived from Williams's interview with Marshall about his early NAACP work.

291 **"our greatest civil rights lawyer"**: *Collier's*, February 23, 1952.

291 **"So go toward them"**: Williams interview with Marshall.

291 **"It shocked me"**: FOHP, Williams.

292 **"a heavy woman in a dark dress":** *New York Daily Compass*, February 12, 1952.

292 **"Well, you got the case":** Williams interview with Marshall.

292 **"clearly implied that":** Greenberg, *Crusaders in the Courts*, p. 144.

292 **"Well," he said:** Williams interview with Marshall.

293 **"Won't say it on myself":** Greenberg, *Crusaders in the Courts*, p. 144.

293 **"who wouldn't confess":** Ibid.

293 **"I'll take a life sentence":** *New York Daily Compass*, February 17, 1952.

294 **shout "Nigger!" over and over:** *Life*, September 20, 1948.

294 **"see it when it was made up":** *Chicago Defender*, February 23, 1952.

294 **"Well, this Deputy Sheriff":** *Fl. v. Irvin*, p. 144.

295 **Marshall had also learned:** Byrd to Carter, LDF, Ocotber 21, 1951.

295 **"best colored man on the panel":** *Chicago Defender*, February 23, 1952.

295 **"If he says the boy is good":** Ibid.

295 **"An ingenious man":** Ibid.

296 **"remarkable," according to one reporter:** *New York Daily Compass*, February 13, 1952.

296 **"hit quite a few licks":** *Fl. v. Irvin*, p. 295.

296 **"Dressed for a party":** Greenberg, *Crusaders in the Courts*, p. 145.

296 **"coral-colored cardigan sweater":** *New York Daily Compass*, February 13, 1952.

297 **"Why would a 'rape victim' strut":** *Crisis*, Vol. 56, October 1949.

297 **"bone-poor":** *New York Daily Compass*, February 13, 1952.

297 **"has the bent carriage":** Ibid.

297 **"which often could not be heard":** Ibid.

297 **"Grab the lady":** *Fl. v. Irvin*, p. 302.

298 **"That's all, brother":** *New York Daily Compass*, February 13, 1952.

298 **"One of them said":** *Fl. v. Irvin*, p. 305.

299 **"*The nigger Shepherd . . .*":** FOHP, Williams.

299 **"Now, Norma, this is":** *FL. vs. Irvin*, p. 310.

299 **"You had a farmer jury":** FHW Papers, Chesley.

300 **"What did you tell him?":** *Fl. v. Irvin*, p. 321.

300 **"You watch her on the witness stand":** *New York Daily Compass*, February 13, 1952.

300 **"gum-chewing husky":** Ibid.

301 **"protecting the integrity":** *Fl. v. Irvin*, p. 339.

301 **"Now, Mr. Yates," Hunter began:** Ibid., p. 341.

302 **"emission of seed"**: Ibid., p. 494.

302 **"the old common Florida way"**: Ibid., p. 513.

302 **"Now, Mr. Yates, is it true"**: Ibid., p. 372.

## Chapter 20: A Genius Here Before Us

303 **"a spread collar"**: *New York Daily Compass*, February 14, 1952.

303 **Howard would break his share of vows:** Author interview with Kim Howard, April 12, 2011.

304 **"Just tell what happened"**: *Fl. v. Irvin*, p. 374.

304 **"Why did you rape"**: MM 44-156, FBI.

305 **"Did you tell them"**: *Fl. v. Irvin*, p. 376.

305 **They had been classmates:** Leesburg High School Yearbook, 1947.

305 **"Well, I asked her"**: *Fl. v. Irvin*, p. 376.

305 **"as smooth as Willie is bucolic"**: *New York Daily Compass*, February 14, 1952.

306 **The Groveland case was never mentioned:** Author interview with Kim Howard, April 12, 1952.

306 **"My mother was a saint"**: Ibid.

306-7 **"The absence of medical proof"**: *New York Daily Compass*, February 17, 1952.

307 **"We need you very much"**: S. Ralph Harlow to Lawrence Burtoft, LDF, January 15, 1952.

307 **"hit over the head"**: *Fl. v. Irvin*, p. 388.

308 **"at least one Ku Klux Klan member"**: *New York Daily Compass*, February 17, 1952.

309 **"genuine fear of reprisals"**: Caxton Doggett to Greenberg, LDF, January 31, 1952.

309 **"wanted him to let his conscience"**: Ibid.

309 **"Now, as a matter of fact"**: *Fl. v. Irvin*, p. 392.

310 **"reported to a man"**: MM 44-156, FBI.

310 **citing the "confidential nature"**: FBI 44-2722-24.

310 **"To tell what I knew"**: Corsair, *The Groveland Four*, p. 318.

310 **"The only chance these Negroes had"**: *Shepherd v. Florida*, 341 U.S. 50 (1951).

312 **"Just a minute"**: *Fl. v. Irvin*, p. 418.

313 **"cracking wise to his friends"**: *New York Daily Compass*, February 14, 1952.

313-14 **"stop the prosecutor"**: Ibid.

314 **"After carefully studying"**: *Fl. v. Irvin*, p. 437.

314 **"Then it is your contention":** Ibid., p. 438.

314 **"ridiculed the testimony":** Greenberg, *Crusaders in the Courts*, p. 146.

314 **"Then, as a matter of fact":** *Fl. v. Irvin*, p. 440.

315 **"chew anything substantial":** Greenberg, *Crusaders in the Courts*, p. 147.

315 **"We do not insist on it":** *Fl. v. Irvin*, p. 446.

316 **"pretty well acquainted":** Ibid., p. 452.

316 **"Gentlemen," he told the jury:** Ibid., p. 464.

316 **"crazy" Herman Bennett:** Ibid., p. 473.

316 **"Now, gentlemen":** Ibid., p. 474.

316 **"They're probably wondering":** *New York Daily Compass*, February 17, 1952.

317 **"in a difficult spot":** Ibid.

317 **"as if they never knew":** *New York Daily Compass*, February 15, 1952.

317 **"Gentlemen of the jury, Marshall began":** *Fl. v. Irvin*, p. 477.

317 **"drumming his fingers":** *New York Daily Compass*, February 15, 1952.

317 **"Now, in cases of this type":** *Fl. v. Irvin*, p. 477.

319 **"patiently, politely":** *New York Daily Compass*, February 15, 1952.

319 **"With Marshall, you really got the impression":** E. Barrett Prettyman, Jr., interview, *Thurgood Marshall: Justice for All*, A&E Biography, 2005.

319 **"best evidence we could find":** *Fl. v. Irvin*, p. 485.

320 **"Damn, that nigger was good":** Greenberg, *Crusaders in the Courts*, p. 157.


## Chapter 21: The Colored Way

321 **"Boy, that's a great man":** FHW Papers, Chesley.

321 **quite "buddy-buddy":** Ibid.

321 **"a terrible racist":** Ibid.

322 **"conned into believing":** Ibid.

322 **"because of its possible good effects":** "Musings," *Mount Dora Topic*, undated clipping. FHW Papers.

322 **"Stay away from that man":** FHW Papers, Chesley.

323 **"We don't say that she was not raped":** *Fl. v. Irvin*, p. 490.

324 **"Gentlemen, although":** Ibid., 505.

325 **"whooped and hollered":** *New York Daily Compass*, February 15, 1952.

325 **"Now, gentlemen, she sat there":** *Fl. v. Irvin*, p. 485.

326–27 **"open up until the case went to the jury":** *New York Post*, February 19. 1952.

327 **"I didn't do it"**: Ibid.

327 **"Judge Futch, I'm quite serious"**: Williams interview with Marshall.

327 **"rigidly scrutinized"**: Corsair, *The Groveland Four*, p. 338.

328 **"How long's the jury"**: Williams interview with Marshall.

329 **"Now when the jury gives its verdict"**: Ibid.

329 **"We the jury find"**: *New York Daily Compass*, February 15, 1952.

329 **"Like a man stunned"**: Ibid.

329 **"Don't you know that"**: *Fl. v. Irvin*, p. 516.

329 the word *criminal*, not *colored*: *New York Daily Compass*, February 15, 1952.

329 **"the reporter who was faithful"**: Ibid.

329 **"Could this be another"**: *New York Daily Compass*, February 17, 1952.

330 **"Say, is that Carter"**: Ibid.

330 **"She had the most impressive face"**: Williams interview with Marshall.

330 **"Lawyer, don't you let"**: Tushnet, *Thurgood Marshall*, p. 455. Also Williams interview with Marshall.

330 **"Don't worry, honey"**: *Chicago Defender*, February 23, 1952.

330 **"Get away," Reese said:** FHW Papers, Chesley.

## Chapter 22: A Place in the Sun

331 **"I don't see how"**: *Baltimore Afro-American*, February 23, 1952.

332 **"All-White Jury"**: *New York Times*, February 15, 1952.

332 praised the **"tranquillity"**: *Ocala Star Banner*, February 15, 1952.

332 **"Brutal and cynical"**: *Daily Worker*, February 28, 1952.

332 **"I'm not sorry,"**: *New York Post*, February 19, 1952.

334 **"If you show your black"**: Kluger, *Simple Justice*, p. 536.

334 **"We could only move"**: COHP, Marshall.

334 Marshall's **"charisma"**: Greenberg, *Crusaders in the Courts*, p. 153.

334 **"fund-raising and organizing potential"**: Ibid., p. 180.

335 **"black people of no great means"**: Ibid.

335 **"He's aged so"**: *Collier's*, February 23, 1952.

335 **"beyond the limits of the human anatomy"**: Kluger, *Simple Justice*, p. 563.

335 Marshall flashed the secret: Greenberg, *Crusaders in the Courts*, p. 170.

336 **"Why don't we take"**: Franklin, *Mirror to America*, p. 157.

337 **"present a case so persuasive"**: Ibid., p. 158.

**337** **"I'm going to be a good butler":** COHP, Marshall.

**337** **"It deserves a place":** Kluger, *Simple Justice*, p. 648.

**337** **"I realized there wasn't":** "Justice Thurgood Marshall," Ken Gormley, *ABA Journal*, June 1992.

**339** **"separate educational facilities":** *Brown v Board of Education*, 347 U.S. 483 (1954).

**339** **"Thurgood was very discreet":** Williams, *Thurgood Marshall*, p. 231.

**340** **"You know, he favors":** "Look At Your Own Child," *Time*, December 13, 1954. Also FHW Papers, Chesley; Berry, *Almost White*, p. 179.

**340** **"Black Angus cattle":** *Daytona Beach Morning Journal*, March 14, 1963.

**340** **"The sheriff is the law here":** *St. Petersburg Times*, October 16, 1955.

**340** **"If the children never":** Berry, *Almost White*, p. 179.

**340** **"people of mixed":** McCall, *Willis V. McCall, Sheriff of Lake County*, p. 70.

**341** **"right to an education":** Bill Maxwell, "Jim Crow Conflict Clouded the Point," *St. Petersburg Times*, February 14, 2001.

**341** **"that if they weren't out by that night":** FHW Papers, Chesley.

**341** **"a man who knows how":** *St. Petersburg Times*, November 7, 1954.

**341** **"I for one, am going to do all I can":** Green, *Before His Time*, p. 196.

**341** **Johns responded by telling reporters:** *Ocala Star Banner*, October 13, 1954.

**341** **"hog and hominy" segregationist:** *New York Times*, May 27, 1956.

**342** **"till the last tick":** *Palm Beach Post*, November 4, 1954.

**342** **"How did you find me?":** Williams, *Thurgood Marshall*, p. 148.

**343** **"He had become cadaverous":** Greenberg, *Crusaders in the Courts*, p. 202.

**343** **"morose and unhappy":** COHP, Greenberg.

**343** **"three sturdy legs":** *Time*, December 19, 1955.

**344** **"ward-heeling, back scratching":** *St. Petersburg Times*, January 5, 1955.

**344** **"were never convinced":** *St. Petersburg Times*, February 21, 1954.

**344** **"get rid of this case":** Corsair, *The Groveland Four*, p. 348.

**344** **In November 1951, only:** Byrd to Marshall, LDF, November 29, 1951.

**344** **"caused him to plot this killing":** Ibid.

**344–45** **"trying to drag Hunter into this killing":** Marshall to Byrd, LDF, November 30, 1951.

**345** **"house might catch fire":** *St. Petersburg Times*, October 19, 1955.

**345** **"out of control":** FHW Papers, Chesley.

**345** **"Much as I hate it":** *St. Petersburg Times*, October 19, 1955.

345 **"The Lord be praised":** Ibid.

345 **"I have no comment":** Ibid.

345 **"night-riding terrorists":** *St. Petersburg Times*, November 13, 1955.

345 **"didn't want to go to school":** *Evening Independent*, December 14, 1962.

346 **"I've got more justice":** *St. Petersburg Times*, November 13, 1955.

346 **The former prosecutor also:** *St. Petersburg Times*, November 14, 1955.

346 **"In my book, they're":** Berry, *Almost White*, p. 182.

346 **"due chiefly to the influence":** FHW Papers, Chesley.

346 **countless "Florida selling" trips:** *Time*, December 19, 1955.

346 **"Is there Negro Blood":** *Ebony*, November 1975.

347 **There are enough staid people:** Gilbert Geis, "A Quarter of a Century for 'Social Justice,'" *Social Justice*, Vol. 26, No. 2 (76), Summer, 1999.

347 **"desperate situation":** Committee of 100 reports, NAACP.

348 **"could have nailed this case down":** Florida State Archives, LeRoy Collins Papers.

348 **"in its best light":** Ibid.

348 **"substantial evidence":** Campbell to Phillips, September 13, 1949, 144-18-117, FBI.

348 **"Since I am your personal friend":** Florida State Archives, Collins.

349 **"In recognizing the humanity":** *Furman v. Georgia*, 408 U.S. 238 (1972).

349 **"Florida's gutter of shame":** *Ocala Star Banner*, September 2, 1987.

349 **"I realized we had to change":** *New York Times*, March 13, 1991.

349 **"offer to the people of the world":** LeRoy Collins, inaugural speech from his den, Florida State Archives, http://www.floridamemory.com/items/show/232461.

349 **"Confess to the rape":** *St. Petersburg Times*, December 16, 1955.

350 **"a demonstration of senility":** Corsair, *The Groveland Four*, p. 352.

351 **It had come to Collins:** *St. Petersburg Times*, February 6, 1956.

## Epilogue

353 **"The State," Governor LeRoy Collins said:** *St. Petersburg Times*, December 16, 1952.

354 **"the victim of a gross miscarriage":** Ibid.

354 **"it took far more political courage":** *Miami News*, February 25, 1956.

354 **"I want you to know":** Corsair, *The Groveland Four*, p. 361.

354 **"Communist pressure tactics":** *St. Petersburg Times*, March 30, 1956.

354 **"the innocent victim":** Ibid.

**355** **"smearing of the good people":** *Sarasota Herald Tribune*, May 5, 1956.

**355** **"obtaining and circulating a petition":** *St. Petersburg Times*, May 5, 1956.

**355** **"when feelings ran high":** *St. Petersburg Times*, September 24, 1955.

**355** **"You're the one who":** *Miami News*, February 23, 1956.

**356** **In March 1960 Deputy James Yates:** *Ocala Star-Banner*, December 21, 1962.

**357** **"I never hurt anyone":** Flores, *Justice Gone Wrong*, p. 187.

**357** **The FBI ultimately laid responsibility:** Moore Report, p. 331.

**357** **"for the 'Tranquility of the South'":** Ibid., p. 123.

**358** **a "model life":** *Daytona Beach Morning Journal*, November 18, 1957.

**358** **"I would put Frank there":** Marshall to Johnson, LBJ tapes.

**358** **"This man is a":** FOHP, Williams.

**359** **Mabel Norris Chesley was suspicious:** FHW Papers, Chesley.

**359** **Ku Klux Klan leader:** *Brandenburg v. Ohio*, 395 U.S. 444 (1969).

**360** **"There is very little truth":** Marshall's speech, 1966 White House conference on civil rights, *Thurgood Marshall: Justice for All*, A&E Biography, 2005.

**360** **Governor LeRoy Collins had done:** Collins later became known as "Liberal LeRoy" after he arrived in Selma, Alabama (dispatched by President Johnson), on March 9, 1965, and successfully negotiated a compromise with police so that Martin Luther King Jr., and the 2,500 marchers could cross the Edmund Pettus Bridge without the police brutality and bloodshed that had marred the first attempt at a Selma-to-Montgomery march two days earlier.

**360** **"did the most immediate good":** Tushnet, *Thurgood Marshall*, p. 455.

**360** **"the sonofabitch":** Williams interview with Marshall.

**361** **My dear Mr. Justice:** Marshall Papers, LOC.

# SELECTED BIBLIOGRAPHY

Aberjhani and S. L. West. *Encyclopedia of the Harlem Renaissance*. New York: Facts on File, 2003.

Andrews, M., and J. Robison. *Flashbacks: The Story of Central Florida's Past*. Orlando, FL: The Orlando Sentinel, 1995.

Arsenault, R. *Freedom Riders: 1961 and the Struggle for Racial Justice*. New York: Oxford University Press, 2006.

Ball, H. *A Defiant Life: Thurgood Marshall and the Persistence of Racism in America*. New York: Crown Publishers, 1998.

———. " 'Thurgood's Coming': Tale of a Hero Lawyer." *Jackson Free Press*, May 13, 2004.

Barnes, J. *Florida's Hurricane History*. Chapel Hill: The University of North Carolina Press, 2007.

Bedau, H. A., C. E. Putnam, and M. L. Radelet. *In Spite of Innocence: The Ordeal of 400 Americans Wrongly Convicted by Crimes Punishable by Death*. Boston: Northeastern University Press, 1992.

Berg, M. *"The Ticket to Freedom": The NAACP and the Struggle for Black Political Integration*. Gainesville: University Press of Florida, 2005.

Berry, B. *Almost White*. London: Collier-Macmillan, 1969.

Black, Elizabeth, and Hugo L. Black. *Mr. Justice and Mrs. Black: The Memoirs of Hugo L. Black and Elizabeth Black*. New York: Random House, 1986.

Blackmon, D. A. *Slavery by Another Name: The Re-Enslavement of Black Americans from the Civil War to World War II*. New York: Anchor Books, 2008.

Bloodsworth, D. *Images of America: Groveland*. Charleston, SC: Arcadia Publishing, 2009.

Carson, C., et al. *Reporting Civil Rights, Part One: American Journalism 1941–1963 (Library of America)*. New York: Library of America, 2003.

Cash, W. J. *The Mind of the South*. New York: Vintage/Random House, 1991.

Chalmers, A. K. *They Shall Be Free*. New York: Doubleday, 1951.

Clark, H. R., and M. D. Davis. *Thurgood Marshall: Warrior at the Bar, Rebel on the Bench.* New York: Birch Lane Press, 1992.

Clark, K. B. *Toward Humanity and Justice: The Writings of Kenneth B. Clark, Scholar of the 1954* Brown v. Board of Education *Decision.* Westport, CT: Praeger Publishers, 2004.

Corsair, G. *The Groveland Four: The Sad Saga of a Legal Lynching.* Bloomington, IN: AuthorHouse, 2004.

Dance, D. C. *From My People: 400 years of African American Folklore.* New York: W.W. Norton, 2002.

Dickerson, J. W. *Remembering Orlando: Tales from Elvis to Disney.* Charleston, SC: The History Press, 2006.

Dray, P. *At the Hands of Persons Unknown: The Lynching of Black America.* New York: Modern Library, 2003.

DuBois, W. E. B. "The Talented Tenth," in B. T. Washington et al., *The Negro Problem.* Charleston, SC: CreateSpace, 2008.

Fairclough, A. *Race & Democracy: The Civil Rights Struggle in Louisiana 1915–1972.* Athens: University of Georgia Press, 1999.

Flores, I. M. *Justice Gone Wrong: A Sheriff's Power of Fear.* New York: iUniverse, 2009.

Franklin, J. H. *Mirror to America: The Autobiography of John Hope Franklin.* New York: Farrar, Straus and Giroux, 2005.

Gallen, D., and R. Goldman. *Thurgood Marshall: Justice for All.* New York: Carroll and Graf Publishers, 1993.

Green, B. *Before His Time: The Untold Story of Harry T. Moore, America's First Civil Rights Martyr.* Gainesville: University Press of Florida, 2005.

Green, V. H. *The Negro Motorist Green Book: An International Travel Guide.* New York: Victor H. Green, 1949.

Greenberg, J. *Crusaders in the Courts: How a Dedicated Band of Lawyers Fought for the Civil Rights Revolution.* New York: Basic Books, 1994.

Hahamovitch, C. *The Fruits of Their Labor: Atlantic Coast Farmworkers and the Making of Migrant Poverty, 1870–1945.* Chapel Hill: University of North Carolina Press, 1997.

Hauke, K. A. *Ted Poston: Pioneer American Journalist.* Athens: University of Georgia Press, 1998.

Hekkanen, E., and E. Roy. *Good Ol' Boy: Willis V. McCall.* Vancouver, BC: New Orphic Publishers, 1999.

Hobbs, Tameka Bradley. "Hitler Is Here: Lynching in Florida During the Era of World War II." Dissertation, Florida State University, Department of History, 2004.

Hurston, Z. N. *Dust Tracks on a Road: An Autobiography.* New York: HarperPerennial, 2006.

———. *Mules and Men.* New York: HarperPerennial, 2008.

———. *Their Eyes Were Watching God: A Novel.* New York: HarperPerennial, 2006.

Ikard, R. W. *No More Social Lynchings.* Franklin, TN: Hillsboro Press, 1997.

Jackson, K. T., and D. Dunbar. *Empire City: New York Through the Centuries.* New York: Columbia University Press, 2002.

James, R., Jr. *Root and Branch: Charles Hamilton Houston, Thurgood Marshall, and the Struggle to End Segregation.* New York: Bloomsbury Press, 2010.

Janken, K. R. *Walter White: Mr. NAACP.* Chapel Hill, NC: University of North Carolina Press, 2006.

Jonas, G. *Freedom's Sword: The NAACP and the Struggle Against Racism in America, 1909–1969.* New York: Routledge, 2005.

Jordan, V. E., Jr. *Make It Plain: Standing Up and Speaking Out.* New York: Public Affairs, 2008.

————. *Vernon Can Read! A Memoir.* New York: Basic Civitas Books, 2001.

Kennedy, S. *The Klan Unmasked.* Tuscaloosa: University of Alabama Press, 1990.

————. *Southern Exposure.* Kila, MT: Kessinger Publishing, 2007.

Kluger, R. *Simple Justice: The History of* Brown v. Board of Education *and Black America's Struggle for Equality.* New York: Vintage Books, 2004.

Lavergne, G. M. *Before Brown: Heman Marion Sweatt, Thurgood Marshall, and the Long Road to Justice.* Austin: University of Texas Press, 2010.

Lawson, S. F. *To Secure These Rights: The Report of President Harry S. Truman's Committee on Civil Rights.* New York: Bedford/St. Martin's, 2003.

Lewis, D. L, ed. *The Portable Harlem Renaissance Reader.* New York: Penguin Books, 1995.

Long, M. G. *Marshalling Justice: The Early Civil Rights Letters of Thurgood Marshall.* New York: Amistad, 2011.

Martin, W. E., Jr. Brown v. Board of Education: *A Brief History with Documents.* New York: Bedford/St. Martin's, 1998.

McCall, W. V. *Willis V. McCall, Sheriff of Lake County: An Autobiography.* Umatilla, FL: Willis V. McCall, 1988.

McCarthy, S. C. *Lay That Trumpet into Our Hands.* New York: Bantam Books, 2003.

McNeil, G. R. *Groundwork: Charles Hamilton Houston and the Struggle for Civil Rights.* Philadelphia: University of Pennsylvania Press, 1983.

Miller, C. C. *Roy Wilkins: Leader of the NAACP.* Greensboro, NC: Morgan Reynolds Publishing, 2005.

Minor, R. *Lynching and Frame-Up in Tennessee.* New York: New Century Publishers, 1946.

Motley, C. B. *Equal Justice Under Law: An Autobiography.* New York: Farrar, Straus and Giroux, 1998.

National Association for the Advancement of Colored People. *NAACP: Celebrating a Century, 100 Years in Pictures.* Layton, UT: Gibbs Smith, 2009.

Newton, M. *The Invisible Empire: The Ku Klux Klan in Florida.* Gainesville: University Press of Florida, 2001.

————. *The Ku Klux Klan: History, Organization, Language, Influence, and Activities of America's Most Secret Society.* Jefferson, NC: McFarland & Company, 2007.

Nieman, D. G. "Black Southerners and the Law, 1865–1900," in A. Hornsby, Jr., *African Americans in the Post-Emancipation South.* Lanham, MD: University Press of America, 2010.

O'Brien, G. W. *The Color of the Law: Race, Violence, and Justice in the Post–World War II South.* Chapel Hill: The University of North Carolina Press, 1999.

O'Reilly, K. *Black Americans: The FBI Files.* New York: Carroll and Graf Publishers, 1994.

Rampersad, A. *The Life of Langston Hughes, Volume I: 1902–1941, I, Too, Sing America.* New York: Oxford University Press, 2002.

Rise, E. W. *The Martinsville Seven: Race, Rape, and Capital Punishment.* Charlottesville: The University Press of Virginia, 1995.

Robeson, P., Jr. *The Undiscovered Paul Robeson: Quest for Freedom, 1939–1976.* Hoboken, NJ: Wiley, 2010.

Robinson, Timothy Brandt. "Law and Order, by Any Means Necessary: The Life and Times of Willis V. McCall, Sheriff of Lake County, Florida." Master's Thesis, Florida State University, 1997.

Rowan, C. T. *Dream Makers, Dream Breakers: The World of Justice Thurgood Marshall.* New York: Welcome Rain, 1993.

Saunders, R. W., Sr. *Bridging the Gap: Continuing the Florida NAACP Legacy of Harry T. Moore.* Tampa, FL: University of Tampa Press, 2000.

Sullivan, P. *Lift Every Voice: The NAACP and the Making of the Civil Rights Movement*. New York: The New Press, 2009.

Tushnet, M. V. *Making Civil Rights Law: Thurgood Marshall and the Supreme Court, 1936–1961*. New York: Oxford University Press, 1994.

———. *Making Constitutional Law: Thurgood Marshall and the Supreme Court, 1961–1991*. New York: Oxford University Press, 1997.

———. *The NAACP's Legal Strategy Against Segregated Education, 1925–1950*. Chapel Hill: The University of North Carolina Press, 1987.

———. ed. *Thurgood Marshall: His Speeches, Writings, Arguments, Opinions, and Reminiscences*. Chicago: Lawrence Hill Books, 2001.

Wald, E. *Josh White: Society Blues*. New York: Routledge, 2002.

Wexler, L. *Fire in a Canebrake: The Last Mass Lynching in America*. New York: Scribner, 2003.

White, W. *A Man Called White: The Autobiography of Walter White*. Bloomington: Indiana University Press, 1970.

Wilkerson, I. *The Warmth of Other Suns: The Epic Story of America's Great Migration*. New York: Random House, 2010.

Williams, J. *Thurgood Marshall: American Revolutionary*. New York: Times Books, 1998.

Wilson, S. K. *Meet Me at the Theresa: The Story of Harlem's Most Famous Hotel*. New York: Atria Books, 2004.

Wormser, R. *The Rise and Fall of Jim Crow: The African-American Struggle Against Discrimination, 1865–1954*. London: Franklin Watts, 1999.

# | INDEX |

*Italicized numbers refer to photographic illustrations*

## | ABOUT THE AUTHOR |

Gilbert King has written about U.S. Supreme Court history and capital punishment for the *New York Times* and the *Washington Post,* and is a featured contributor to *Smithsonian* magazine's history blog, *Past Imperfect.* He is the author of *The Execution of Willie Francis: Race, Murder, and the Search for Justice in the American South.* He lives in New York City with his wife and two daughters.

## About the author

## About the book

## Read on

Insights,
Interviews
& More . . .

# A Conversation with Gilbert King

**Where does the title, Devil in the Grove come from?**

I'd been trying to come up with something for a very long time. This book was untitled for several years while I was researching and writing it. I liked what Hampton Sides did with his book about the assassination of Martin Luther King, Jr., *Hellhound on His Trail*. It was taken from an old Mississippi blues song by Robert Johnson, *Hellhound on My Trail*. I'm embarrassed to admit how much time I spent listening to classic blues music and African-American folk songs, hoping to find something "grove-oriented" that I liked. I listened to countless Works Progress Administration recordings made by Zora Neale Hurston and Stetson Kennedy during the 1930s, where they traveled the backroads of Florida, recording work songs sung on chain gangs, turpentine camps, and citrus groves. Time well-spent, but I never did find a title for the book.

I did manage to find the phrase, "beneath a ruthless sun" from a James Weldon Johnson poem, *Fifty Years*, which describes the backbreaking work still being done by blacks in the fields on the occasion of the fiftieth anniversary of the signing of the Emancipation Proclamation. But *Beneath a Ruthless Sun*, while nice, didn't really speak to the danger and violence in my book, and we wanted something stronger. Then, I began to think of words that fit the story—words like "devil, blood, fire, grove, death," etc. *Devil in the Grove* popped up, and it sounded like it could be an old blues song, so we went with it.

### Is Willis McCall the "Devil" in the Grove?

Believe it or not, that really didn't occur to me at the time. Certainly, it's an easy connection to make, especially with Sheriff McCall appearing on the cover. But I always thought of the "Devil" as something more abstract, like the forces of oppression and the legalized white supremacy that forms the backdrop for this story.

### You spent nearly four years working on this book. Is there anything you wish you'd done differently?

Not differently. I'm very pleased with the way the story unfolds on these pages. I think it was important for readers to understand the historical context of what was happening in the South after World War II, but I also wanted to tell that story in a suspenseful way. I really had a lot to work with in that regard. I do wish that I had been able to speak with Norma Padgett in much greater depth. I did meet her when I showed up at her home in the South, but she was not willing to discuss the case with me. The message she gave me was, "let sleeping dogs lie."

The more I looked into this story, the more I came to believe that Norma Padgett was also a victim of the "Devil in the Grove." Certainly not to the extent of those men and women who were killed, and the people who lost their homes at the hands of the Ku Klux Klan in the aftermath of her rape allegations. But a seventeen year-old girl could never have caused all of this violence and death on her own. Had I been able to talk to her, not necessarily about the case, but about her life in Bay Lake, I think I would have been able to create a richer and perhaps more sympathetic figure. Instead, I mostly had to rely on her court testimony and statements to the FBI, as well as the statements of those close to her at the time. ▶

**A Conversation with Gilbert King** *(continued)*

*You were also granted access to the NAACP's Legal Defense Fund files, which have not been viewed by many historians or journalists.*

Yes, I was very fortunate in that regard. I think because the scope of my request was fairly narrow, and I wasn't seeking boxes and boxes of files, the LDF eventually vetted the materials and allowed me to see them. I can't tell you how exciting it was for me to read the minutes from legal strategy meetings on the Groveland case, where Marshall and his staff were trying to develop a defense, as well as a continuing public relations campaign to bring attention to events in Lake County. It was a researcher's dream come true—like being a fly on a conference room wall for these essential conversations. I was continually impressed at the high ethical standards that Marshall had insisted on. It was obvious that he knew the organization could not afford to cut any corners or do anything morally questionable.

I have since spoken at LDF conferences and at their offices, and to see brilliant young lawyers like Debo Adegbile, Jeffrey Robinson, Christina Swarns, and Elise Boddie continuing in the tradition of the LDF pioneers of the pre–Civil Rights era is inspiring. I was also pleased to see that Thurgood Marshall's desk is still at the LDF's downtown Manhattan offices, along with many other historical photographs and documents.

*Can you talk about your writing process, and how you transition from research to the actual writing of the book? You've done a great deal of research on this case, but critics have described* Devil in the Grove *as a "thriller" that "reads more like a Southern Gothic novel than a work of history."*

I love the groundwork. In order for me to spend years on a story, I have to sort of trick myself into believing that I'm a detective attempting to solve a mysterious criminal case from the past. For me to read every single document and explore every possible lead requires a certain level of obsession, so I don't go into my research casually!

But it's also important to understand that, while detail is important, my ultimate responsibility is to write a story that keeps readers turning the pages. Because I was able to acquire so many primary sources, like the unredacted FBI files, the LDF files, and even audio recordings of interrogations, I had an abundance of quotes that I was able to use as dialogue in some very chilling scenes. Once I actually began writing, I had these larger-than-life characters like Sheriff Willis McCall and Thurgood Marshall to work with, and I was able to present the story using their actual words.

At one point, I quickly sketched an outline of the story and it became very obvious to me that there were twists and turns in this case that would seem unbelievable if they appeared in a novel. Most notably, the scene when Sheriff McCall arrives at Raiford to bring Walter Irvin and Samuel Shepherd back to Lake County for the retrial, and he ends up shooting them in an alleged escape attempt. That Irvin survived and was able to recount his thoughts and observations at the time McCall was trying to kill him on that dark night on the side of a quiet road, definitely adds to the "thriller" or "Gothic" aspect of the book. And there were quite a few dramatic scenes like this in the story, where those involved gave detailed interviews to FBI field agents. The most fascinating ones were those given off-the-record, usually by law enforcement agents who provided signed statements, but then told FBI agents "what really happened," even though they were refusing to include that information in their statements. Those off-the-record conversations are documented in the FBI reports, and they helped accentuate the mystery and intrigue in *Devil in the Grove*. ∾

# The Last Word . . .

IN MY PREVIOUS BOOK, *The Execution of Willie Francis*, I took careful pride in selecting what I thought was the perfect epigraph—a brief passage from Robert Penn Warren's classic American novel, *All the King's Men*. Aside from the Louisiana setting, it touched on all of the elements of the Willie Francis story—mystery, truth, shame, and historical research that gives voice to the dead. Above all, Warren's words are poetry and more beautiful than anything I could write, which is why and how writers often select epigraphs. I liked Robert Penn Warren's words so much that I ended up paying for permission to publish them, since I wanted to include more than just a few lines. I'd show you here, but it would cost me again!

Once I started work on *Devil in the Grove*, I was a bit disappointed that in all of my research, nothing had jumped out at me the way Warren's passage had. Yet I was confident something would eventually appear. Then, something strange happened. In February of 2012, the first hardcovers of *Devil in the Grove* arrived at my house. I cracked one open and immediately noticed the lack of an epigraph in the first few pages. I was so busy with last minute edits on the book that I simply forgot!

I didn't feel too bad about it, as nothing had materialized. But recently, I came across a passage written in the early twentieth century by John Jay Chapman, in his essay, *The Negro Problem*. I'd never seen it before, and I thought it was most appropriate for the story in these pages. So here's my epigraph for *Devil in the Grove*, tucked away in the postscript of the paperback edition. Better late than never.

*There is a law governing the meeting of the races. When a powerful race meets a helpless race, two things happen. First, there is a carnival of crime. Cruelty and*

*oppression take place: some men in each*
*race become hard-hearted. But the reverse*
*also happens thereafter; goodness and*
*mercy are developed; certain men become*
*saints and heroes.*

—John Jay Chapman,
*The Negro Problem*, 1915

In thinking about this P.S. section,
I decided I wanted to do something different.
Secretly, I had hoped, now that the book had
been published, that Norma Padgett might
want to break her silence on the case and
agree to an interview. I gave that one more
try, to no avail.

Then, something else came to me. Like
most writers, (if they are lucky) I heard from
quite a few people who wrote to tell me that
they were moved by *Devil in the Grove*. One
afternoon in March of 2012, I received an
email from David Dow, the author, professor
at the University of Houston Law Center, and
a renowned defender of death row inmates.
Harper had sent him a copy of my book, and
he was sitting by the phone, he said, waiting for
the Supreme Court to call to tell him whether
or not his client, Keith Thurmond, would be
executed later that day.

Most times, David said, he just "twiddles
his thumbs," because there's nothing left to
do, and it's hard to concentrate on anything
else. But on that particular afternoon, he
picked up *Devil in the Grove*, figuring he'd
just flip through it while he waited for the
call. Instead, he started reading and couldn't
stop. He said he was probably going to be up
very late with the book. He just wanted to let
me know that, and he thanked me for telling
the story.

His compliments passed right over my
head. Immediately, I did a search on Keith
Thurmond, who was within hours of his
death by lethal injection. It was my first real
connection, however small, to a death penalty
case that wasn't a part of history. I wrote ▶

back to David and told him that I hoped he was up very late, but only because the Supreme Court had called with news of a stay and prison guards were leading his client back to his cell.

That would not be the case. Thurmond was strapped to a gurney later that afternoon of March 7, 2012 in Huntsville, Texas, in "the busiest death chamber in the industrialized West."

"I didn't kill my wife . . . I swear to God I didn't kill her," he said, and eleven minutes later, at 6:22 pm, Thurmond was pronounced dead.

Following the drama online was an odd and grim experience. Unable to concentrate on anything else, I kept clicking the refresh arrow on my screen, awaiting updates from Texas as the clock ticked down to that fatal hour. I knew nothing of Thurmond's case until that day. Just that he was a fifty-two year-old white mechanic, accused and convicted of killing his wife and her boyfriend more than ten years ago. He lost his federal appeal when a court-appointed attorney missed a filing deadline, and Dow finally entered the case, arguing that Thurmond's earlier appeals were "grossly deficient."

Thurmond's execution was a dark reminder that even today, without competent representation, justice can be mercilessly uneven in America. It also reminded me that the work of dedicated attorneys like David Dow, as well as the brilliant and tireless lawyers at the Legal Defense and Education Fund, is no less important today than it was when Thurgood Marshall, Jack Greenberg, Franklin Williams, and the other LDF pioneers were defending innocent men in capital cases.

In letters and email, I also heard from young law students who were moved by the stories of Marshall and the LDF, and inspired to practice civil rights law upon graduation. They wanted me to know that there were still important battles to be won, and that the civil rights struggle hadn't ended with the election of Barack Obama. I heard from the African-American mother of a fifteen-year-old son who had just moved to Lake County, Florida from Chicago. She was very concerned about the slaying of Trayvon Martin, and since their new home wasn't far from Sanford, Florida, (where Martin was fatally shot) she wanted her son to read the book so that he had some sense of the area's history. She wanted him to know that in 2012, as a young black man in America, he still had to be careful and smart.

There were, however, two letters that came to me—letters that left me breathless. Both writers had connections to Lake County and to people in the book, and they do not require much in the way of introduction. The letters are extraordinarily descriptive and well-written, and in spite of the pain they evoke, they are also immeasurably profound and optimistic. I could not be more grateful to both authors, Lawrence King and Anne Pattillo Kail, for sharing their memories and their very personal stories.

Sometimes, in the form of an epigraph, a book may begin with the meaningful words of writers like Robert Penn Warren and John Jay Chapman. And sometimes, an author is contented to give others the last words as well.

April 11, 2012
Dear Mr. King:

I was born in 1962 at the clinic at Teresa Holland in Leesburg, Florida, delivered by Dr. Geoffrey Binneveld, grew up in Leesburg and Okahumpka, and attended Leesburg High School. I spent my formative years all over Groveland, Mascotte, Eustis, Umatilla, Tavares, Fruitland Park—even Stuckey Still. I remember fondly drinking fountain Cokes at Carney's Drug Store on West Main Street in Leesburg. I remember all too well the sweet smell of concentrate being packed at the Minute Maid plant on East Main Street. I knew Coach Hubert Dabney—of Dabney Funeral Home—for whom my middle school is now named. I knew Herlongs, and I knew Ydes; in fact, everyone in town knew that Emil Yde set the record (which still stands) for highest winning percentage by a major league pitcher in a season (when he was 18-1).

My paternal grandfather worked as a supervisor in citrus packing houses in Leesburg most of his adult life. My maternal grandfather founded and owned Blue Sink Groves; after he died in 1967, my father managed them until the freezes of the 1980's finally did them in. I spent my childhood riding the groves (as a little boy), hoeing them (during about puberty), and working tractors and trucks in them (from about age thirteen on—and during summers home from college). My blood, my sweat, and my tears are in that white sugar sand of Lake County. My second job was pitching in at Lasher Feeds in Okahumpka—or the nearby watermelon fields. I am one of a very few people who will ever write to you, and honestly lay claim to being a fourth generation Floridian.

In law school, I first became acquainted with Thurgood Marshall. While previously I had known his name as having been associated with the civil rights movement, I did not come to appreciate much about him until I began the study of the law. Until I read your book, however— last week—I never knew he had set foot in Lake County. I was stunned. I knew Sheriff Willis McCall, and I knew his son (later sheriff) Malcolm McCall, and I knew from school Willis's grandson Spence McCall. I was ten when Willis left office. I can remember the crackers—of which I suppose I am one—conversationally using the word "Nigra" to refer to the "good blacks," and I remember, too, the similar word used to refer to the "bad ones." I remember "colored restrooms" and I remember "colored" water fountains. I remember one lynch mob forming and dispersing in the mid-1970's when Mack Ruffin and Freddie Lee Hall ▶

kidnaped, raped, tortured, and killed a pregnant woman. I remember as a young teenager seeing a Klan meeting in a field near Okahumpka. And I knew about the Scottsboro case, because it was taught at school.

The Leesburg I grew up in was bucolic; Venetian Gardens was made as a WPA project in the 1930's, and is a lovely area of reclaimed swampland featuring landscaping, bridges, benches, and a beautiful lakefront beach. Throughout school, I had black friends and white friends; my mother approved—but was surprised—when I thought nothing of bringing home a friend from fourth grade to play; he was black. The Big Bass Motel, on U.S. 27 in Leesburg, was frequently targeted by teenagers who loved shooting out the second "B." My family was worth money on paper (the orange groves made that so), but, as most farmers know, we didn't always have much "extra." In fact, I never knew how small our house was at 1300 square feet with parents and two brothers, until I was in law school (when I also first saw snow). Church softball was big, and in 1976, Leesburg won the State 3-A championships in baseball and basketball. I was Methodist, and the Baptist preacher required Methodist boys to attend his sermons at least once a month to qualify to date a Baptist girl. I knew one Mormon family, and one Greek Orthodox family, and the Tender Pig had the best barbecue in all the world. We bought shoes from Ezell's Department Store, went to movies at the Tropic Twin, and bought groceries on Main Street at Eddie's Groceteria (which featured hardwood floors). I would not have traded my childhood for anyone's.

A lot of my family (the older ones, and some of the younger) are still hard-right wing people; I cannot say that I know too many of those still around to be racist. I never had reason to think that any in my immediate family were racists. And whereas, as a child, I had some vague sense of racial tension in the United States, it was mostly from TV news reports from such far off places as Mississippi, Georgia, and my hometown since 1985 (save three years)—Birmingham, Alabama (which, until I moved here for law school, I wrongly believed to be little more than smokestacks from the steel mills and Bull Connor's fire-hoses and German Shepherds).

My parents never spoke of the case involving the Groveland Boys—even though the cry of rape was merely thirteen years before Dr. Binneveld brought me into the world. Groveland was little more than a stone's throw from where I grew up, but its lessons were never mentioned in school. Indeed, I had never heard of that case until I read your book. Despite having heard all my life about how Sheriff Willis McCall once "shot two colored boys, chained together, trying to 'escape' near the Ocala National Forest," I never knew the circumstances of those two young men and what brought them together with the sheriff. While I knew all my life that the sheriff was a racist, my knowledge largely came from anecdotal accounts of what I heard a scattered few adults say about him. Until I read your book, I never knew how unenlightened I was.

Your book unsettled me. You wrote of people I knew, places in which I had spent my entire youth running barefooted, fishing, and toiling. You wrote of the citrus industry that kept boots on my feet and chicken on my table throughout my childhood. I never until now knew that I grew up in the presence of the *Devil in the Grove*, down the road from where neighbors whispered, "Thurgood's coming. . . ." My perception of reality is now different.

Your book has made me think, and caused me to reflect. Things were not as innocent as maybe I had thought. For a while, I was mad at you; your book changed what I thought of my childhood milieu. I am not mad at you anymore; you have opened my eyes in a way that a man needs his eyes opened. For a while, I was mad at my parents; they withheld the truth from me. I am not mad at them anymore, either; they raised me in a way that permits me to (most of the time) see past color, and gave me the foundation to know the truth that all men are created in the image of God, who sent His Son to save all the world (and not just the white Republican world).

I know how hard you worked on your book. I enjoyed it, and I appreciate you having written it. Next time I go to Lake County to visit the cemeteries where my mother, all four grandparents, and a raft of aunts, uncles, and cousins are buried, I plan on talking to them some about your book. They lived in the moment, and they knew. They could have told me, but didn't. And I will thank them in a different way for giving me the underpinning that lets me try to make a positive difference in the world in which I live until I see them again.

In sum, I am sure that your book made some people angry. I am equally sure that, for some, it will bring enlightenment. I don't know how many of my home-folks you will hear from, but from me, I will just say, sincerely, "Thank you, sir," and leave it there.

Sincerely yours,
Lawrence T. King

July 9, 2012
Dear Mr. King,

Researching my home state of Florida recently, I came across your "citrus baron" blog post on A.S. Herlong. I was heartbroken reading about the Groveland incident and the policies of A.S. Herlong & Company during the late '40s. It was an intimate heartache, as A.S. Herlong was my great grandfather. His son, A.S. Herlong, Jr., was my grandfather, who I admired and loved dearly. ▶

I immediately bought and read *Devil in the Grove*. I started my read prepared to defend and preserve my wonderful memories of times spent in the groves surrounding my grandparents' house in Leesburg, Florida. I quickly realized I was going to have to accept those early memories for what they were—the memories of a child; a version of history not fully informed. As far removed as I was from the injustices that occurred the need I felt to make amends was very strong. In the end, the only restitution I felt I could possibly offer, however feeble, was to share the story of where my family ended up. That is my intention in writing to you.

My grandfather was one of four sons. He was less involved with A.S. Herlong & Company and more active in politics. He practiced law until 1937 when he left to serve as Leesburg city attorney then county judge and finally as a U.S. Representative elected in 1949 where he served for ten terms. He stepped into the national political scene when the issue of civil rights was really heating up. His election in 1949 followed the surge of registered black voters in Florida mentioned in your book. I have wondered if that correlation bodes well for his esteem among blacks in his community—a hint, perhaps, that his position on civil rights stood apart from other white leaders in the South. I will never know, because the only perspective I had was that of a small girl. I did not know my grandfather politically. What I do know is that he made it very clear he loved and cherished each of his thirteen grandchildren and valued and encouraged qualities of love and kindness in us.

My mother, the oldest daughter of A.S. Herlong, Jr. and Mary Alice Youmans Herlong, grew up in Leesburg. My dad was born in Daytona and grew up mostly in Live Oak and Orlando. They married in 1953 and after a year in Lake Charles, Louisiana settled in Ocala. My dad was an attorney and eventually established his own practice in Ocala. The message in our house was, unequivocally, that we were to love and appreciate all people, regardless of the color of their skin. I'm grateful for this standard, because it spared me the disgrace of sharing gross attitudes of superiority many white people had during that time. My older brother, Pat, said it best: "I see a lot of people who are overtly or subliminally racist, and I think what an awful disease that is and how much it warps the soul. That disease is inherited. Glad I didn't have it."

My fondest memories of being with my grandparents in Leesburg were of running barefoot through the groves around their house with my siblings and cousins. We would fill our red wooden wagon with as many oranges as we could pull through the sand. My grandmother, Mimi, and her maid Pearline would meet us at the kitchen door to help unload the oranges into the kitchen sink, slice them in half and squeeze our own orange juice. My mother made the best homemade orange sherbet from that juice you have ever put in your mouth. We always had a box of grapefruit or oranges outside our back door, and I didn't know what store-bought juice was until after a bad freeze that left the trees unable to produce sweet fruit. My grandparents had a magical home— a Mediterranean style house, complete with the best banister I've yet to slide down and an old cage-door Otis elevator. Every trip down Shore Acres Drive to their house started by rolling down the windows to let in the heavenly scent of orange blossoms. There was nothing like it! The power of that scent so impacted me, that on an elementary school field trip to Homosassa Springs, I found and bought a tube of Orange Blossom perfume gel as a gift for my mother. I just knew she would love it, since it smelled so much like home. As I remember it, she was thrilled, though I do recall the tube took years to empty; I think she was more inclined toward Chanel No. 5. Again, mine was a child's view of life.

There were many memories that gave me clear insight into the hearts of my grandparents and parents and what they wanted us to know and feel:

- On my 9-year-old trip with my grandparents in 1969 (a rite of passage for each grandchild at that age), we traveled up the east coast from Florida to Washington, DC, where my grandfather was serving as a member of the Securities & Exchange Commission. My grandmother asked my grandfather to pull to the side of the road in Georgia next to a cotton field. She got me out of the car, walked me over to the field and picked a piece of cotton so I could see all the parts of it and how the seeds are buried deep in the cotton. She had grown up in South Carolina where cotton was a major crop. I can still feel and see the emotion with which she explained how backbreaking it was for workers to pick this cotton in the hot sun and how fingers were often left bloody from the effort. I think I still have that piece of cotton stuck in a scrapbook in my attic. I will never, ever forget that moment. Ever.

- My mother recalls a conversation she had with my grandfather driving to school one chilly morning. She was complaining of being cold, and he quickly directed her attention to a little girl walking to school with no sweater and said, "Imagine how she feels and think about how lucky you are." She remembers his words shut her up pretty quickly. She also recalled her grandmother stopping to offer rides to women walking with heavy loads of groceries. She asked her grandmother why she did that, and her grandmother explained, "It's a long way to walk, and they get so tired." It has always bewildered my mother how she grew up without an ounce of prejudice, clearly seeing the escape from those attitudes as something profound, given the time. ▶

## The Last Word . . . *(continued)*

- My father discarded more than escaped the attitudes of his generation. Late in life, he shared that at one point he held attitudes he came to deride as shameful. I was astounded, because he was a huge moral compass in our lives, insisting that we show love and respect to ALL people and pulling us out of private schools to join desegregated classrooms in our public school system. When a local attorney advertised he would defend anyone wanting to make a case against desegregation, my dad responded with a letter to the editor offering to defend anyone whose right to integrate white schools were being denied or challenged. His extensive annotated library shows he was in a constant conversation with God, searching and yearning to be who God called him to be. This journey had to include a rejection of prejudice. I also think he was influenced by my mom, and I know his love for us would not allow him to pass along attitudes or actions of superiority or hatred.

It is this family that taught me to think and love in a way that eventually gave me the tools to cope with one of the most difficult experiences of my life. As a freshman student at the University of Florida, one early morning I was waiting for a ride in front of my dorm when I was kidnapped and raped at gunpoint. My attacker was a black man, but I never once considered the color of his skin. My immediate concern was whether they would catch him, which they did. After that, the question that persisted was what awful things happened in his life to make him want to hurt people the way he hurt me. It wasn't his skin color that was to blame, it was his heart. As far as I know every human heart has the potential for darkness or light, influenced largely by how we are raised and how thoroughly we are loved—or at some point whether we come to know how worthy we are of that love. When I had to identify my attacker in a police line-up, fear that hadn't been there suddenly gripped me. The overwhelming authority I was being handed to affect another person's fate and the possibility that I could make a mistake was absolutely frightening. This makes the swift, unlawful convictions of the '40s and '50s unfathomable and the empty, unchecked accusations of Norma Padgett truly unbelievable. I was only one year older than she was when this happened to me, and the contrast in our stories is stark.

Reading this book raised questions I needed answered. On a trip home to Florida, I sat down to visit with my "second mother," Betty Cook, to ask some of those questions. Betty came to work for our family in 1963 at the age of 21, when I (the fourth of five kids) was eighteen months old. She was my mom's right-hand helper and second mother to all five of us. You name it, she did it to take care of us and set us straight when necessary. At seventy, she still shows up to help my mother, now almost eighty. Their relationship is a unique and tender friendship. We call Betty on Mother's Day, and sometimes she calls us. She was not married, and besides a few nieces and nephews she loves dearly, she had no children of her own. We were the closest thing to it on a daily basis.

Betty didn't recall the specific incidents in your book. She told me that adults shooed young people out of the room when heavy subjects were discussed. She did, however, show a proud familiarity with the legendary Thurgood Marshall. Betty was, and is, a strong, confident woman. She didn't let injustice go unchecked, once marching in to tell a local merchant whose children had thrown live firecrackers at her and her brother on their front porch one evening, "I threw a flower pot at their car and missed, but I promise you I won't miss next time!"

I needed to know if Betty's love for us was as color blind as our love for her, given what she must have witnessed and experienced as a black female during this time. We sat down to talk, and I asked her, "Do you remember the day we drove you home and passed the black lady carrying an umbrella with her head wrapped in a bandana?" She grinned and started to laugh, because she remembered the story well. "Remember, I said, 'Mom, mom, look, look is that Little Black Sambo's mother? Is it? Is it mom? It looks just like her. Mom, mom. . . . teeeellll me . . . !" You can picture it; I was relentless. Betty said, "Oh, do I ever remember," and went on to finish the story. As my childish persistence intensified, so did my mom's embarrassment. Betty held her breath until we pulled up to her house where she quickly escaped the confines of our station wagon. Her family thought she'd gone crazy when she stormed in and threw herself on her bed, laughing hysterically. Once she got the story out, they laughed right along with her.

"How did you laugh instead of being resentful?" I needed to know. "That was a stereotype that should not have been perpetuated." Years later, I felt like a player, albeit a very young one, in the game of stereotypes that dishonored the God-given intellect and talents of black people. I have to wonder how many great smart, young leaders we deprived ourselves of because of the roles and abilities we assigned based on skin color. Betty recovered from laughing, softened and said, "You were all so sweet. You were just a little girl, and it was just something you had read in a book." So there it was. She saw me as just the little girl I was, nothing more, nothing less. And I saw her as a guiding authority figure in my life who loved me unconditionally. Nothing more, nothing less. My love and respect for her remain as huge, genuine and pure as they were then.

Today, I teach seventh graders of many different cultures and colors in a public school in a suburb of Houston, now considered to be one of the most culturally diverse cities in our country. On any day, you could enter my classroom and sit next to children who are fresh in this country ▶

### The Last Word . . . *(continued)*

from Mexico, India, China, Nigeria, and many other countries. Many come speaking very little English, but we all speak the language of a smile and a warm, kind word. My three sons are fourth generation Floridians who, thanks to their Texas public school education, do not consider color; few of their friends look anything like them. It is only one example of the distance my family has come over the years.

I have to believe that a different lesson was being taught in my grandparent's house for us to be where we are today. Hopefully, it speaks positively about the legacy my grandfather left. I am grateful for my extended family and where they have brought me. I will be forever grateful for the lifetime of sacrifices made by the heroes of the civil rights movement, particularly Thurgood Marshall, whose intellect, wisdom and intense devotion to constitutional law saved so many lives and forced us all to think differently. Finally, I am grateful you decided to research and retell this story so that we might never forget the gross injustices of the past in order that they will never be a part of our future.

Sincerely,
Anne Pattillo Kail

# Questions for Discussion

1. Was there anything that made you think about Thurgood Marshall differently in terms of his role in American history based on what you've read in *Devil in the Grove*?

2. The author devotes a large part of this story describing the forces of laws and justice in Jim Crow South, and he makes a point to describe Florida as "South of the South." Does this fit your vision of what Florida was like in the pre-Civil Rights era?

3. The citrus industry plays an important role in this story, and with labor such an essential part of production, were you surprised to learn about "work or fight" laws that allowed sheriffs like Willis McCall the ability to arrest men who weren't working? Were you aware that "debt slavery" and peonage conditions were still in place, where arrested men would be made to work in the groves to pay bail or fines?

4. Willis McCall held a tight reign on Lake County. In the beginning of the book, he prevents the men of Bay Lake from storming the jail and possibly lynching the Groveland suspects. But clearly, he was also capable of violence against those same men. What do you think Sheriff McCall's motivations were throughout the story, and why do you think he was able to remain county sheriff for twenty-eight years?

5. The author makes a point to describe Norma Padgett differently in the two trials of the Groveland Boys. In the first trial, she wears a fancy dress and proudly marches up to the stand to point out her alleged rapists. But by the second trial, she's described as gaunt, worn down ▶

17

and tired, and doesn't seem to have much interest in the case anymore. What do you think happened on the night of the alleged rape? Do you believe the suspects were strangers to her?

6. The author points to Curtis Howard, the gas station attendant who spots Norma Padgett on the side of the road on the morning of the alleged rape. Yet Howard doesn't mention his observation until later that morning. What are your thoughts about Curtis Howard's role in this case?

7. Walter Irvin described being shot by both Sheriff McCall and his deputy, James Yates. Yet despite having evidence that supported Irvin's story rather than McCall's, the FBI was able to hold onto this evidence for years, and neither McCall nor Yates were ever charged. Discuss the role of the FBI in this case and how it fits with your expectations?

8. Reviewers have commented that *Devil in the Grove* has the narrative drive of a thriller. Did this book read or feel differently than other nonfiction books you've read in the past?

9. In the end, Governor LeRoy Collins commuted Walter Irvin's sentence. He'd spend nearly twenty years in jail after being beaten and shot three times. Four people were killed during this case, yet Marshall still saw it as a victory. Why do you think that was so?

10. The case of the Groveland Boys was significant because it led to the NAACP's Legal Defense Fund program to invalidate the use of the death penalty for rape. Discuss the ways you think the legal system has changed since then, and how a rape case like this would be both prosecuted and defended today. ✑